MW01626319

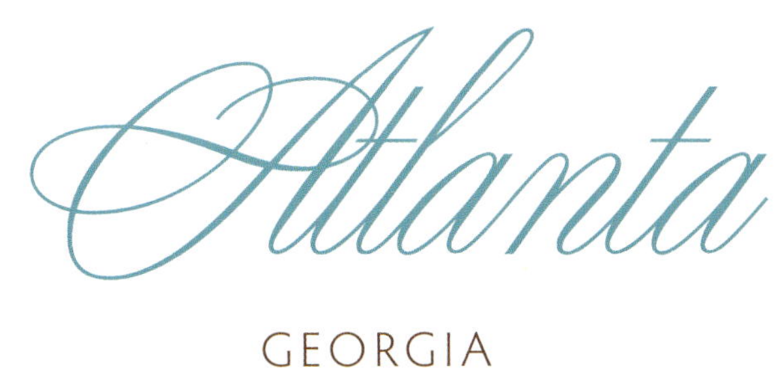

GEORGIA

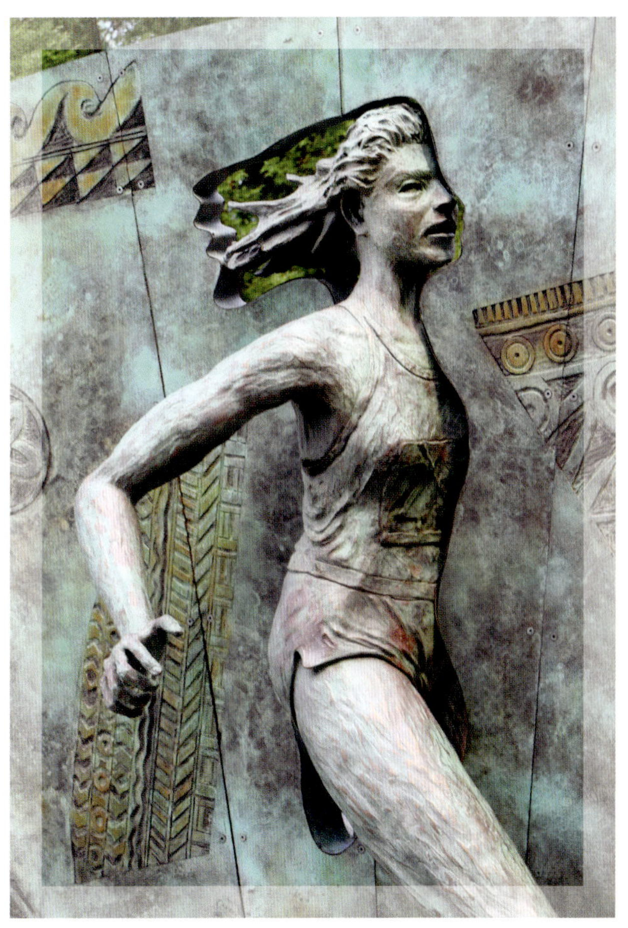

A PHOTOGRAPHIC PORTRAIT

PHOTOGRAPHY BY PAUL SCHARFF
NARRATIVE BY KATHRYN WITT

TWIN LIGHTS PUBLISHERS • ROCKPORT, MASSACHUSETTS

First published in the United States of America by:

Twin Lights Publishers, Inc.
8 Hale Street
Rockport, Massachusetts 01966
Telephone: (978) 546-7398
http://www.twinlightspub.com

ISBN: 978-1-934907-13-9

10 9 8 7 6 5 4 3 2 1

(*opposite*)
Downtown Atlanta

(*frontispiece*)
Centennial Oylmpic Park

(*jacket front*)
In Reflection

(*jacket back*)
Symphony Tower
International Peace Fountain
The Chattahoochee River National Recreation Area

Book design by:
SYP Design & Production, Inc.
www.sypdesign.com

Printed in China

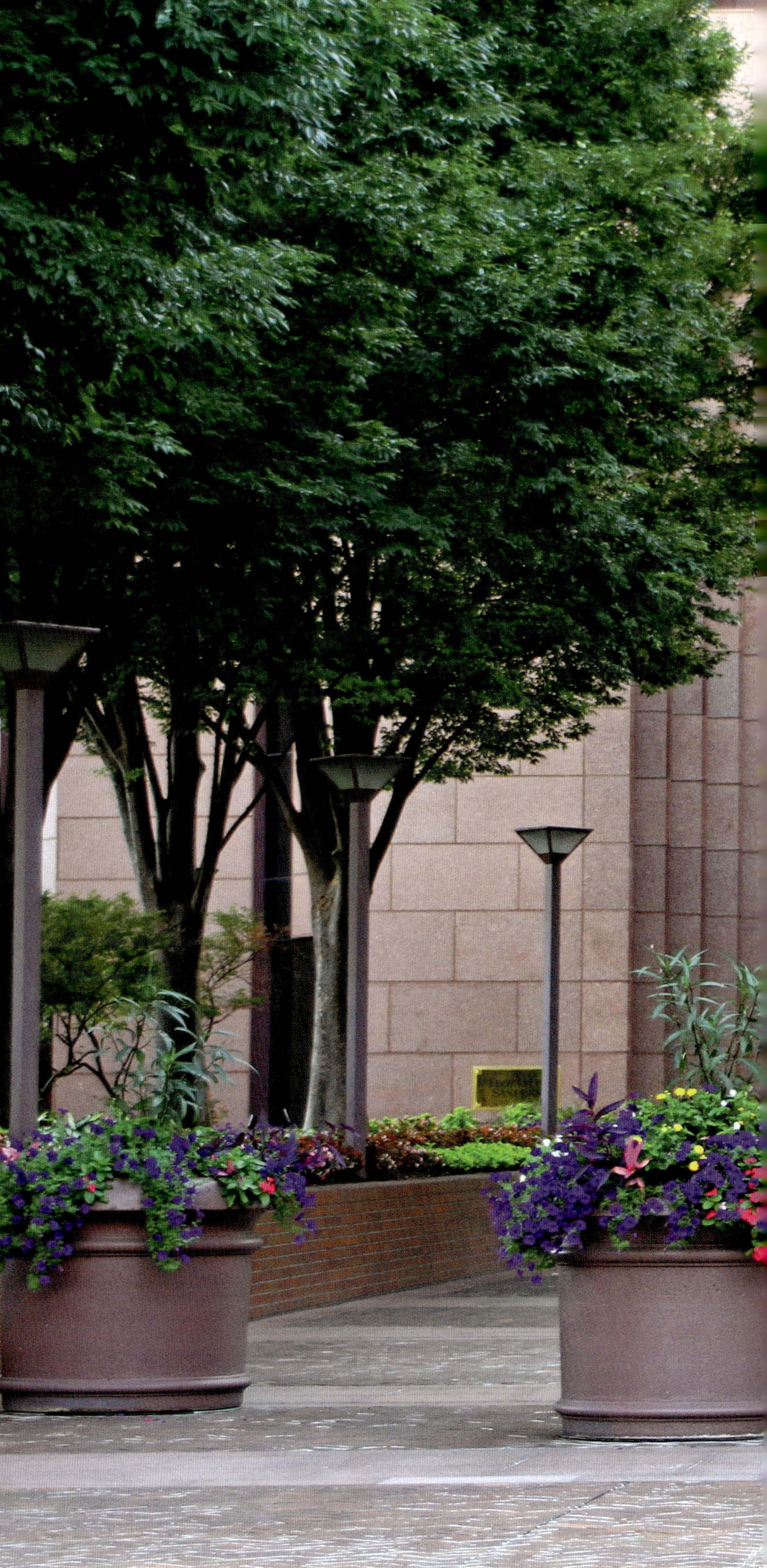

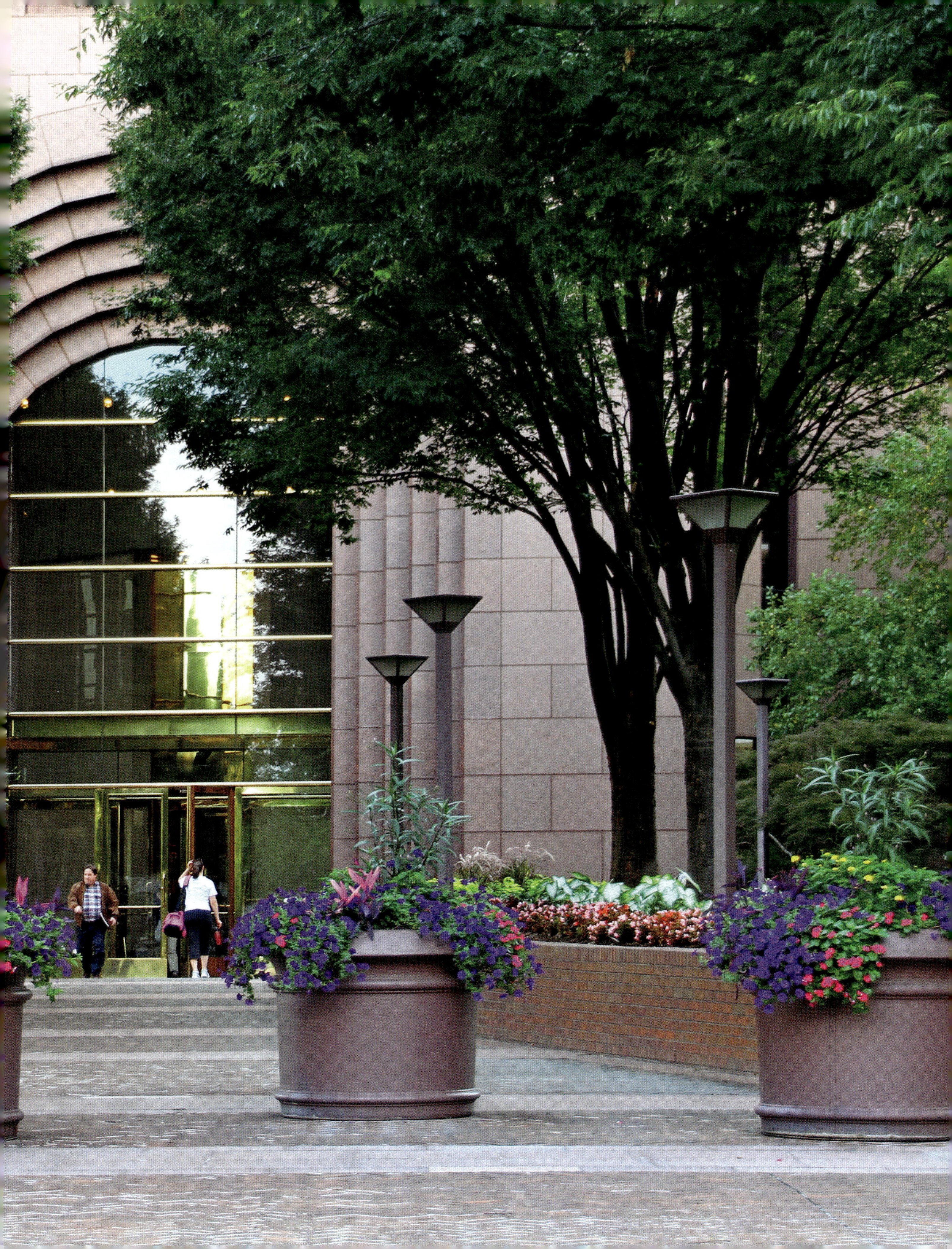

Atlanta. Southern-bred and worldly-wise, this densely forested urban dynamo is an international cultural melting pot renowned for its world-class attractions, culinary and shopping landscapes, and neighborhoods as individual in spirit and mien as the people who make up Atlanta's diverse communities.

Located in the foothills of the Appalachian Mountain range, the Atlanta metropolitan region encompasses 28 counties, stretches languidly across more than 6,000 square miles, and is called home by more than 5 million residents – a population that swells to accommodate some 35 million visitors annually from across the U.S. and around the world.

Founded in 1837, Georgia's capital and the state's largest city is a robust financial center and a major transportation hub, a leader in higher education and medical research, and an innovator in information technology. Atlanta is a visionary whose story is written on her skyline. And she is a survivor.

Like the phoenix of ancient mythology that is her symbol, Atlanta rose from the ashes of the conflagration that burned the city to the ground and brought the community to its knees during General Sherman's Civil War March to the Sea. And she rose heroically – ascending to skyscraping heights in her architecture, gleaming modern and postmodern structures housing a heavy concentration of Fortune 1000 and Fortune 500 companies. Atlanta has achieved superlative triumphs in attractions that include the world's largest aquarium, world headquarters for the first all-news television channel in the United States, and an entire "world" feting a beverage. She has attained the upper reaches of the cultural stratosphere in gems that include the leading art museum in the southeastern United States, one of the oldest zoos in the country, a garden nurturing the nation's foremost collection of species orchids, and a public art program whose sculptures enrich streetscapes throughout the city.

Once the homeland of Native Americans, Atlanta has risen to history's challenges from the Civil War to the Civil Rights Movement and emerged an important international city with an excellent quality of life. It is a place on history's timeline marked with names like Jimmy Carter, Margaret Mitchell, Martin Luther King, Jr., Joel Chandler Harris, Coca-Cola founder Asa Candler, and renowned architect John Portman.

Those who call Atlanta home and those who are welcomed as visitors will see, through this brilliant collection of images by Paul Scharff, a bold survivor with Southern grace and charm and international aspirations and achievements.

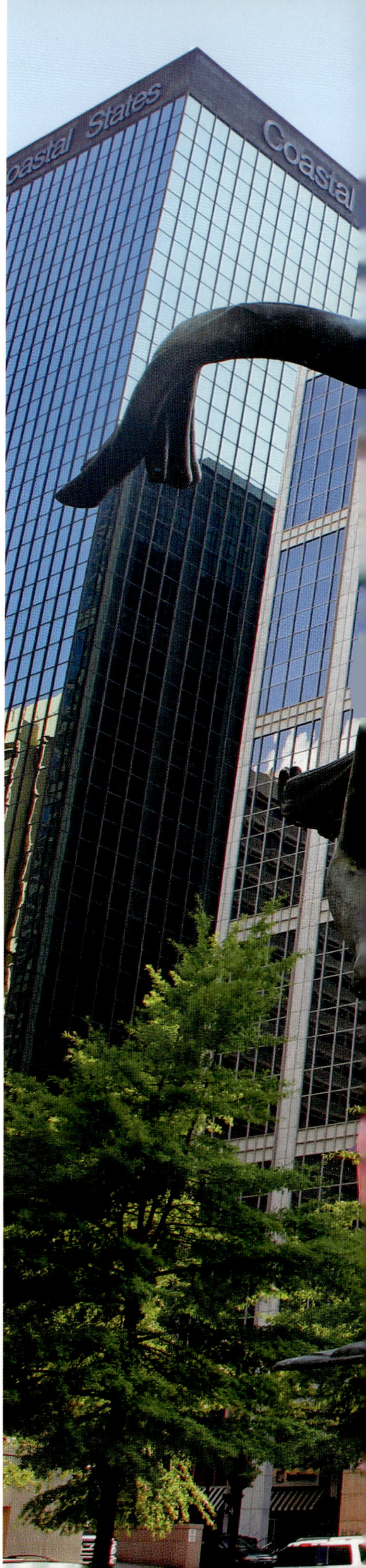

Ballet Olympia

Adapted from Art Deco sculptor Paul Manship's bronze *Maenad* figure by John Portman, one of America's most influential architects, *Ballet Olympia* depicts two spirited dancers, resplendent in their nudity, exuberantly tossing ribbons as they look skyward. This bronze sculpture, unveiled in 1992, is located at the SunTrust Plaza.

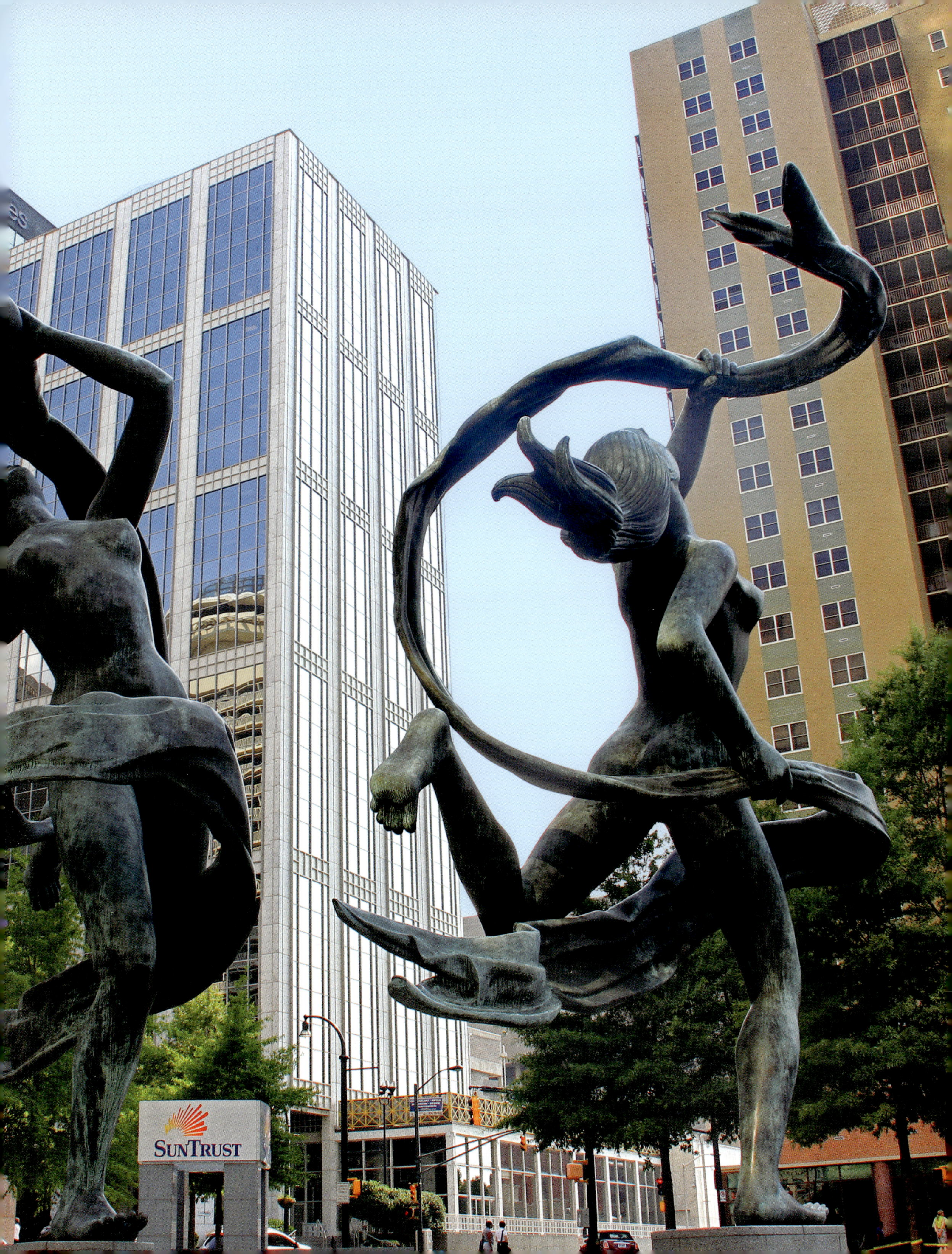
SunTrust

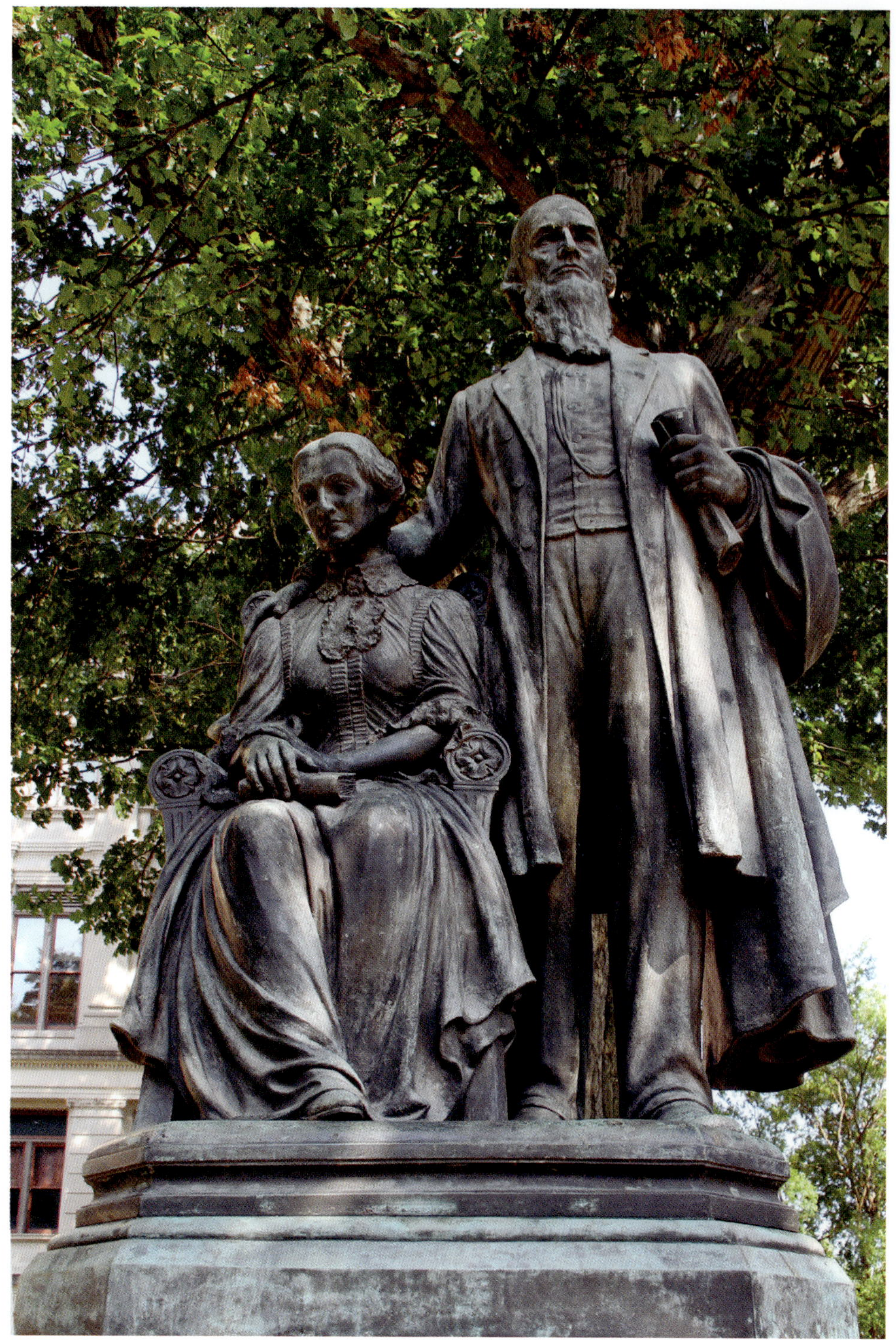

Governor Joseph Brown *(above)*

Considered one of the most successful politicians in Georgia's history, Civil War governor Joseph Emerson Brown (1821-1894) is memorialized with his wife, Elizabeth Grisham Brown, in one of the few husband-and-wife statues in the world. The sculpture is located on the southwest corner of the Georgia state capitol square.

John Brown Gordon *(opposite)*

In 1907, the statue of John Brown Gordon was the first monument to be placed on the Capitol grounds. Gordon is one of Georgia's most renowned political and military figures of the 19th century, serving as captain of the "Raccoon Roughs" and eventually rising to major general in command of half of Confederate general Robert E. Lee's army.

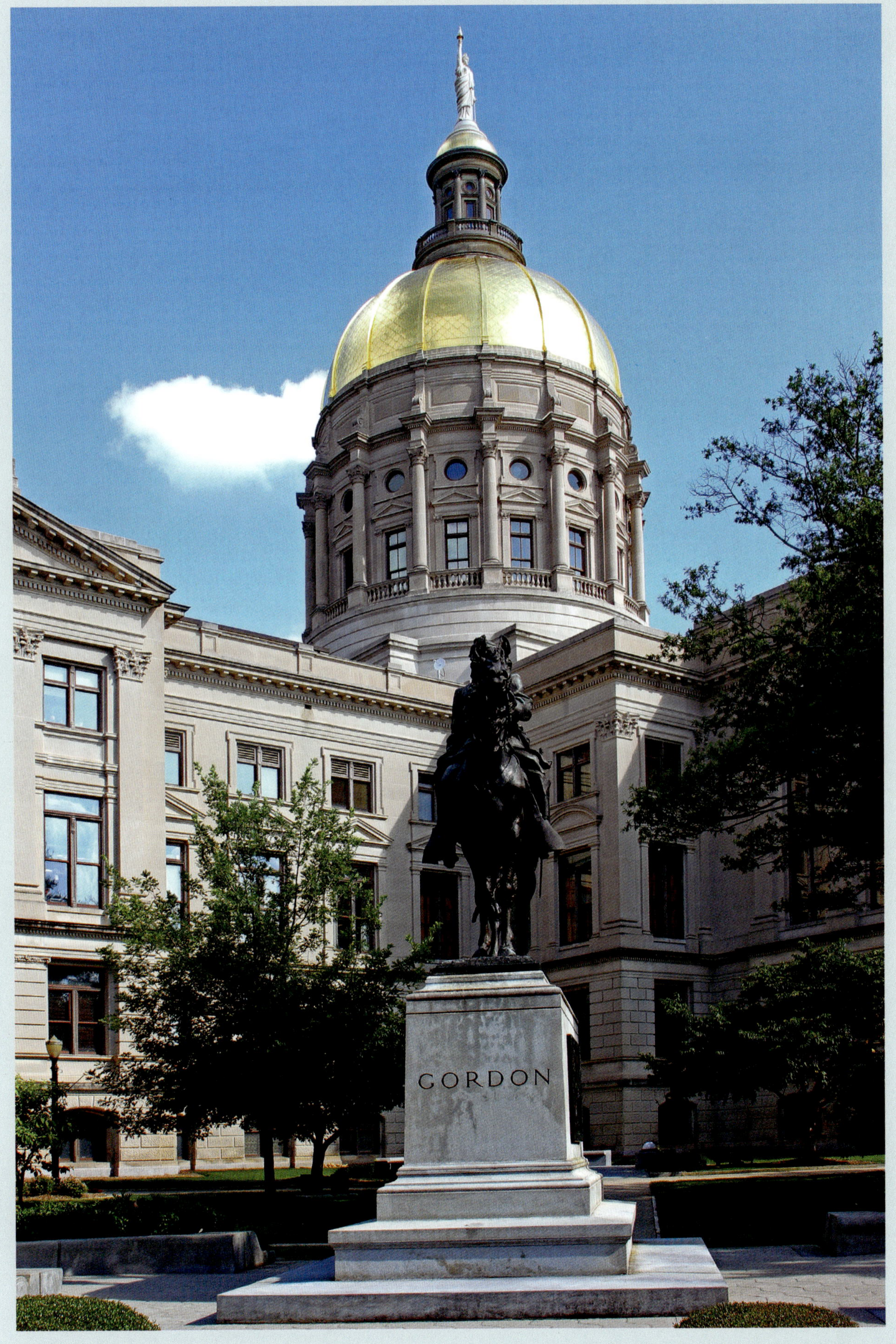
GORDON

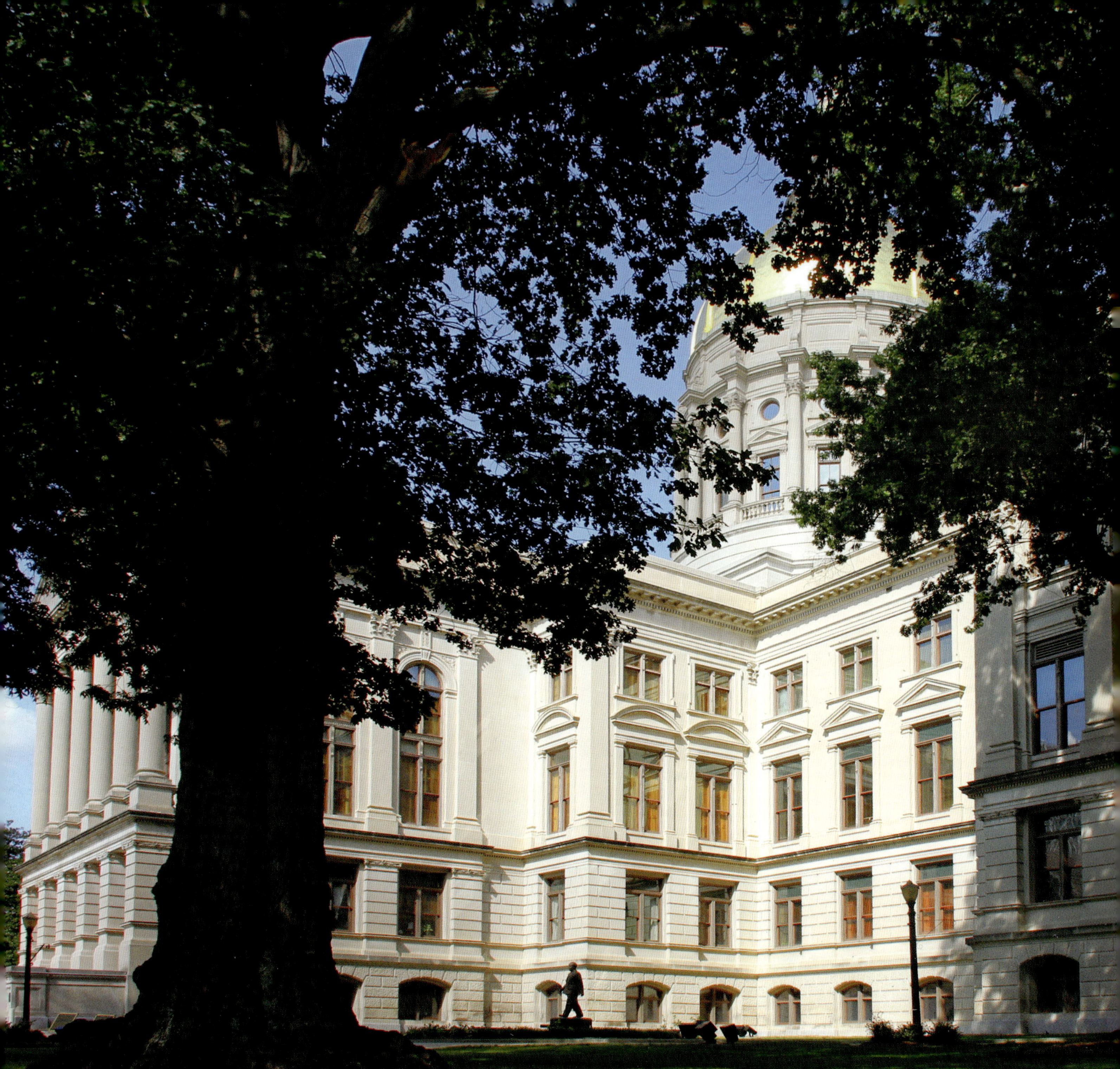

Georgia State Capitol

The building for Georgia's fifth permanent capital city boasts a Neo-Classical design, whose facade features a four-story portico with stone pediment supported by six Corinthian columns. Built from 1884 to 1889, it has an open rotunda extending from the second floor through the upper stories and a gilded dome measuring 75 feet in diameter.

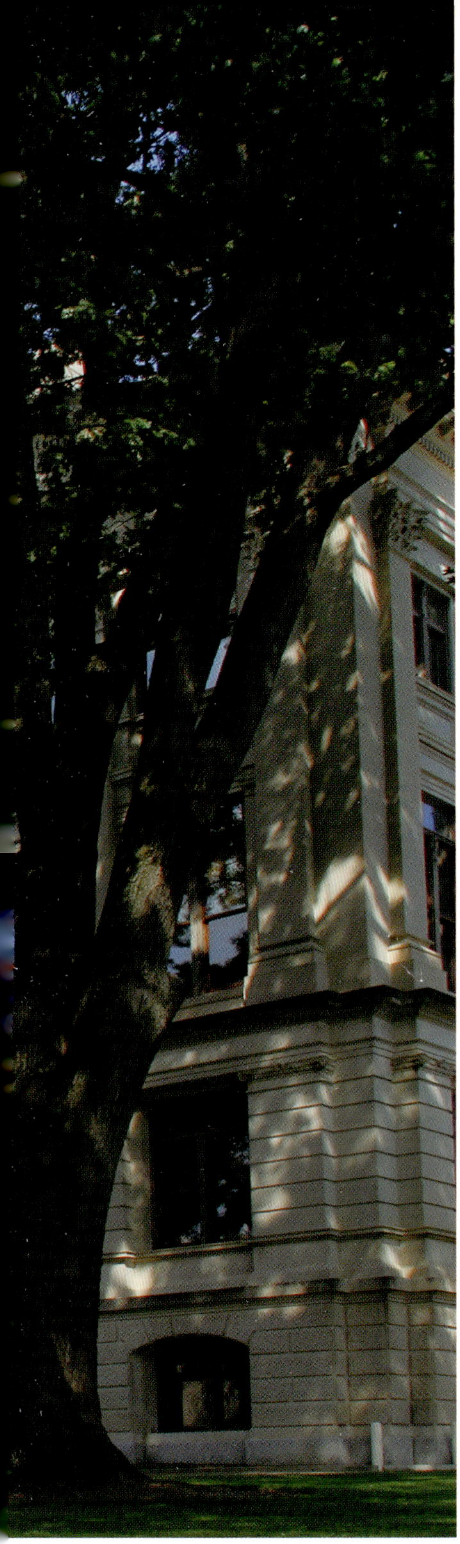

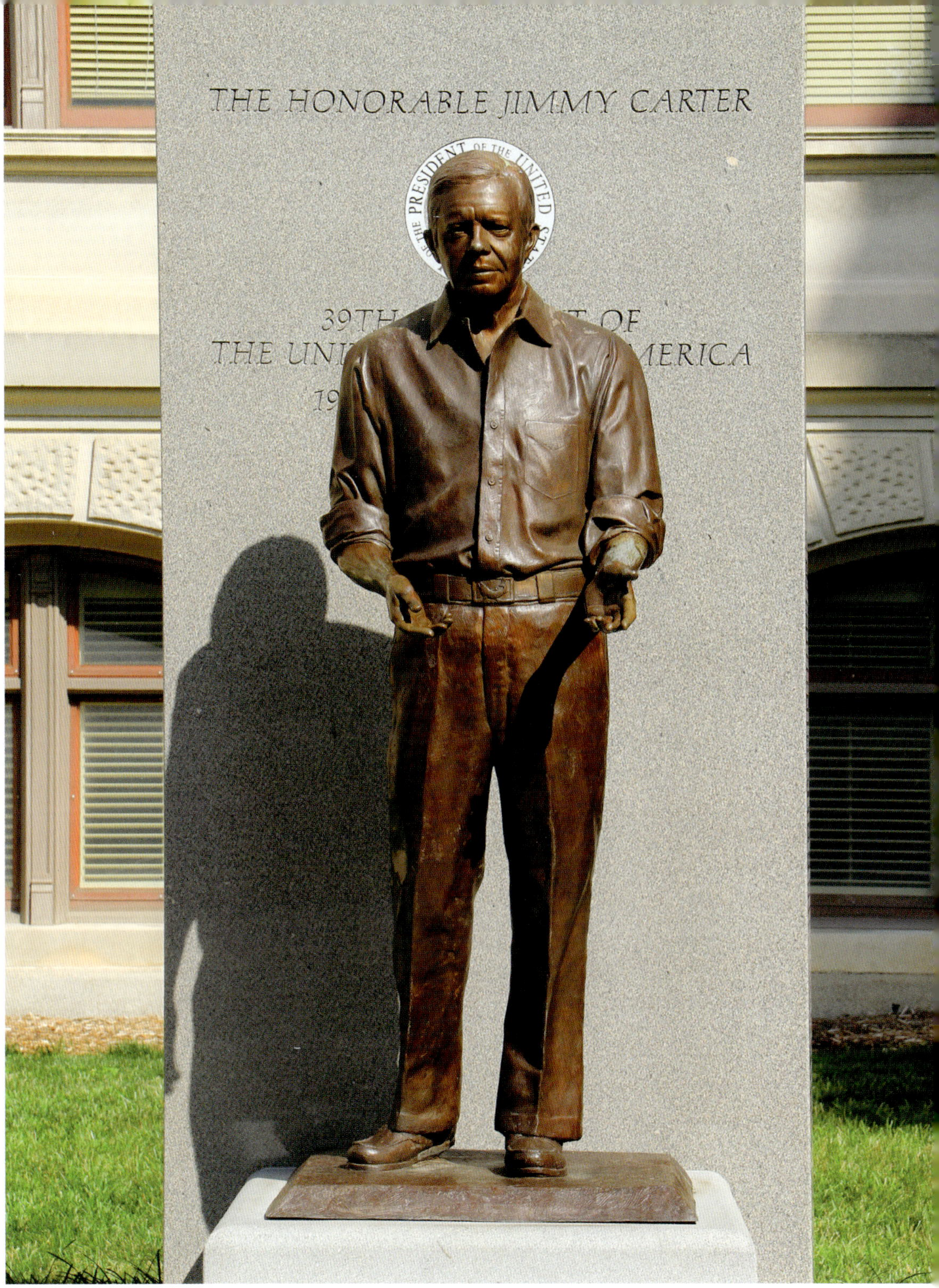

President Jimmy Carter

Looking unpretentious in khakis and with his sleeves rolled up, the bronze statue of James Earl Carter captures the essence of the "peanut farmer from Georgia," the 39th president of the United States. Even Carter's belt buckle with carved trout underscores the humble nature of the highly regarded elder statesman and humanitarian.

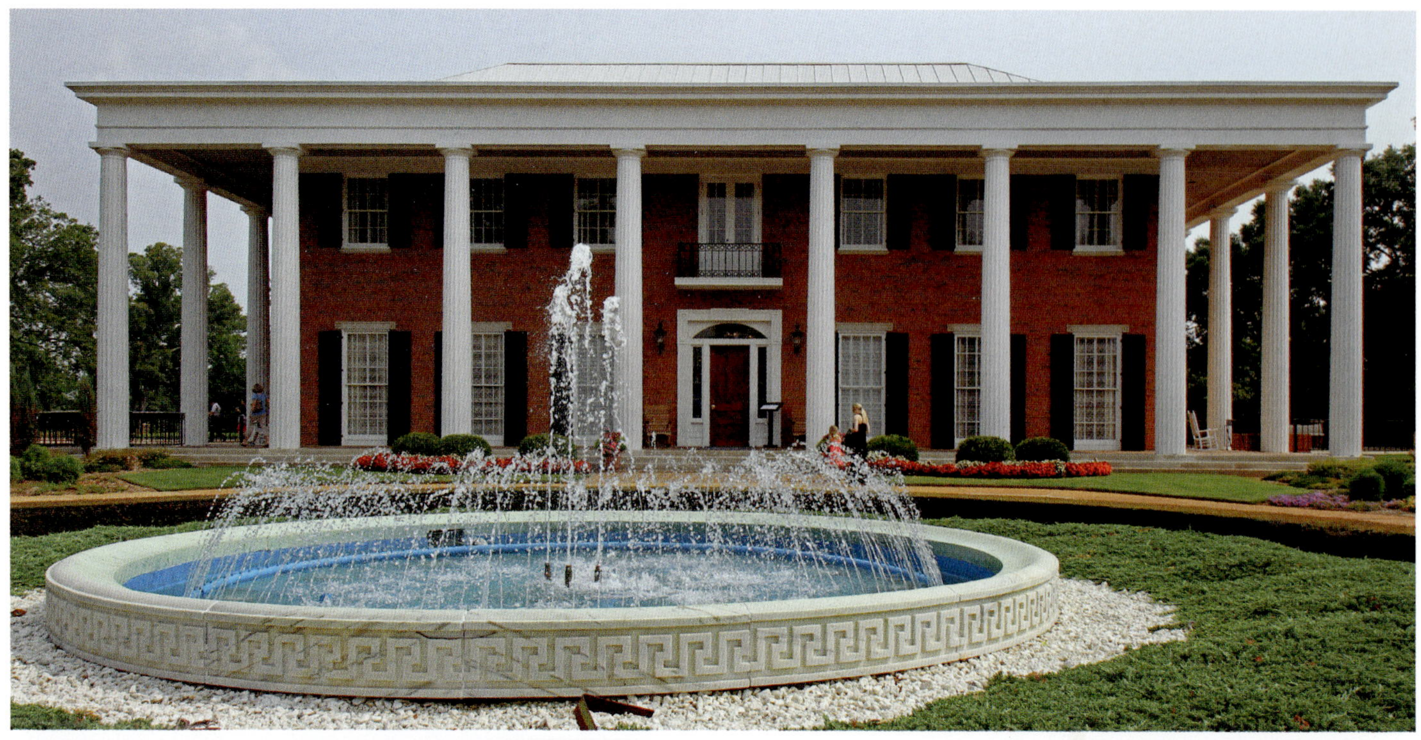

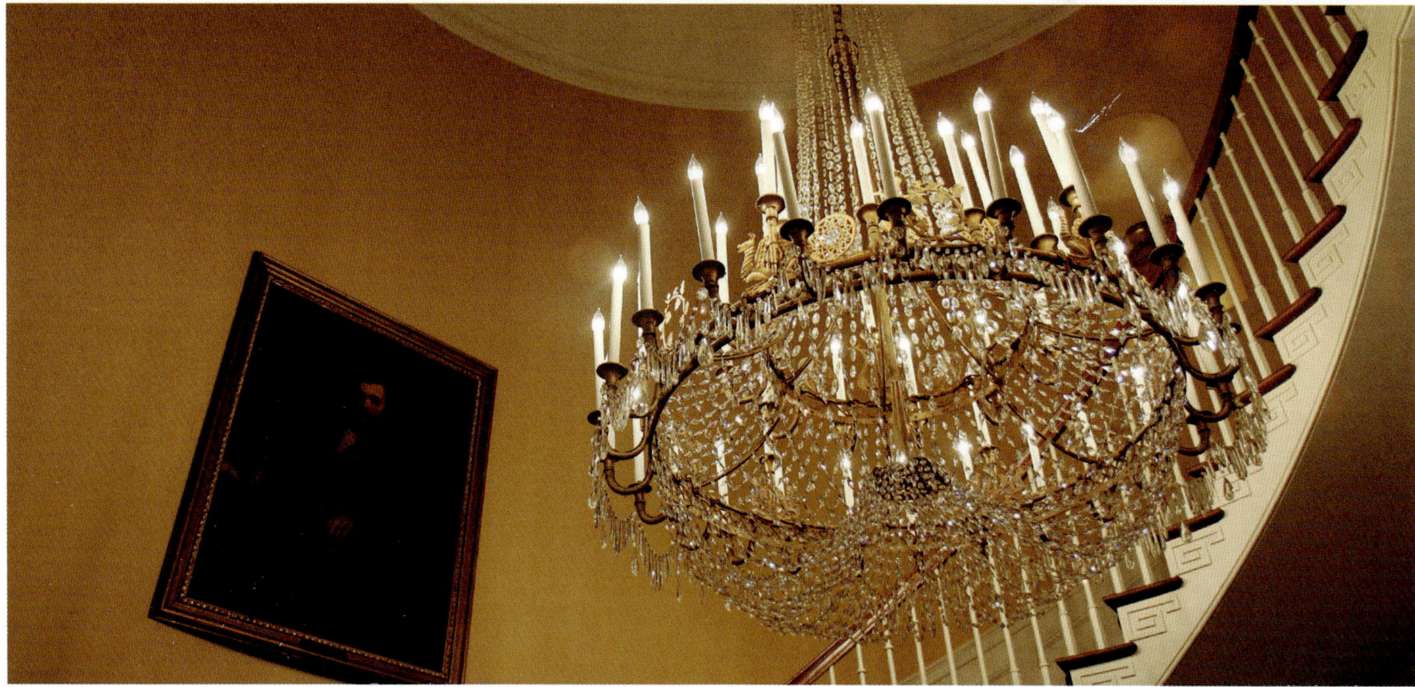

Governor's Mansion *(top)*

Built in 1967, this Greek Revival-style home, owned by former Atlanta Mayor Robert F. Maddox, was built amongst terraced gardens, statuary, and fountains. Landscape architect Edward Daugherty created the master landscaping plan for the new mansion, located in Atlanta's Buckhead area and first occupied by Governor Lester Maddox.

Governor's Mansion Chandelier *(bottom)*

Among the museum-quality art and furnishings in the Governor's Mansion is a chandelier created by combining pieces from two distinctly dissimilar chandeliers – a modern American piece and a 19th-century Italian chandelier – both of which were salvaged from the former and prestigious Standard Club in Atlanta.

Art Museum in a Mansion *(opposite)*

Designed by Thomas Bradbury, the 24,000-square-foot Governor's Mansion features 30 Doric columns, made from California redwoods. Interior furnishings comprise one of the finest Federal Period collections in the country, including a rare, circa 1810 Old Paris porcelain vase with a hand-painted medallion of Benjamin Franklin.

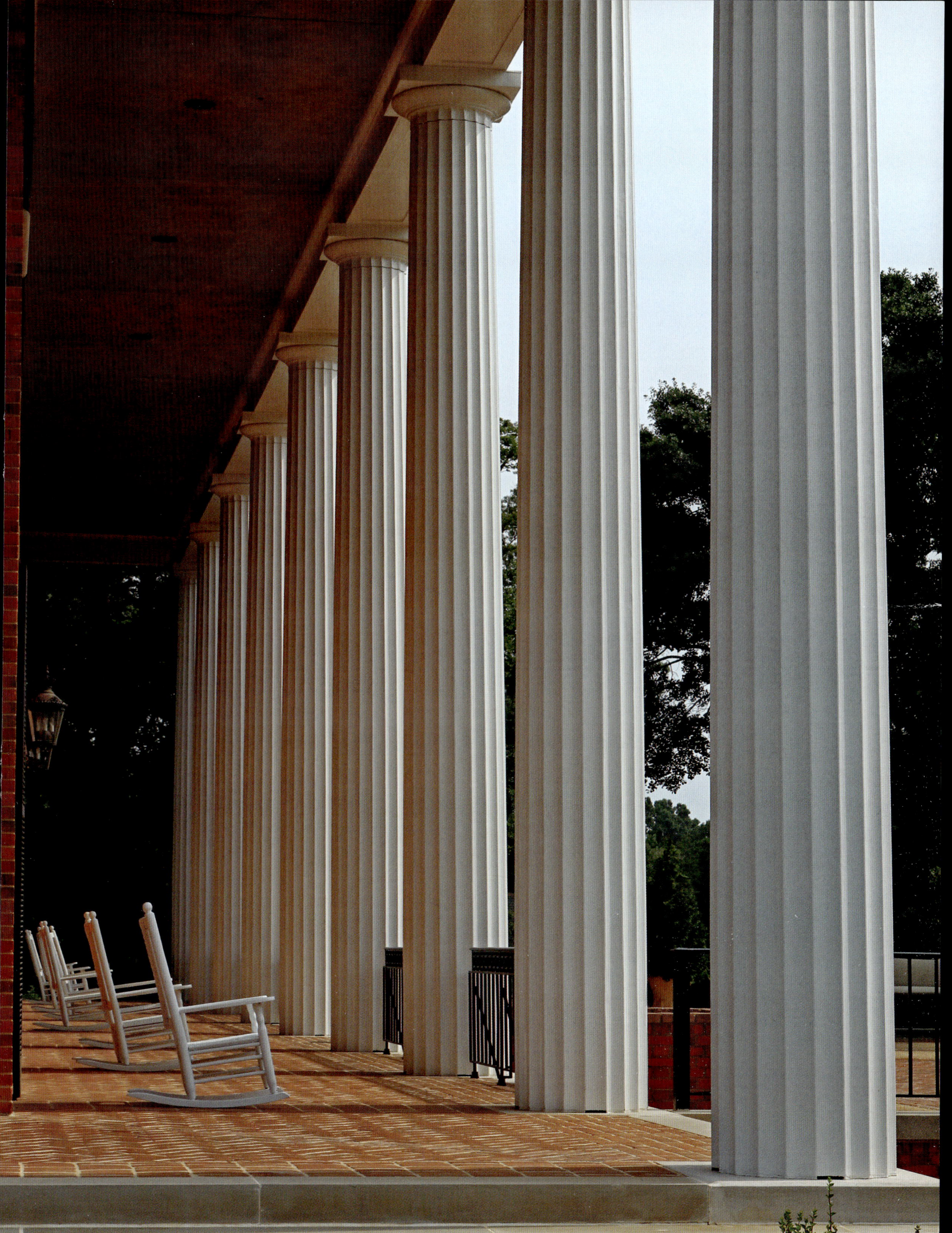

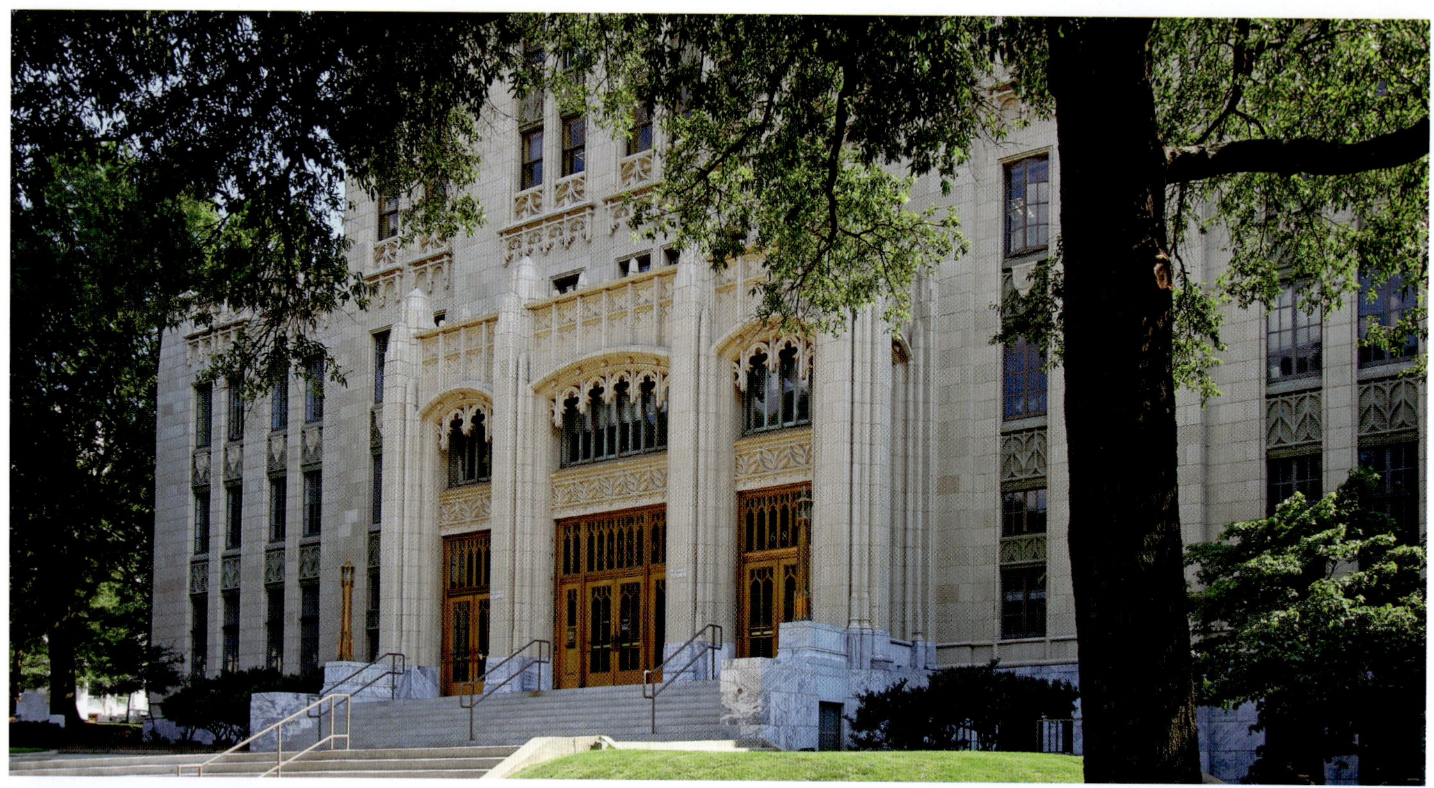

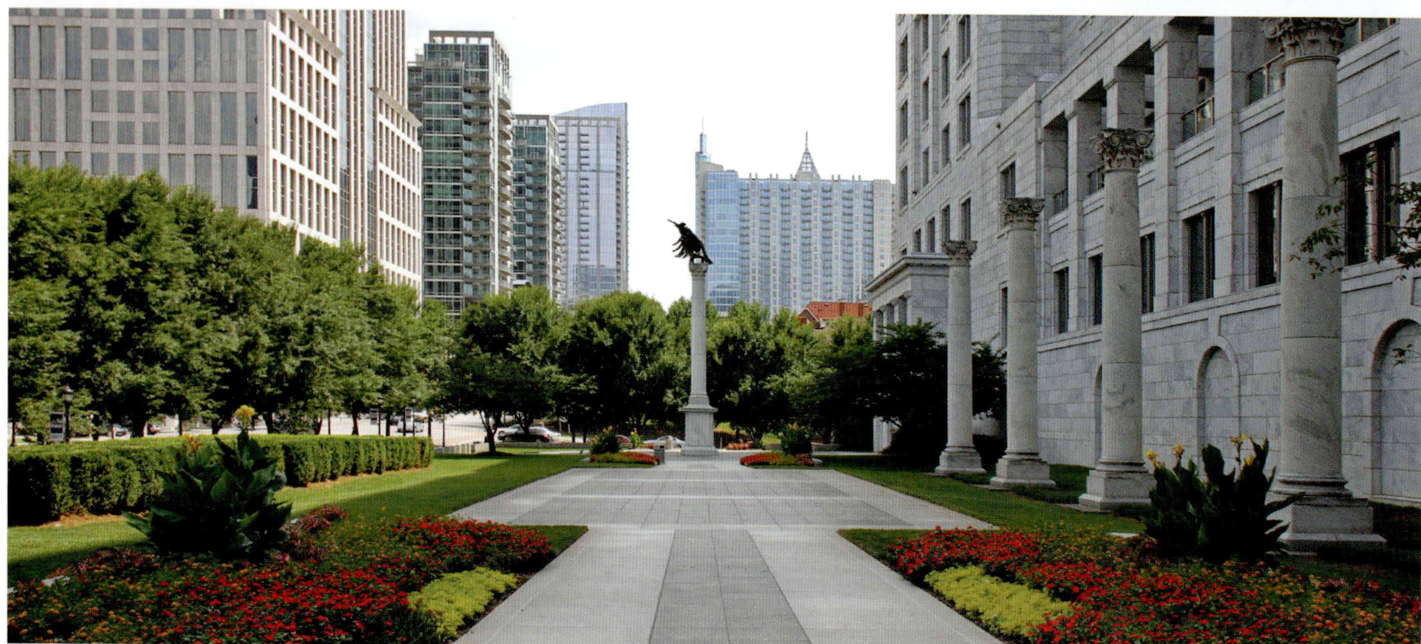

City Hall *(top)*

Built in 1930, Atlanta City Hall was designed by local architect G. Lloyd Preacher, most famous for his commercial office, hotel, and apartment building designs. Listed on the National Register of Historic Places, the neo-Gothic-style building is 11 stories tall and set on a four-story base. Today, it serves as the Council Chambers for City Hall.

Federal Reserve Bank *(bottom)*

One of 12 regional Reserve Banks in the country, the Federal Reserve Bank of Atlanta, with its White Cherokee marble exterior, sits on eight acres – three devoted to green-space and public plazas. It comprises a general office, operations center, and education center. A Visitors Center and Monetary Museum are housed in the 10-story tower.

Lift *(opposite)*

Commissioned by The Federal Reserve Bank of Atlanta and Holder Properties, *Lift* rises nearly 30 feet high on the grounds of this Atlanta landmark. The sculpture was created by Andrew Crawford who works primarily in bronze and iron, exploring the aesthetics of functional objects, ornamental ironwork, and industrial fabrication.

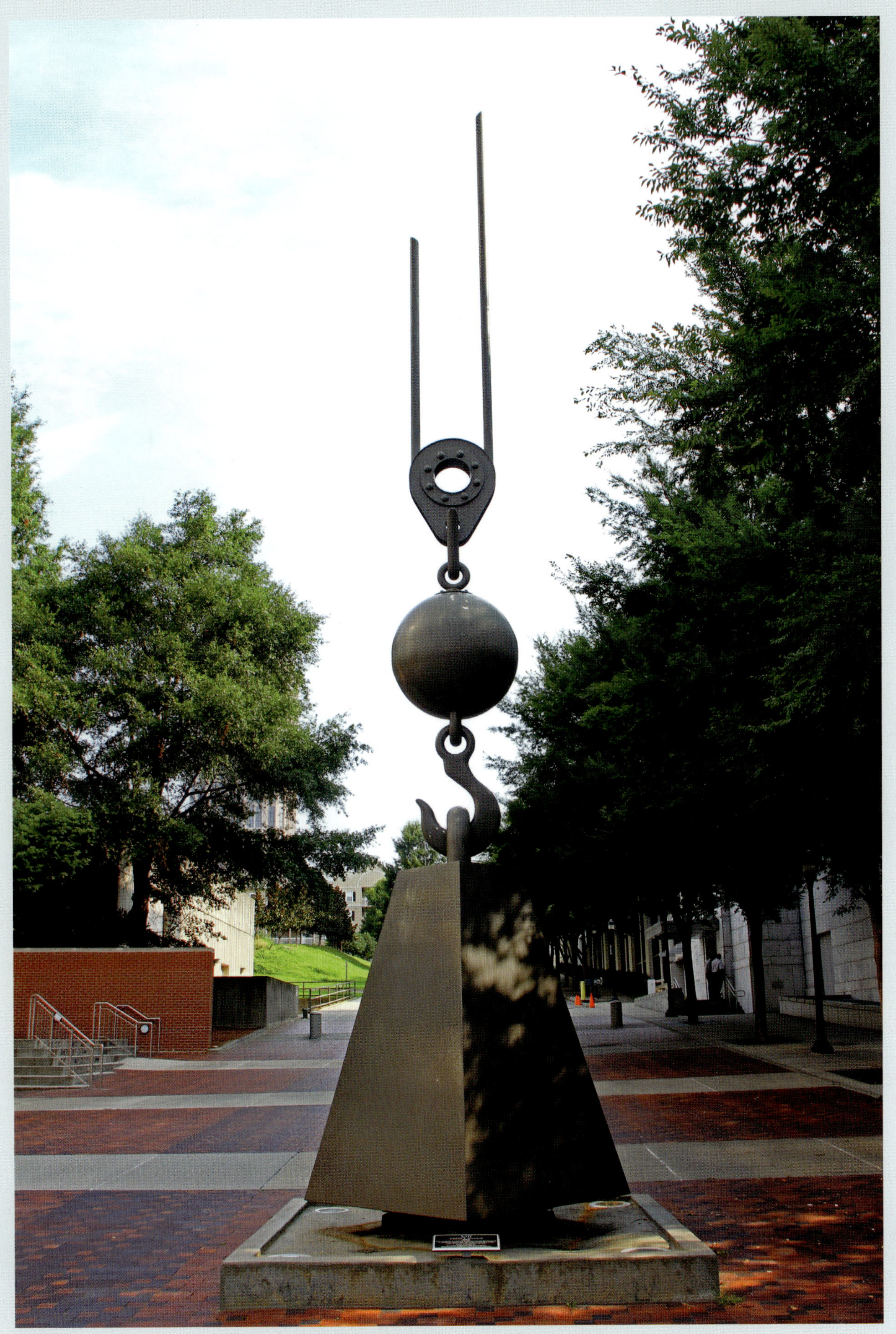

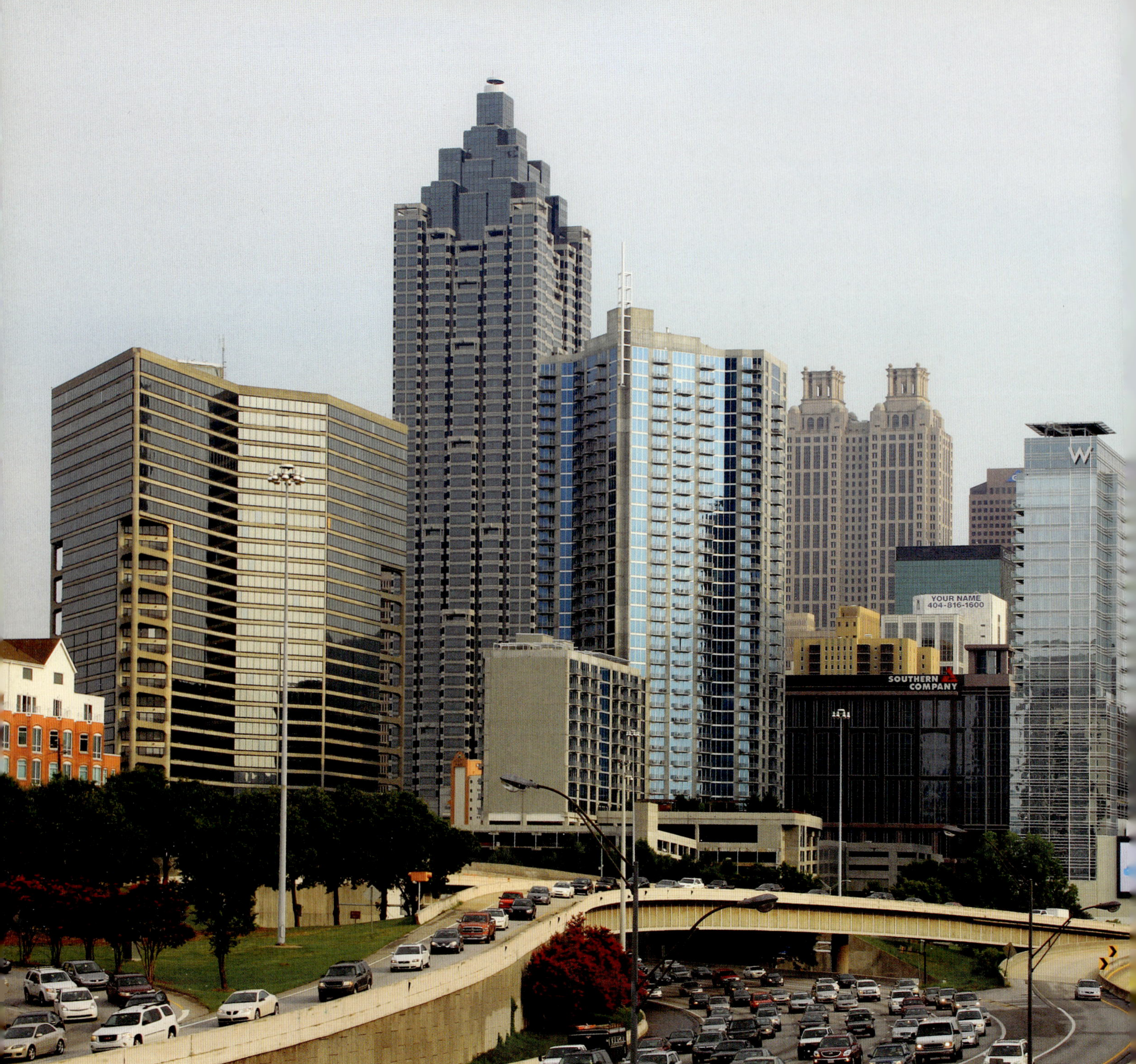

Atlanta Skyline

Dynamic, historic, and urbane, metro Atlanta pulsates with possibility. Home to numerous Fortune 1000 and Fortune 500 companies, as well as eclectic neighborhoods whose vibe swings from business to Bohemian, upscale to arts-centric, a beguiling dining and shopping landscape, and an exceptionally high quality of life, Atlanta's skyline reflects its promise.

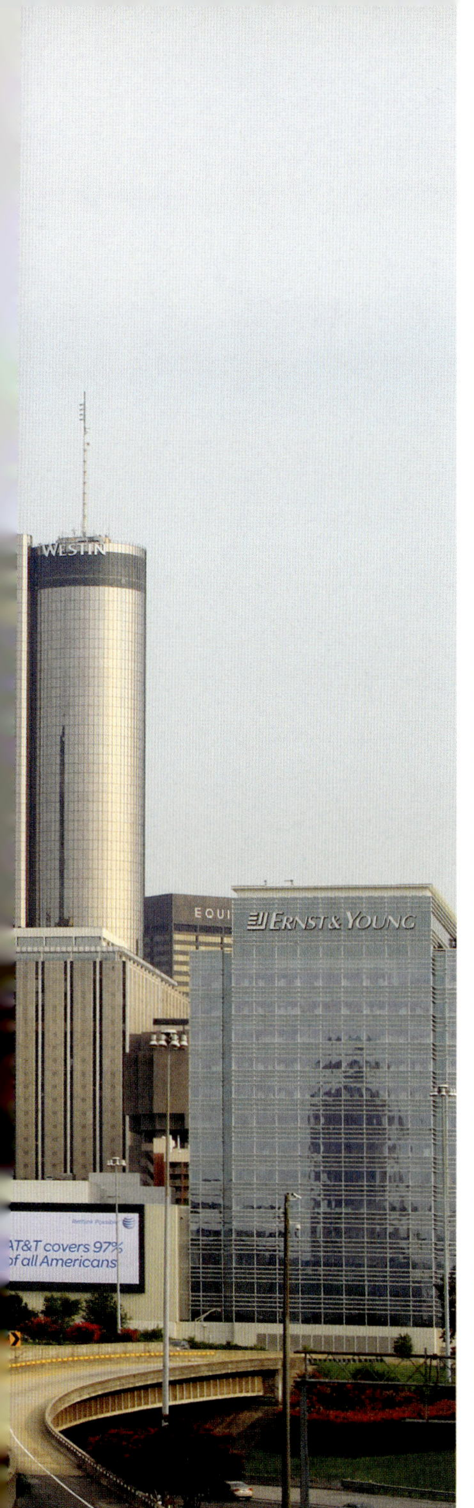

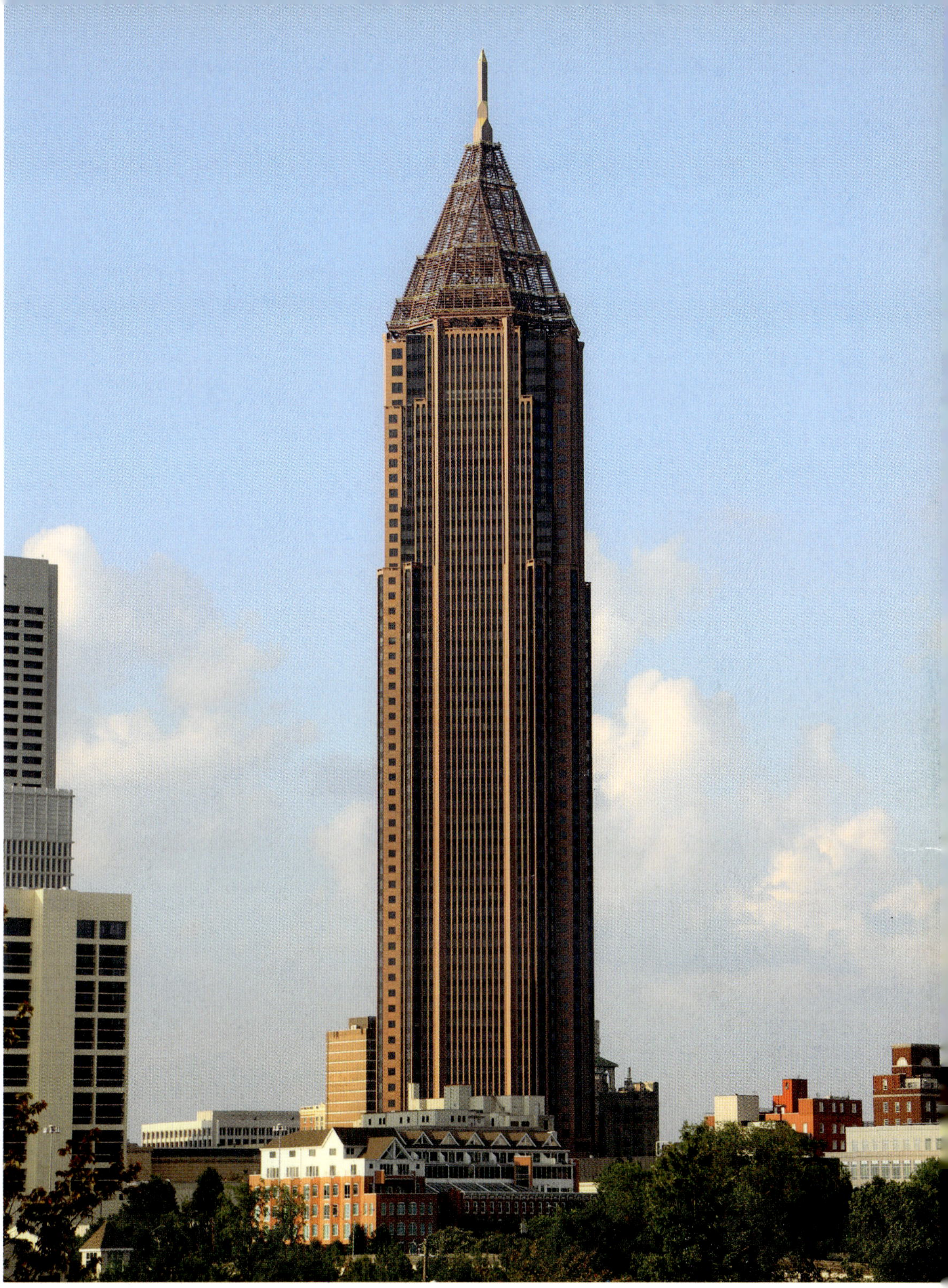

Bank of America Plaza *(above)*

The tallest building in the southern United States, this 55-story postmodern skyscraper embodies Atlanta's progressive, modern aesthetic and sensibility. The steel structure is distinguished with a granite facade crowned by a stepped pyramid whose steel frame tapers to a 90-foot high spire, much of it enrobed in 23-karat gold leaf.

Evening Skyline *(pages 16–17)*

Illuminated beneath an evening sky, Atlanta's impressive skyline is a dichotomy of New South and Old. Its eight skyscrapers along Peachtree Street, marvels of modern architectural styles, tower over a lush tree canopy that includes magnificent oaks. A former railroad town, Atlanta retains its Southern flair in spite of its growth.

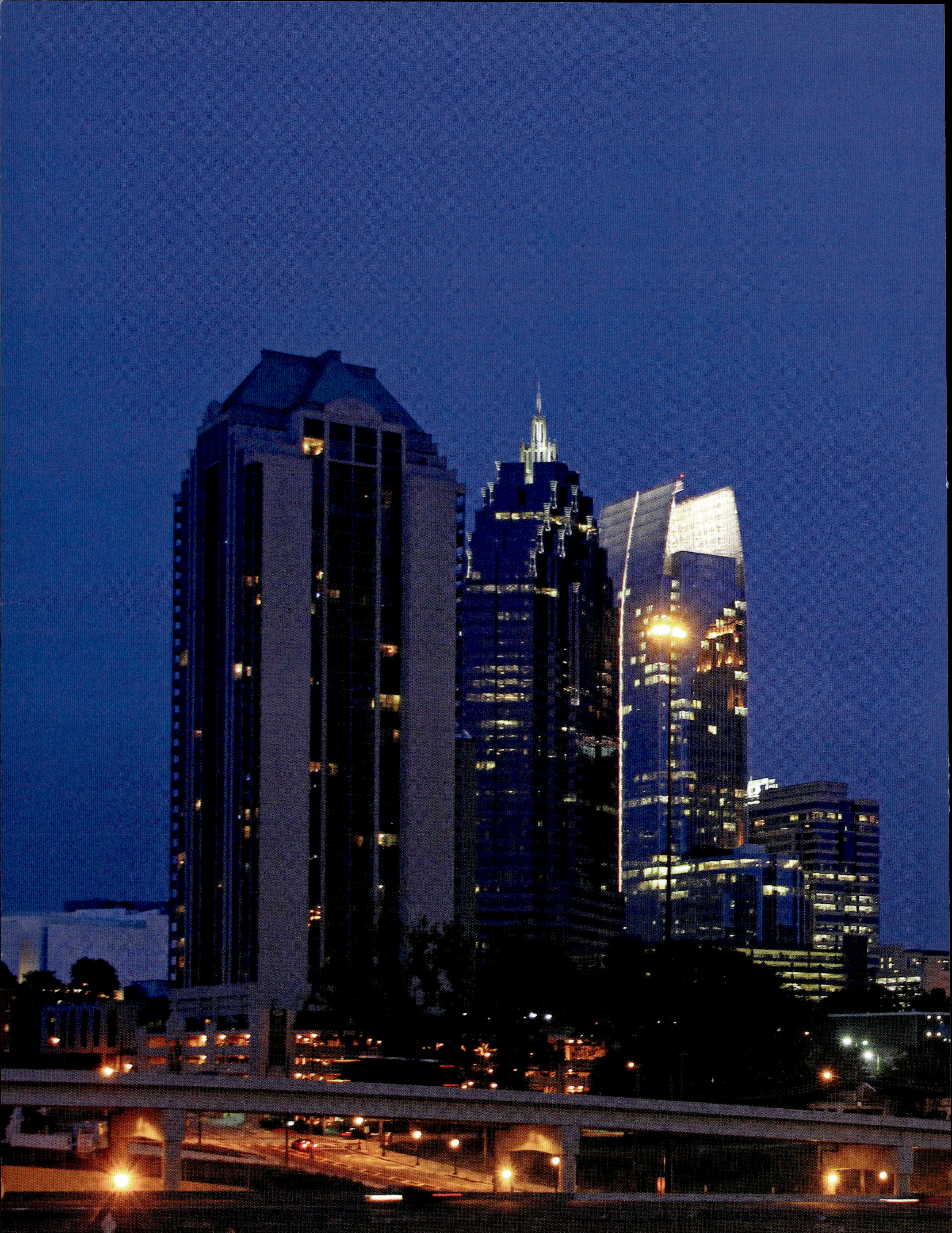

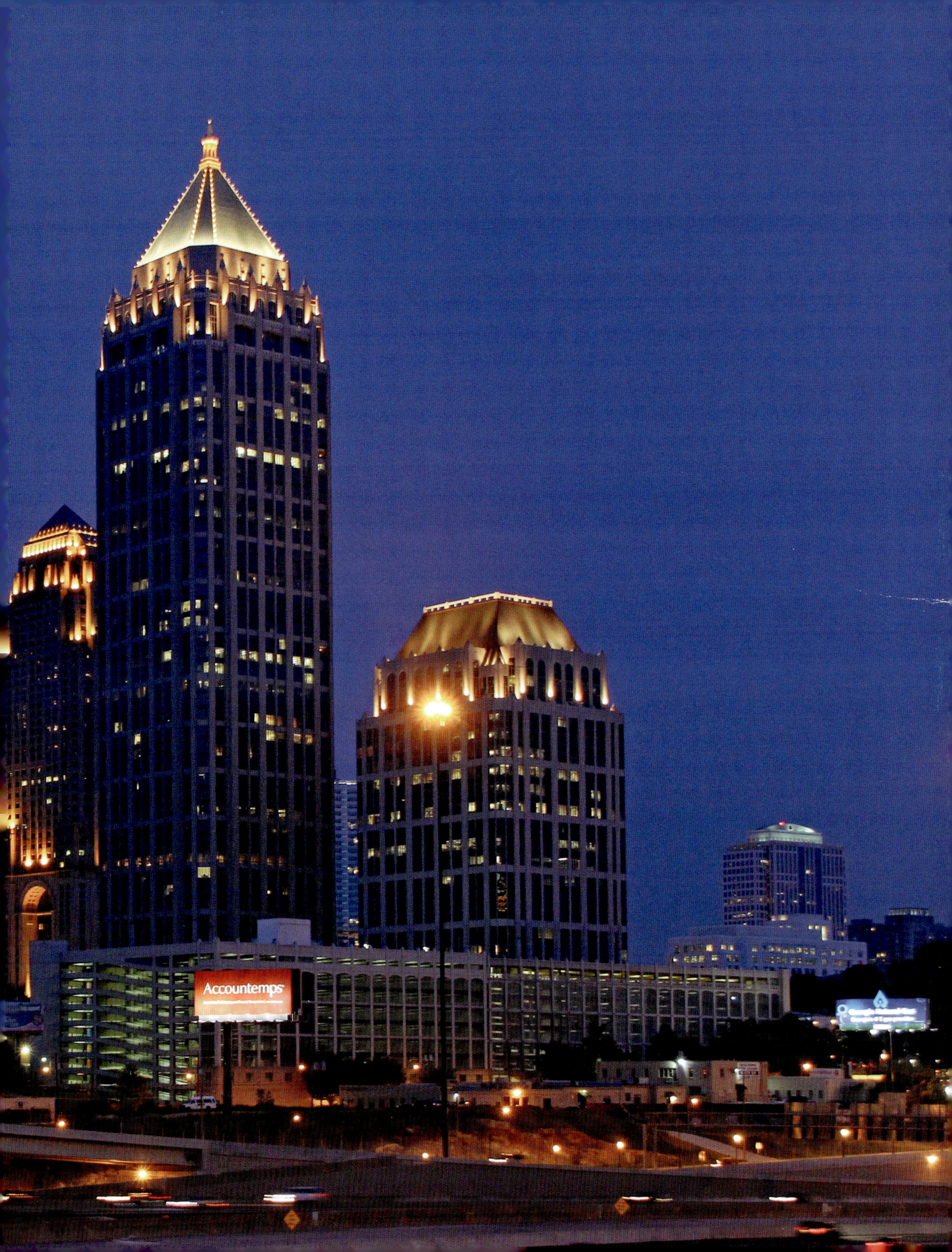
Accountemps

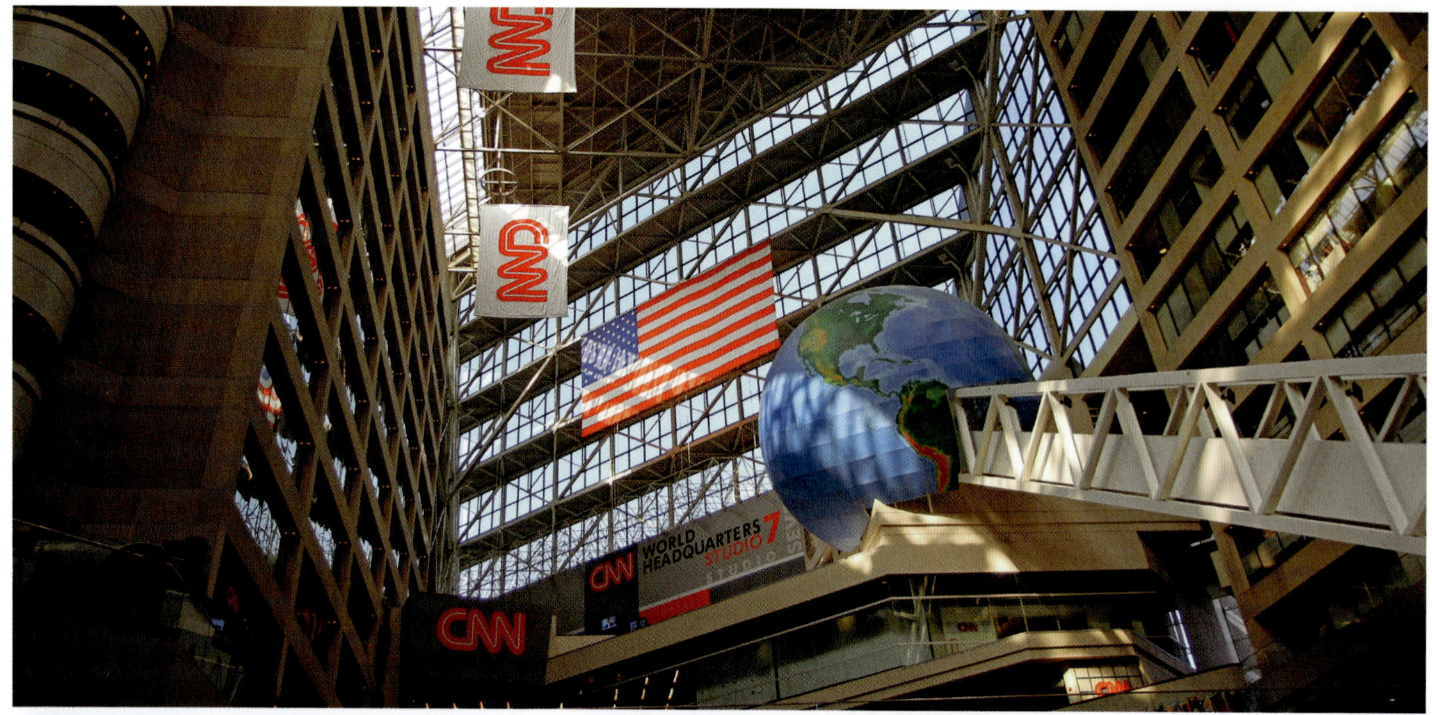

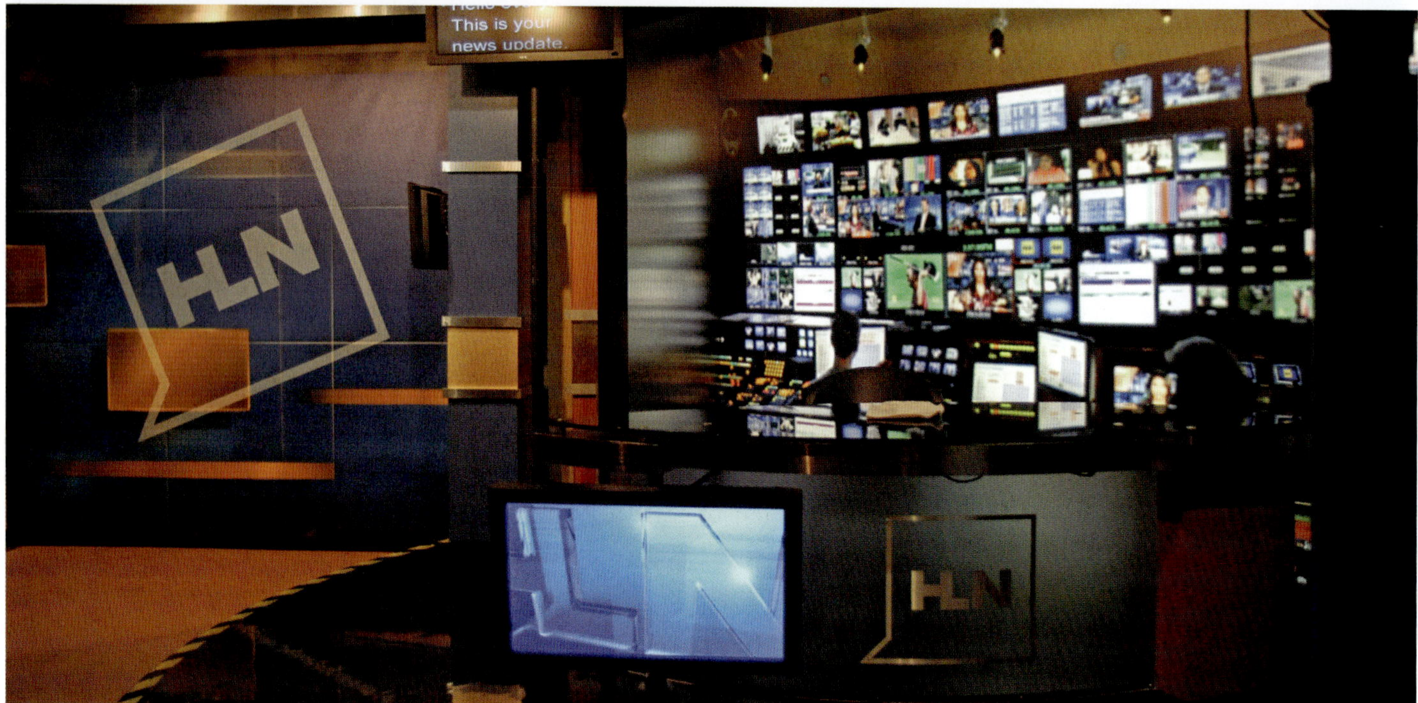

CNN Center *(top and bottom)*

CNN's global headquarters is home to the state-of-the-art HD Studio 7, where most of CNN's daytime broadcasting takes place. The Center also houses the Omni Hotel Downtown, an atrium food court, and multiple retail shops. Guided behind-the-scenes walking and VIP tours are available and include tours of the HLN control room.

Symphony Tower *(opposite)*

Shining like a beacon amidst Atlanta's skyscrapers, 1180 Peachtree, otherwise known as Symphony Tower, is a paean to the city's 21st-century mien. Portraying a modernist approach to natural lighting and a welcoming environment, the steel and concrete tower has gently curving facade, illuminated fins, and a 35,000-square-foot roof garden.

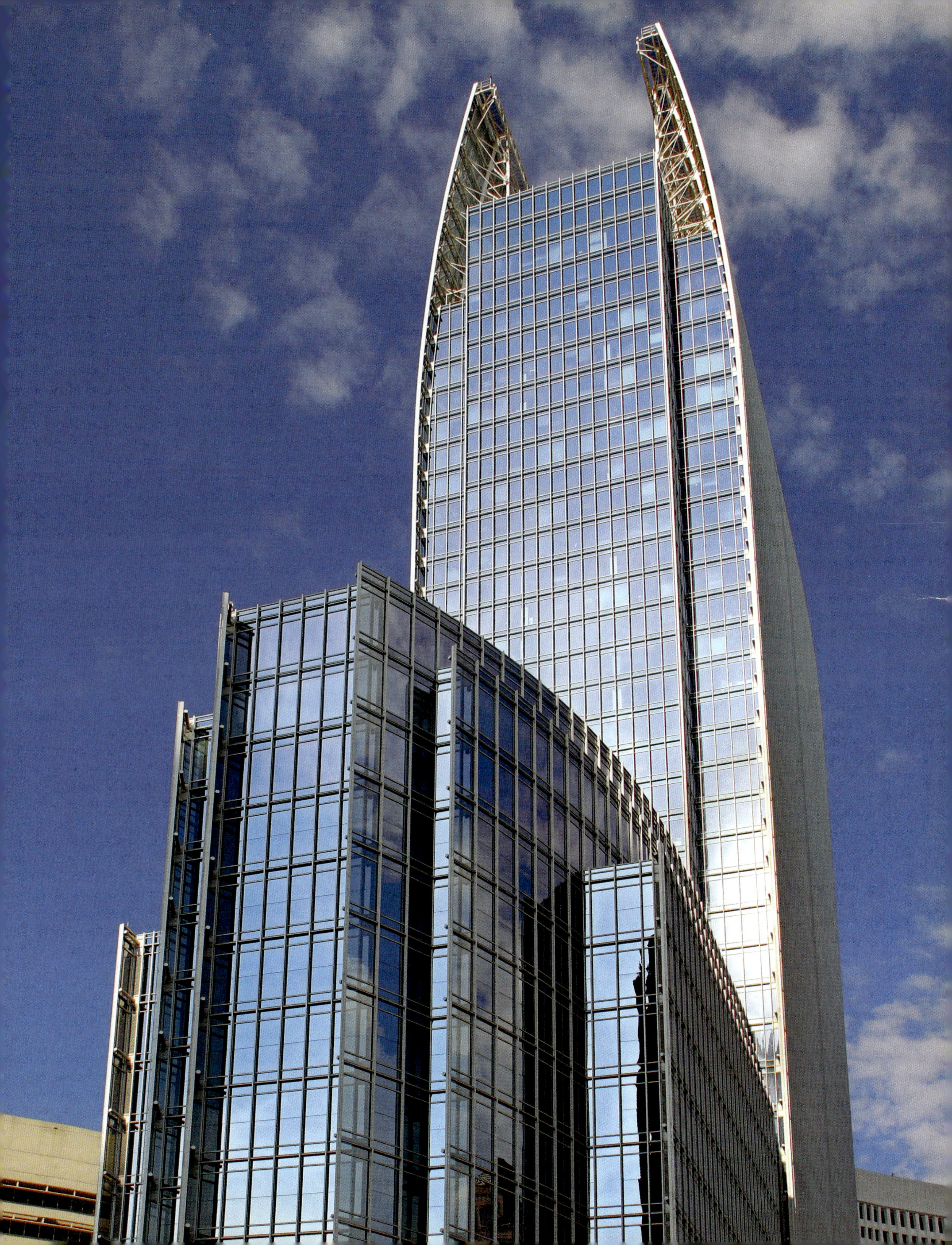

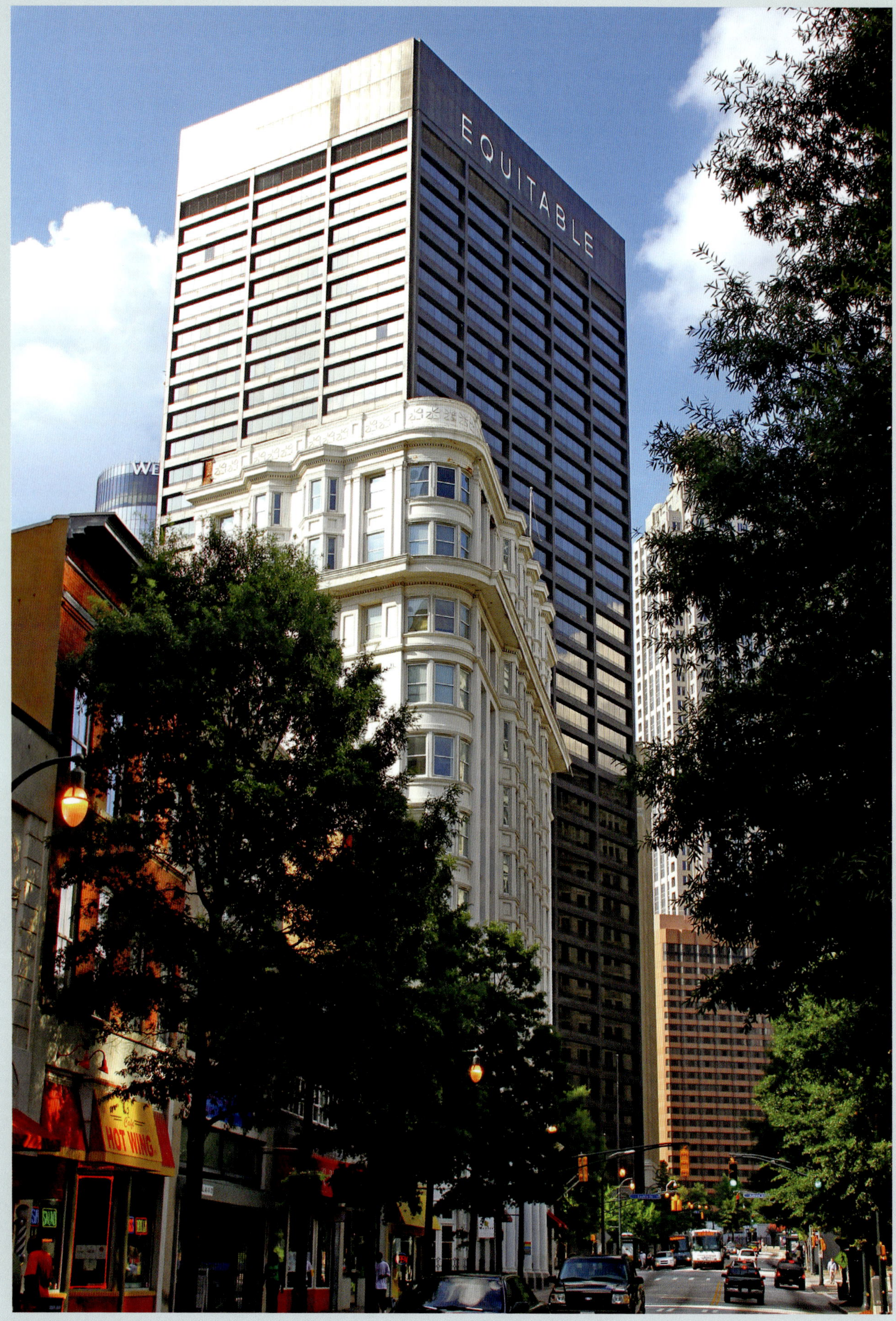
EQUITABLE
HOT WING

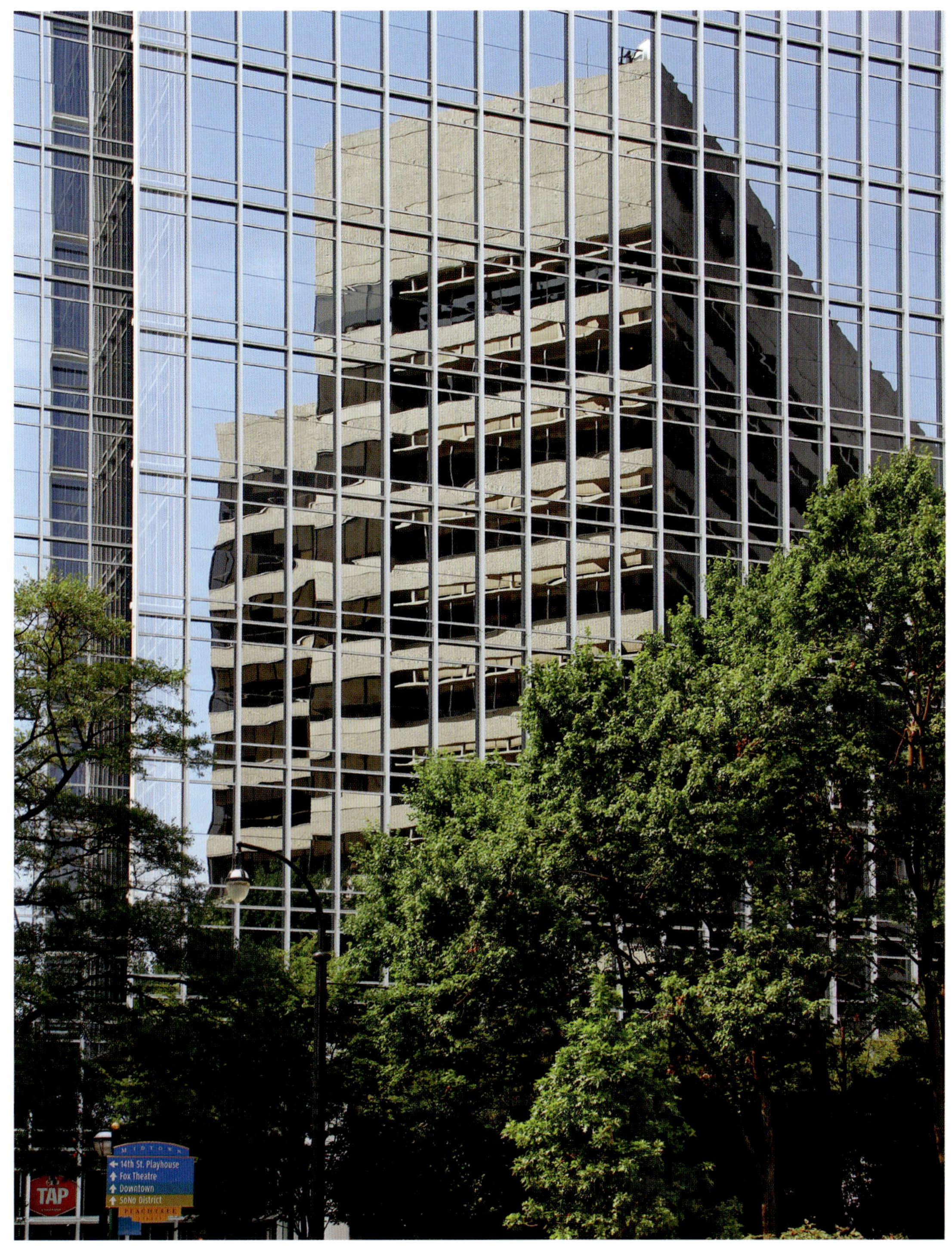

International City *(opposite)*

Dynamic, urbane and constantly in motion: Having risen from the ashes after being the only U.S. city ever destroyed by fire as an act of war, Atlanta's own long march transformed the former railroad town into a business and cultural mecca, an international city with a diverse population that is home to the world's busiest passenger airport.

The Evolution of Terminus *(above)*

Once known as the town of Terminus because of its railroading origins, the city was renamed Atlanta in 1845. A fusion of soaring office buildings and softer greenspaces, financial districts feature striking architecture and neighborhoods that articulate an ambience of Victorian charm, cultural verve, and artistic élan.

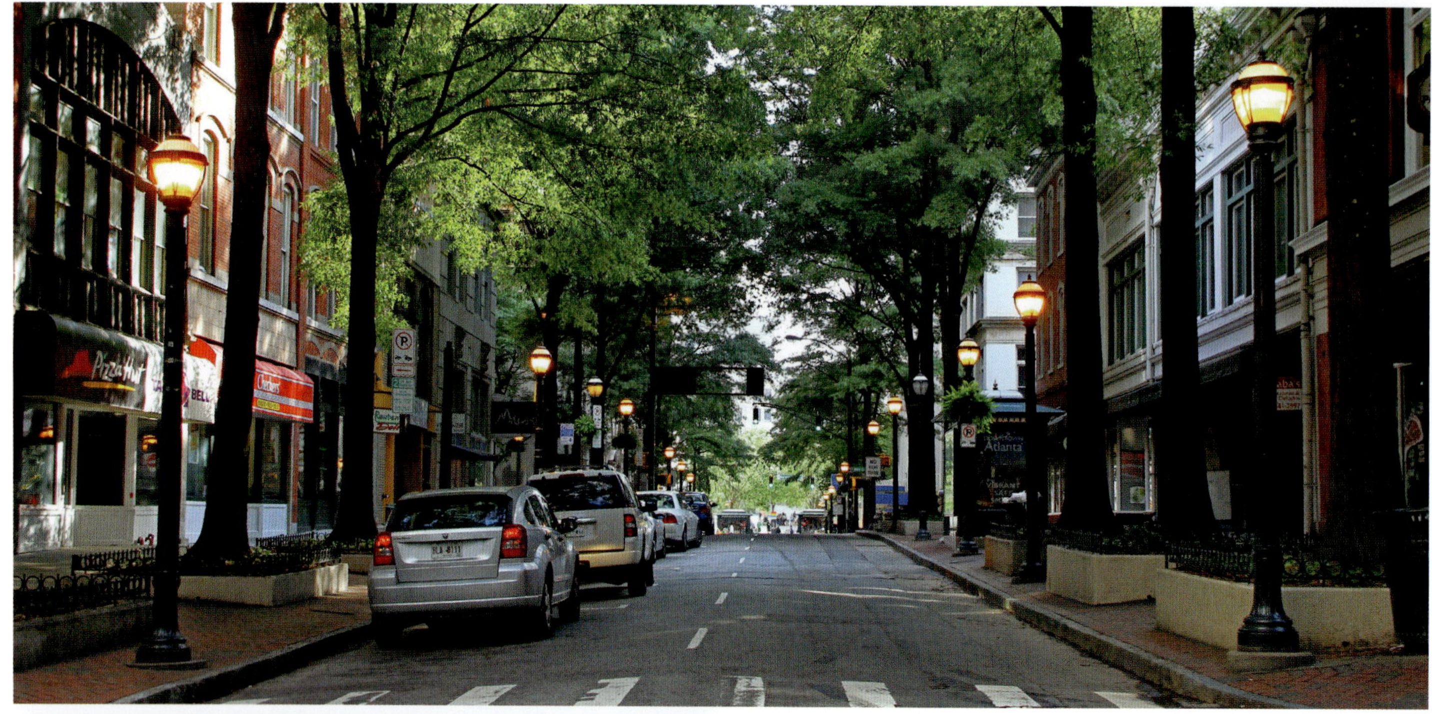

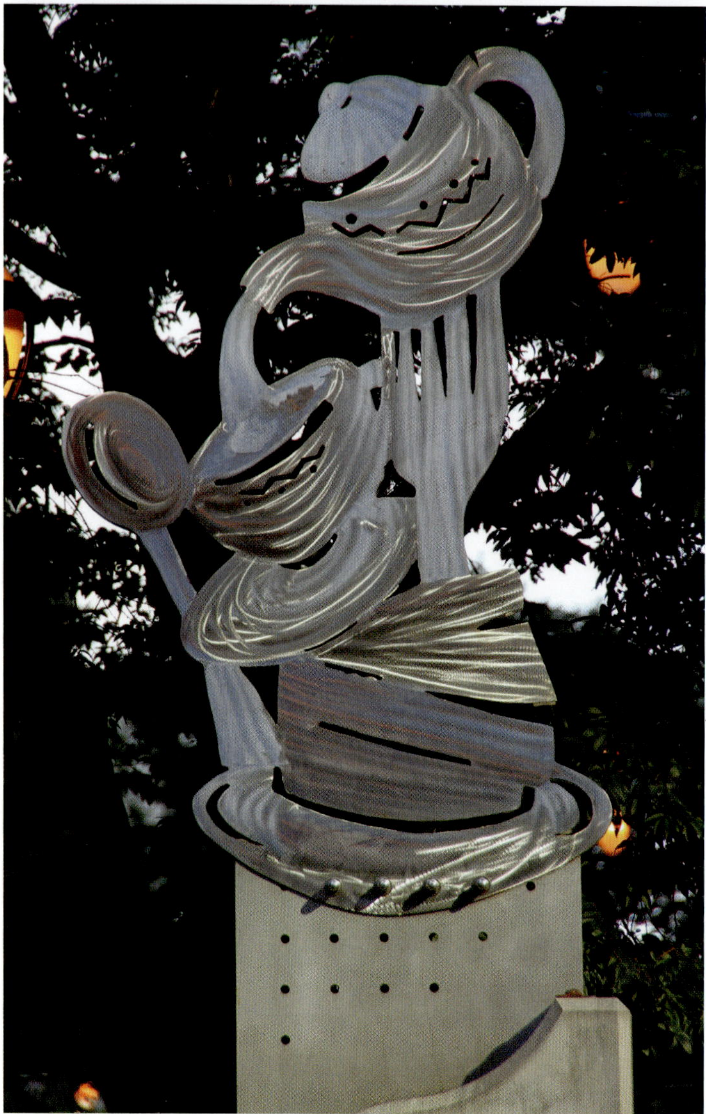

Atlanta's Diverse Neighborhoods *(top)*

Atlanta's neighborhoods are as distinct as the ethos that characterizes them: business-minded Downtown; cultured, cosmopolitan Midtown; affluent Buckhead, legendary for its shopping; quietly hip Virginia-Highland; East Atlanta and its gentrified neighborhoods; Little Five Points with its alternative edge; urban SoNo (South of North Avenue); the historic African-American community of Sweet Auburn; and the Frederick Law Olmsted-designed Druid Hills.

Cultural Atlanta *(left)*

The scents of countless restaurants – hundreds Zagat-rated – including everything from international fine dining to soul food, mingle into an intoxicating culinary olio. Equally enticing is Atlanta's arts and culture scene: gallery strolls, museum exhibits, visual and performing arts, and world-class attractions, including the High Museum of Art, the Fox Theatre, World of Coca-Cola, CNN Center, and the Georgia Aquarium.

Peachtree Building *(opposite)*

The 20-story Peachtree Building pays tribute to Georgian architecture with Corinthian-style columns, a brick veneer and century cobblestone, and granite curbing. The interior lobby has three towers with a connecting atrium of glass, ornate millwork, and coffered ceilings. Slate walkways and a formal English garden lend a sophisticated air.

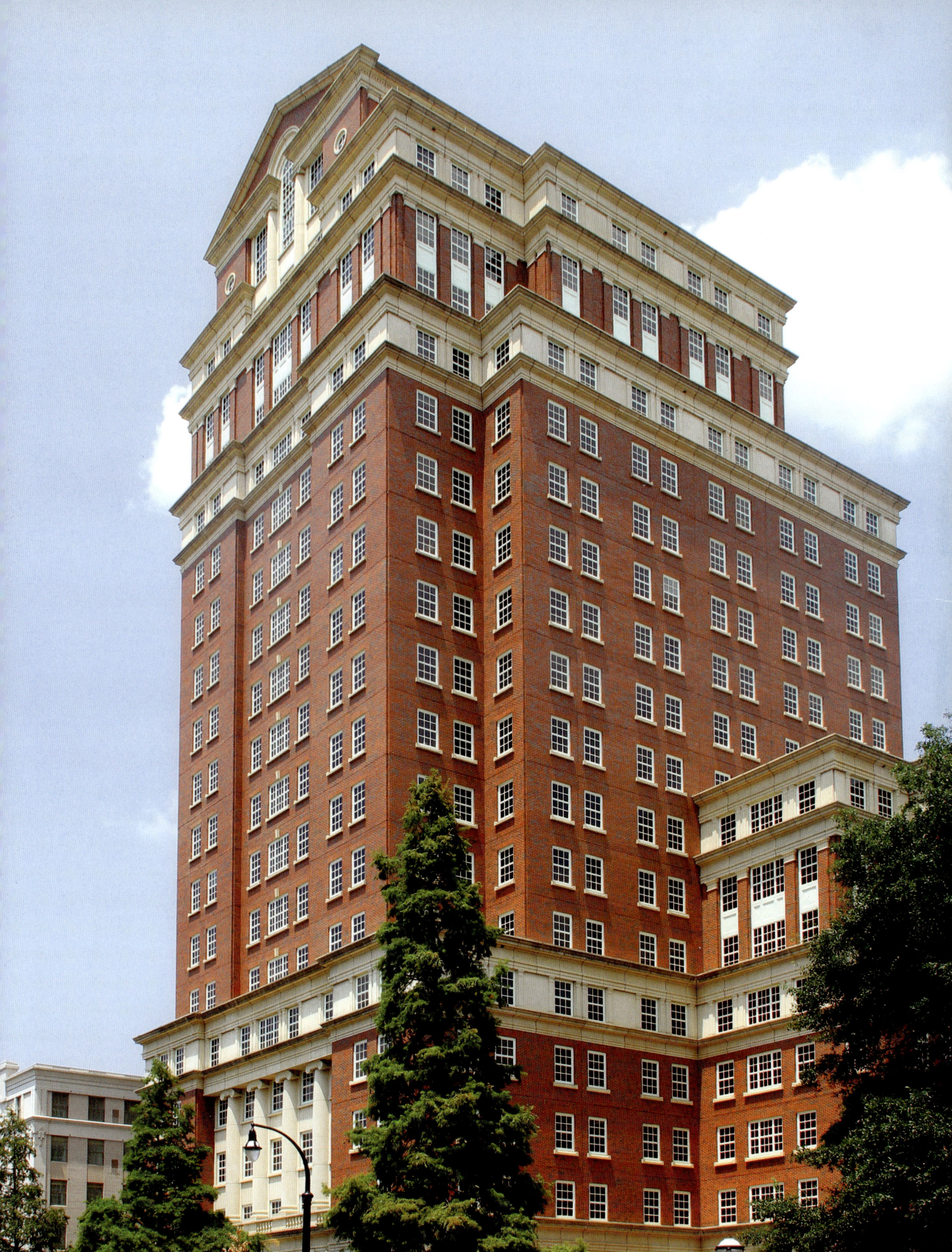

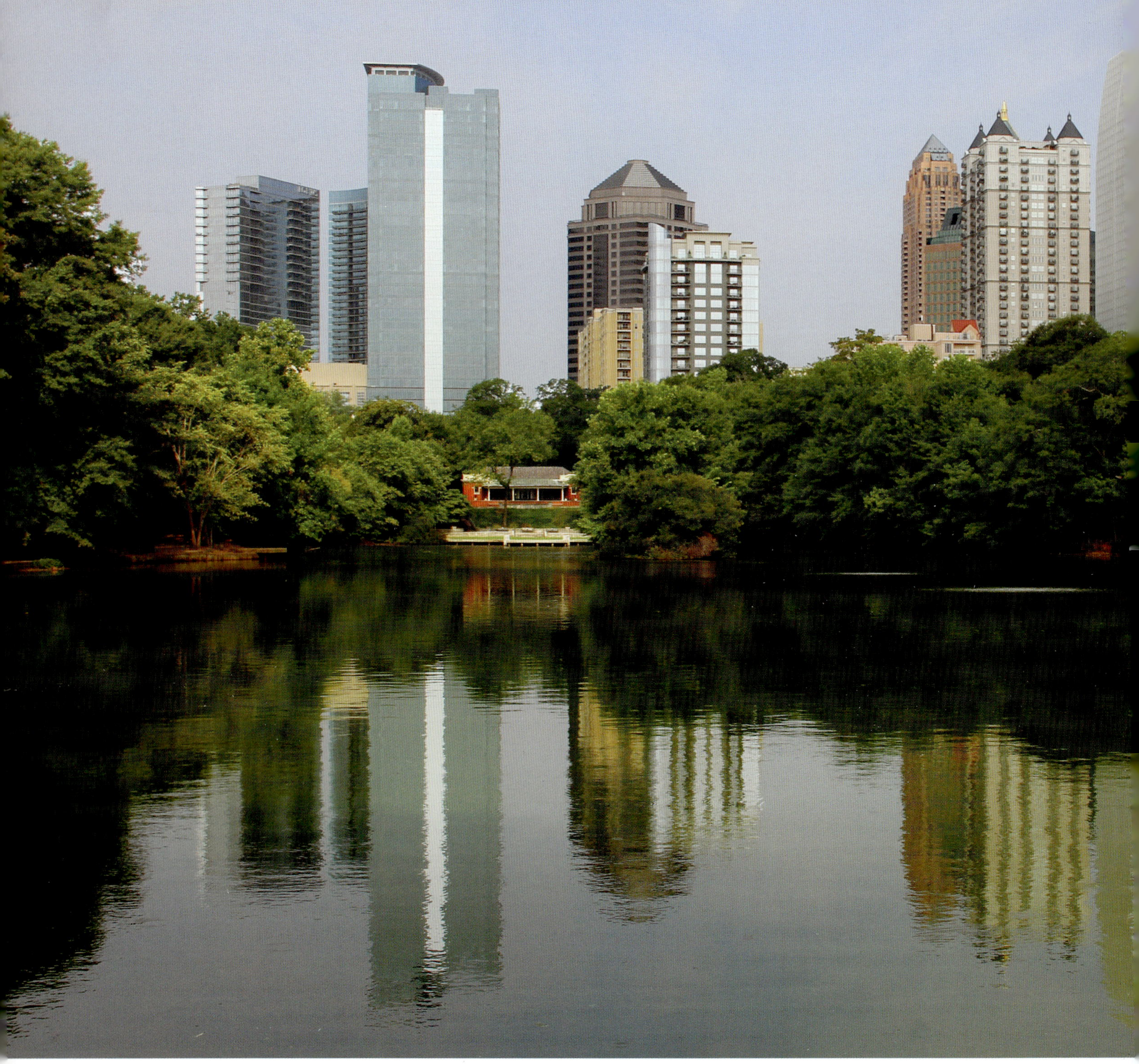

In Reflection

Atlanta is America's most forested city, with more than 25 percent of the city covered with trees – magnolias, pines, hickories, and hundred-year-old oaks. Here, the waters of Lake Clara Meer in Piedmont Park, which was designed by the sons of famed landscape architect Frederick Law Olmsted, mirror skyline and foliage.

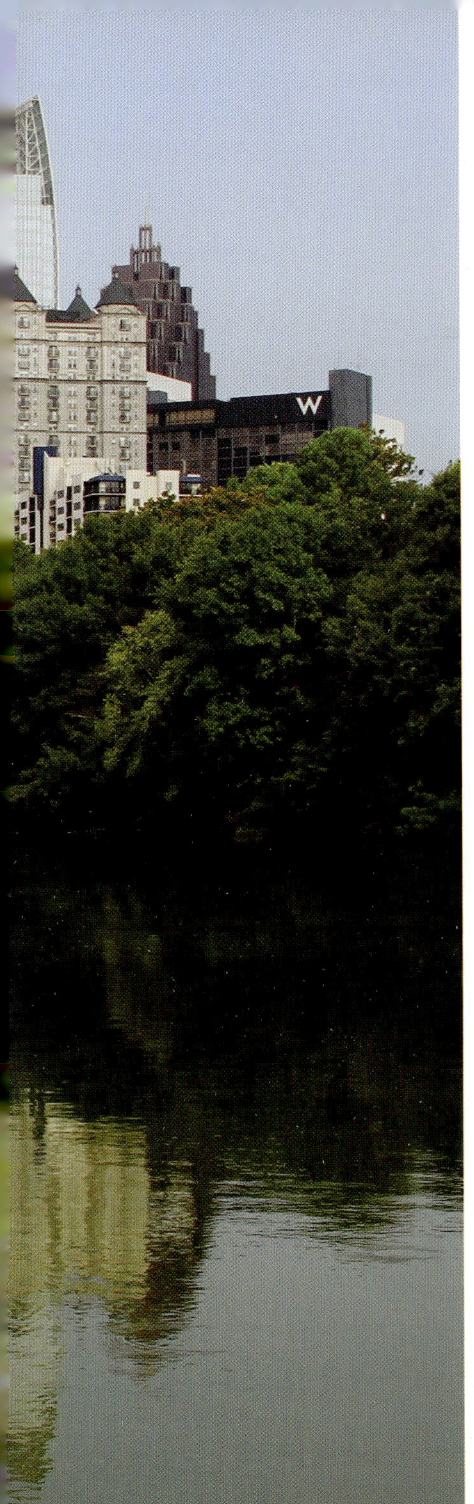

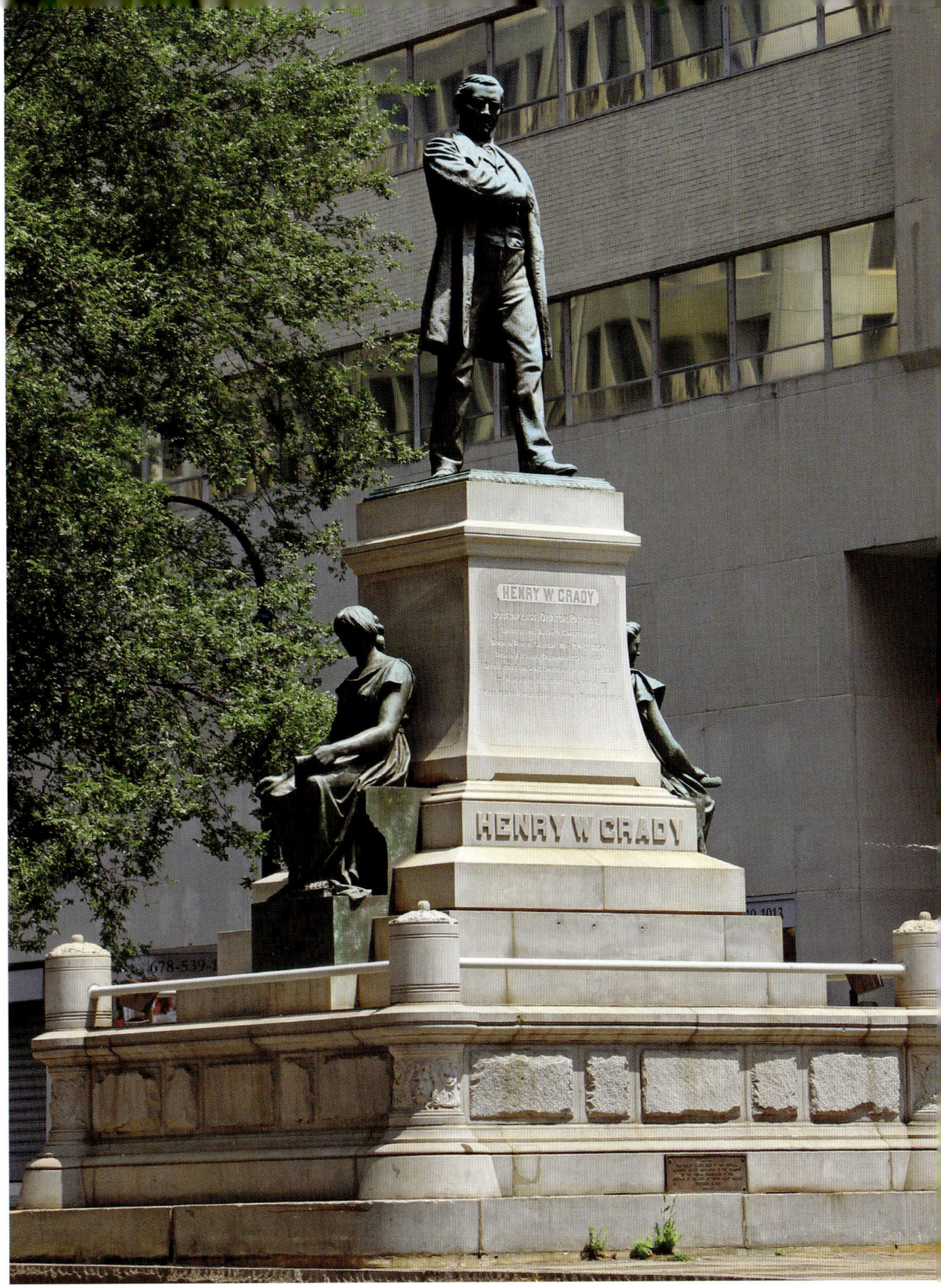

Henry W. Grady Sculpture

As dynamic as Atlanta itself, Henry W. Grady (1850-1889), the "Spokesman of the New South," was the managing editor for, and eventually part owner of, the *Atlanta Constitution* in the 1880s. An advocate for industrial development in the post-Civil War South, Grady was inducted into the Georgia Writers Hall of Fame in 2004.

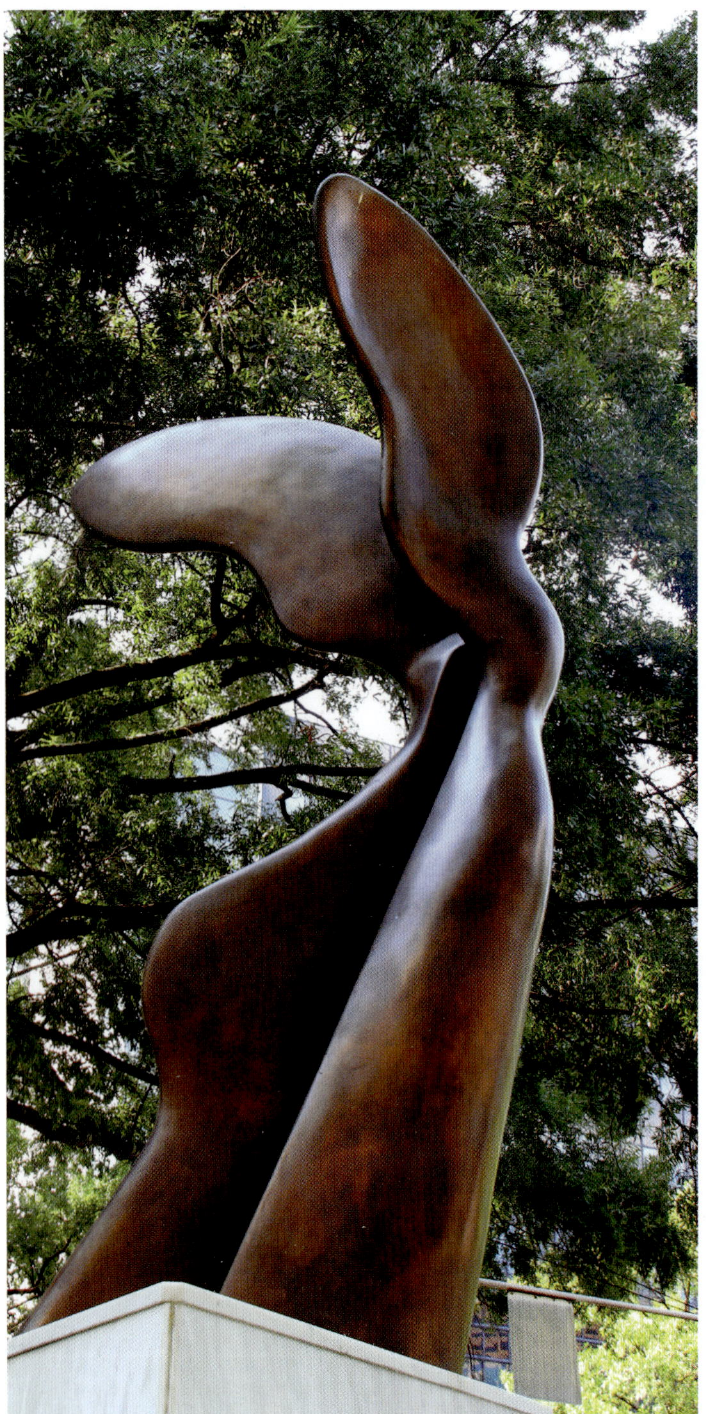

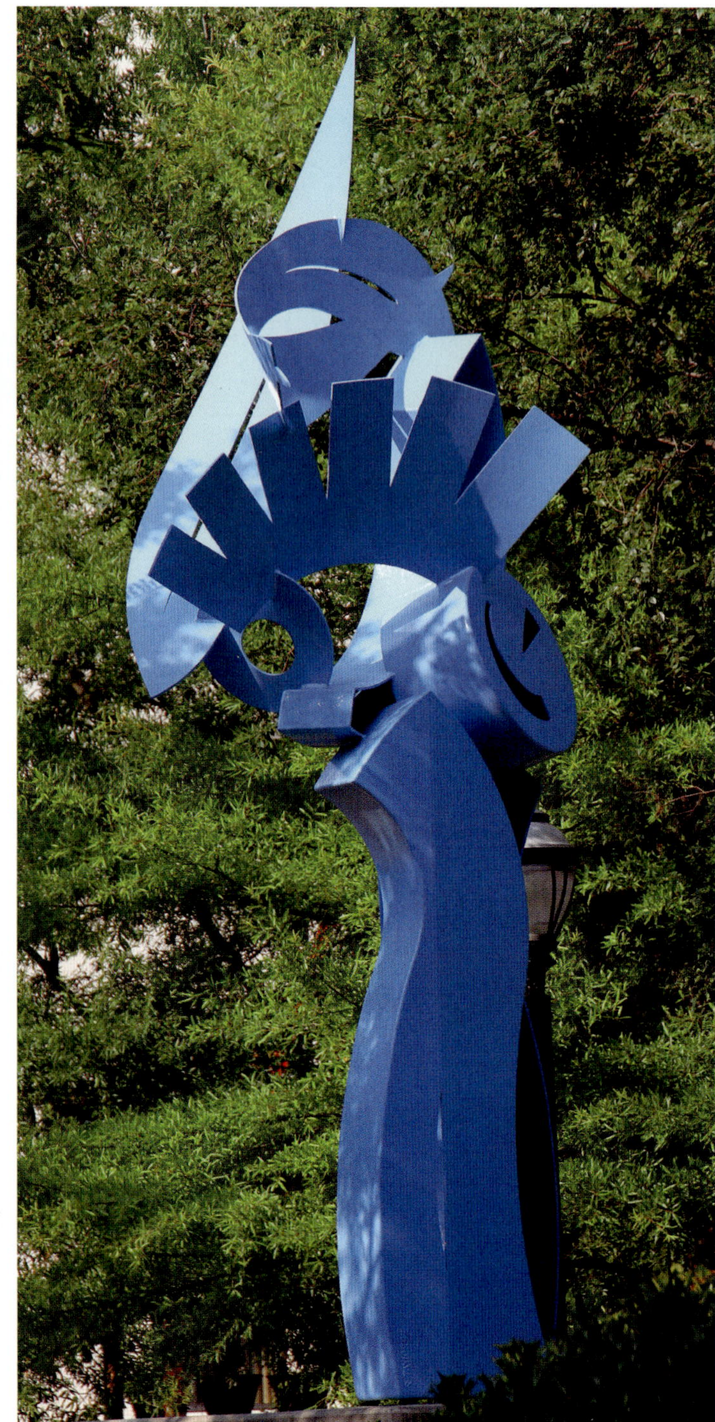

Nike *(above left)*

A contemporary adaption of the *Winged Victory of Samothrace* statue – a masterpiece of Greek sculpture on exhibit at the Louvre in Paris – this bronze and marble sculpture by Pavlos Kougioumtzis was a permanent gift to Atlanta from the City of Athens, Greece. Located at City Hall, it symbolizes the ideals of the Olympics.

The River Sings *(above right)*

Created by Richard Taylor, a Milwaukee sculptor whose art "allows the cadences, rhythms and syncopations of music and poetry to find themselves" in his work, the 15-foot *The River Sings* holds court in Hardy Ivy Park. It references the power and vitality of a river's flow and its presence and optimism in the world.

Grand Mercy *(opposite)*

Artist Jerry Peart, who has created more than 35 large-scale public sculptures, unveiled *Grand Mercy* in 1996. This lyrical abstract sculpture, evocative of classical and historical images, is intended as a salute to the people of Atlanta. It was commissioned by Hyatt Corporate and stands on the grounds of the Hyatt Regency Atlanta.

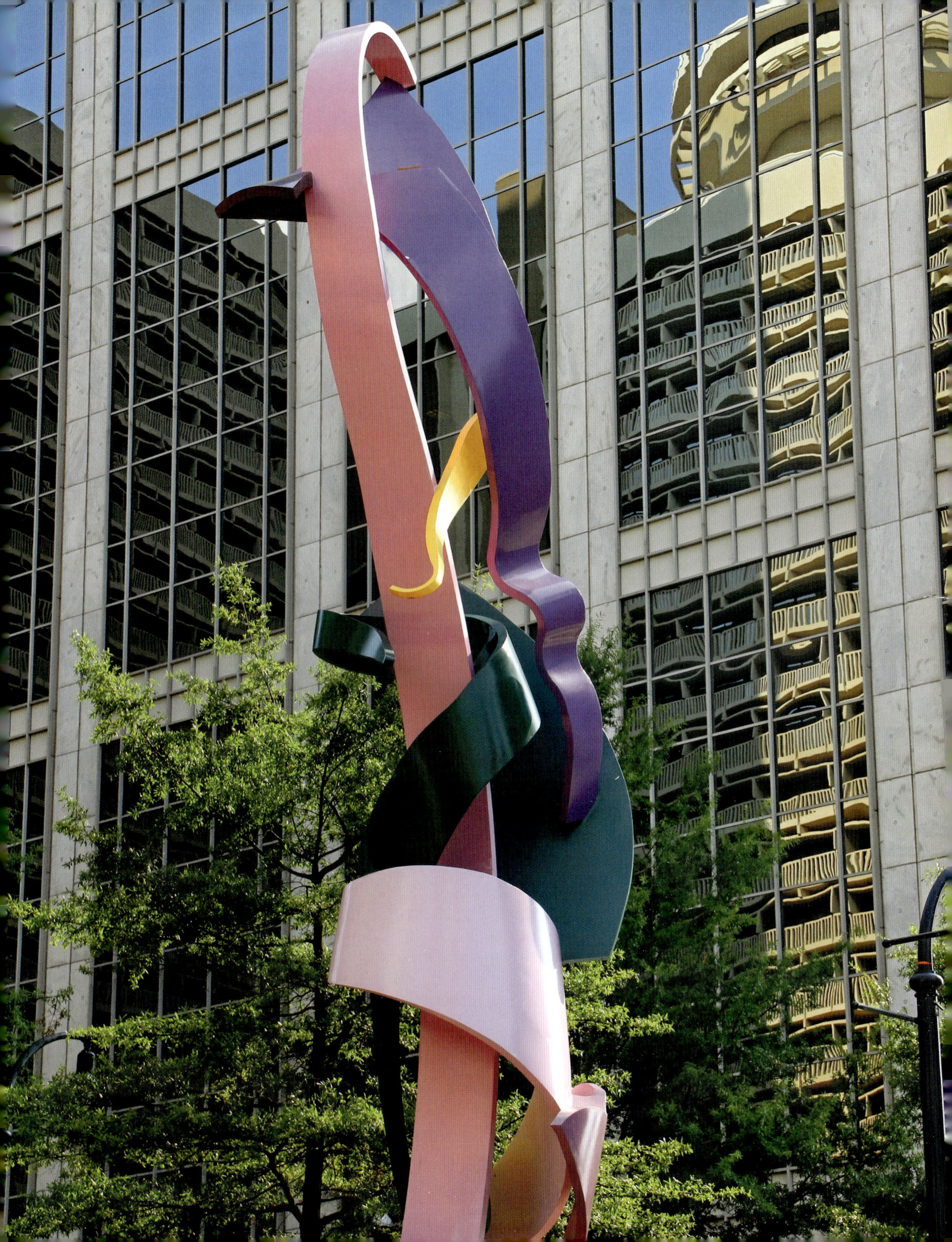

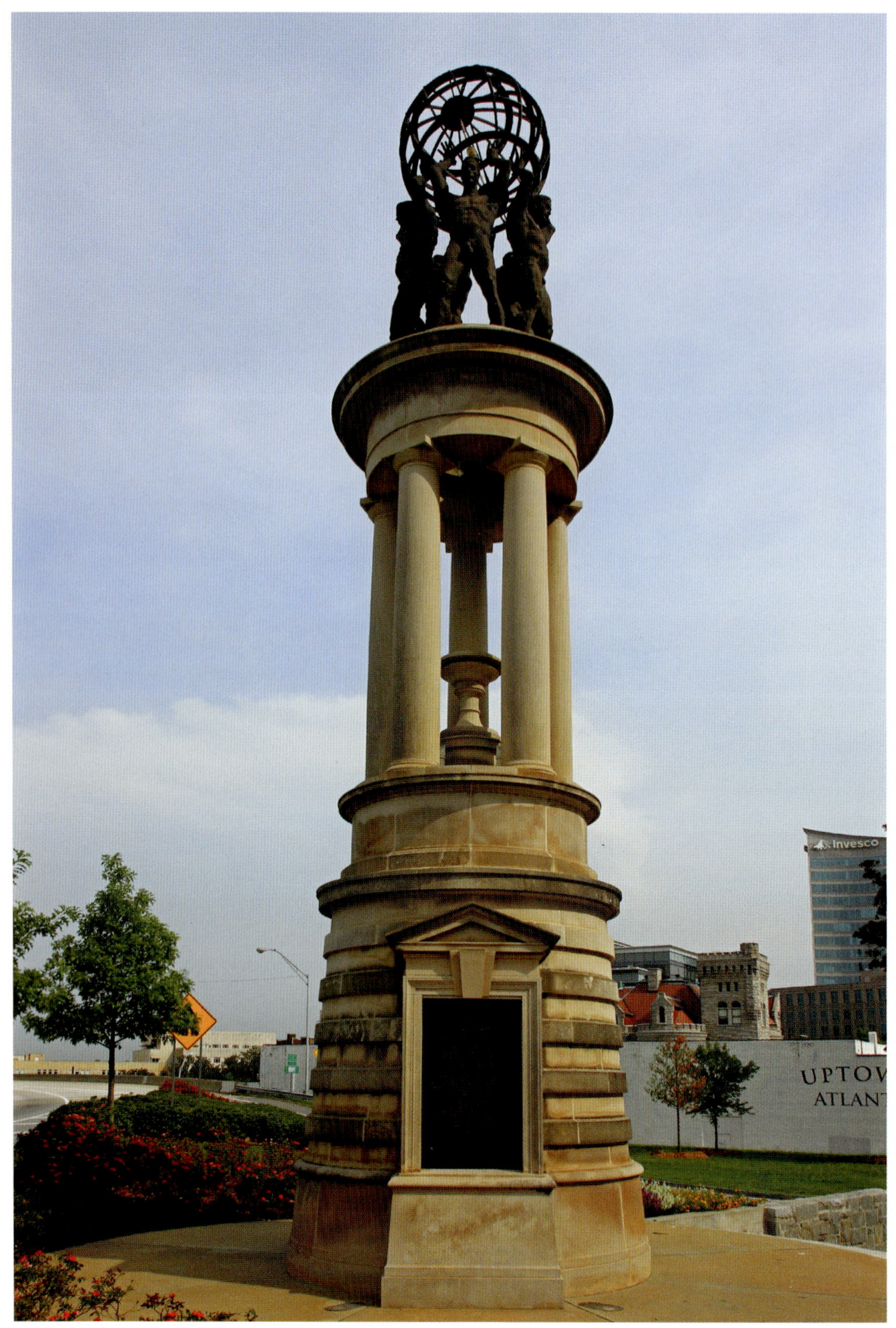

World Athletes Monument *(above)*

This monument to the 1996 Olympic Games, also known as the Prince of Wales's Monument and the Olympic Monument, is carved of Indiana limestone. Rising 55 feet in Midtown, its *tholos* (ancient Greek building) is circled by five Doric columns, which represent the five continents, and support five titans who together carry a globe.

The Flair *(opposite)*

Celebrating the triumph of the human spirit, *The Flair* reflects the Olympic credo of *citius, altius, fortius* (swifter, higher, stronger) and is dedicated not only to Olympic athletes but to all who pursue excellence and the "heroic possibilities of mankind." It stands east of the Georgia Dome in the Georgia World Congress Center complex.

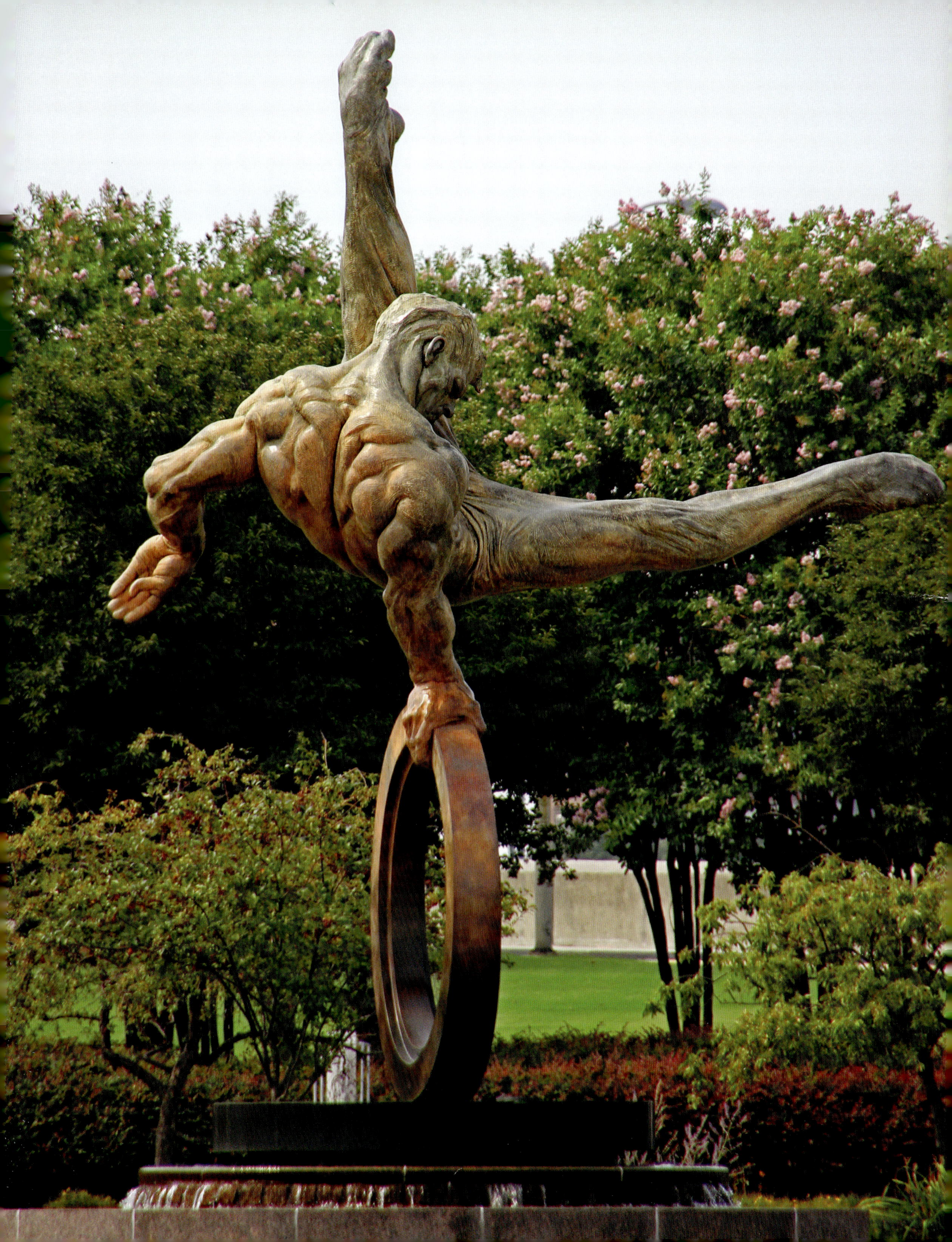

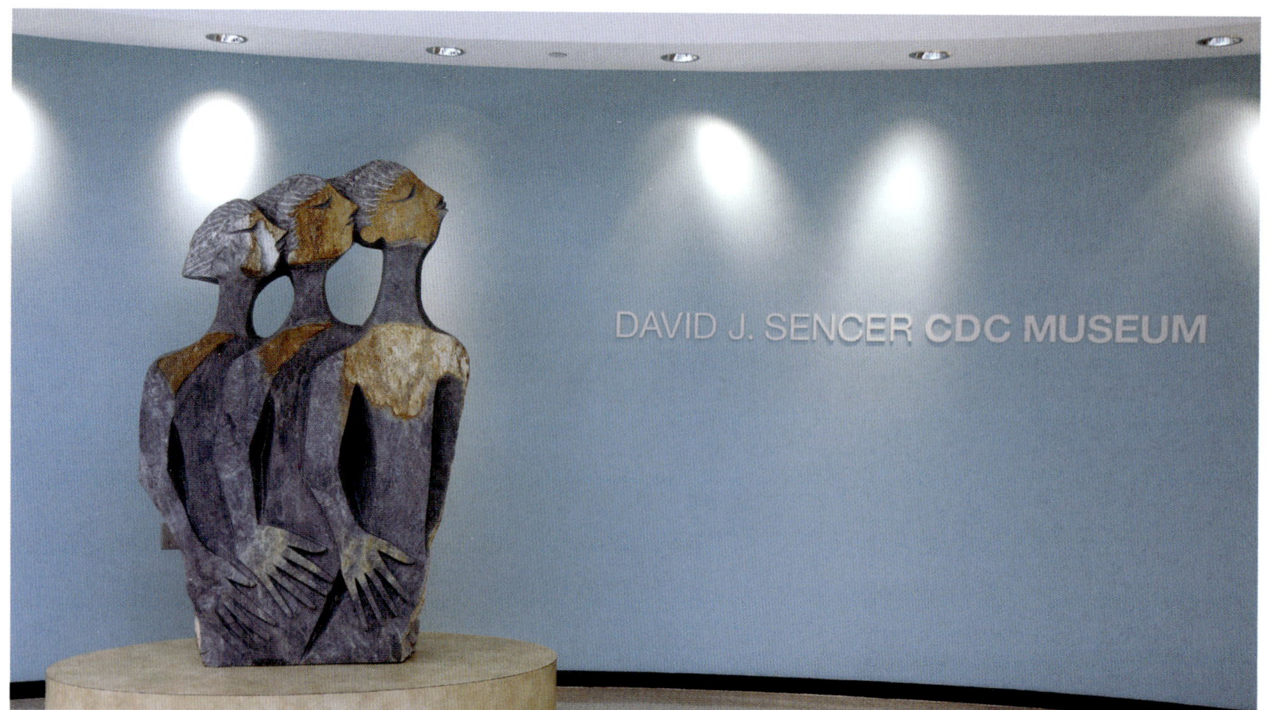

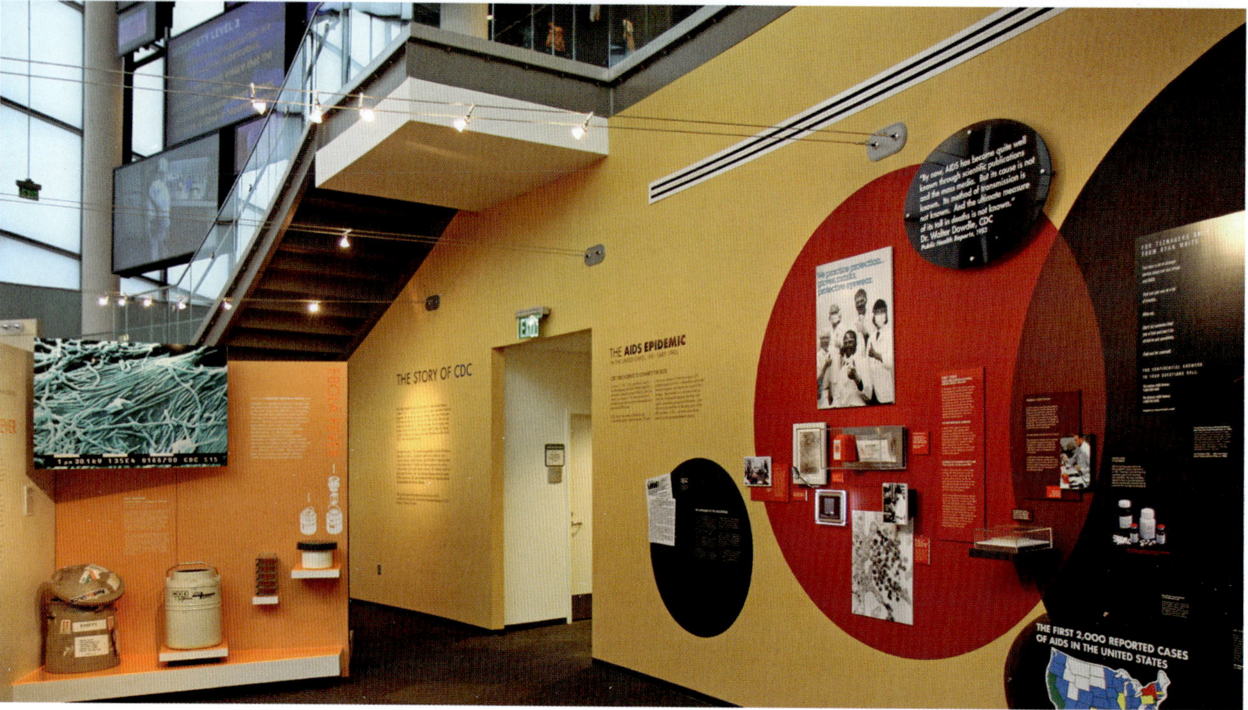

David J. Sencer CDC Museum *(top)*

The David J. Sencer CDC Museum features high-tech, hands-on exhibits focusing on the history of CDC and a variety of public health topics. Interactive timelines and displays show how scientists crack the cases of mystery diseases. Changing exhibits throughout the year supplement permanent installations, including the multimedia *Global Symphony*.

Rotating Exhibitions *(bottom)*

Originally the Global Health Odyssey, the David J. Sencer CDC Museum teaches CDC, public health, and the benefits of prevention. A Smithsonian Institution Affiliate, it has changing exhibitions of both CDC-curated and traveling exhibitions, and offers educational programming, research opportunities, tours, and an annual CDC Disease Detective Camp.

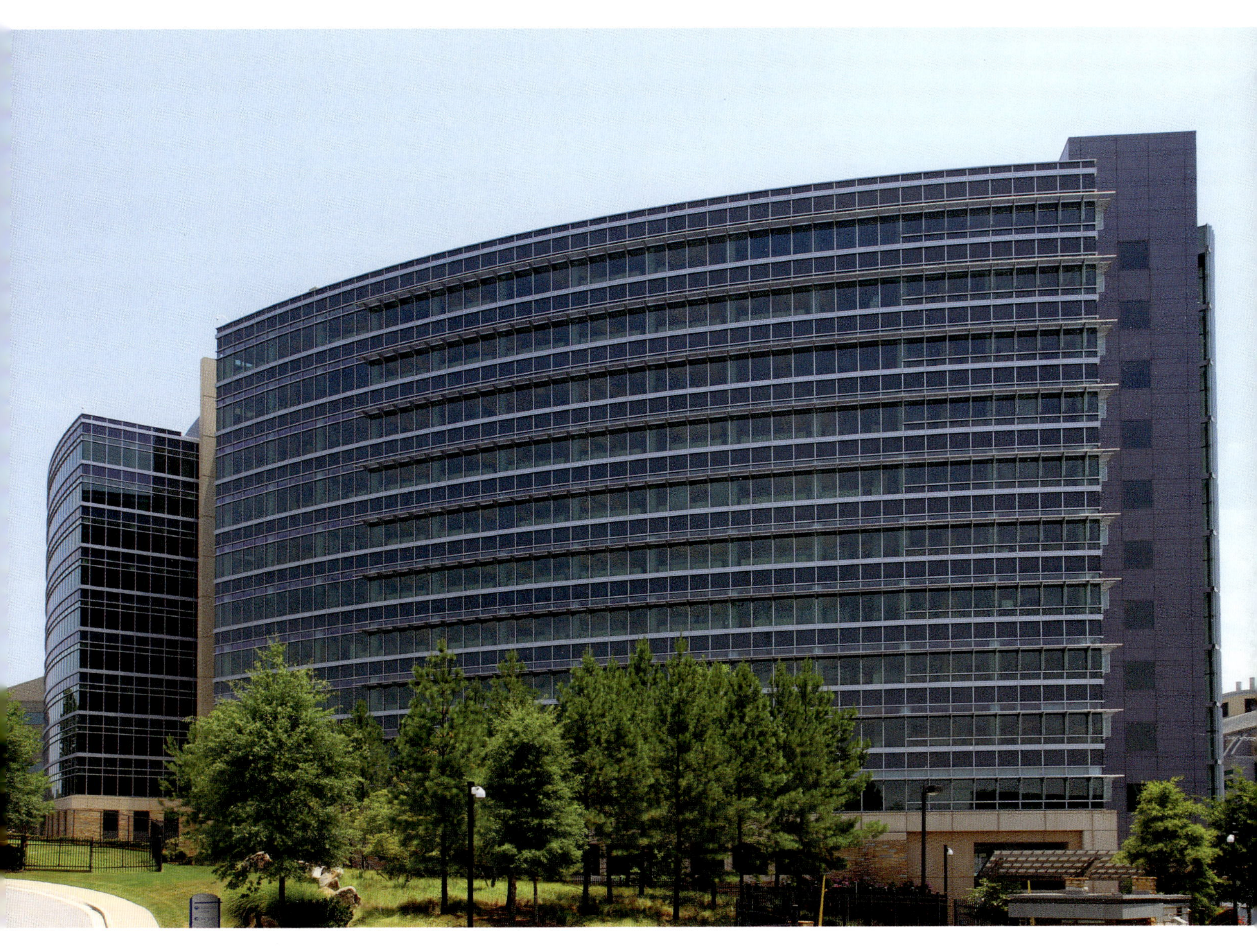

Centers for Disease Control and Prevention

Headquartered in Atlanta, the Centers for Disease Control and Prevention (CDC) was founded in 1946. It is the nation's premier health promotion, prevention, and preparedness agency and a global leader in public health, recognized for its action-oriented approach to conducting research.

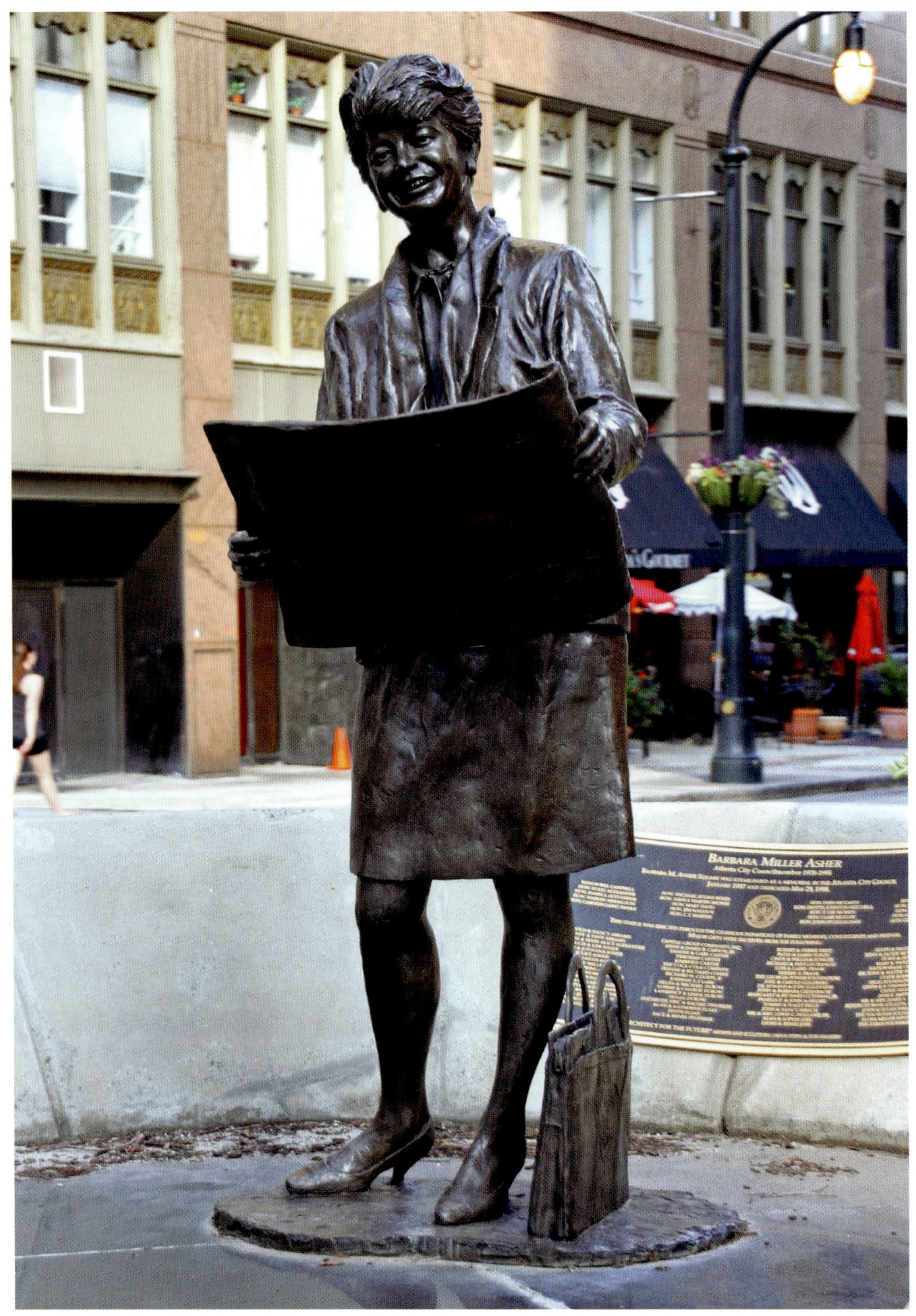

Barbara Miller Asher *(above)*

Smiling widely on a pedestrian plaza at Five Points is Barbara Miller Asher, a progressive-minded Atlanta councilwoman who served from 1978 to 1995 and who was one of the driving forces for the city's downtown revitalization. The memorial, called *Architect for the Future* and crafted by Don Haugen, was installed in 1997 at Asher Square.

Promenade II *(opposite)*

Soaring nearly 700 feet into Midtown Atlanta's skyline is Promenade II, also known as the AT&T Building. Constructed of granite and glass, this postmodern marvel, set diagonally to the street grid to maximize its impact on the skyline, has a ziggurat-like tapering spire with stainless steel fins that are illuminated at night.

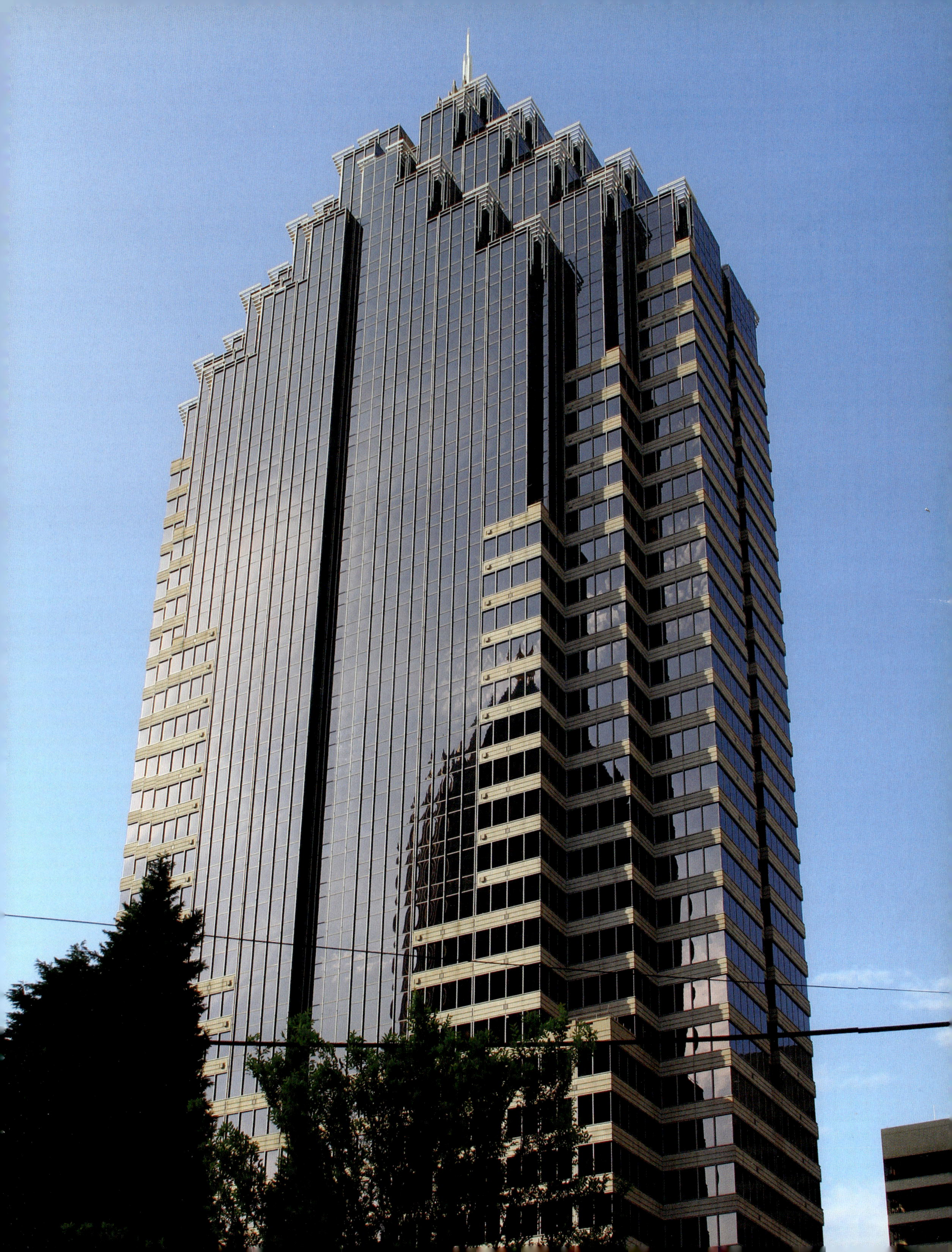

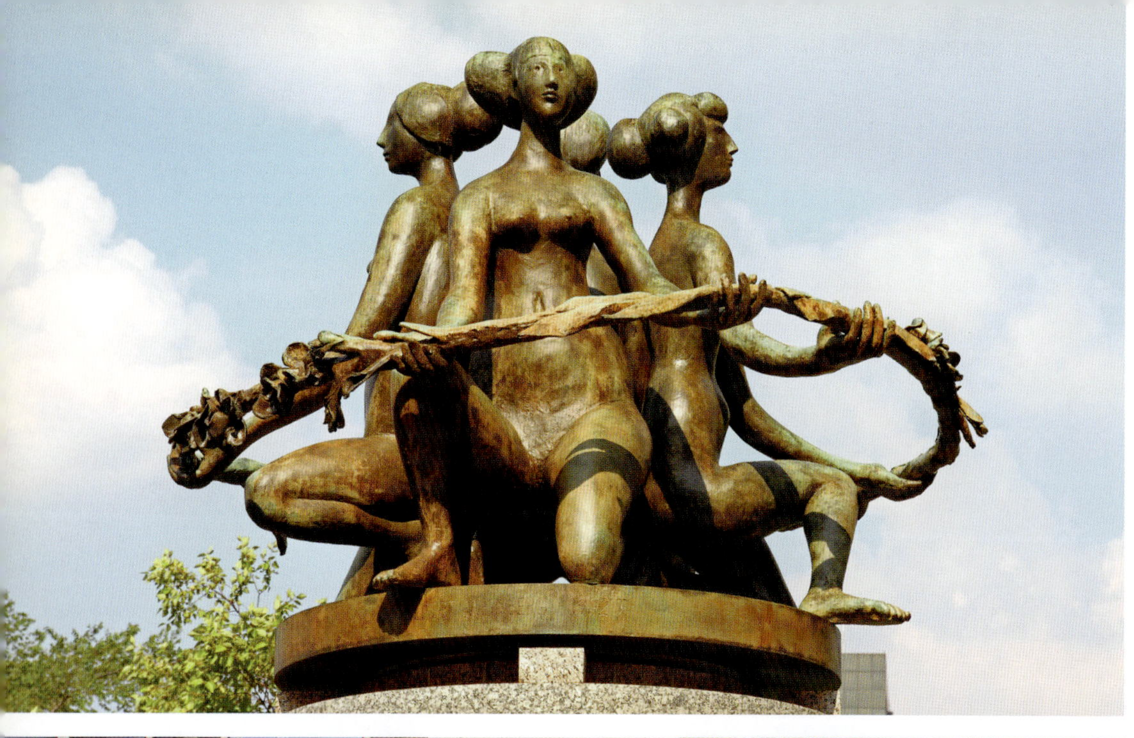

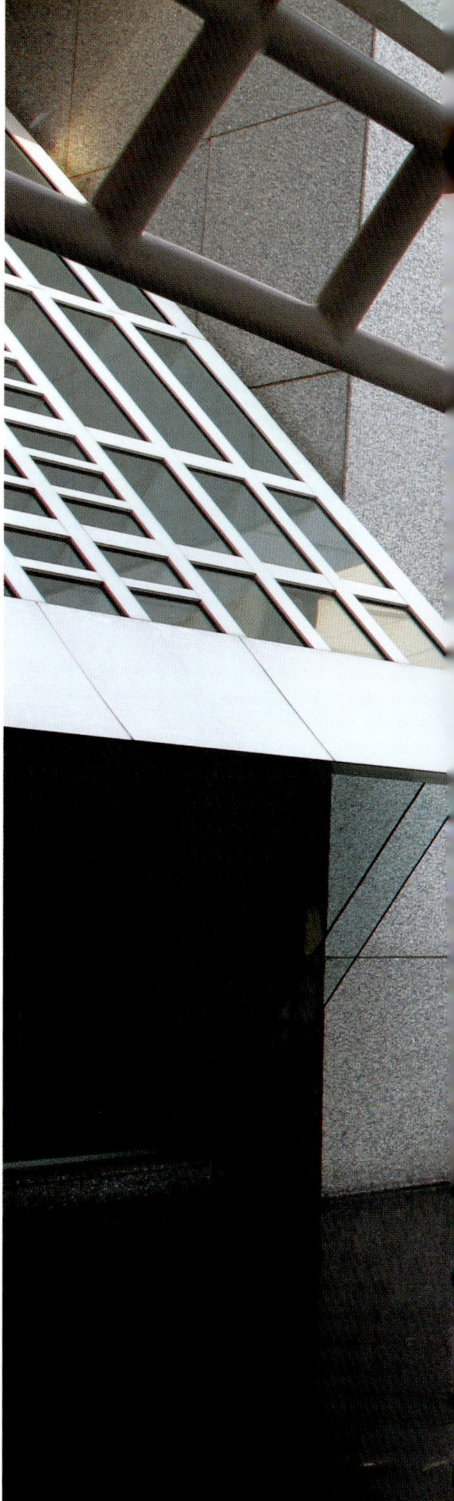

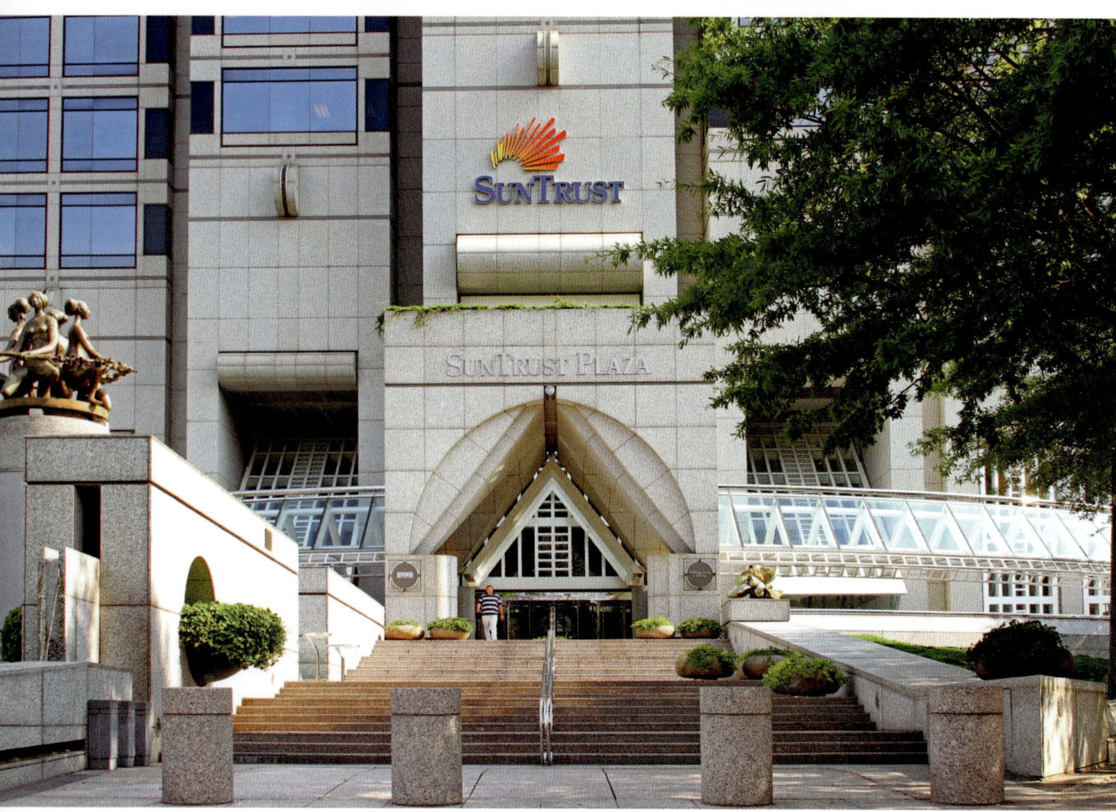

Rites of Spring *(top)*

SunTrust Plaza has an art gallery in its lower lobby and other fine art on display in the tower's Grand Lobby. Among permanent exhibits is the bronze *Rites of Spring* by sculptor and storyteller Albert Weinberg. Commissioned by John Portman, it carries an "aura that's very special," as the architect described Weinberg's collective works.

60-Story Skyscraper *(bottom)*

Towering 871-plus feet above the Central Business District, the award-winning SunTrust Plaza was designed by internationally prominent 20th-century architect, John Portman. This signature centerpiece of the SunTrust Plaza office, retail, and parking complex rises 60 stories and offers world-class shopping and dining and spectacular city views.

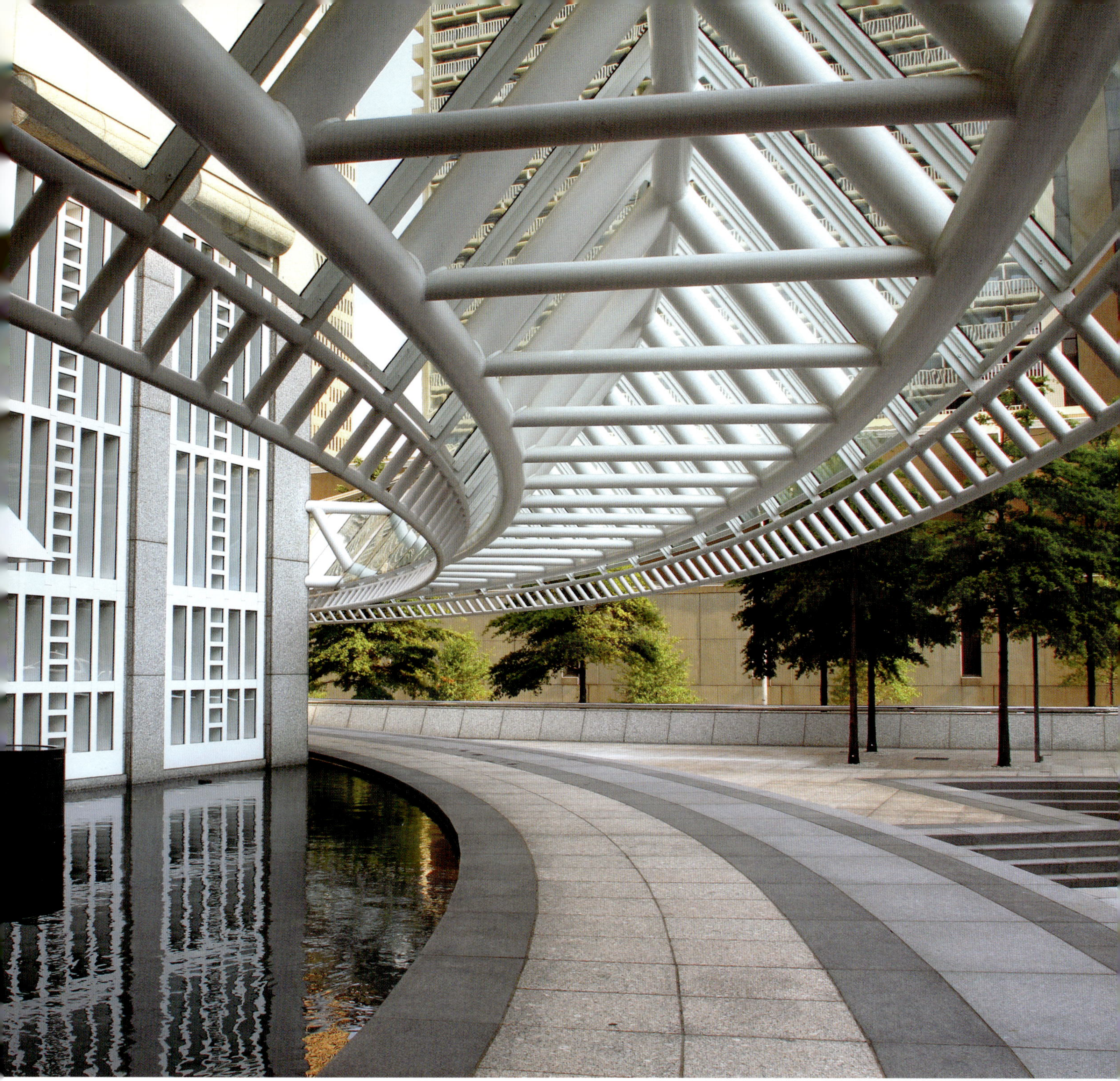

SunTrust Plaza

Atlanta's second tallest building and the headquarters for Atlanta's World Trade Center, the SunTrust Plaza is a postmodern glass and granite behemoth. Its faceted exterior provides up to 36 corner offices on an average floor and finishes throughout convey a classic elegance in step with this high-end executive environment.

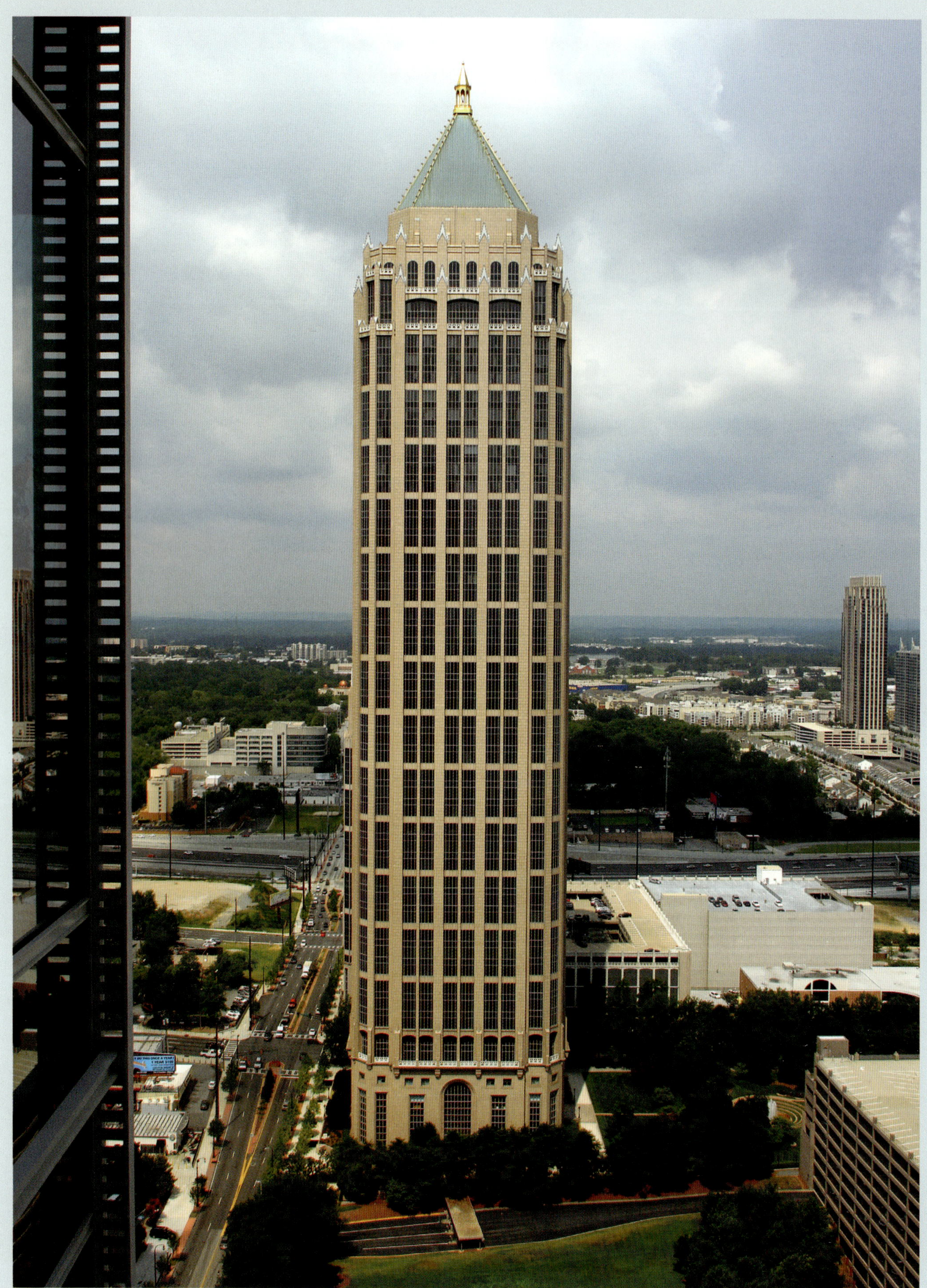

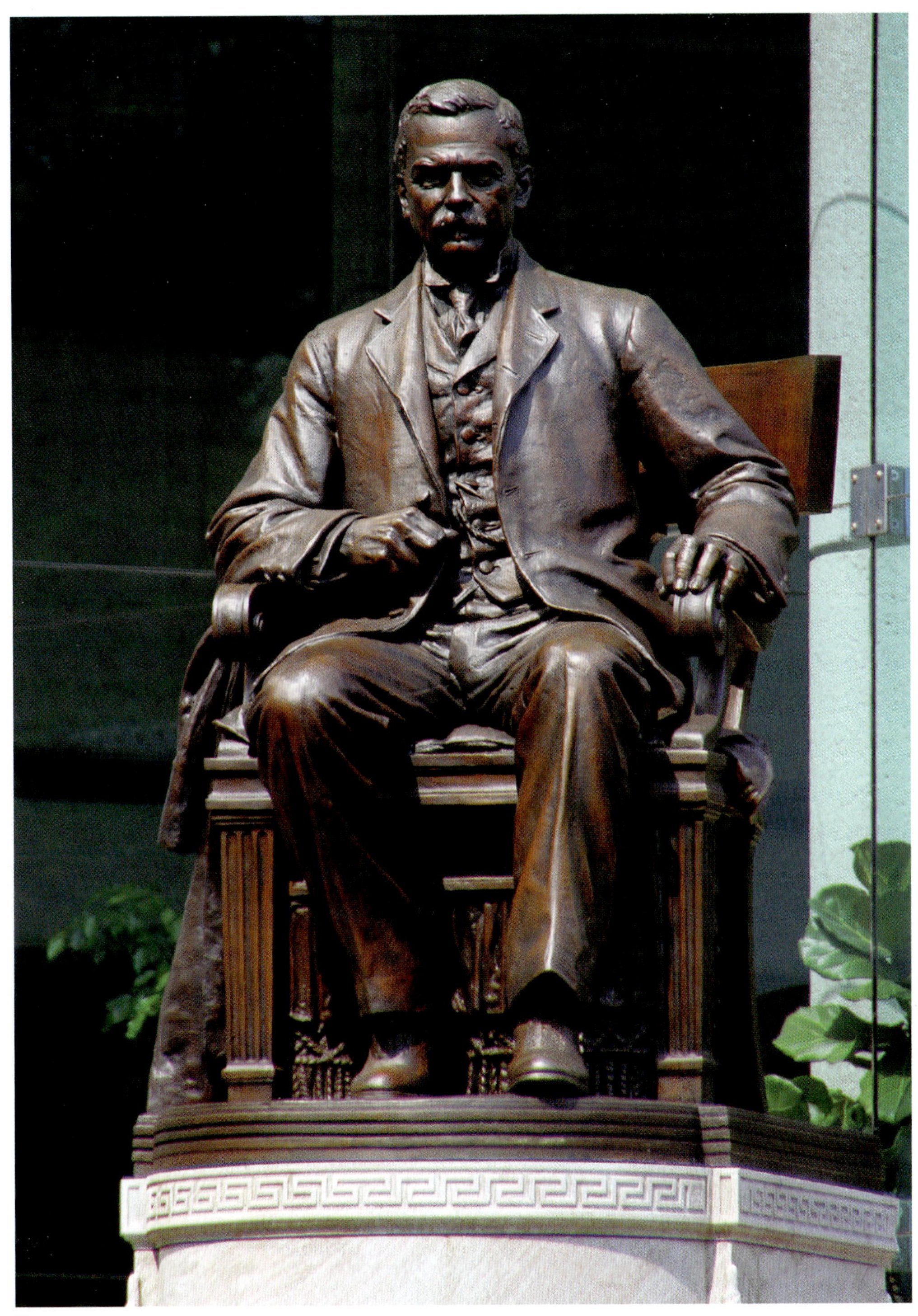

One Atlantic Center *(opposite)*

Atlanta's tallest building until 1992, iconic One Atlantic Center, designed by preeminent 20th-century architects Philip Johnson and John Burgee, rises 820-plus feet. The 50-story postmodern landmark with a lush park, grand lobby, and original frescoes houses some of the city's most influential movers and shakers.

Samuel Spencer *(above)*

Dedicated in 1910, the Samuel Spencer Monument was originally erected at Atlanta's Terminal Station and now stands in Hardy Ivy Park. This Confederate soldier became a railroad surveyor and president of the Southern Railway. His untimely death in 1906 at age 59 was ironic, as he was killed in a railway accident in Virginia.

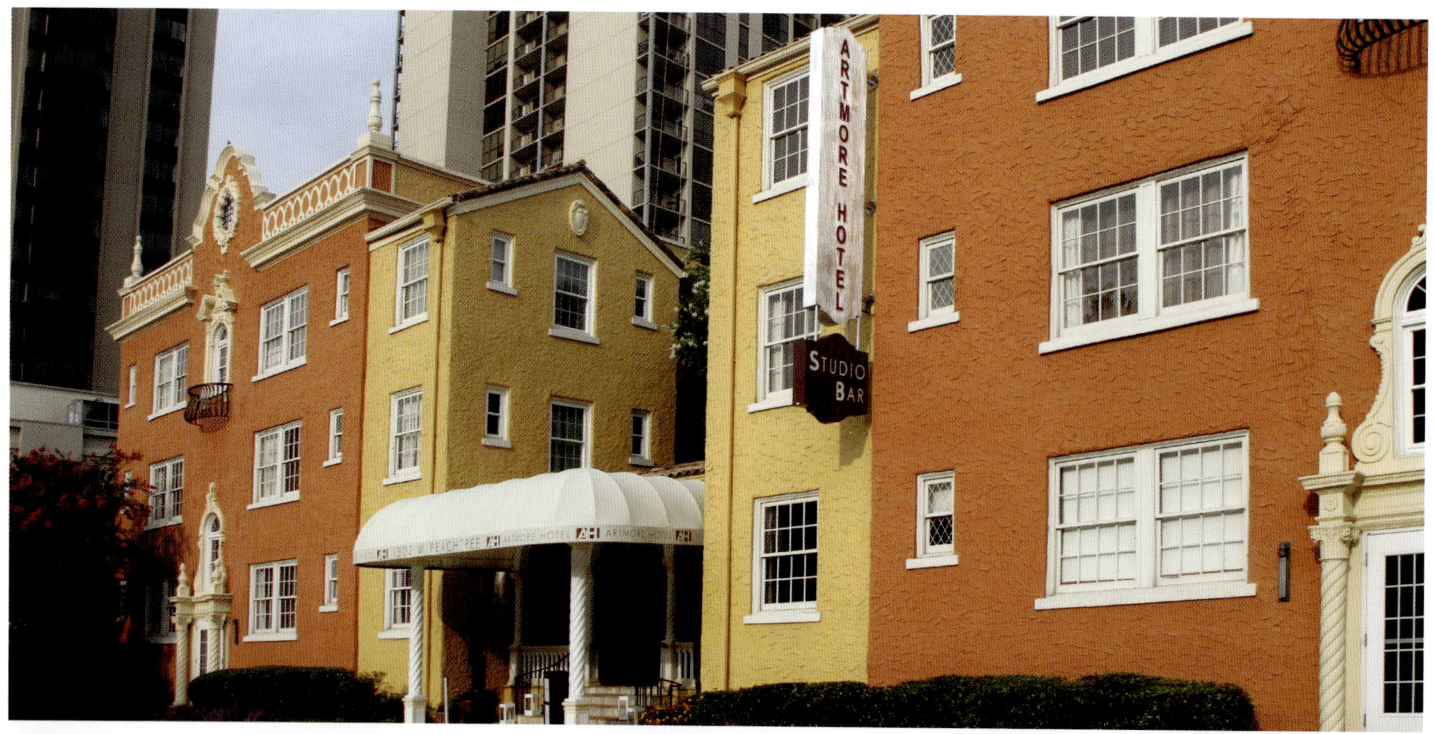

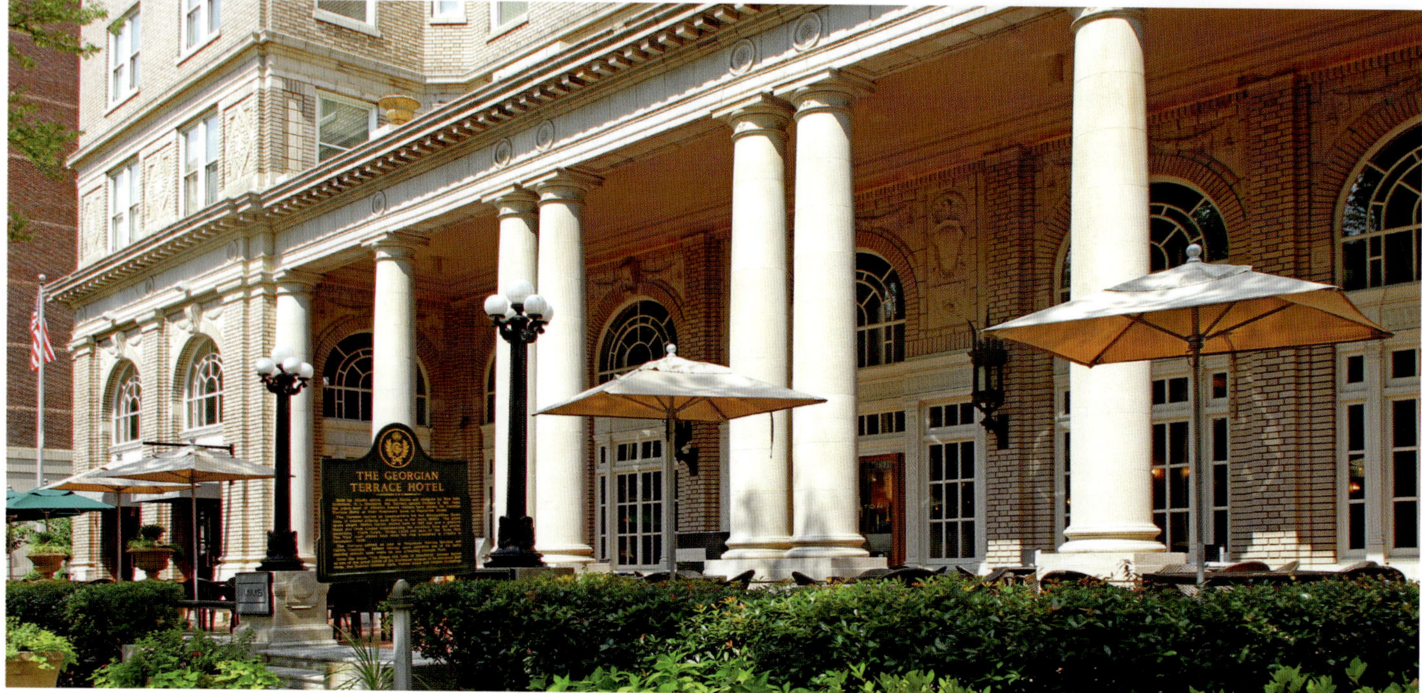

Artmore Hotel *(top)*

An architectural treasure in the midst of Atlanta's Cultural Arts District, the Artmore Hotel, formerly the Granada Suites Hotel, is tucked into an historic 1924 building whose design is based on Spanish Mediterranean aesthetics. The independent boutique hotel is known for its dedication to and delivery of the personalized guest experience.

Georgian Terrace Hotel *(bottom)*

A circa 1911 luxury hotel with crystal chandeliers, floor-to-ceiling windows, and white marble columns, the Georgian Terrace Hotel has hosted such notables as President Calvin Coolidge and author F. Scott Fitzgerald. It hosted the premiere of *Gone with the Wind* in 1939 and is listed on the National Register of Historic Places.

Westin Peachtree Plaza *(opposite)*

The tallest hotel in the world when it opened in 1976, the John Portman-designed Westin Peachtree Plaza ascends 73 floors in the heart of downtown. A cylindrical tower clad in reflective glass, it has a 90-foot sky-lit lobby and some 5,600 windows. It was famously featured in the 1981 Burt Reynolds movie, *Sharky's Machine*.

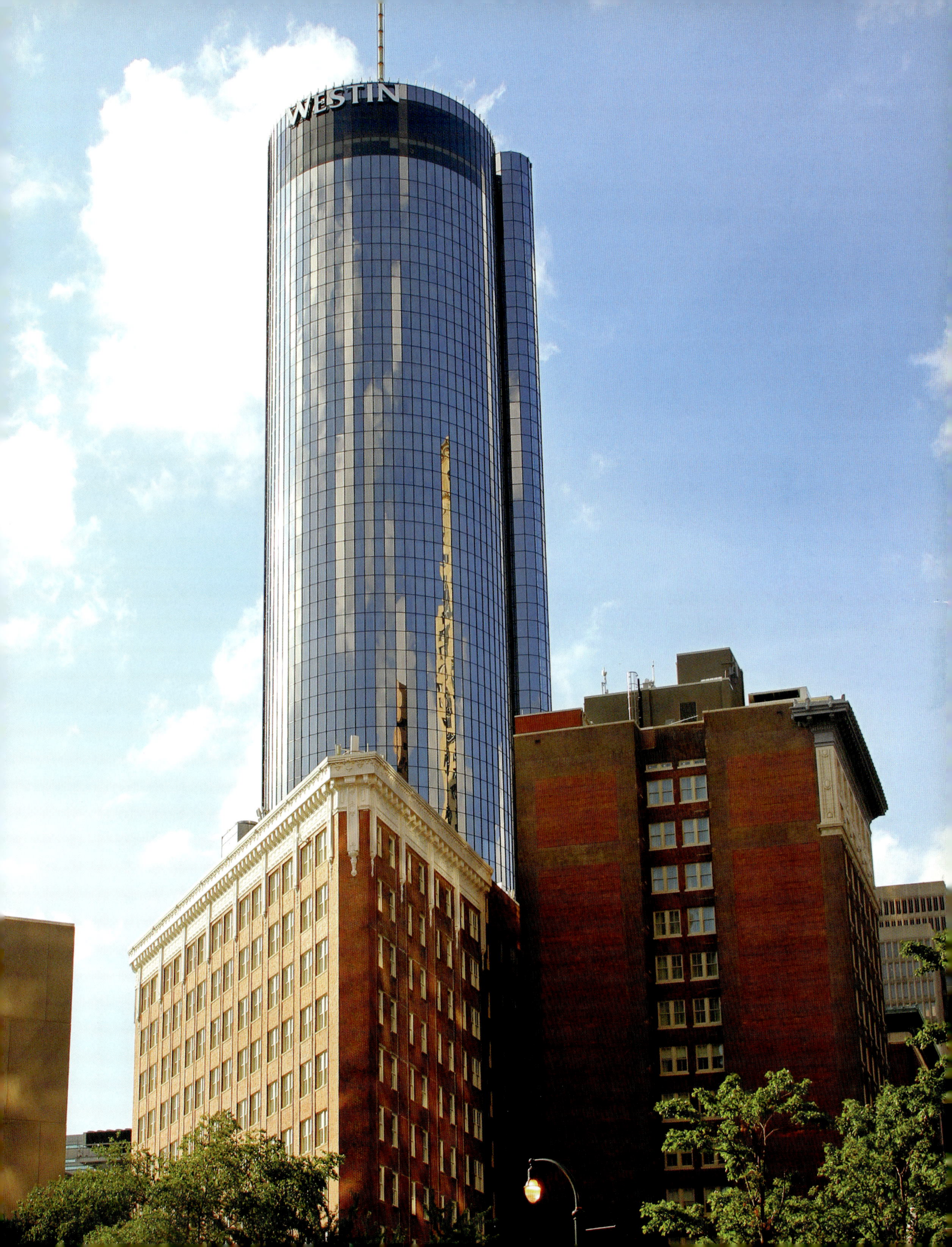
WESTIN

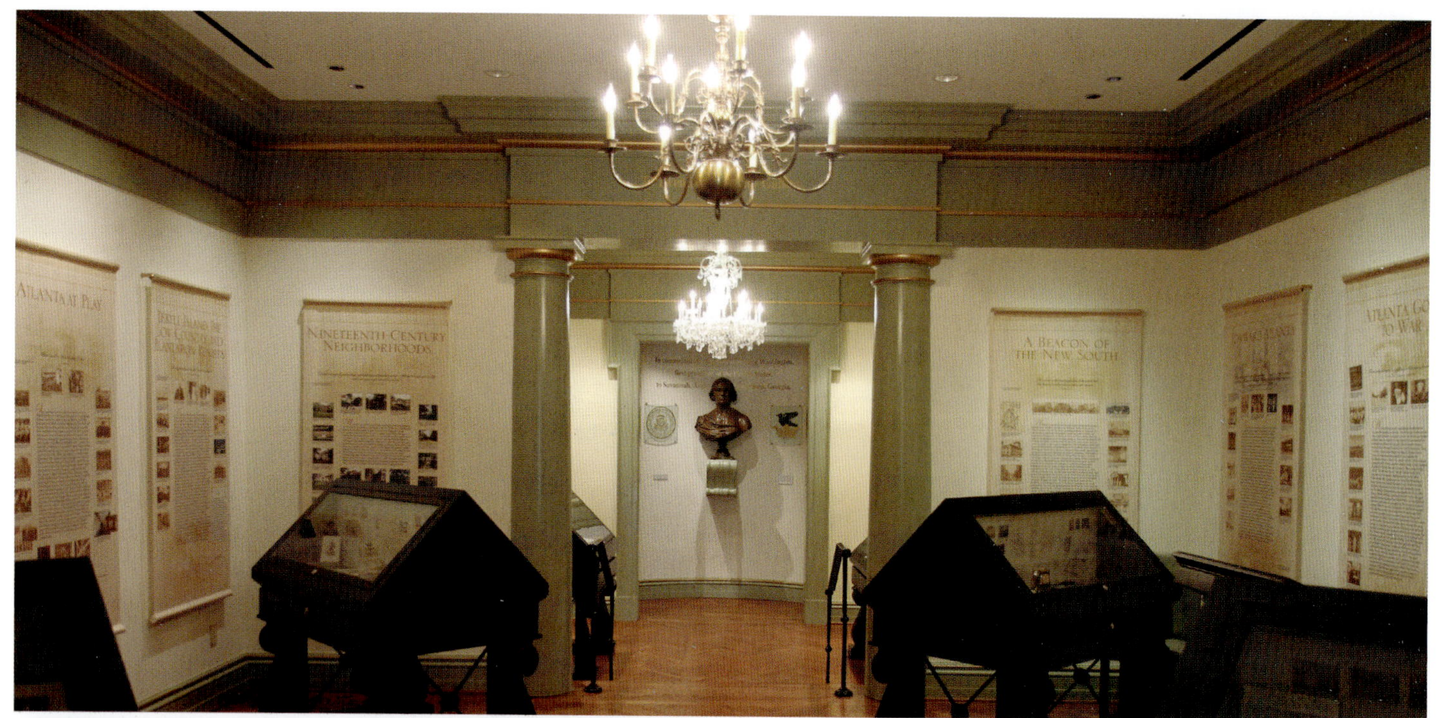

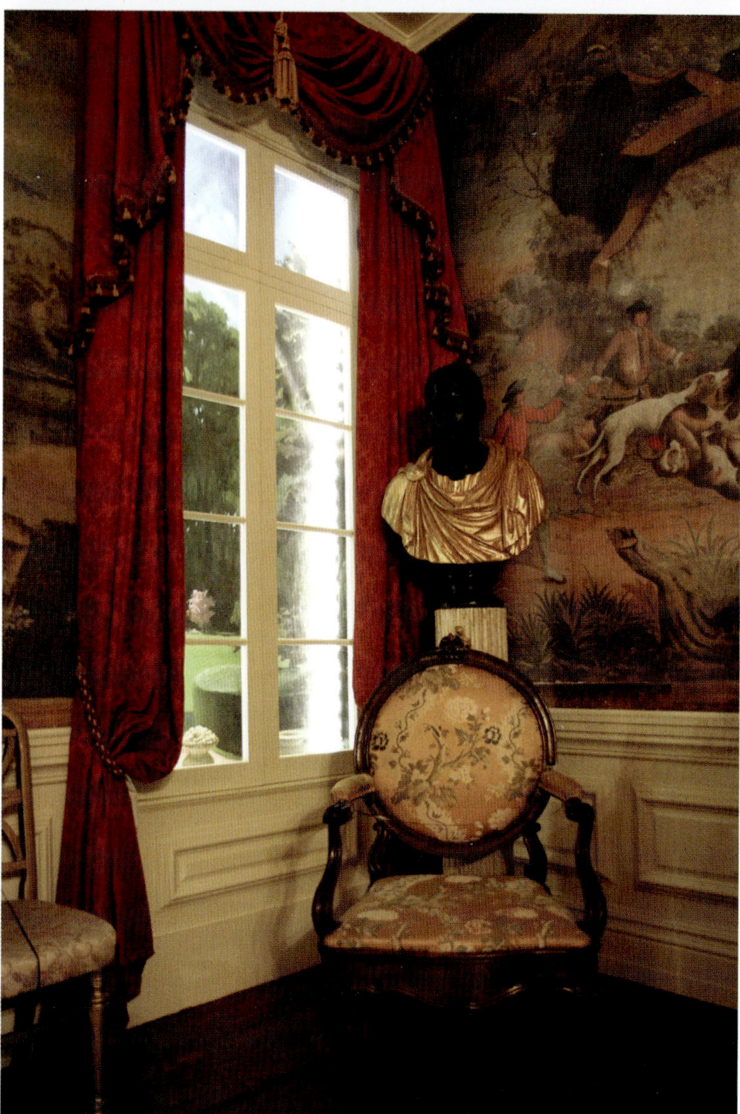

Museum at Millennium Gate *(above)*

With a mission to "preserve and interpret Georgia history, architecture, culture, and philanthropic heritage as well as highlight Georgia's historical and aesthetic relevance to the United States and to the world," the Millennium Gate, located inside Atlantic Station in Midtown, houses a 12,000-square-foot museum encompassing historical documents and artifacts, interactive technology, period rooms, and exhibitions.

Atlanta's History *(left)*

The classic monumental arch narrates Georgia's and Atlanta's history in gallery settings that begin with Native American history, segue into General Oglethorpe's creation of the Colony of Georgia and the state's pioneering past, and continue into the 20th century through rooms furnished with period furniture.

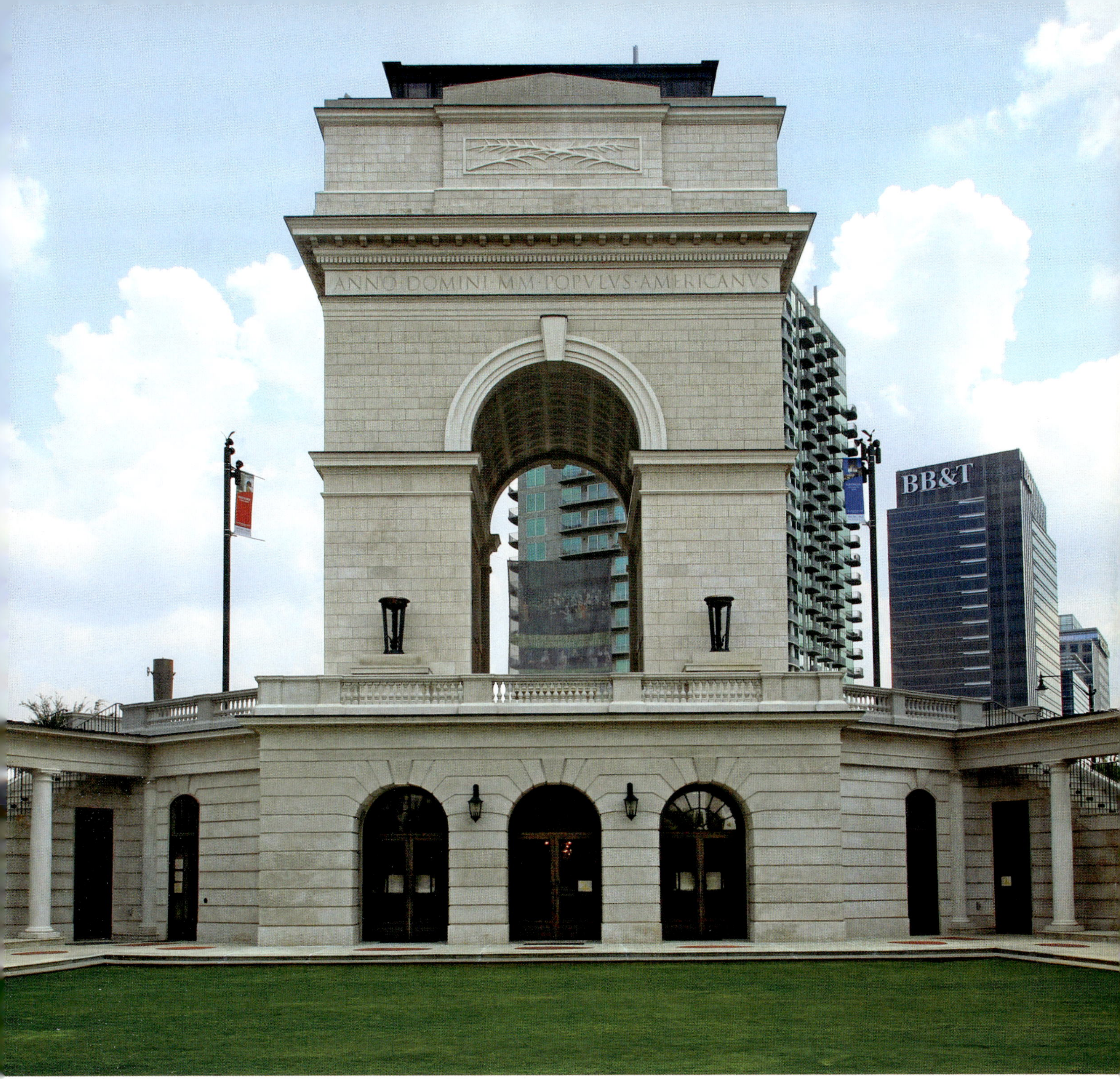

Gate City

In a place once called "The Gate City," the seven-level, 100-foot-tall Millennium Gate has a 360-degree view of the city. The Latin inscription translates, "This American monument commemorates all peaceful accomplishment since the birth of Jesus Christ in the year of our Lord, MM." Its bronze *Justice* and *Peace* statues each weigh two tons.

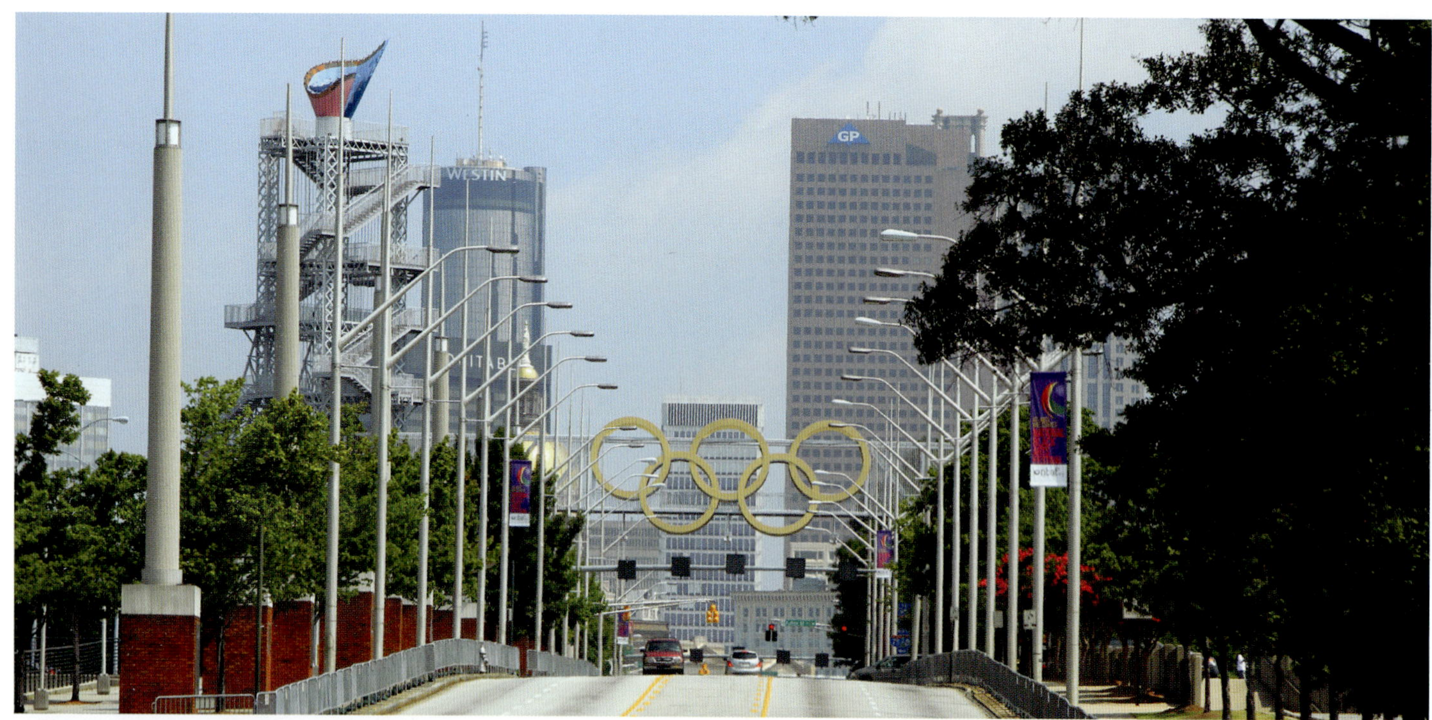

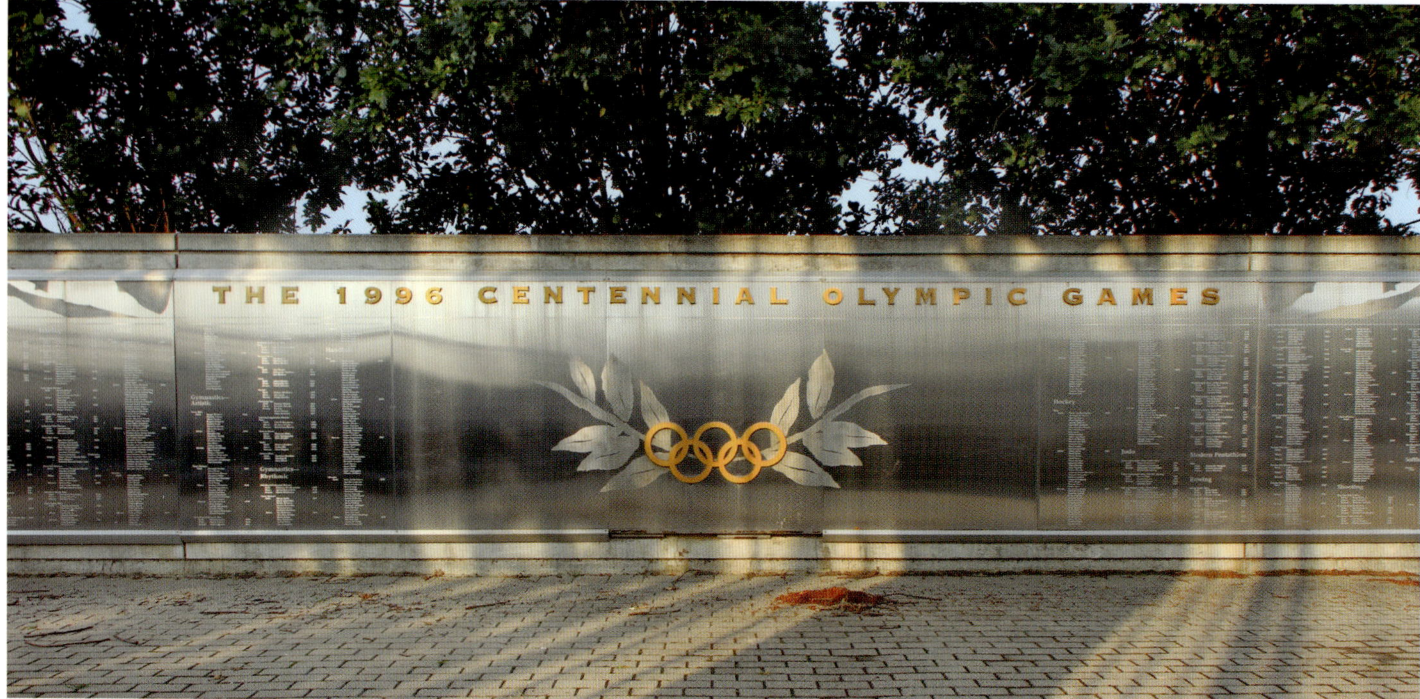

The Olympic Bridge *(top)*

Designed by Iranian-born American sculptor Siah Armajani, the Olympic bridge linked the former Olympic Stadium to the tower that housed the Olympic flame. Following the 1996 Olympic Games it became Turner Field, home of the Atlanta Braves. The Olympic Rings on the bridge are structural components symbolizing international unity.

Olympic Flame Tower and Bridge *(bottom)*

From July 19 until August 4, 1996, Atlanta hosted the Centennial Summer Olympic Games, which honored the 100th anniversary of the modern Olympic movement. The Games showcased 10,318 competitors representing 197 nations in 26 sports. The tower and bridge are now among Atlanta's most famous landmarks.

Torch Memorial Tower *(opposite)*

A legacy of the 1996 Olympics that stood in Olympic Stadium, the majestic caldron – a three-dimensional Cultural Olympiad logo – rises 116 feet above ground. It was lit by boxing legend Muhammad Ali, using a self-propelling fuse ball that transported the flame upward to open the Olympics. It was later moved one block north of the stadium.

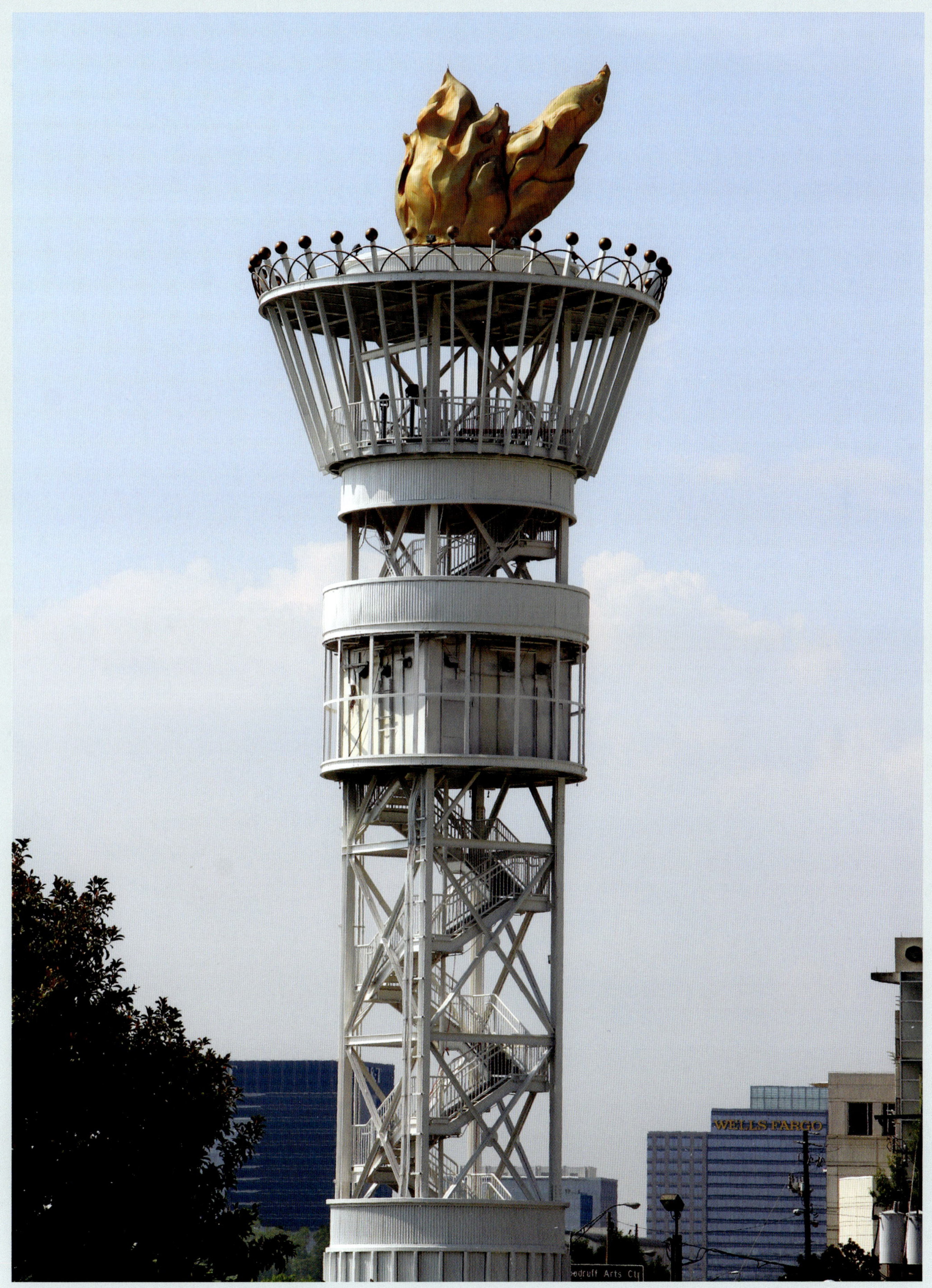
WELLS FARGO

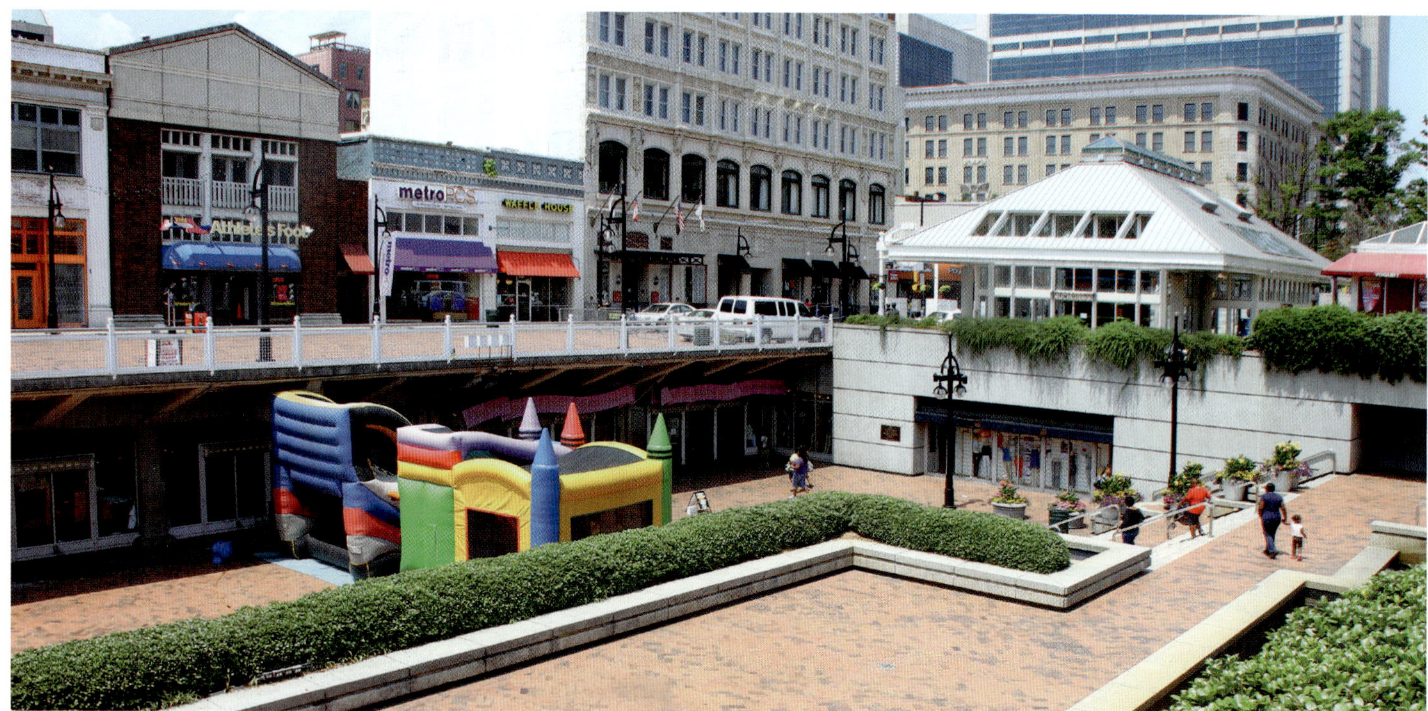

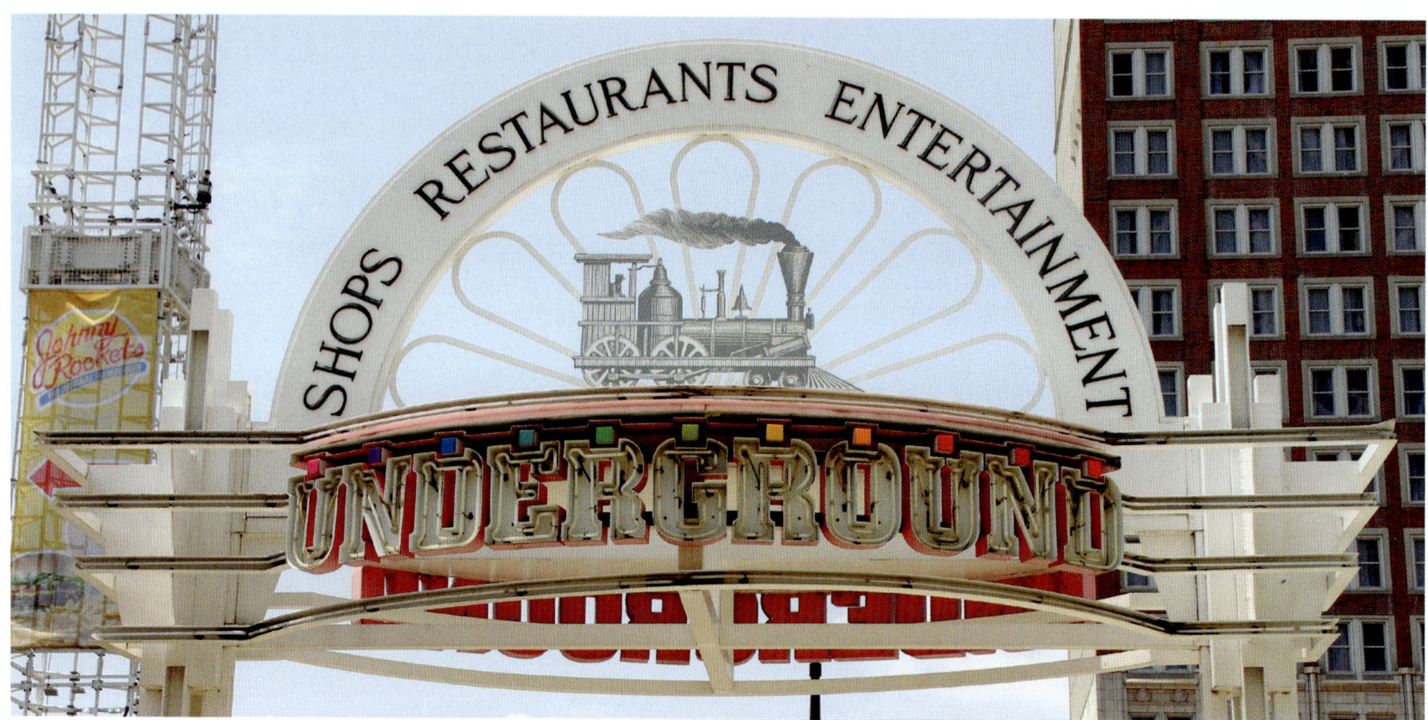

Original Streets of Atlanta *(top)*

Step back in time in this bustling retail and entertainment center located in the heart of Downtown and built on Atlanta's original streets. Underground Atlanta is at the Zero Milepost, located on the basement level of the circa 1869 Georgia Railroad Freight Depot and marking the spot where the railroad stopped in the 1830s.

Subterranean Complex *(bottom)*

Family-friendly Underground Atlanta is abuzz with daily entertainment, fast and fine dining, fortune telling, spas, shopping, live music, and special events. A National Register of Historic Places, Underground Atlanta sports original storefronts, including ornate marble, granite archways, decorative brickwork, and hand-carved wood posts.

Underground Atlanta *(opposite)*

Head underground and into Atlanta's past on a guided history tour, *From Civil War to Civil Rights*, to hear stories of what life was like in the 1800s. Venture into Kenny's Alley after dark to join the nightlife crowd. Browse Humbug Square Street Market for one-of-a-kind specialty items, including handmade jewelry and scented crystals.

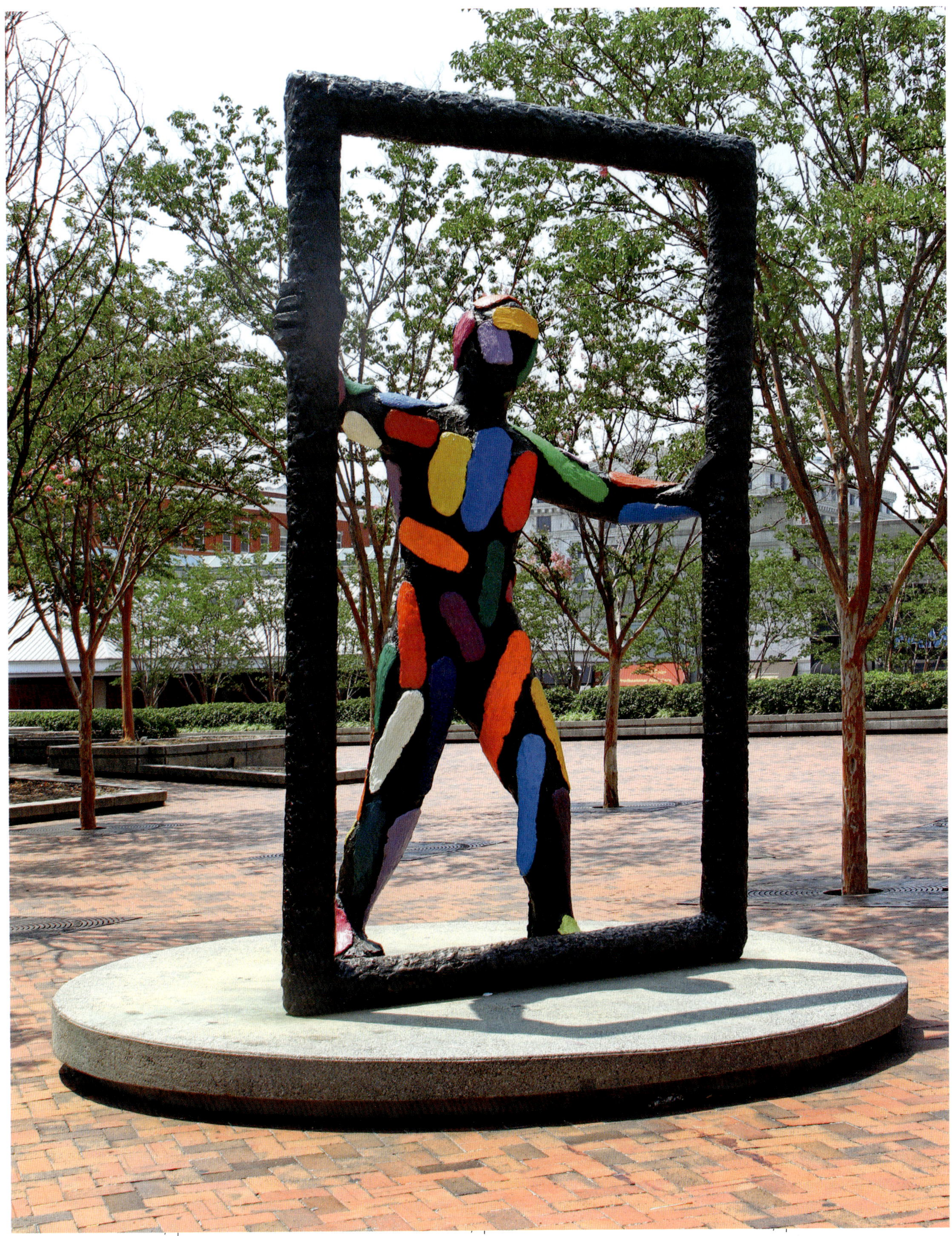

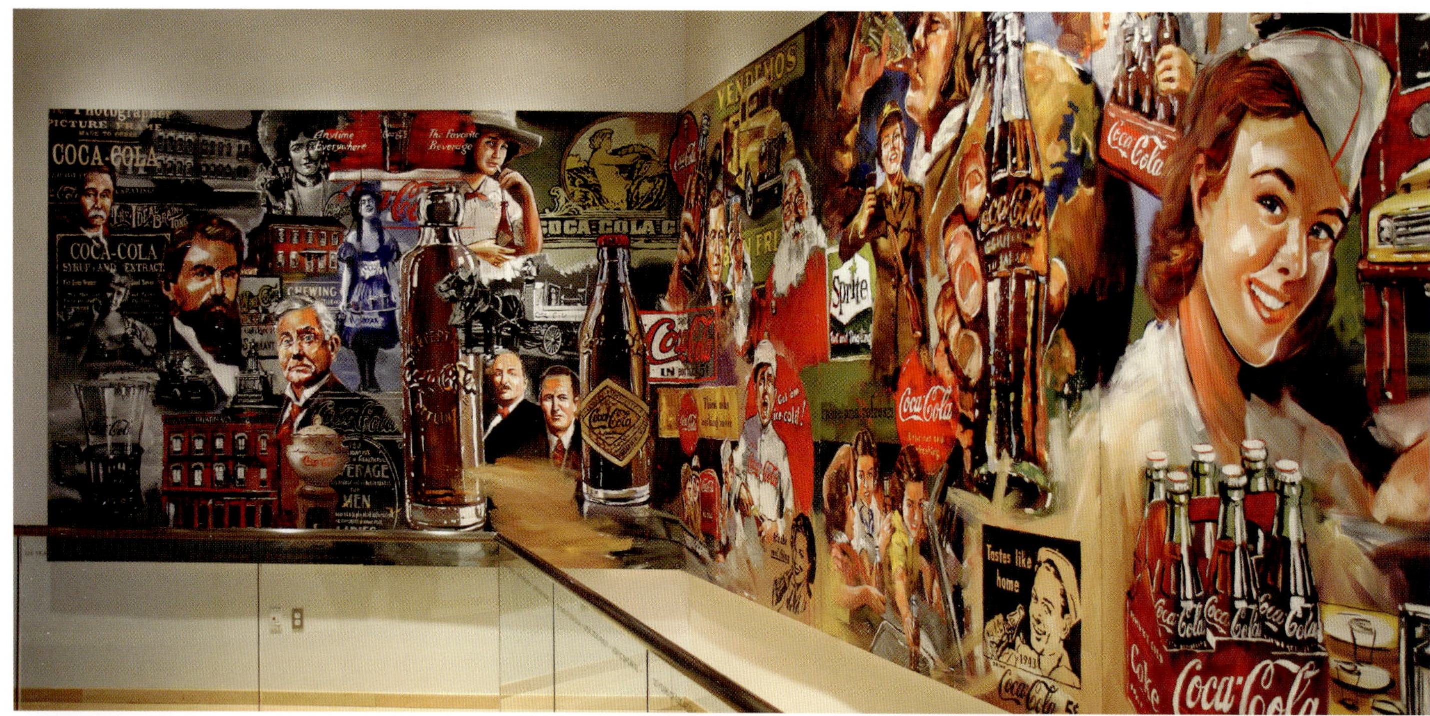

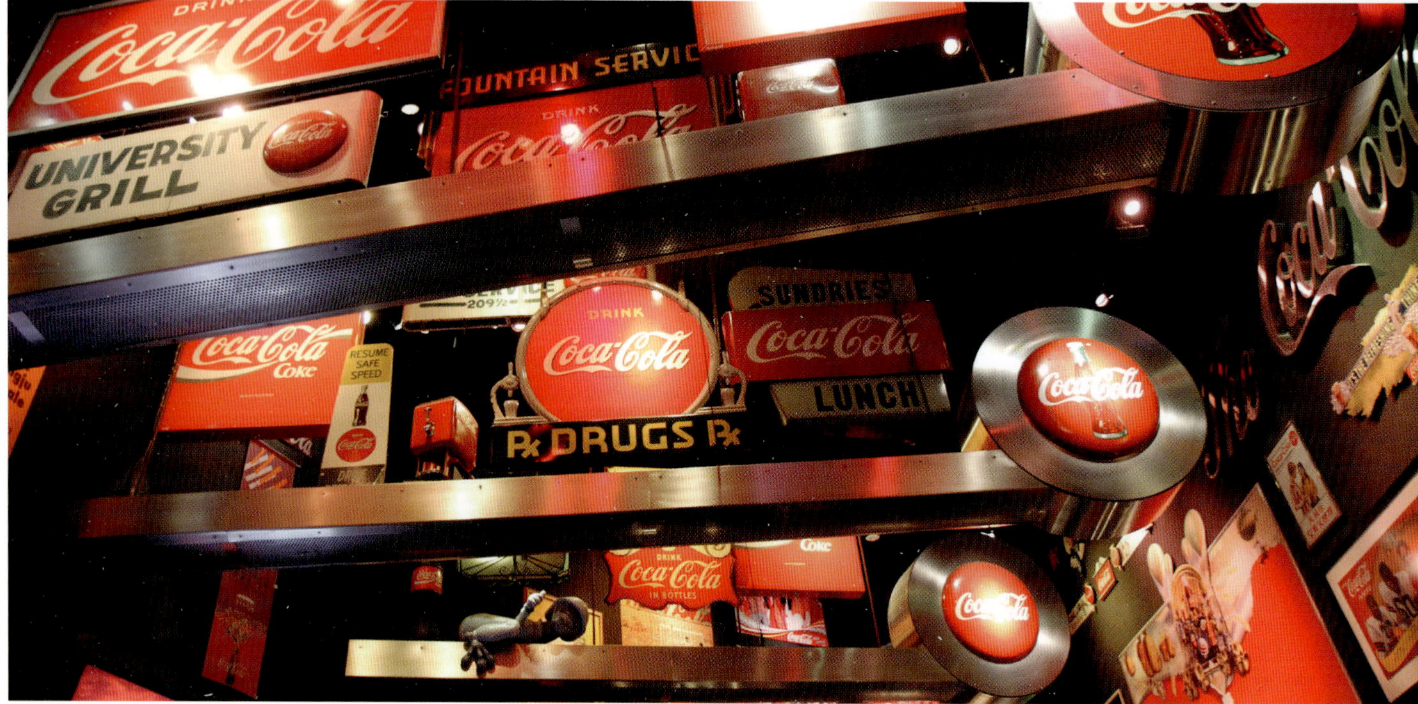

The Story of Coca-Cola *(top)*

This 92,000-square-foot behemoth is the only place in the world you can explore the story of Coca Cola. Located at Pemberton Place, the World of Coca-Cola, which welcomed its three millionth guest in 2010, features more than 1,200 artifacts including relics from 20 different countries representing 17 different languages.

World of Coca-Cola *(bottom)*

Step into an interactive world: a multi-sensory 4-D movie with eccentric scientist and chairs that go bump in the dark; a fully functioning bottling line; the huggable seven-foot Coca-Cola Polar Bear; the new Vault of the Secret Formula immersive experience; and a chance to taste 60-plus different beverages from around the world.

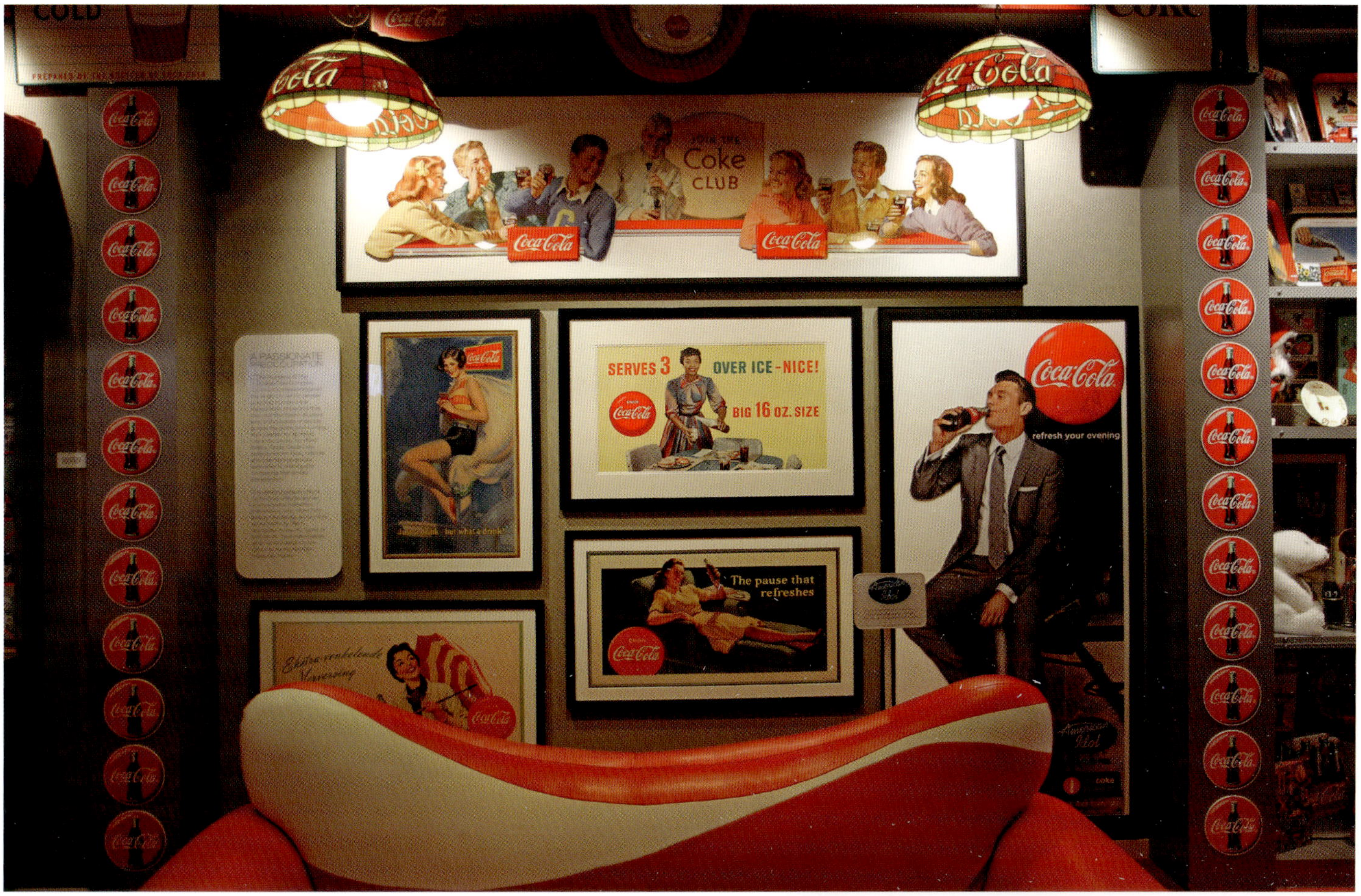

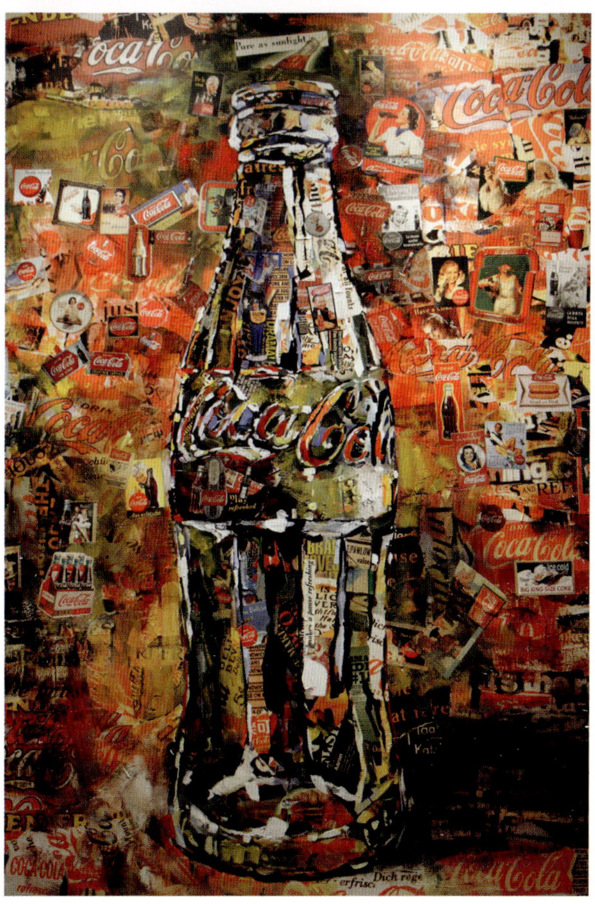

A World of Treasures *(above)*

Housed in the Coca-Cola loft are some of the brand's most prized possessions: Norman Rockwell's 1931 *Barefoot Boy*, one of six Rockwells painted for the company; an 1896 syrup urn that was given to pharmacists who purchased 100 gallons of Coca-Cola syrup from Asa Candler; and the weathered Coca-Cola Company logo silver letters, 1919-1979, from the previous world headquarters building.

Pop Culture *(right)*

In the Pop Culture Gallery, take a musical journey inside a Coca-Cola vending machine during the new animated film, *Happyfication*, in the Happiness Factory Theater. Follow the Live Positively Portrait Wall, a motion-activated media experience, to hear how Coca-Cola has touched people the world over. And, be sure to enter the Secret Formula 4-D Theater (alas, you will not learn the secret formula).

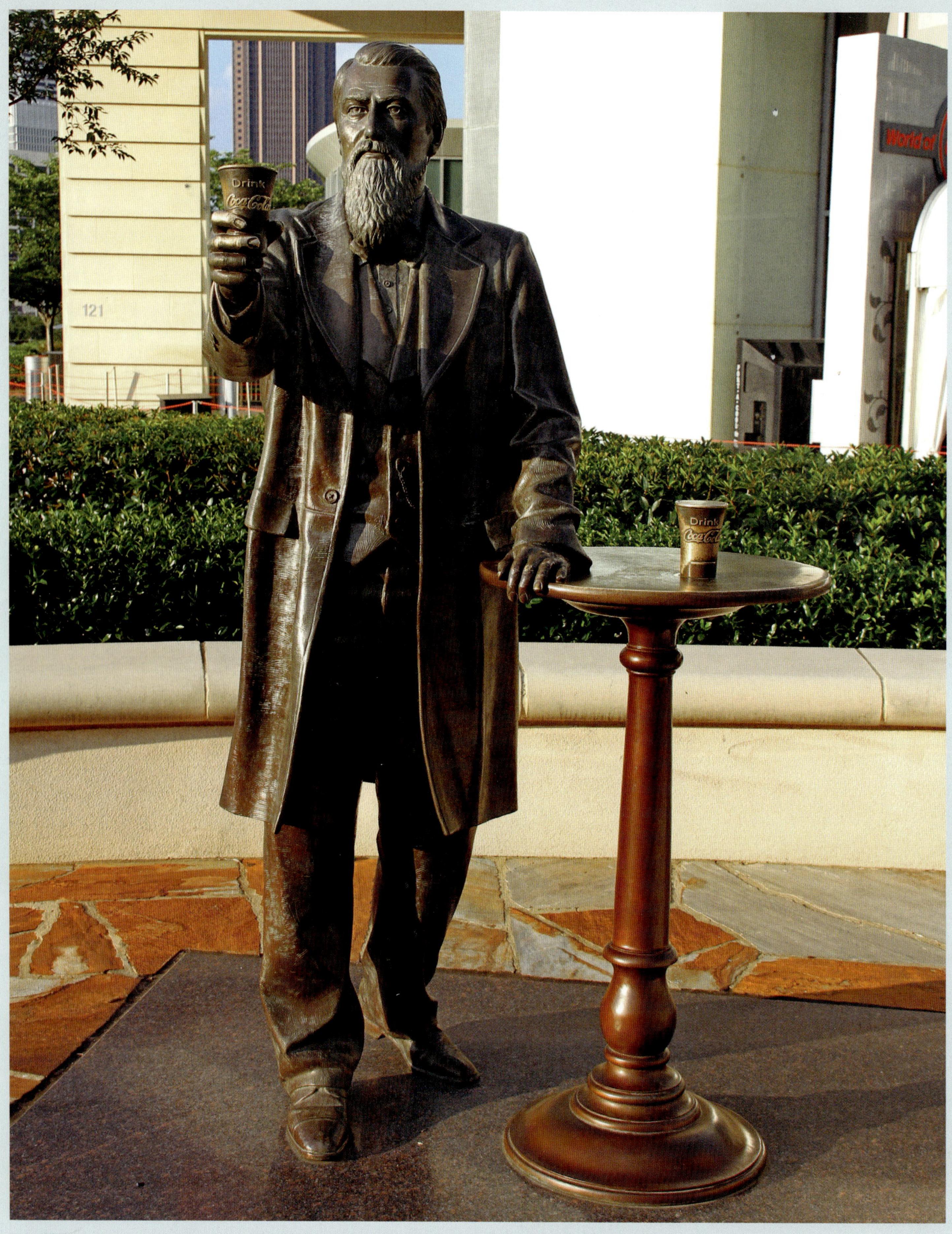
Drink
Coca-Cola
121
World of

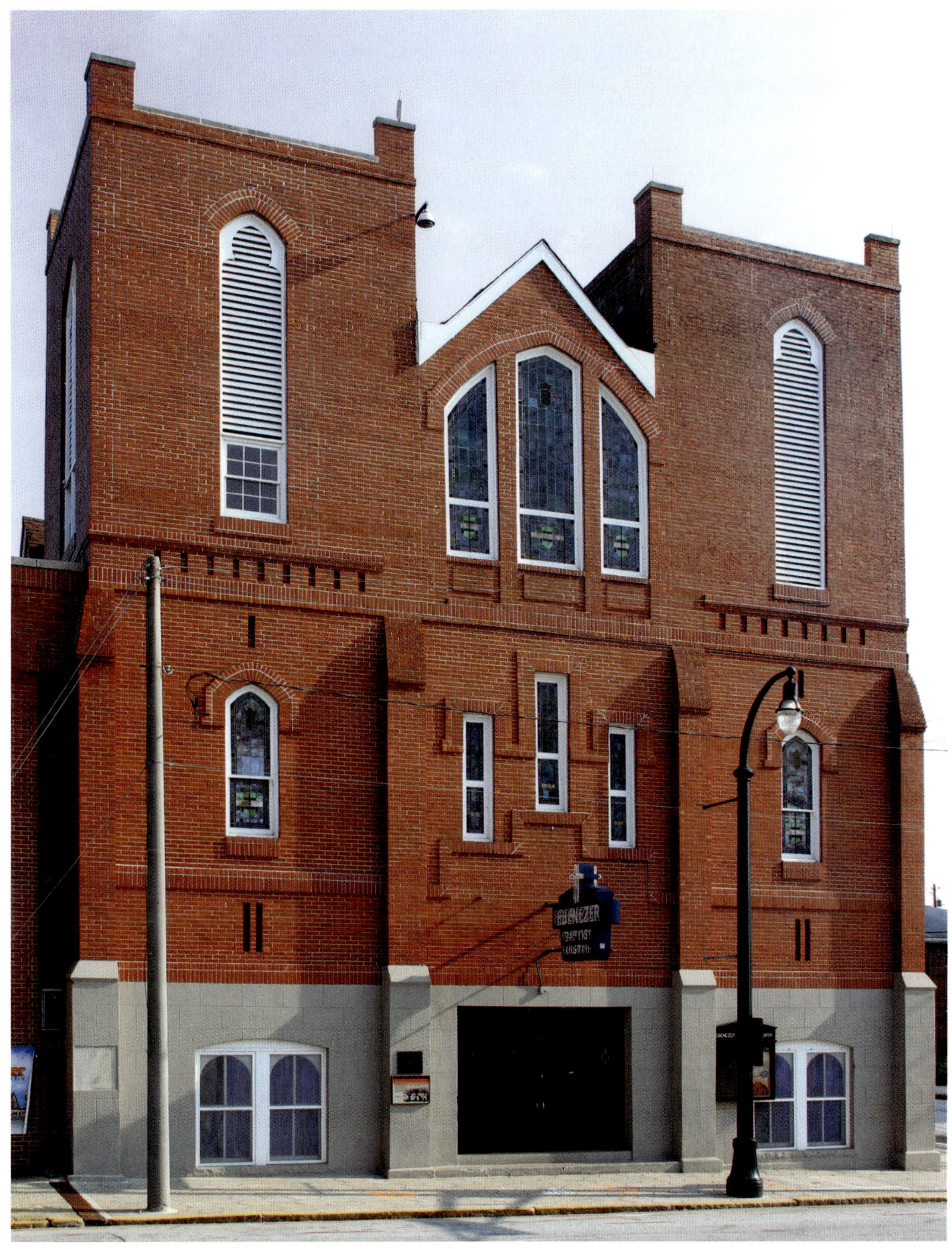

Pemberton Place *(opposite)*

Named in honor of John S. Pemberton, the pharmacist who created Coca-Cola in 1886, Pemberton Place stretches over 20 acres of downtown Atlanta across from Centennial Olympic Park and is home to the World of Coca-Cola, the Georgia Aquarium, and a five-acre swatch of greenspace.

Ebenezer Baptist Church *(above)*

The Ebenezer Baptist Church was the home church of Rev. Dr. Martin Luther King, Jr., from where he preached his ministry of nonviolence. Founded in 1886, it is located within Atlanta's Sweet Auburn District, considered to be the cradle of the Civil Rights Movement. John A. Parker, who had been born into slavery, served as its first pastor.

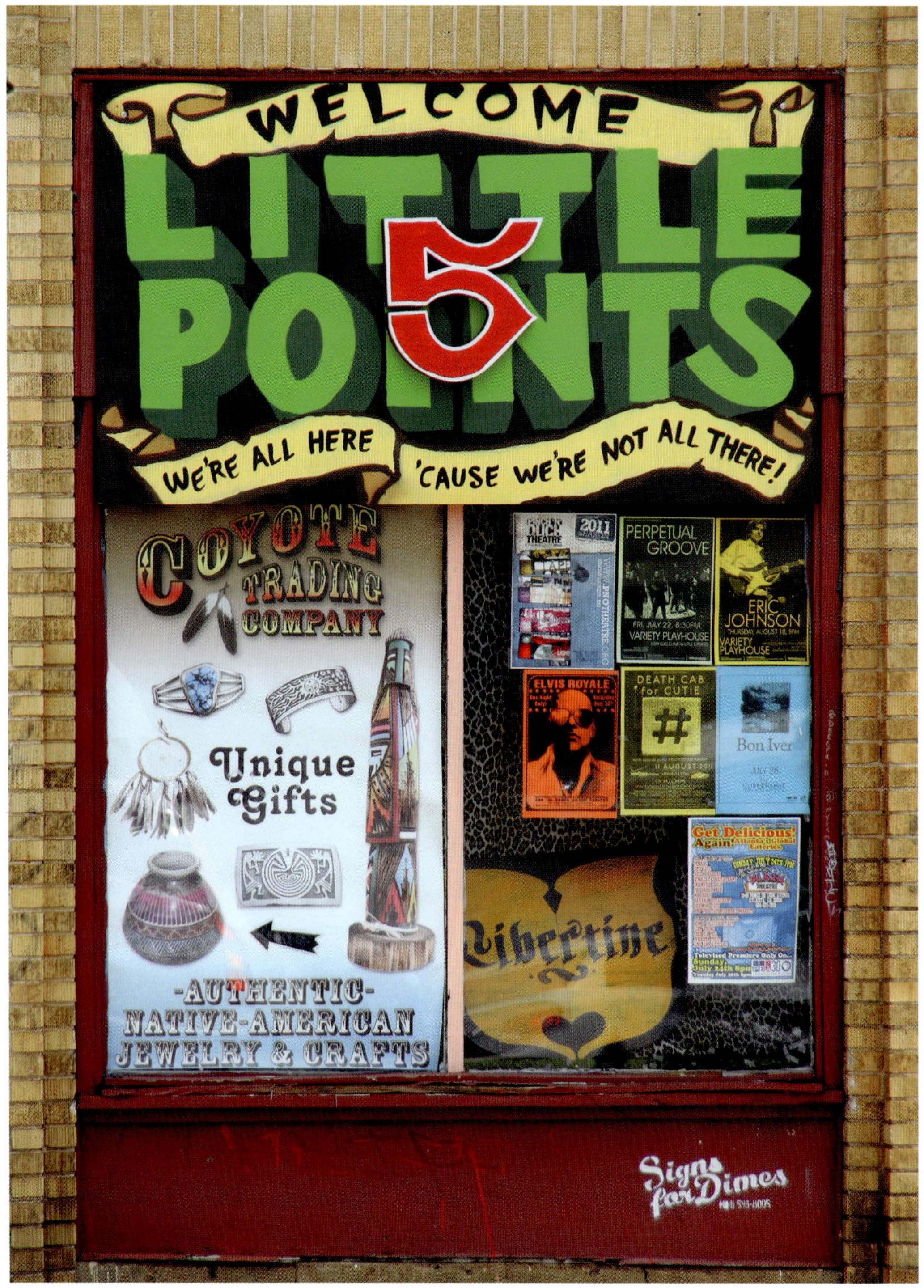

Little Five Points *(above)*

Essence of cool, epicenter of alternative, Little Five Points, or L5P, is a mélange of retail shops, eateries, arts venues, theatre, and services (think tattoo parlors) representing interests that run the flavor gamut: funky, hippie, indie, eccentric. This thriving district in the middle of Moreland, Euclid, and McLendon Avenues is a world of eclectica.

Rising from the Ashes *(opposite)*

Atlanta from the Ashes personifies Atlanta's rebirth after the city was burned to the ground during the Civil War. Also known as *The Phoenix*, the 21-foot bronze statue at the Five Points entrance of Woodruff Park, depicts a woman holding a phoenix, the mythological bird that, once consumed by flames, arose again from the ashes – like Atlanta.

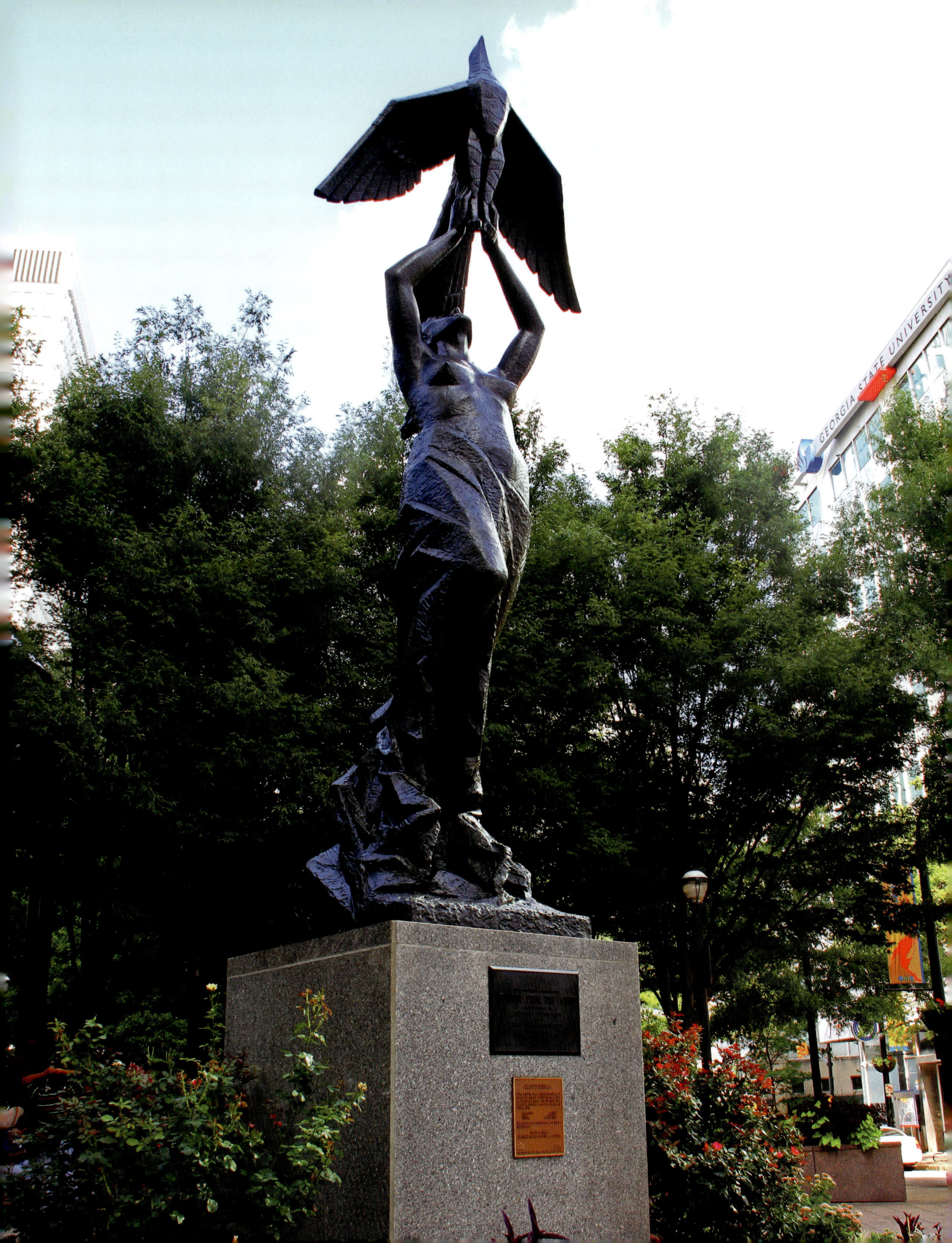
GEORGIA STATE UNIVERSITY

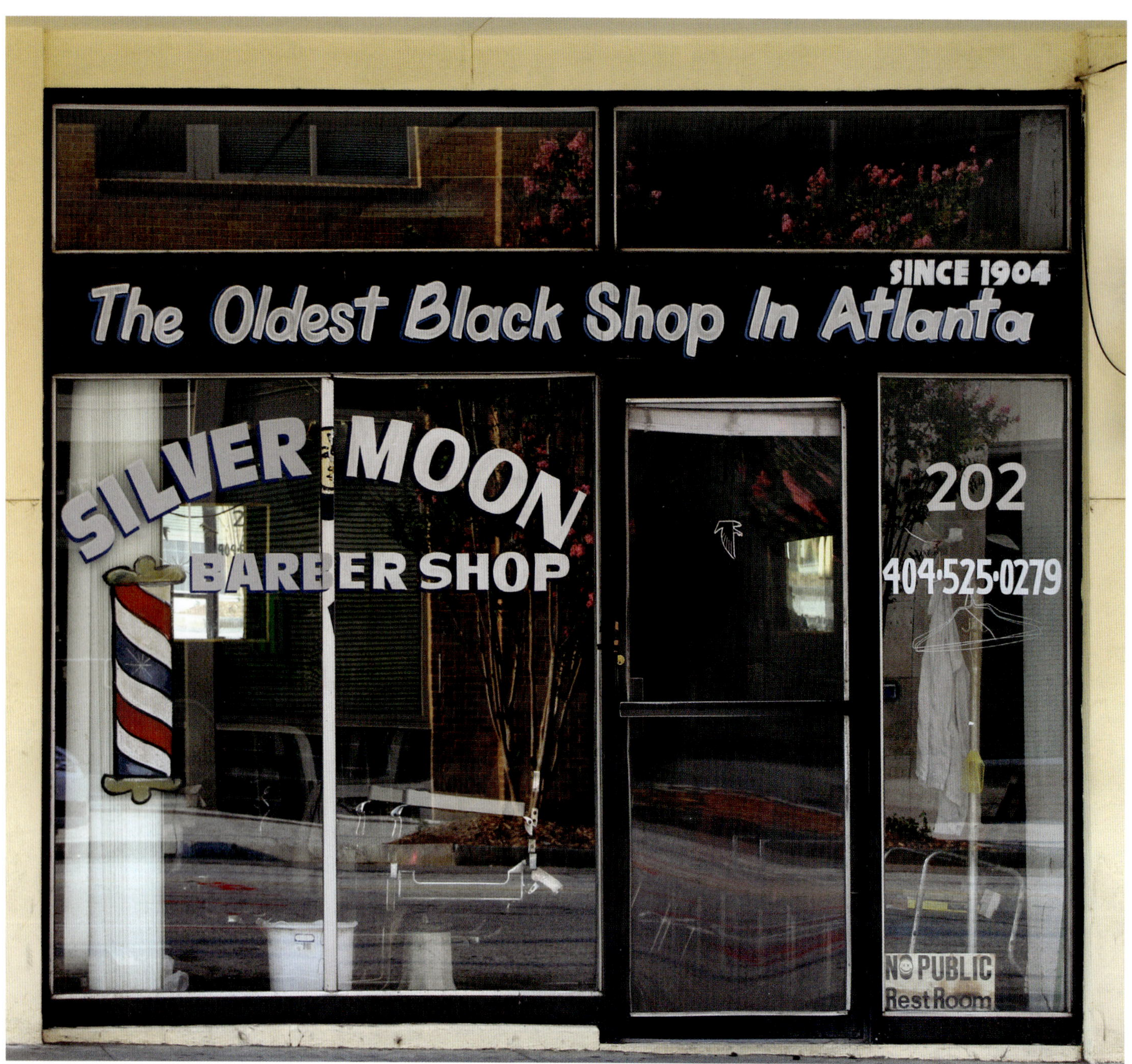

Sweet Auburn *(above)*

The Sweet Auburn Historic District, a National Historic Landmark, reflects a rich history of Atlanta's African Americans. Within this community is the second largest black insurance company in the country; Atlanta's first black-owned office building; and a club showcasing B.B. King, the Four Tops, and Atlanta's own Gladys Knight.

Through His Eyes *(opposite)*

This seven-foot-tall portrait head of civil rights activist John Wesley Dobbs invites visitors to walk into the sculpture and view the Auburn Avenue neighborhood where Dobbs once lived through the eyes of the figure. Designed as a mask by Ralph Helmick, the piece was installed atop a circular base at Dobbs Plaza in 1996.

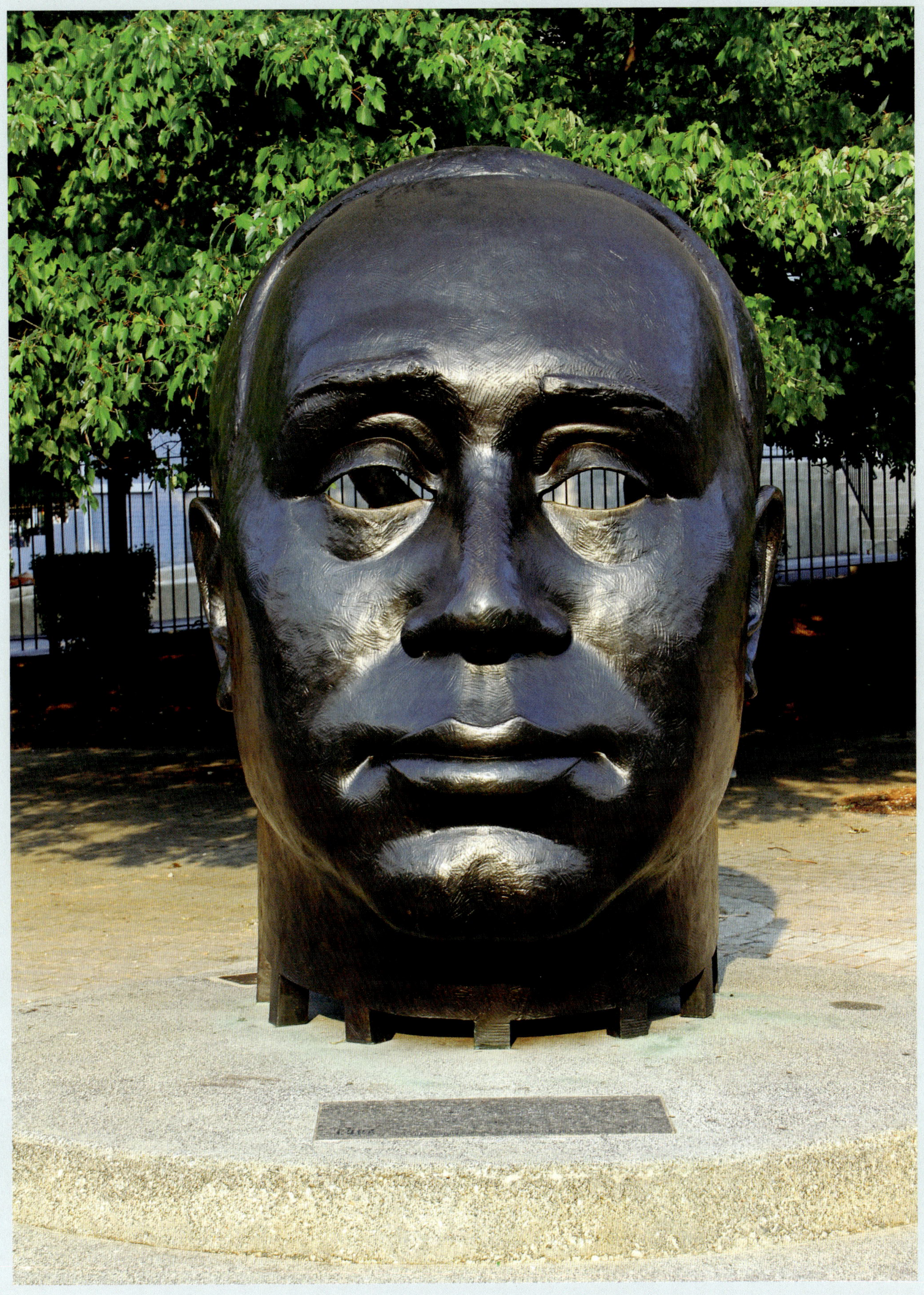

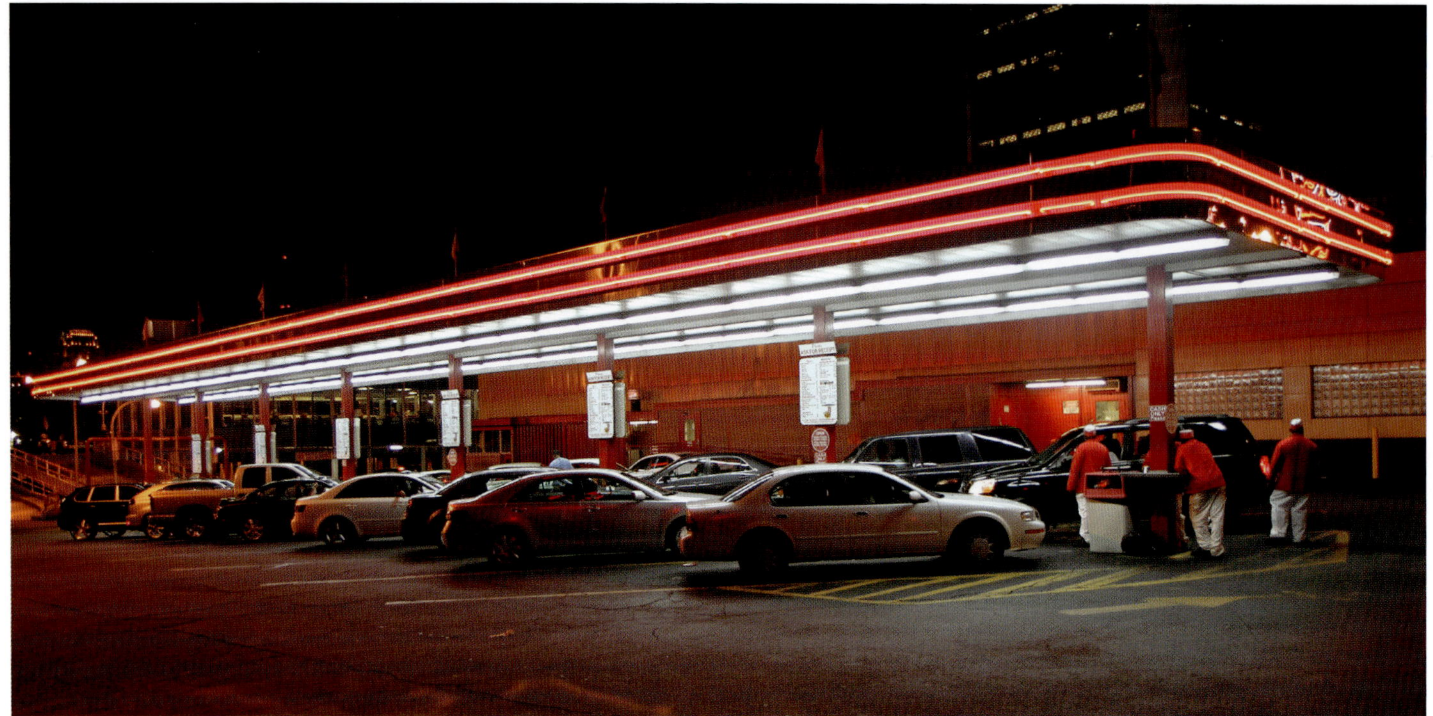

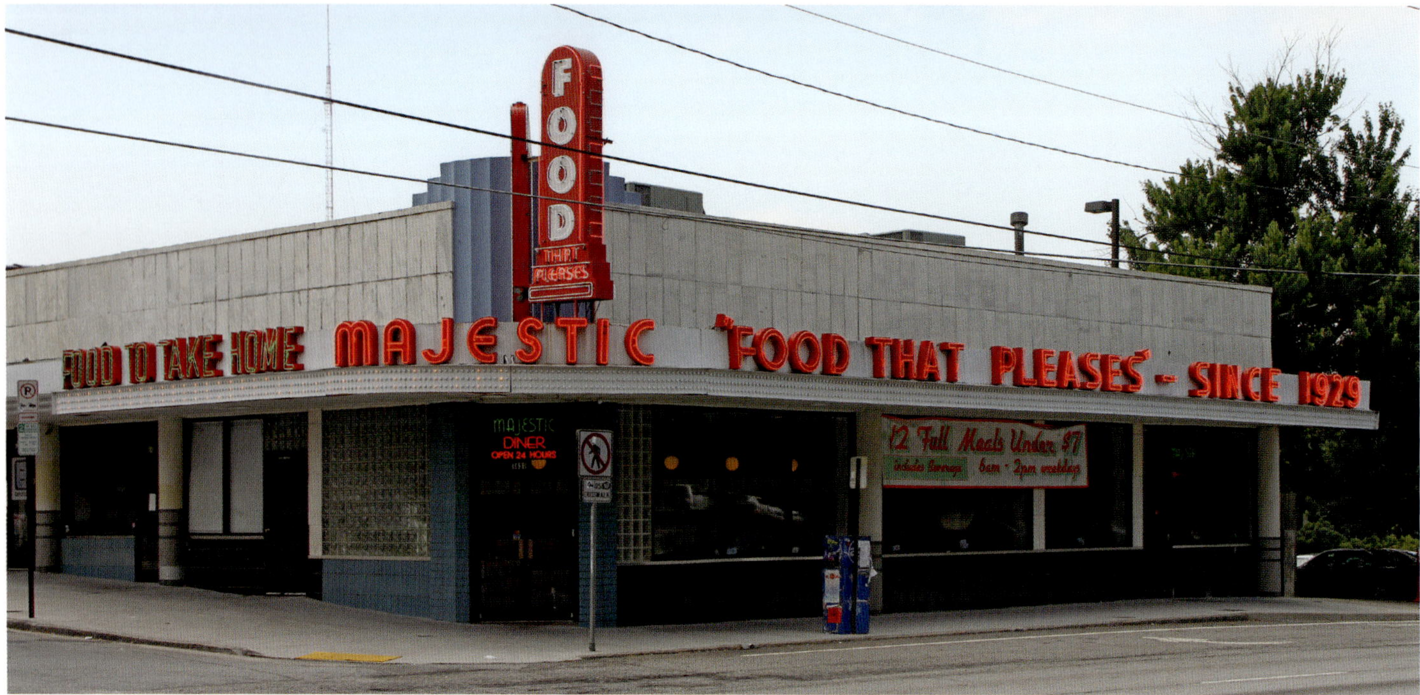

Varsity *(top and opposite)*

"What'll ya have?!" Famous for its screaming waiters, chili cheese dogs, onion rings, fried pies, and Frosted Orange drinks, this Atlanta institution is the world's largest drive-in eatery. Established in 1928, the Varsity has fed the locals and those from the White House and around the world. TV and movie star Nipsy Russell was once car hop #46.

Majestic Diner *(bottom)*

Generations of Atlantans have grown up on the "food that pleases," served at the Majestic Diner with a smile and a side of nostalgia. Established in 1929, the diner is known for the Majestic Special: a double burger with American or Swiss cheese, lettuce, tomato and mayo, and served with French fries. It is open 24 hours a day.

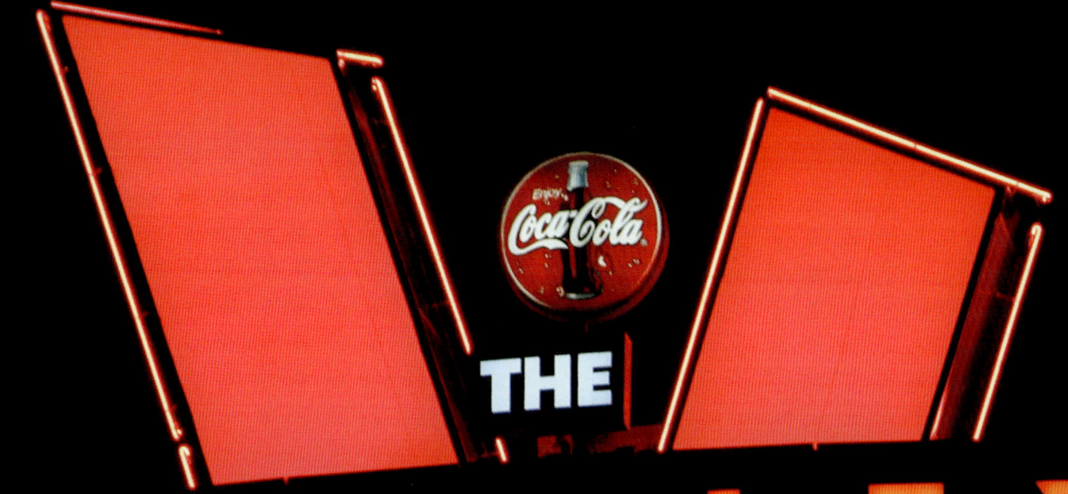
Coca-Cola
THE
VARSITY
Coca-Cola Salutes THE VARSITY Since 1928

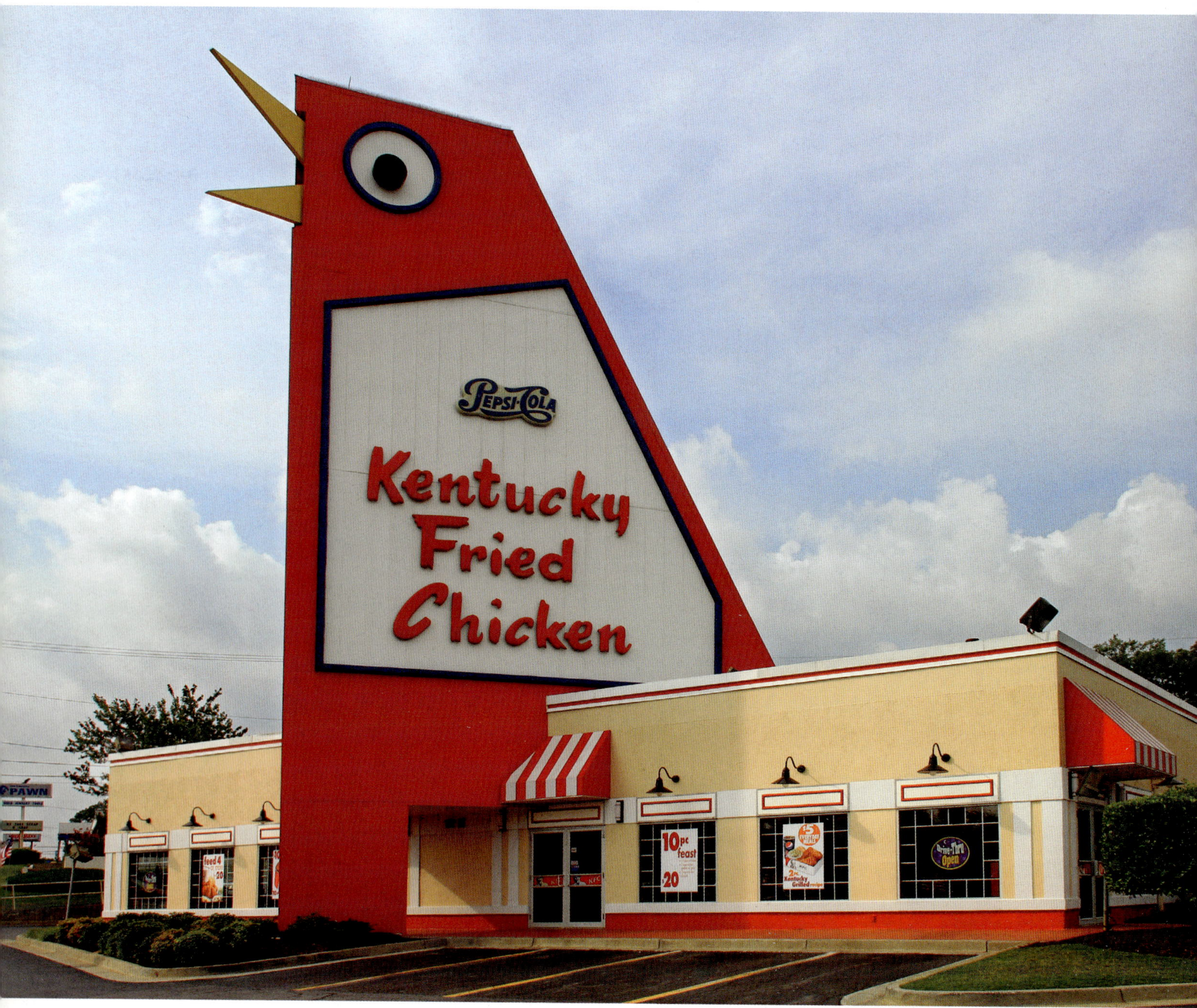

The Big Chicken

Holding court on a fast food highway in Marietta, the 56-foot-tall Big Chicken has been a quirky and navigational landmark since 1963 when it was erected by S.R. "Tubby" Davis to advertise his restaurant, now a KFC franchise. An abstract metal structure, it has moving eyes and a bright yellow beak. The KFC gift shop sells Big Chicken souvenirs.

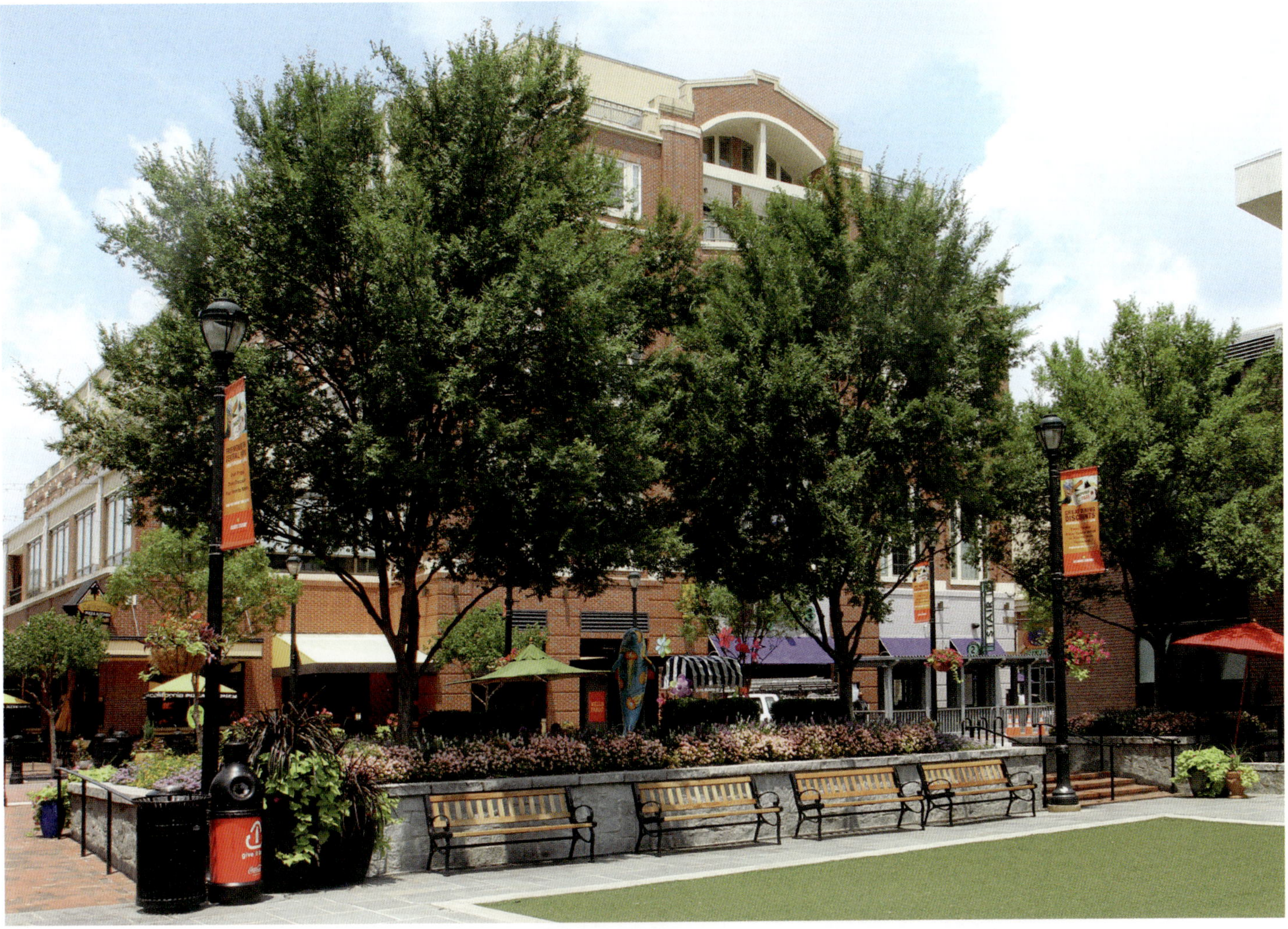

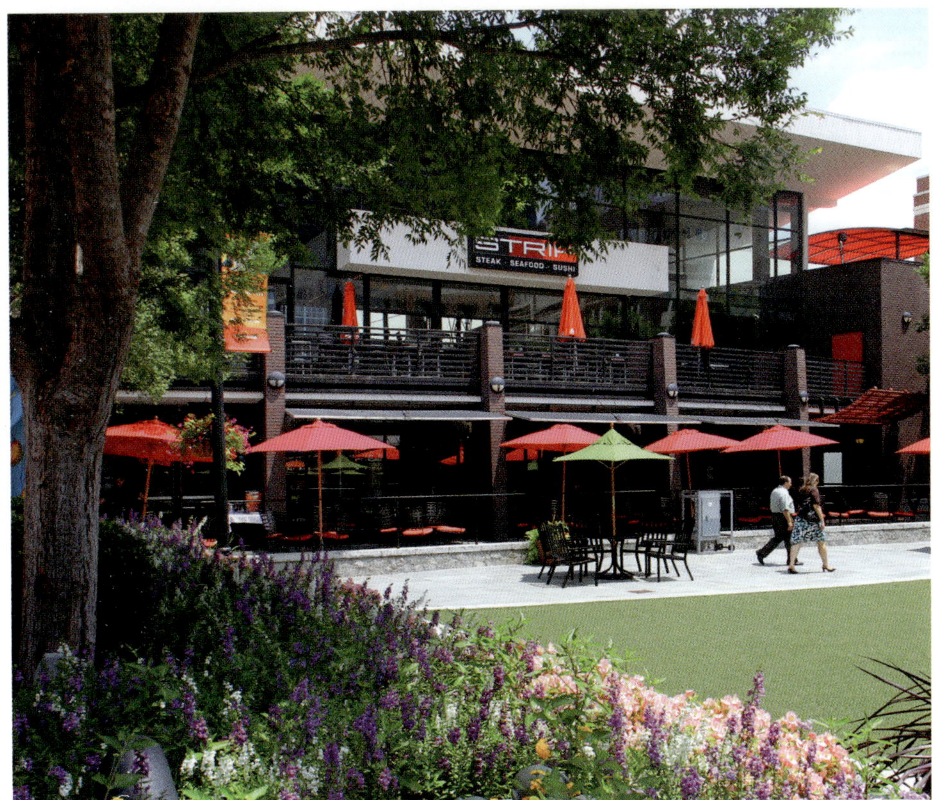

Atlantic Station *(above and right)*

A national model for smart growth and sustainable development, the architecturally striking Atlantic Station community combines upscale residential areas with world-class shopping, dining, theatre, and employment opportunities for pedestrian-friendly, round-the-clock living, playing, and working. A former steel mill site, this 138-acre reclaimed brownfield is environmentally-friendly with wide boulevards, sidewalk cafes, and expansive parks.

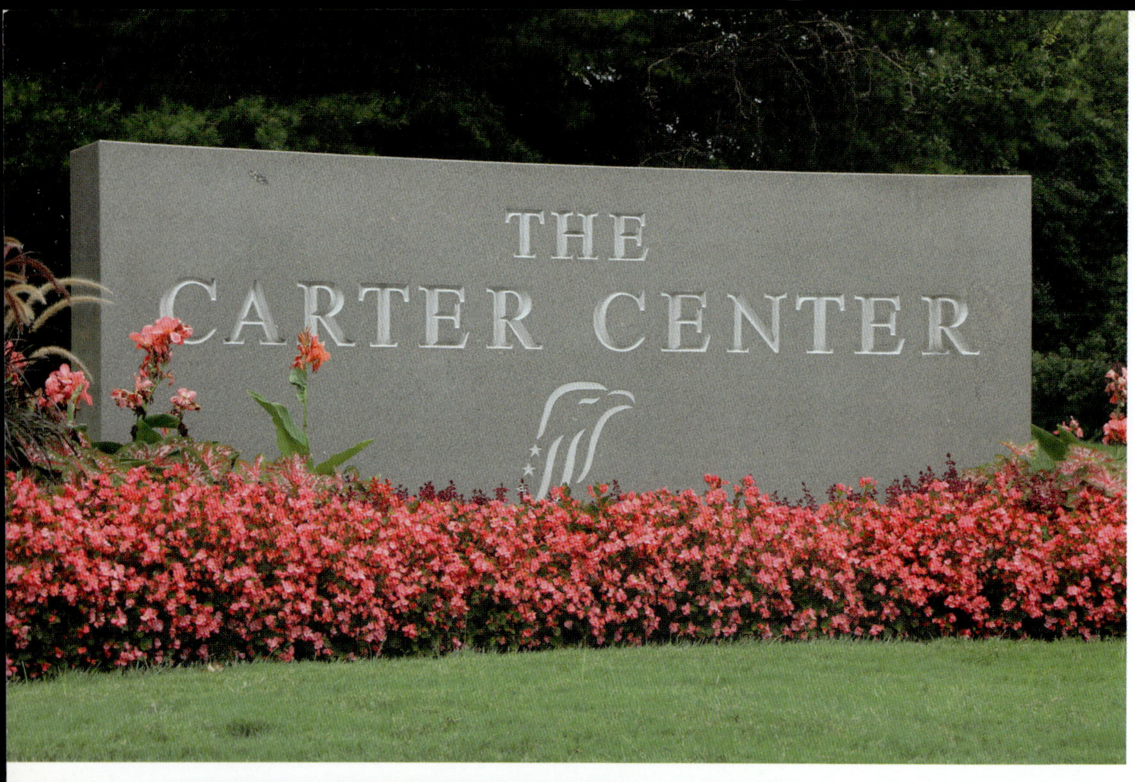

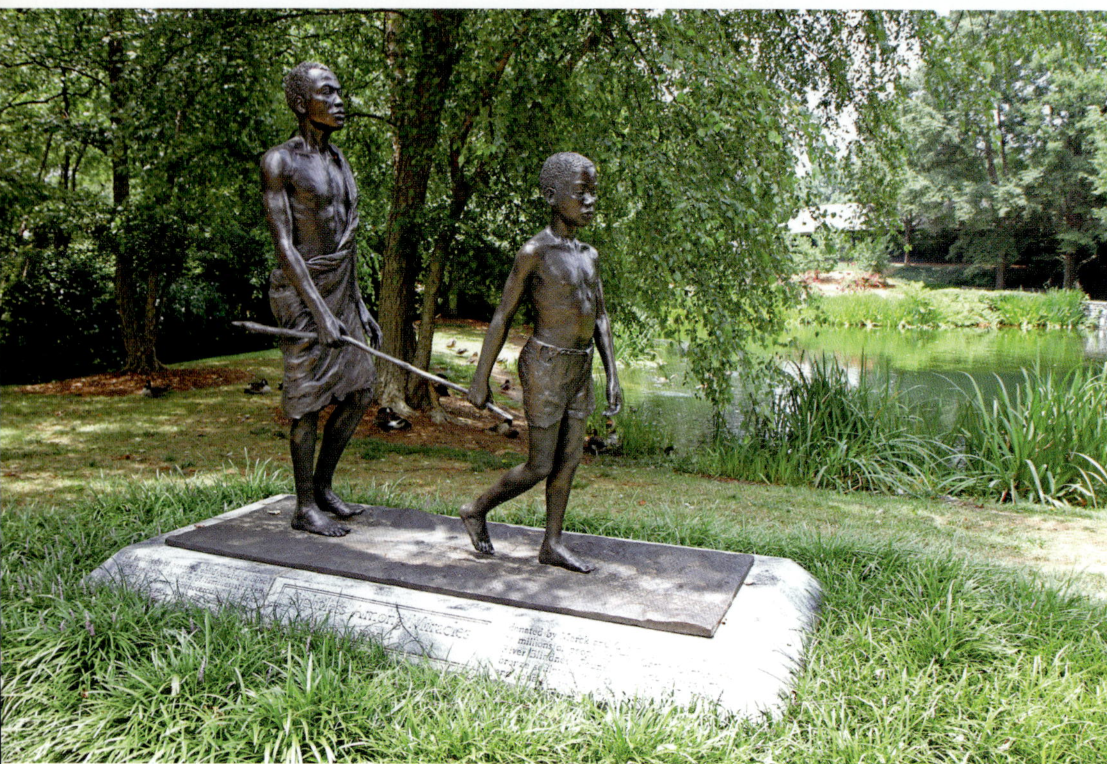

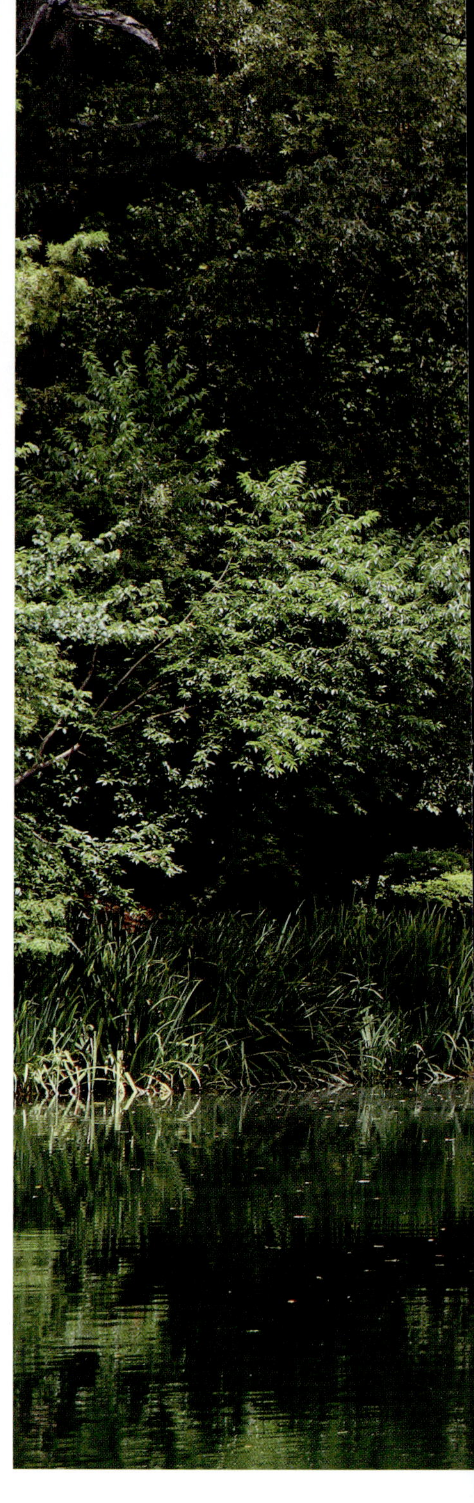

The Carter Center *(top)*

Opened in 1986, the 35-acre Carter Presidential Center includes both The Carter Center, which is the headquarters for Jimmy and Rosalynn Carter's work to promote peace, health, and human rights, and the Jimmy Carter Presidential Library and Museum, which is part of the National Archives and Records Administration.

Sightless Among Miracles *(bottom)*

Sightless Among Miracles, located in the gardens of The Carter Center, is a striking sculpture donated by John and Rebecca Moores that depicts a child leading a blind man, a sight often seen in countries whose populations are vulnerable to river blindness disease. The Carter Center has led efforts to control or eliminate this disease.

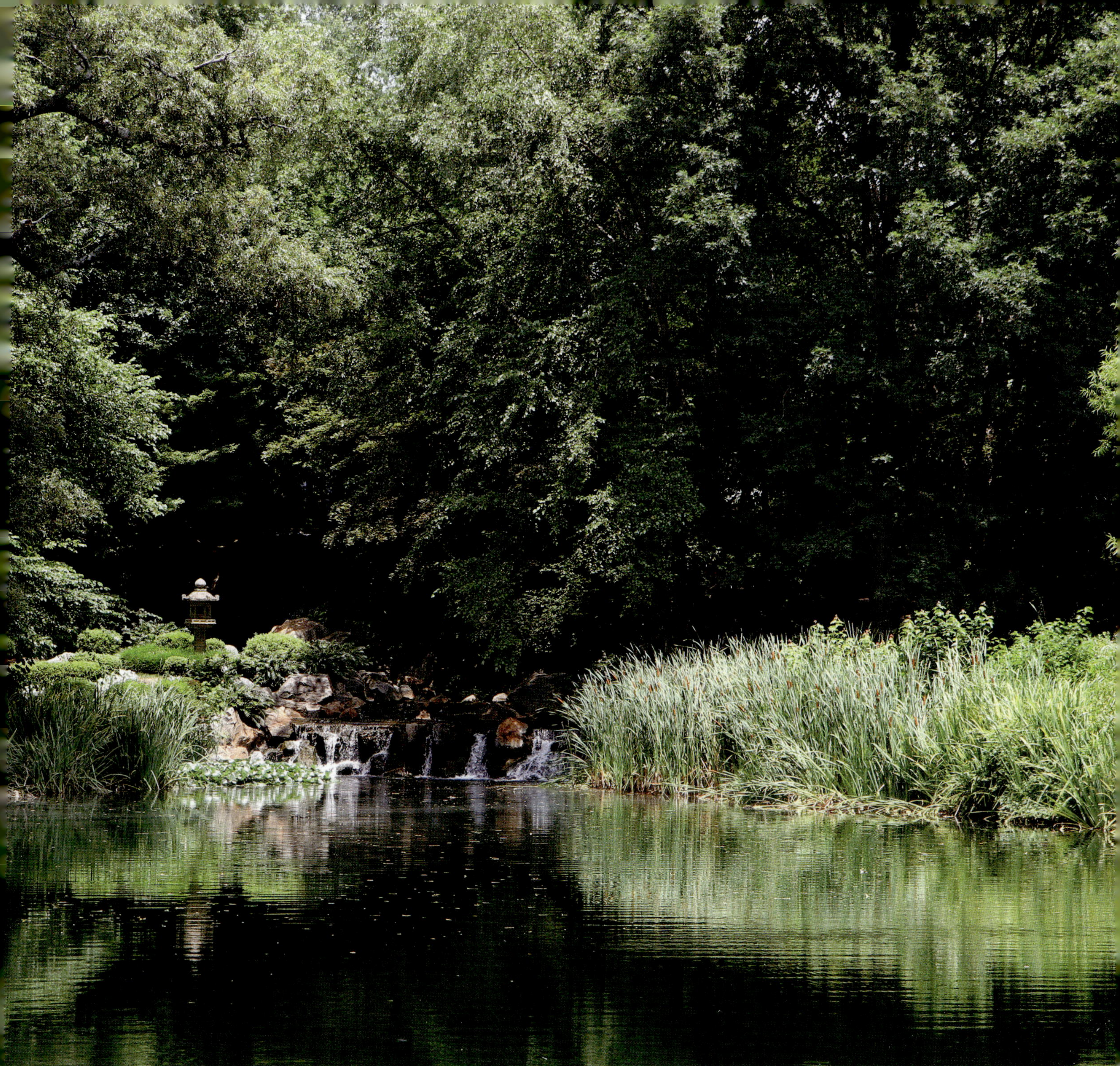

Japanese Garden

At The Carter Center, tucked between two small lakes, is a peaceful Japanese garden, designed by Japanese Master Kinsaku Nakane. It features a large waterfall representing President Jimmy Carter and a smaller one symbolizing Rosalynn Carter. The grounds also include an oak forest, rose garden, cherry tree orchard, and koi pond.

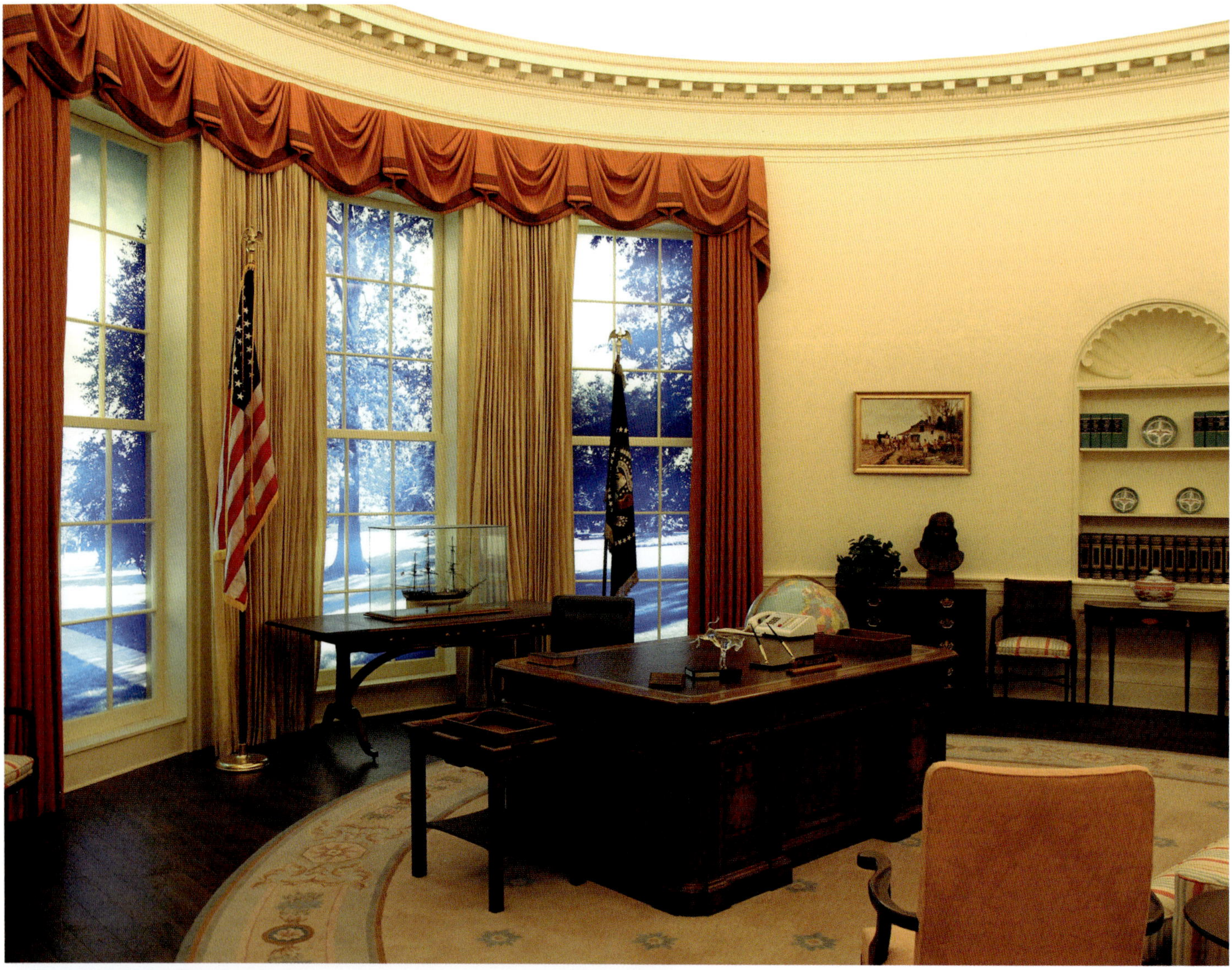

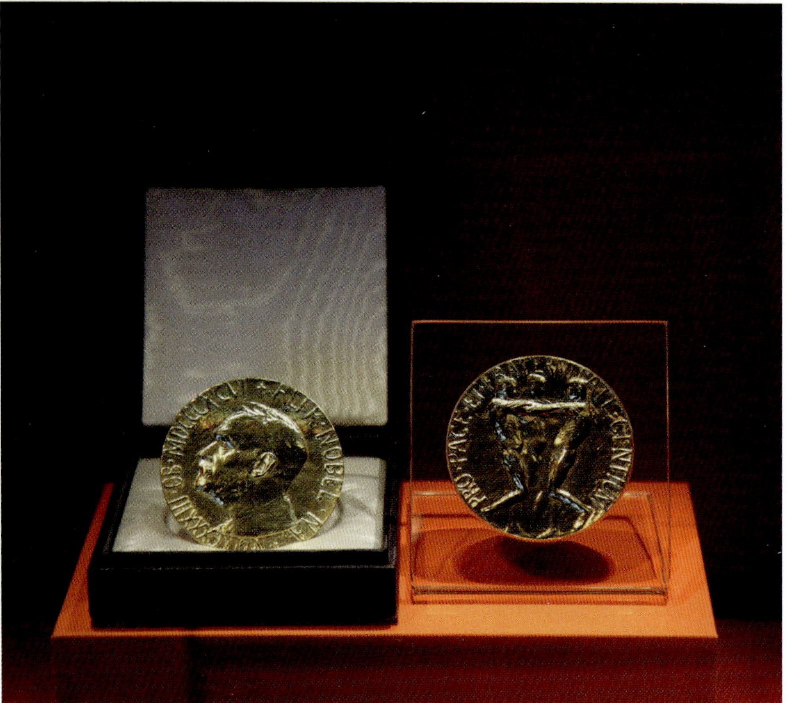

Jimmy Carter Library and Museum *(above)*

Highly interactive and family-friendly, the Jimmy Carter Library and Museum includes an exact replica of the Oval Office, decorated as it was during the Carter Administration. President Carter can be heard describing it and some of his memories. A replica of the "Resolute Desk," made famous by President Kennedy's son John who used it to play "hide-and-seek," is the centerpiece.

Peace Medallion *(left)*

The Nobel Peace Prize was awarded to President Carter in 2002 for his "decades of untiring effort to find peaceful solutions to international conflicts, to advance democracy and human rights, and to promote economic and social development." On display are both the Gold Medallion and one of Carter's two Bronze Medallions, giving visitors the opportunity to see both sides of the medal.

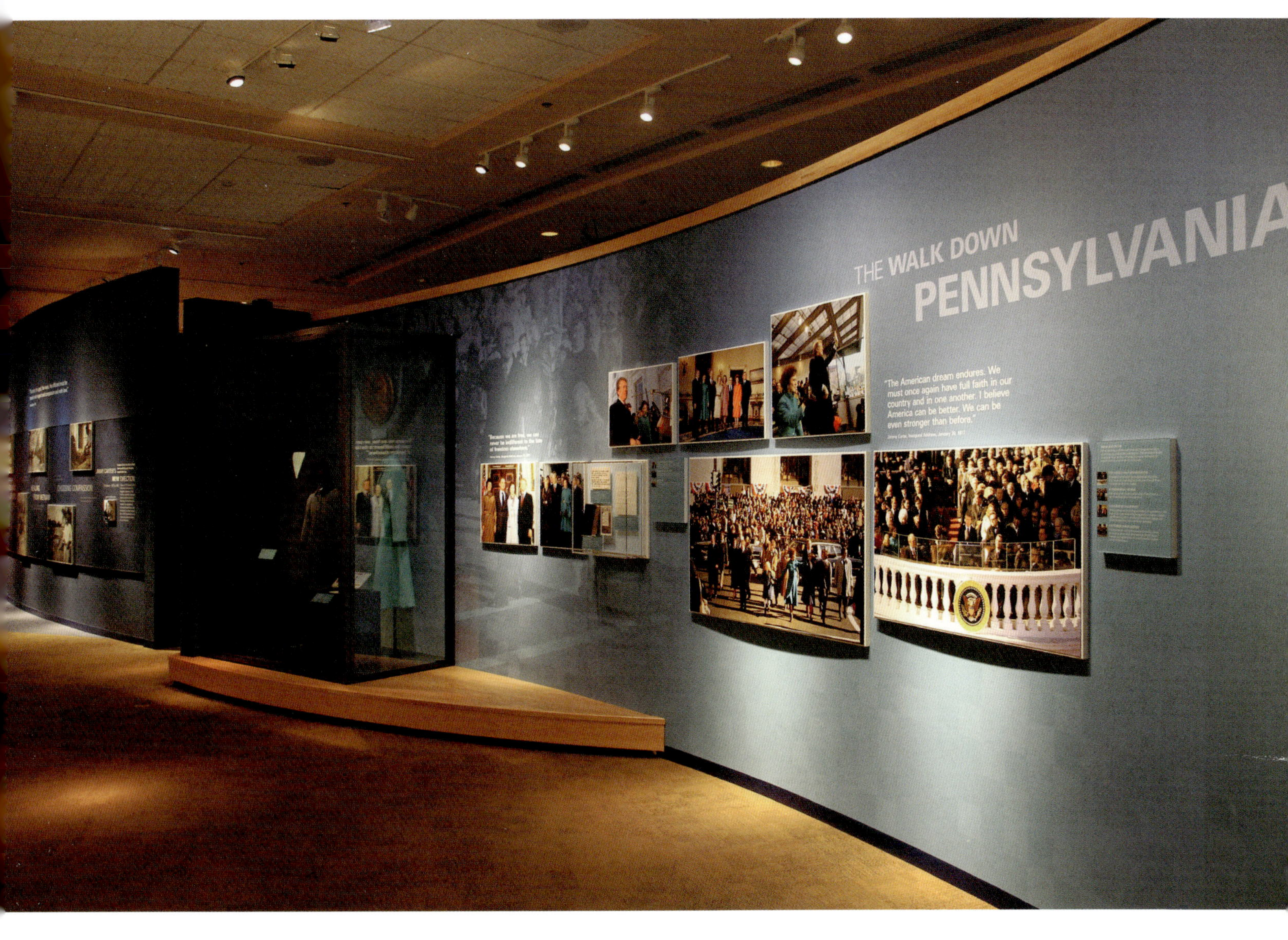

Carter Inauguration

The Walk Down Pennsylvania Avenue is one of many galleries in the museum that depicts the career of President Carter. Among the artifacts are the coats worn by the Carter family during the inauguration. Interestingly, the coat Carter wore actually belonged to his media advisor, Gerald Raftshoon – borrowed for an outdoor television interview.

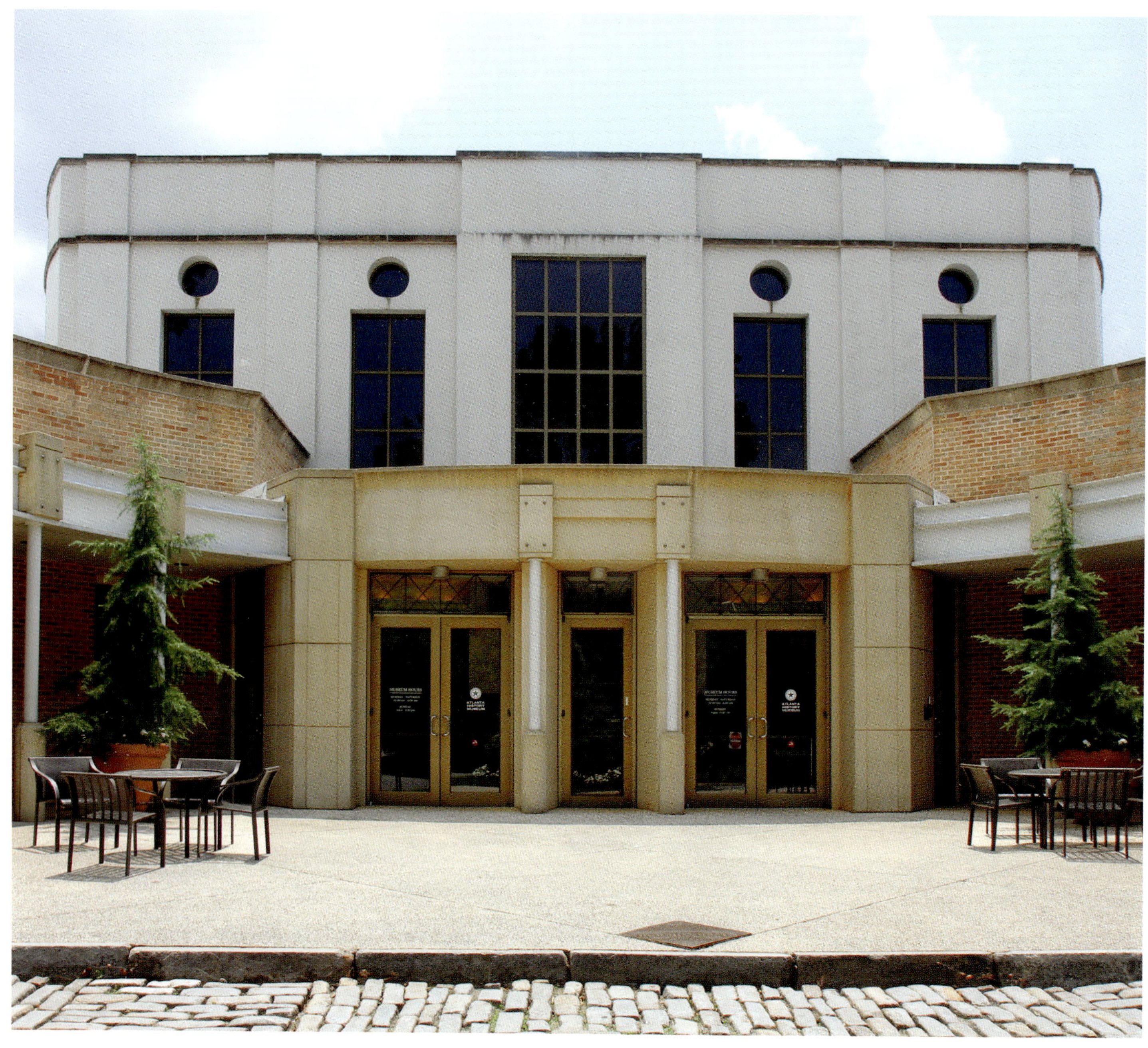

Atlanta History Center

Located in Buckhead, the Atlanta History Center includes the Atlanta History Museum; Centennial Olympic Games Museum, one of the most significant exhibitions on Olympic history in the United States; three historic homes – Swan House, Smith Family Farm, Margaret Mitchell House; six historic gardens; and the Kenan Research Center.

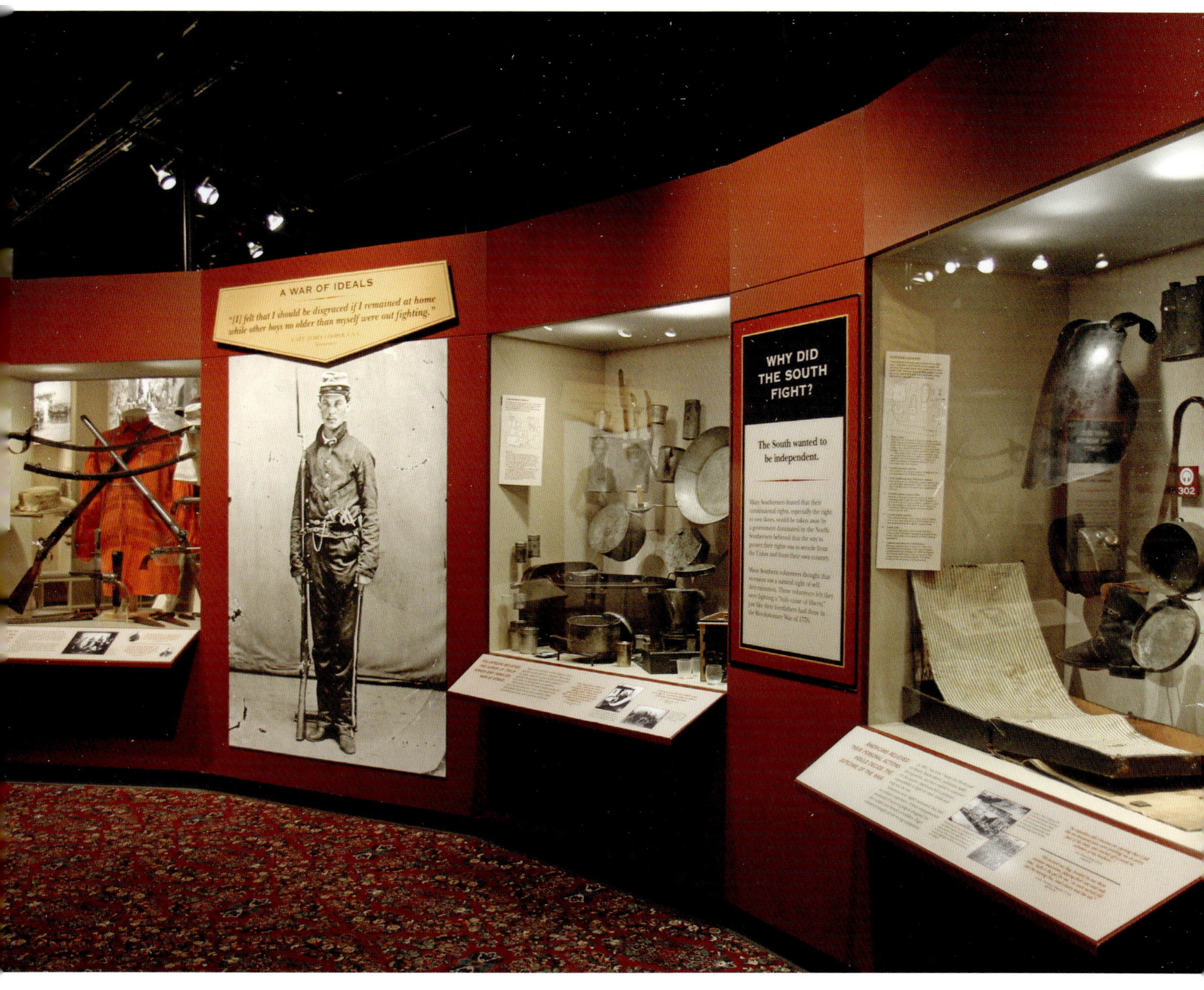

History Preserved

Forty thousand items dating from the early 19th century to the present comprise exhibits covering Urban History, Decorative Arts and Material Culture, Textile and Social History, and the Civil War. The Civil War and Military Collection has at least one of nearly every type of weapon, uniform, and accessory used by Union and Confederate forces.

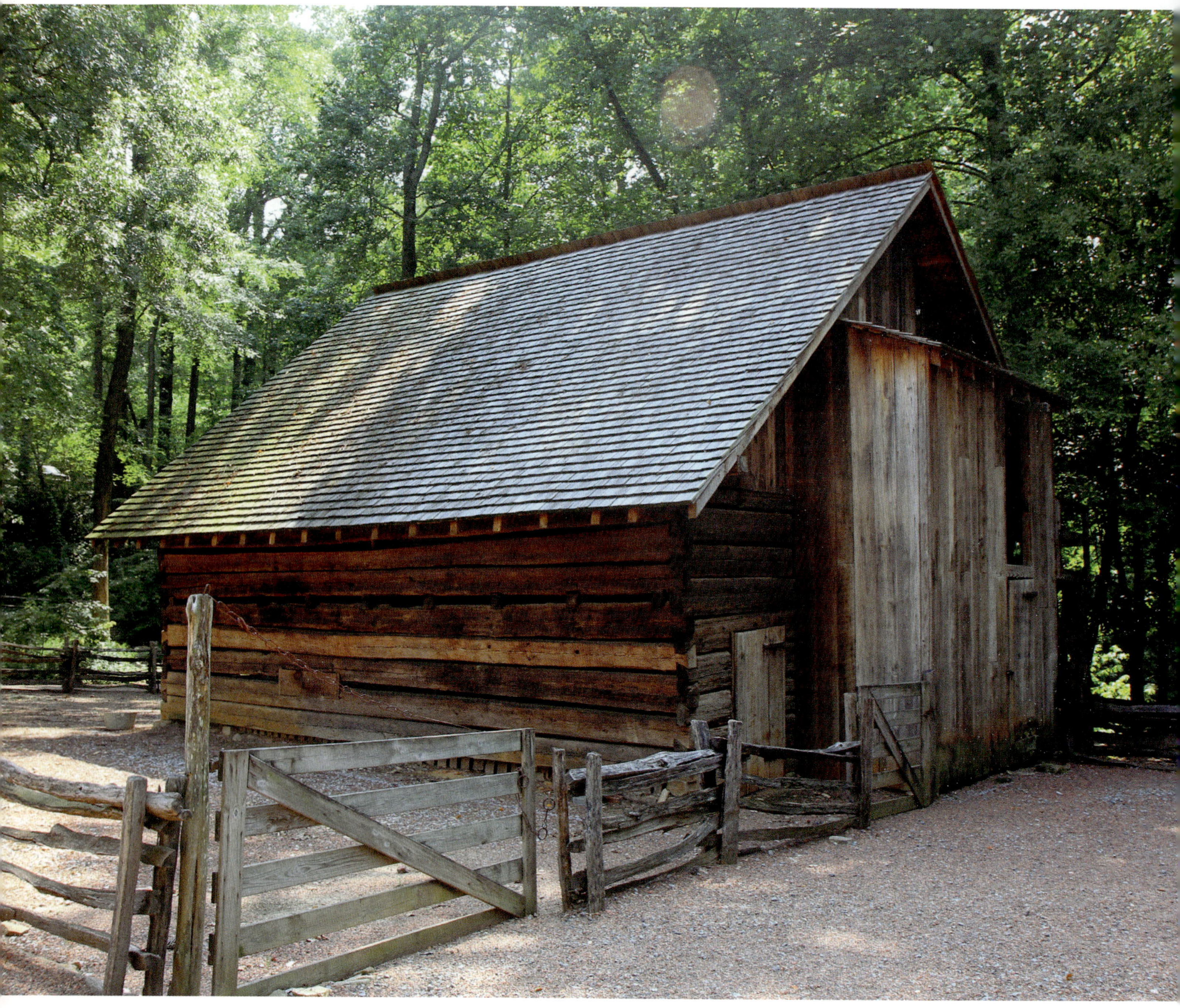

Tullie Smith Farm

The circa 1840s "plantation-plain" house built by the Robert Smith family is on the National Register of Historic Places. It is located on the Atlanta History Center's Buckhead campus amidst a dairy, blacksmith shop, smokehouse, double corncrib, slave cabin, and gardens. Costumed interpreters conduct tours and 19th-century rural Georgia programs.

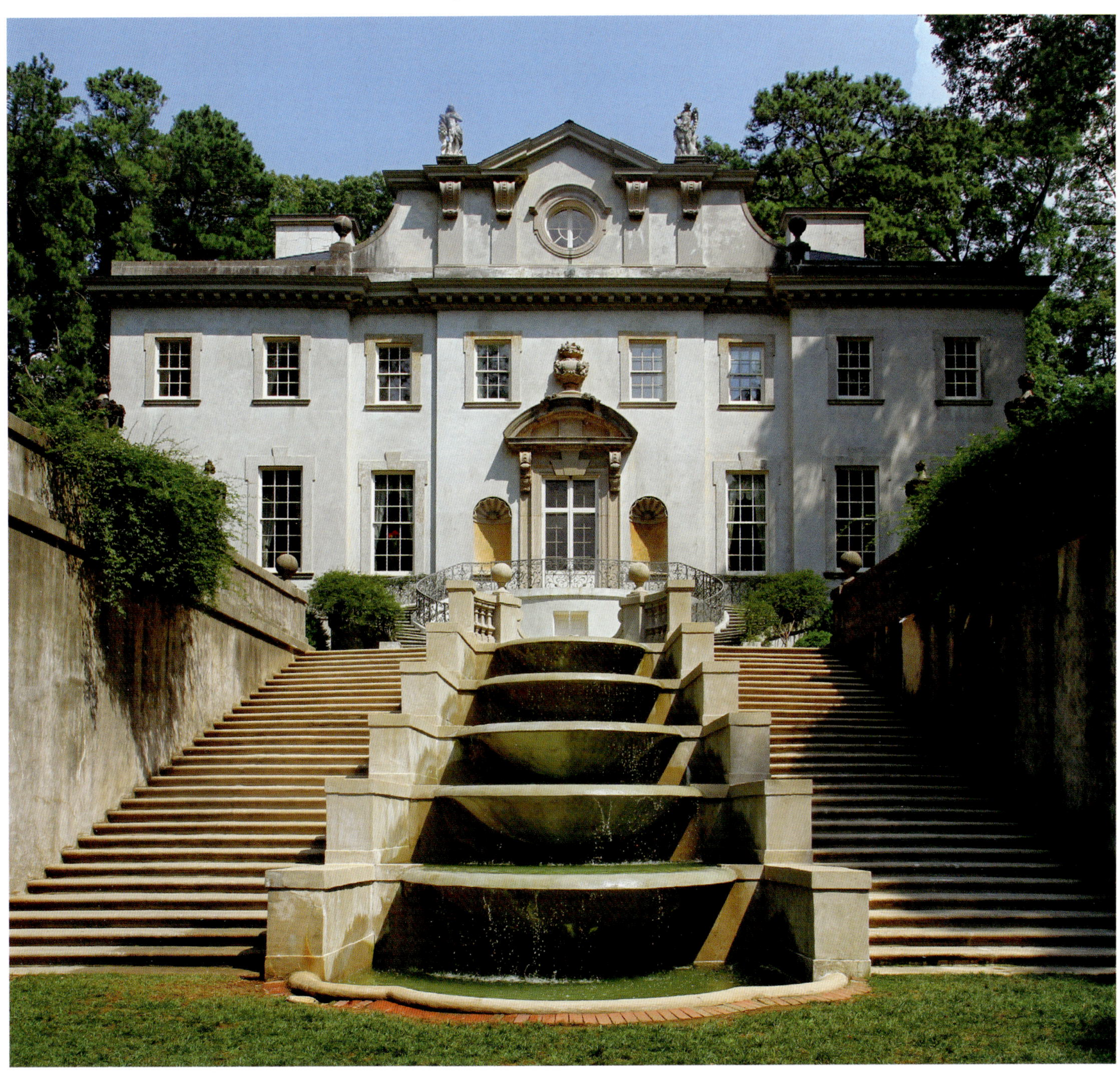

Swan House

As elegant as the Tullie Smith House is rustic, this 1928 classically styled mansion – one of the most photographed landmarks in Atlanta – is also located on the Atlanta History Center's Buckhead campus and listed on the National Register of Historic Places. Glimpse at the 1920s and 1930s lifestyle of heirs to a cotton brokerage fortune.

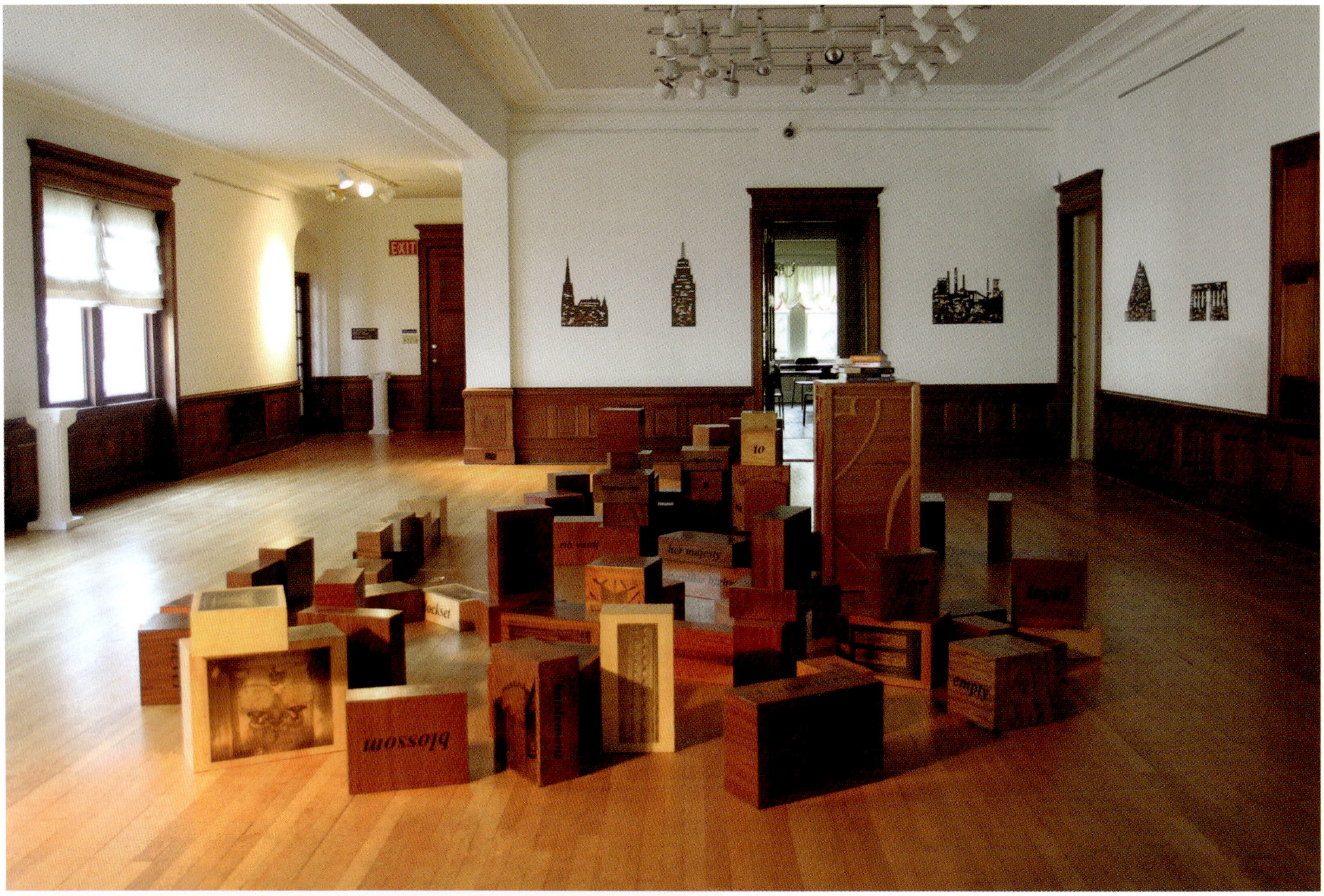

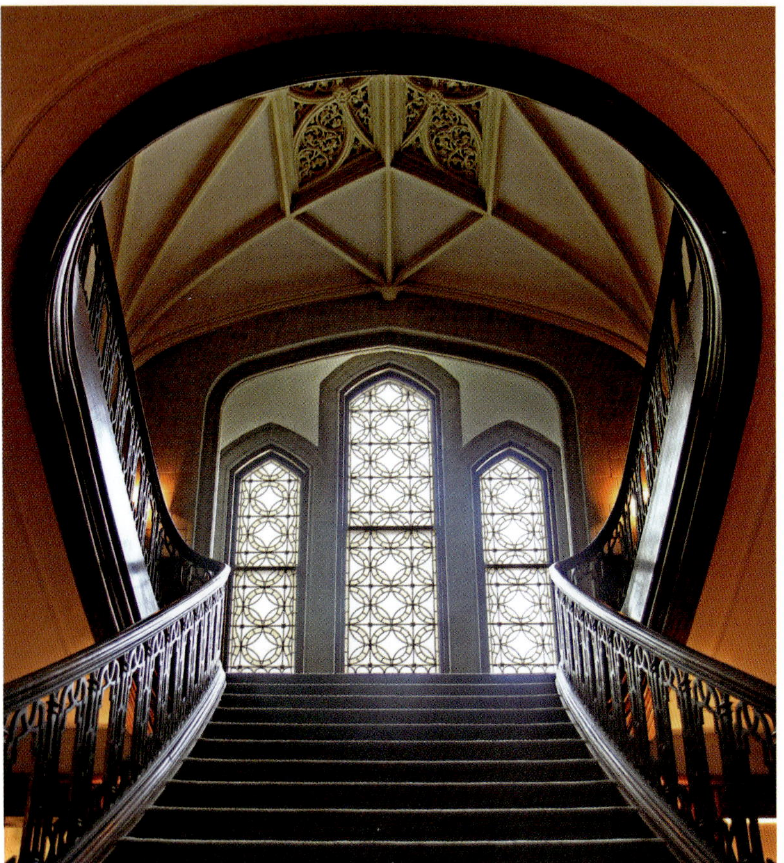

Gallery Exhibit *(above)*

Situated on a 12.5-acre estate landscaped with sculptured lawns, formal gardens, nature trails, and rock garden, the Callanwolde Fine Arts Center is a unique art center that combines history, architecture, and art education in a magnificent 27,000-square-foot Gothic-Tudor style mansion. Special performances, gallery exhibits, and outreach programs are presented throughout the year.

Home of Coca-Cola President *(left)*

Callanwolde, home of the Charles Howard Candler family, was completed in 1920. Located in Atlanta's Druid Hills neighborhood, the estate was planned by the firm of Frederick Law Olmsted. Howard Candler, eldest son of Coca-Cola Company founder Asa Candler, was the president of the company from 1916 to 1923.

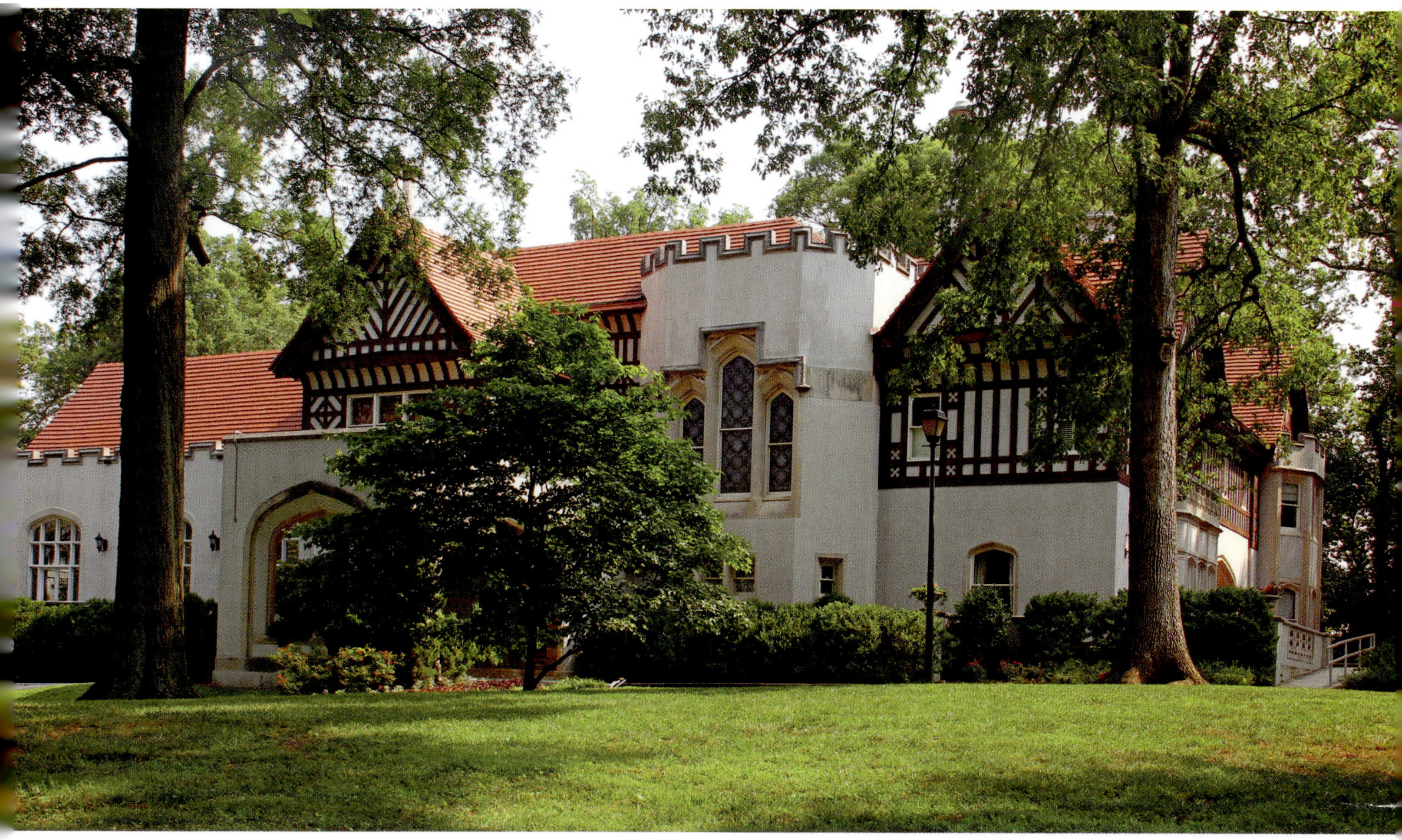

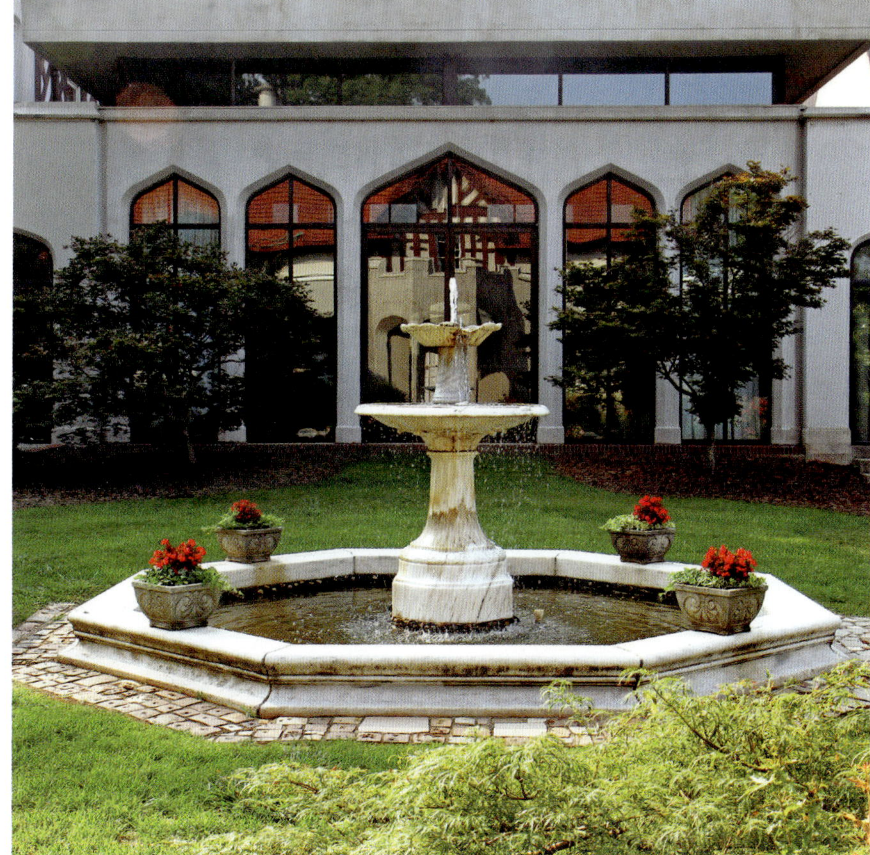

Callanwolde Fine Arts Center

(above and right)

Donated to Emory University in 1959, two years after Howard Candler's death, the estate includes many of the furnishings original to the home. The windows in the Billiard Room carry the Candler Family crest with the motto, "Faithful Unto Death." An Aeolian organ console, specially designed for the house and installed during its construction, resides in the Great Hall.

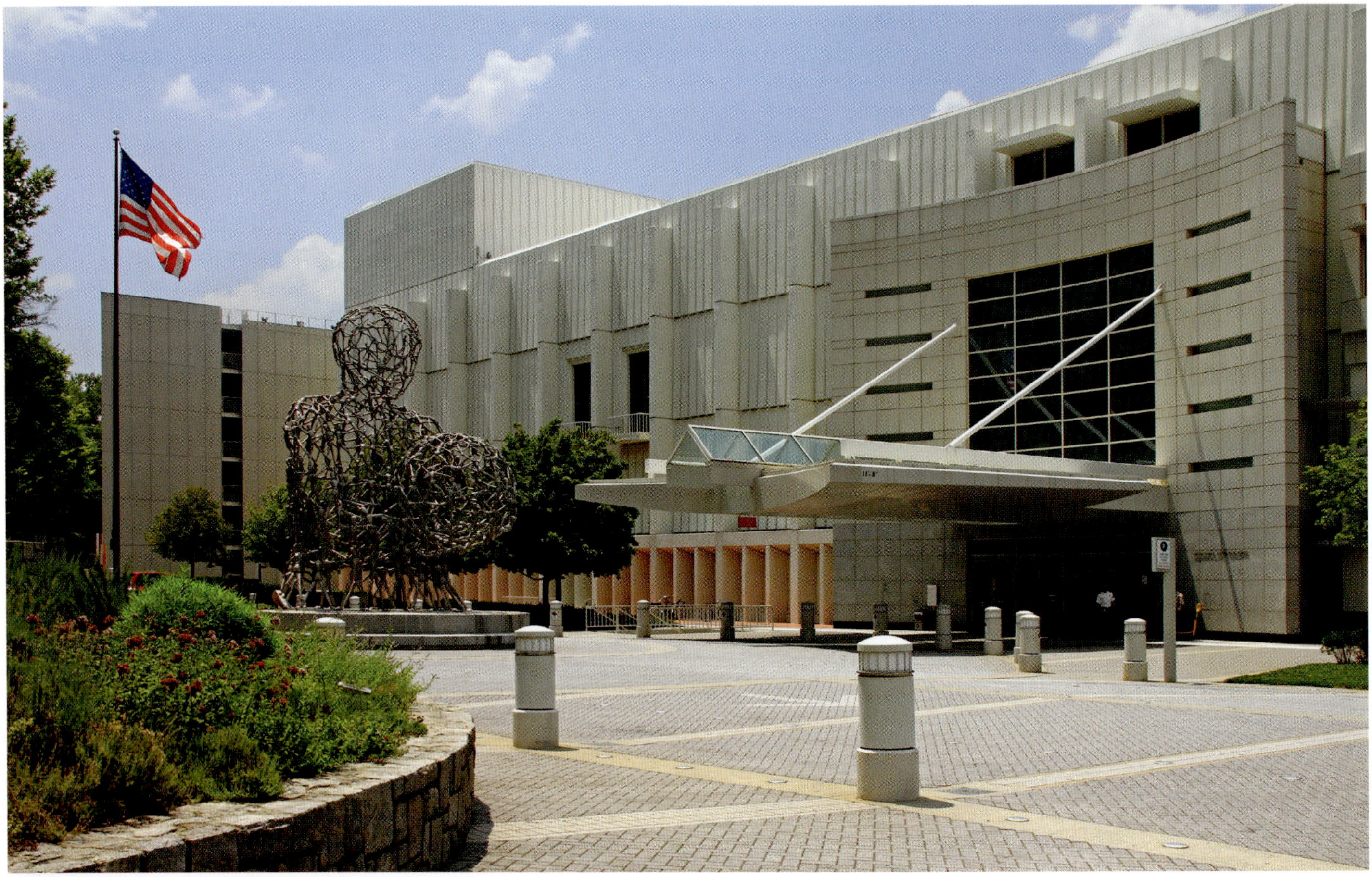

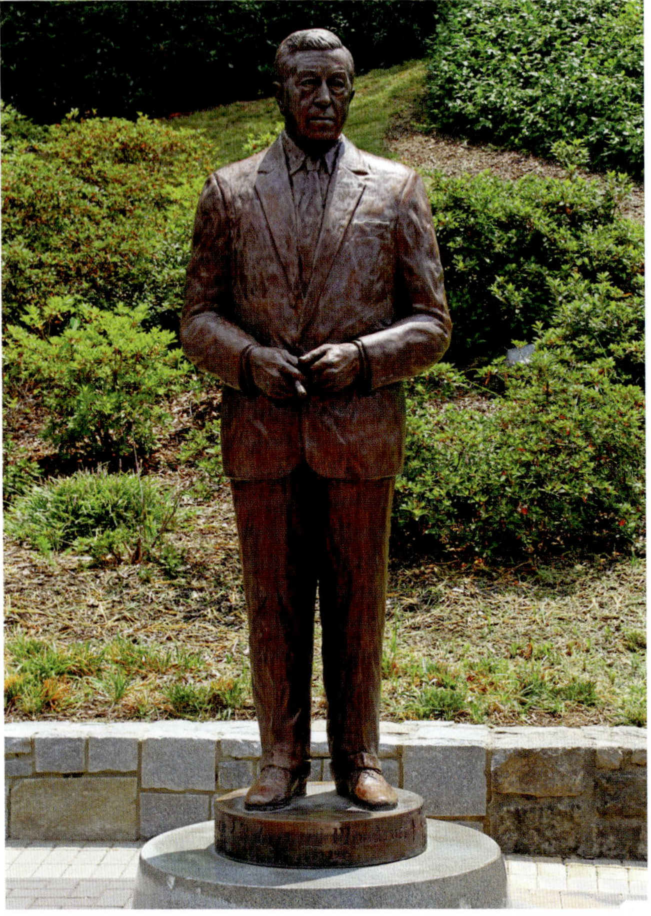

Woodruff Arts Center *(above and opposite)*

The epicenter of Atlanta's arts community is the Woodruff Arts Center in Midtown, which includes the Tony Award-winning Alliance Theatre, High Museum of Art, Young Audiences, 14th Street Playhouse, and Atlanta Symphony Orchestra. It is considered the most dynamic center for the visual and performing arts in the South and is among the top such centers in the nation.

Beverage Baron *(left)*

Making the dream of combining the cream of Atlanta's performing and visual arts venues into a center for the arts was made possible by the Woodruff Foundation, which had been established by Atlanta-based Coca-Cola magnate Robert W. Woodruff – the man responsible for turning a fledgling soft drink enterprise into a corporate giant.

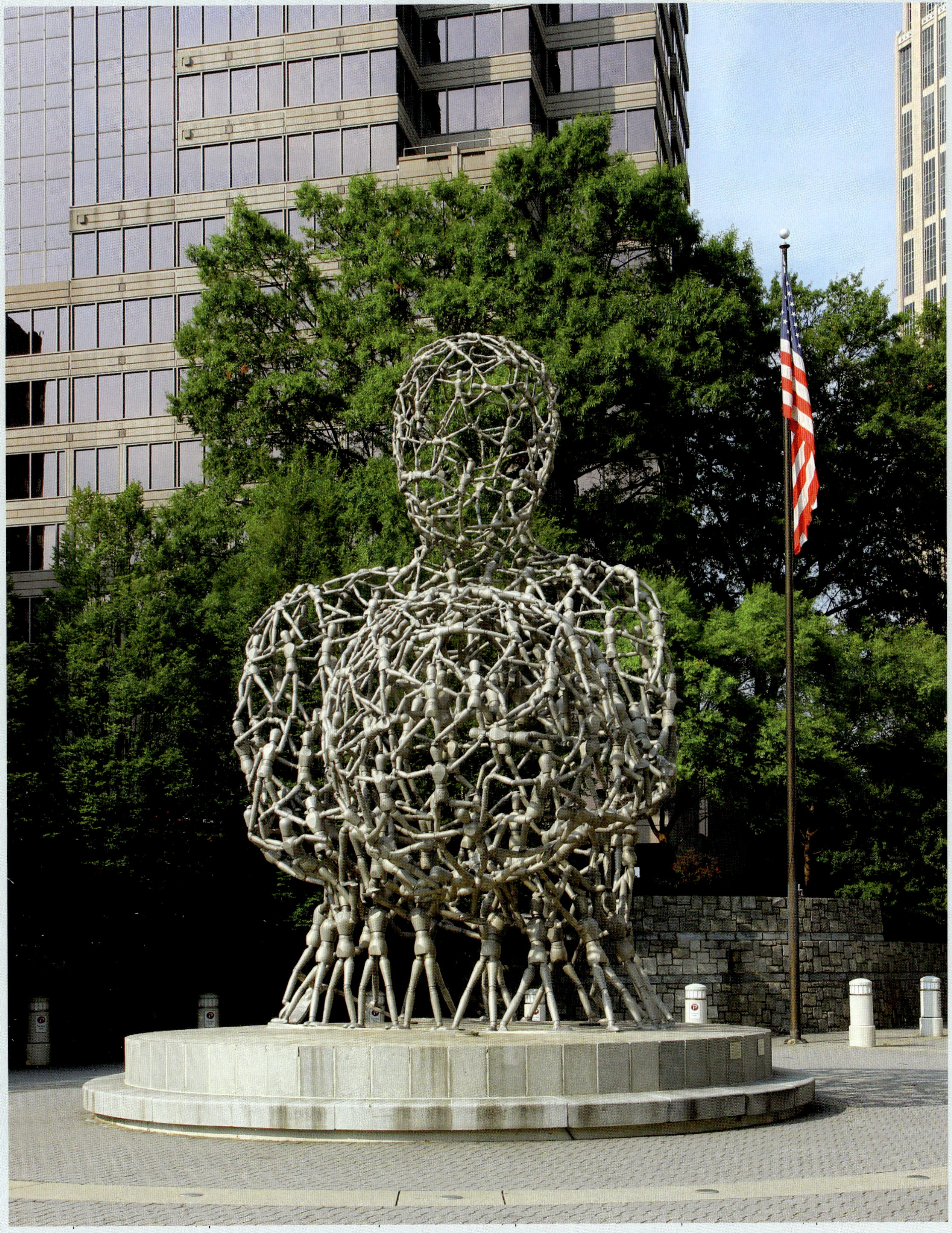

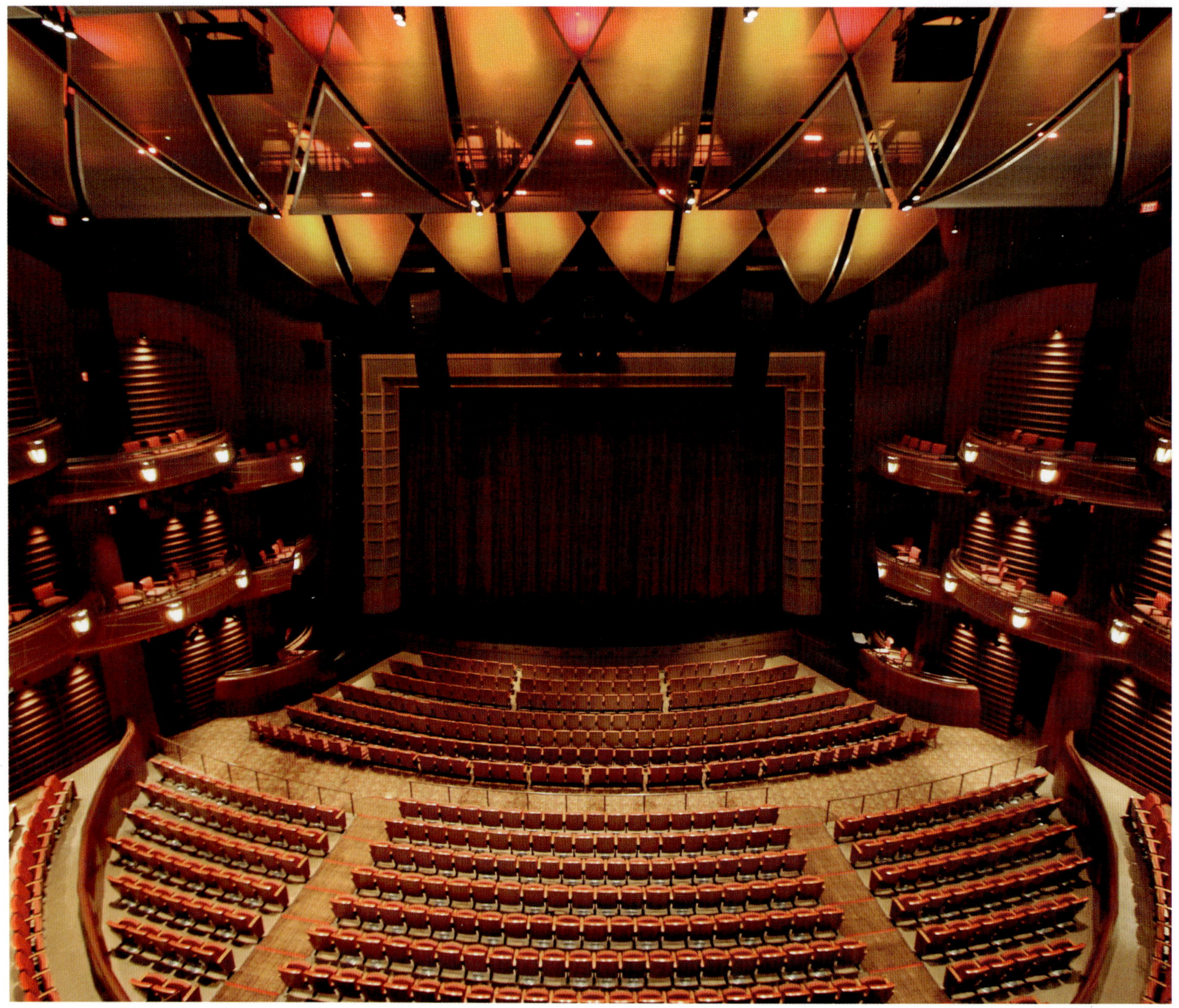

John A. Williams Theatre

Home of the opulent 2,750-seat John A. Williams Theatre, a multi-purpose venue that blends striking architectural elements with ultra-modern theater systems, the Cobb Energy Performing Arts Center is noted for its curved roof structure and glass entrance. It also has a 10,000-square-foot ballroom, as well as courtyard and terrace.

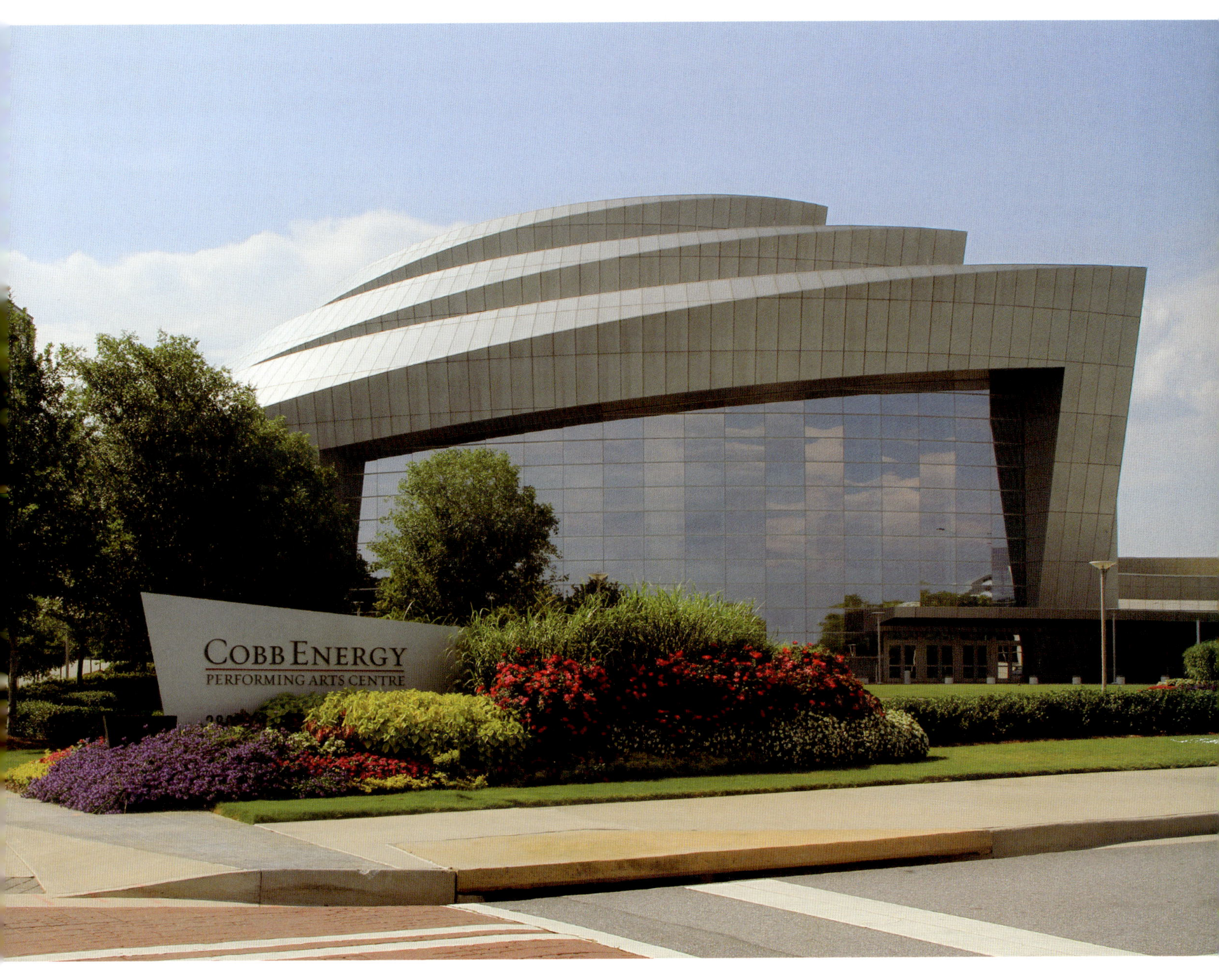

Cobb Energy Performing Arts Centre

The Cobb Energy Performing Arts Centre – a premier venue for Broadway shows, ballet, concerts, educational shows, opera, corporate meetings, and events – is home to resident companies Atlanta Opera, Atlanta Ballet, and Gas South Broadway Series. It was the first major performing arts facility built in metro Atlanta in four decades.

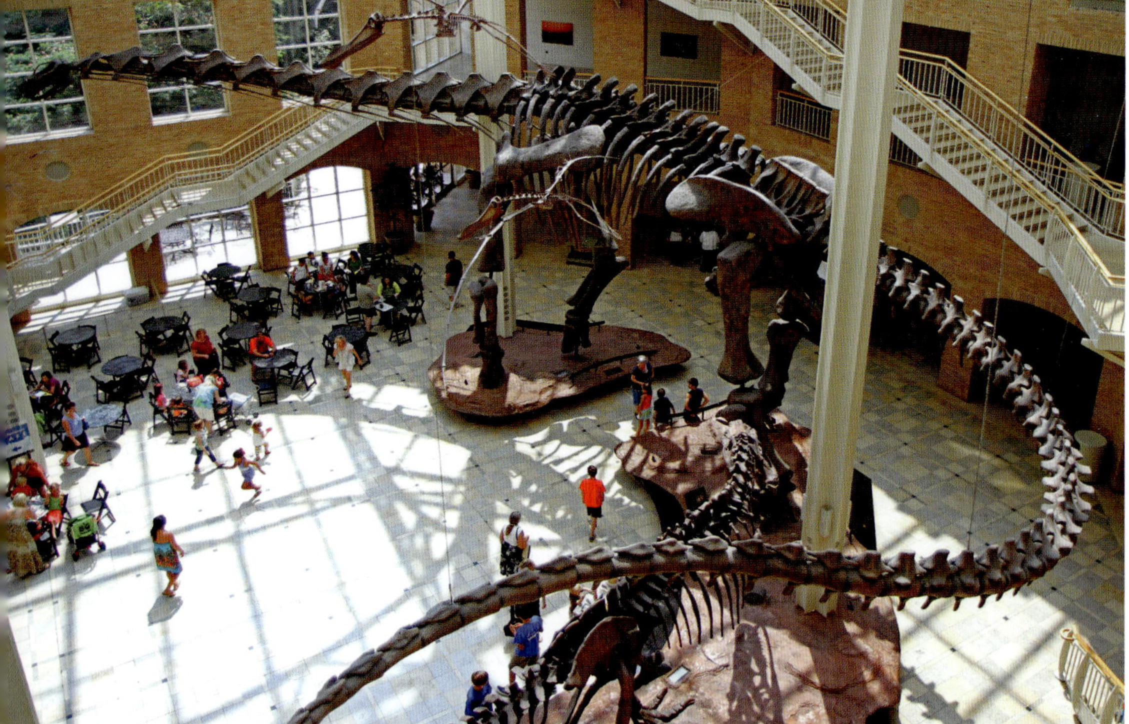

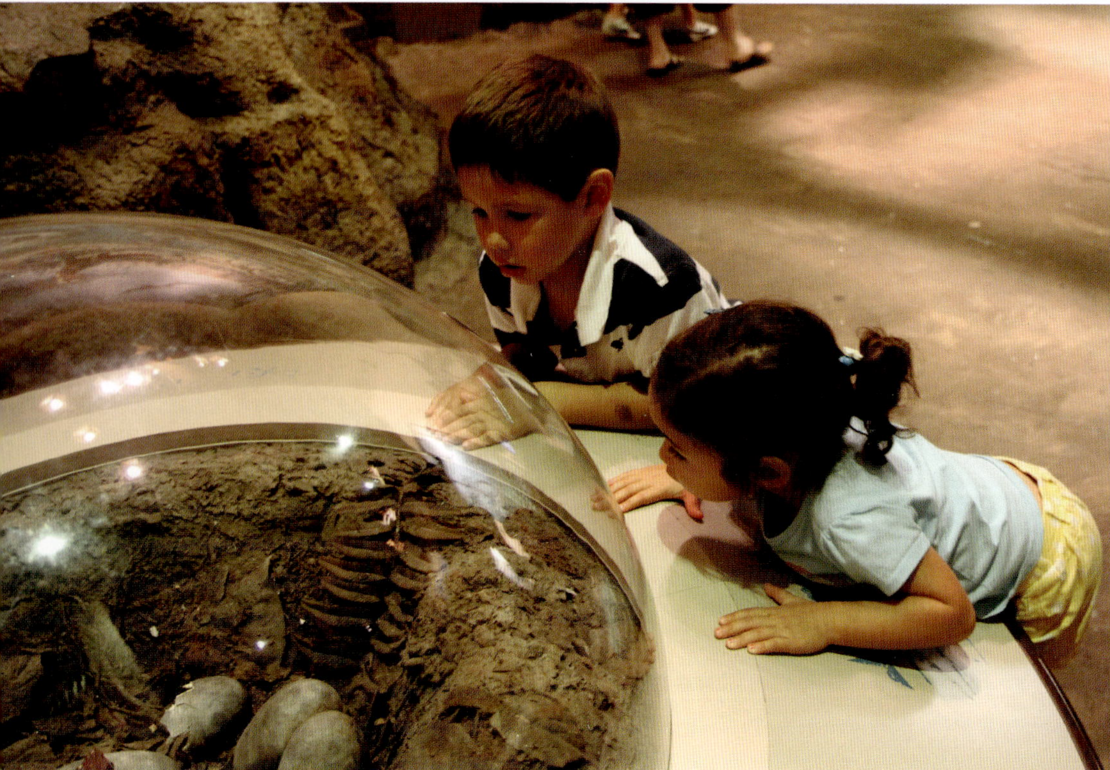

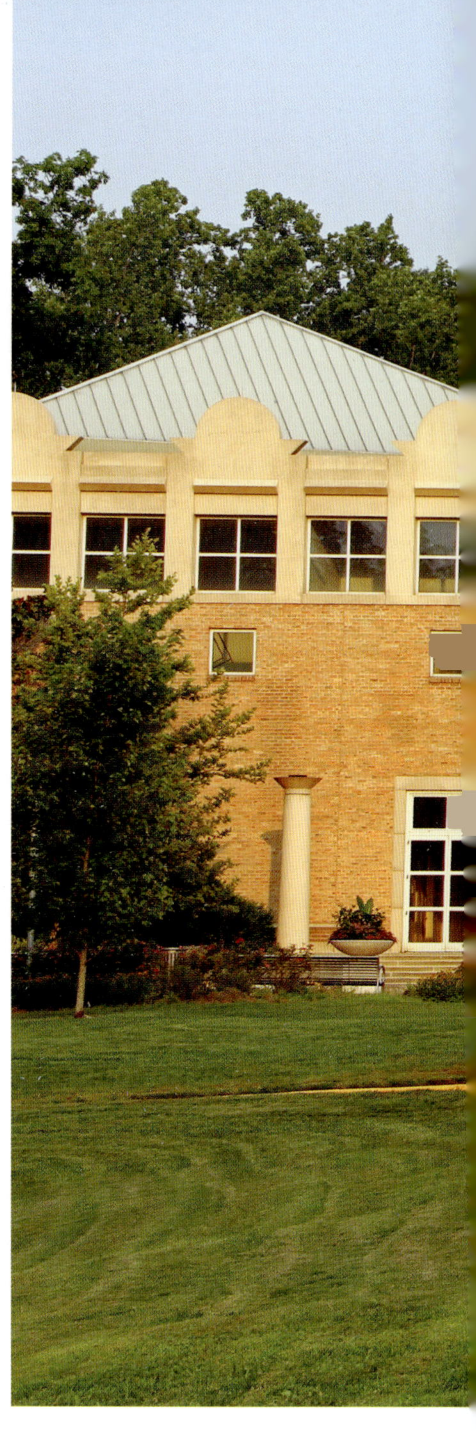

The World's Largest Dinosaurs *(top)*

Fernbank Museum of Natural History is where the world's largest dinosaurs roam. It was the first museum to display these superlative prehistoric beings in a permanent exhibition. At Giants of the Mesozoic, meet Argentinosaurus – the length of nearly four school buses and weighing 100 tons – and Giganotosaurus, at 47 feet and eight tons.

Walk Through Time *(bottom)*

Follow the fossils to see a cave, a giant sloth, and a re-creation of a nest of dinosaur eggs in Fernbank's signature exhibition, A Walk Through Time in Georgia. Tour the night sky, witness a tornado, stop and smell the roses in the Rose Garden, get blown away in the five-story IMAX Theatre, and embark on an interactive NatureQuest.

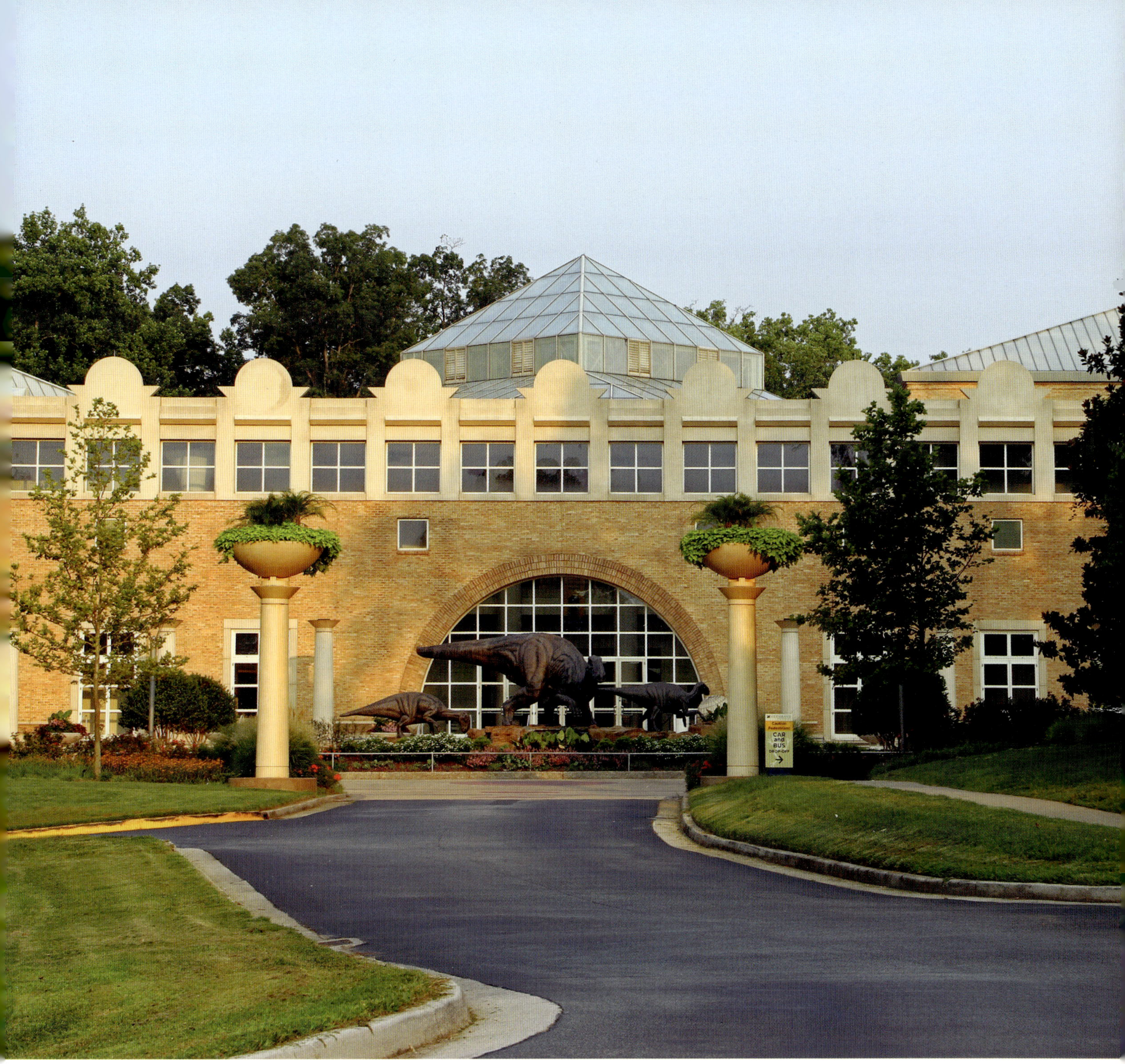

Fernbank Museum of Natural History

Step beneath the family of bronze dinosaurs and into a world where the past roars to life amidst the 65-acre Fernbank Forest, the largest old-growth urban Piedmont forest in the country. Tread carefully: You're walking on 40,000 limestone tiles, each containing fossil remains of animals that lived in a shallow reef more than 150 million years ago.

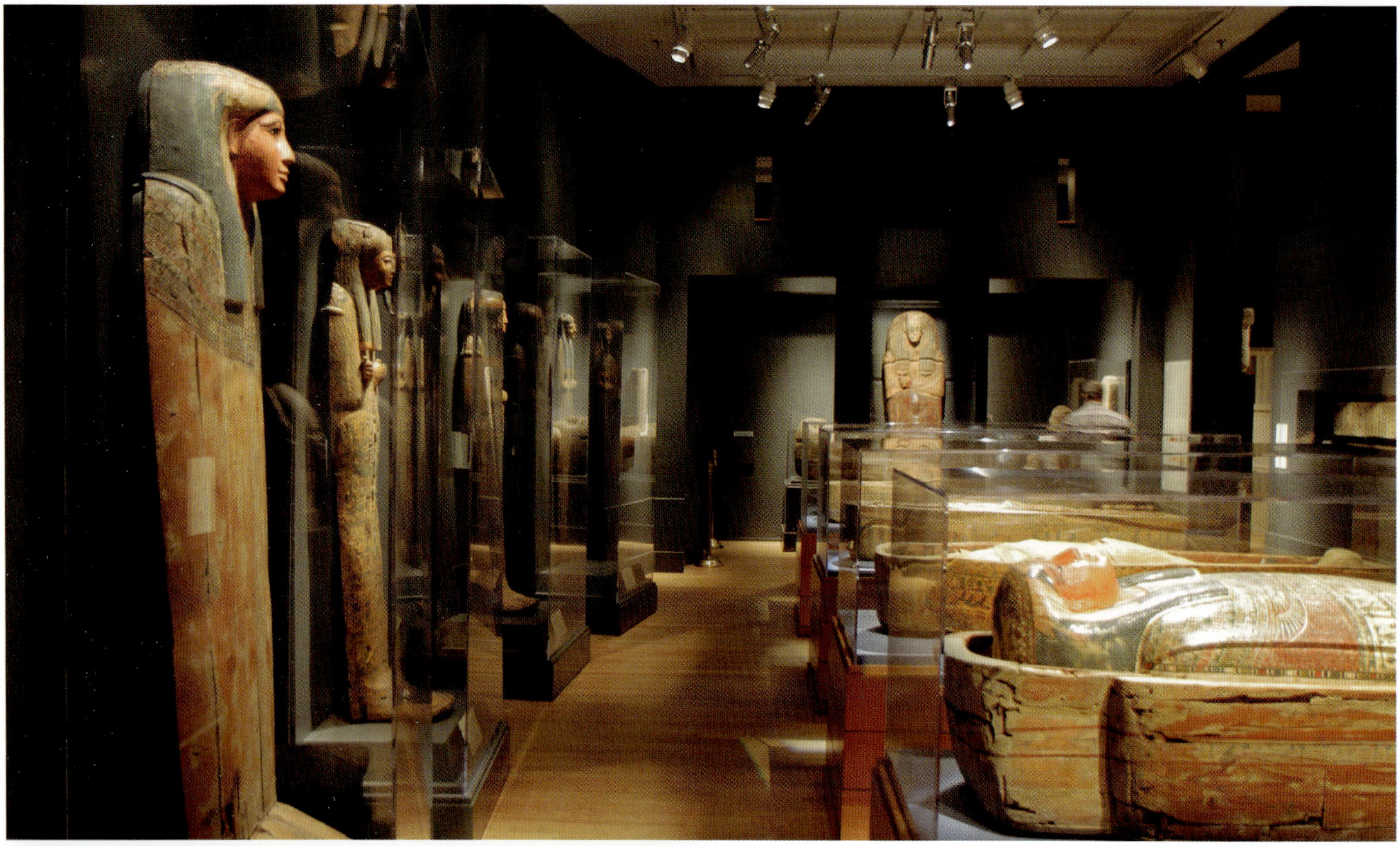

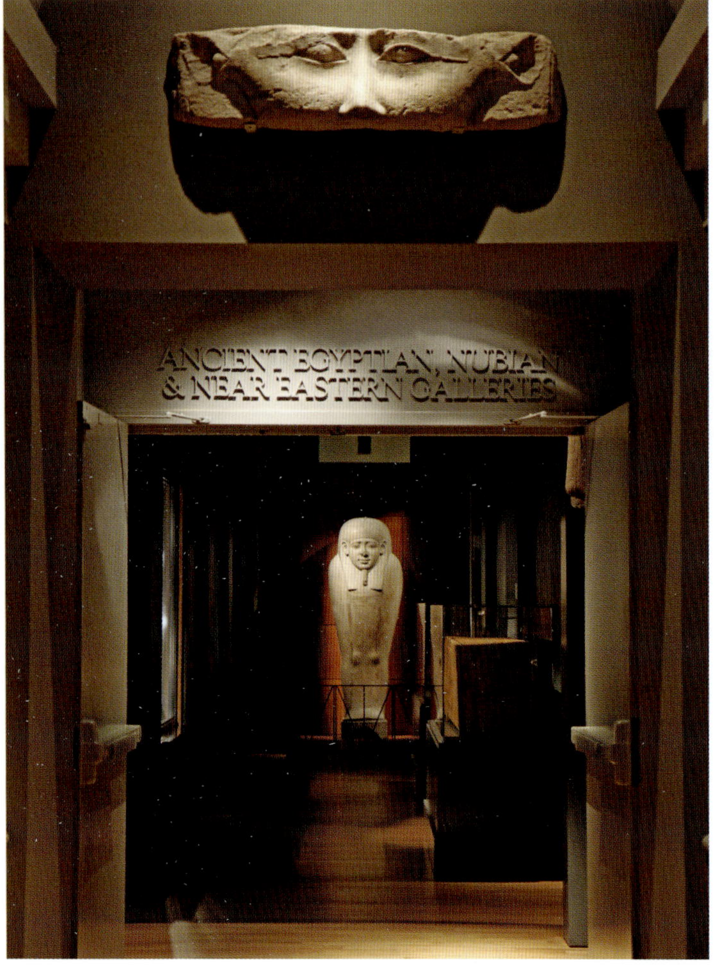

Michael C. Carlos Museum *(above)*

Located at Emory University, the Carlos Museum is one of the Southeast's premier ancient art museums with major collections of art objects from ancient Egypt, Nubia, Near East, Greece, Rome, ancient Americas, Africa, and Asia; a collection of works on paper from the Renaissance to the present; and a distinguished exhibition calendar and teaching laboratory and conservation center.

Egyptian Art Collection *(left)*

Covering the full spectrum of Nile Valley civilization, from prehistory to Roman domination, is the Egyptian, Nubian, and Near Eastern Art collection. Its centerpiece is the oldest Egyptian mummy in the Americas and other artifacts Emory Professor William Shelton acquired during a 1920 Egypt expedition. Additionally, the Niagara collection comprises 10 mummies, nine coffins, and an array of funerary artifacts.

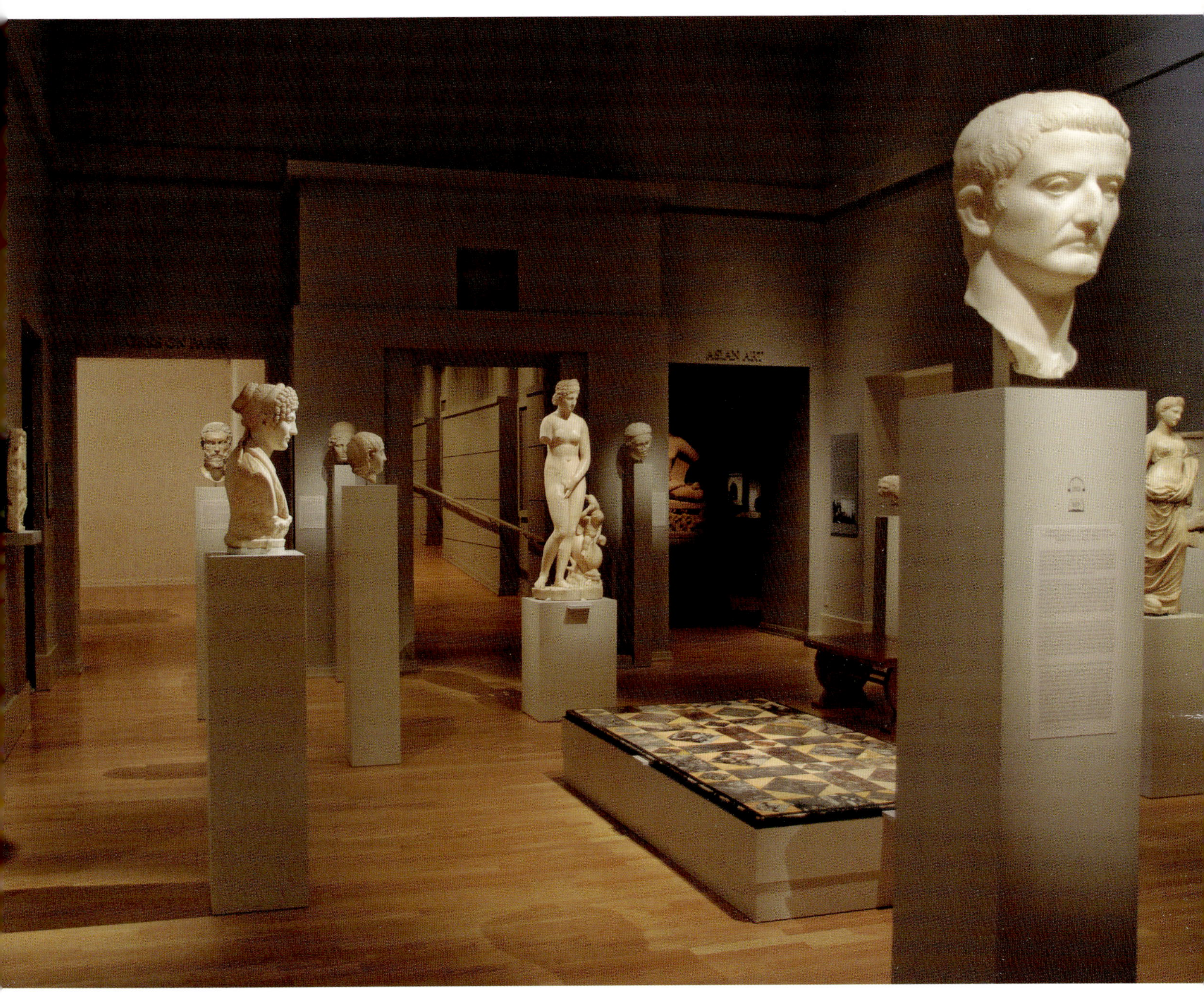

4000 BC

Collections of Greek and Roman art span over four millennia and provide snapshots of life as far back as 4000 BC: a bathtub from Bronze Age Greece; a circa 480 BC symposion cup depicting a spirited drinking party; a seventh century BC vessel that recalls the mythology of Pandora's box; and the classical world's stunning triumphs in portraiture.

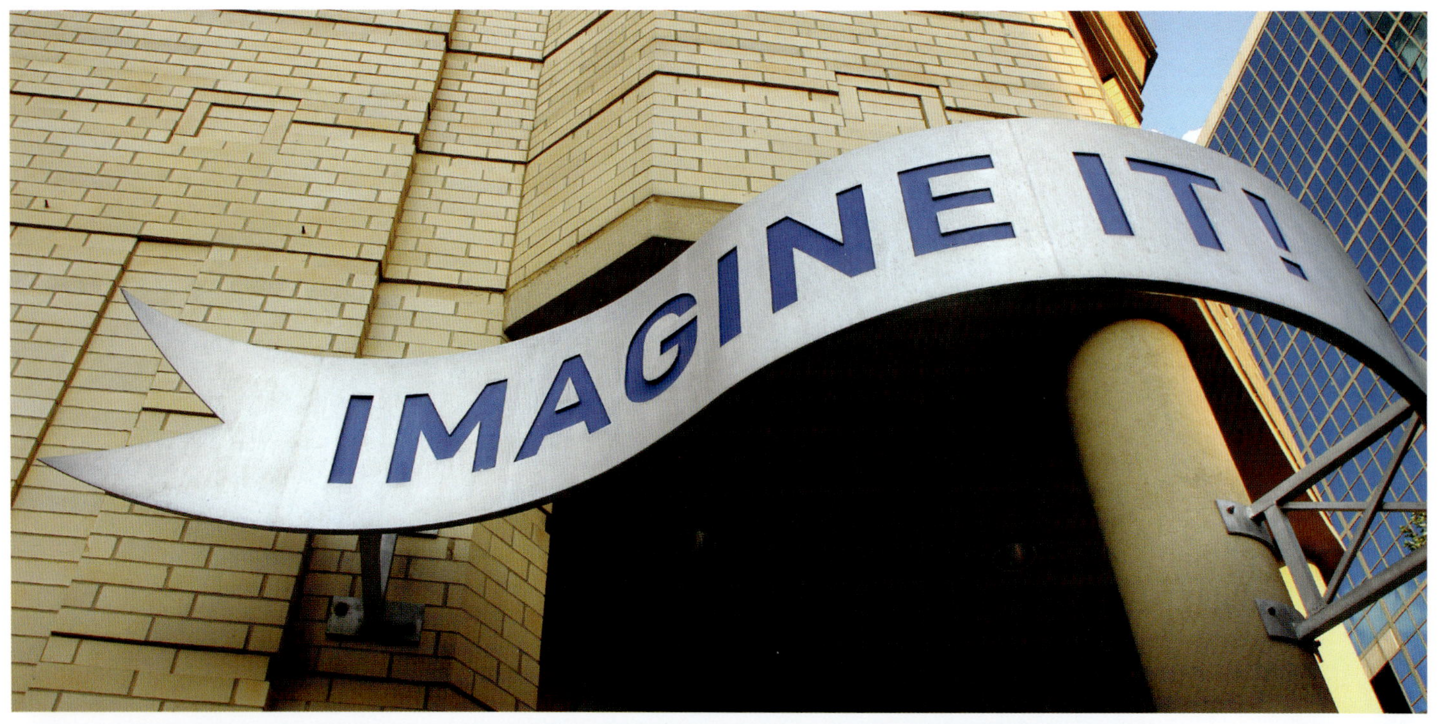

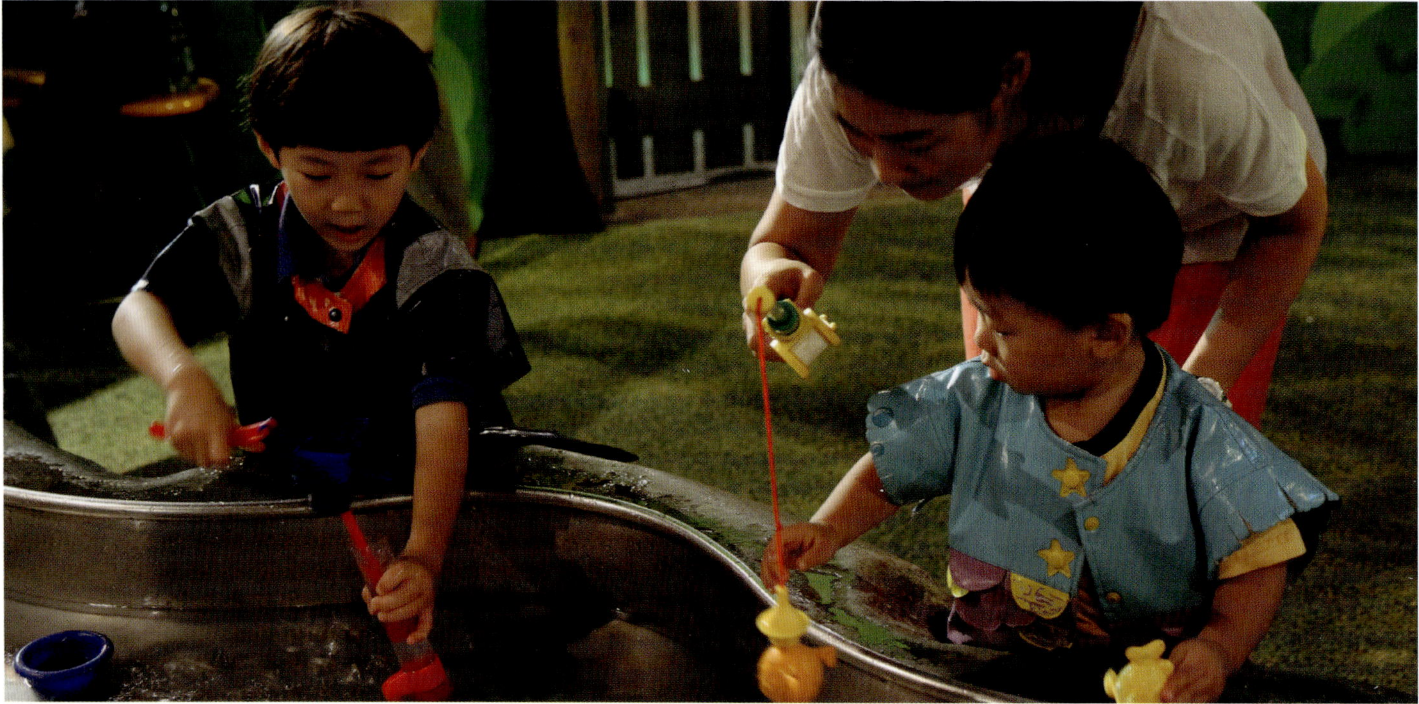

Busy Exploration *(top)*

Family-friendly spaces, bursting with creative interactive exhibits and play areas, include a colorful crawl space, a magical forest, a tree house, and a giant painting wall. Located at Centennial Olympic Park, Imagine It! The Children's Museum of Atlanta invites busy exploration in bright hands-on exhibits that are both entertaining and educational.

Splash It! *(bottom)*

With programming designed to engage all the senses, unique and interactive Imagine It! helps children develop knowledge and skills in reading, social studies, math, science, language arts, and the arts. Don a raincoat in the Leaping into Learning exhibit to splish-splash in a stream or cast a fishing rod to catch colorful fish.

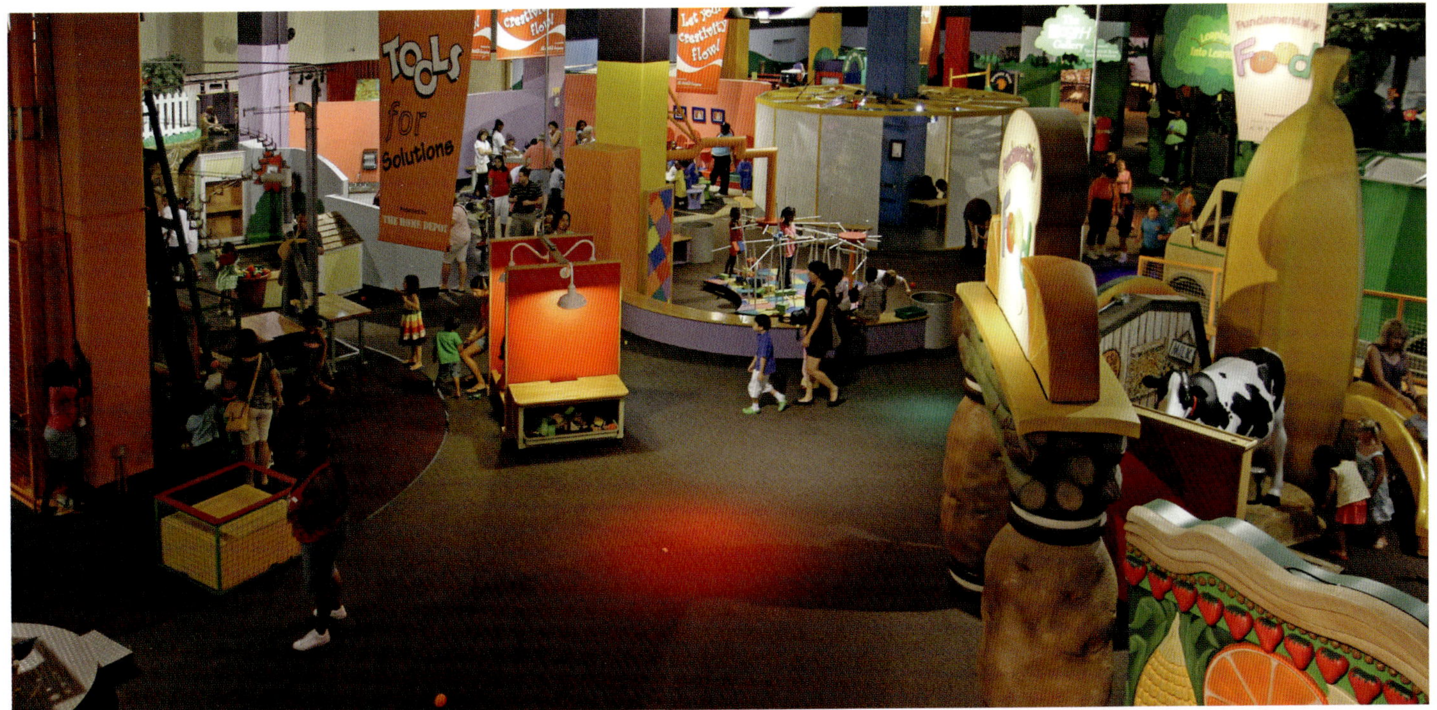

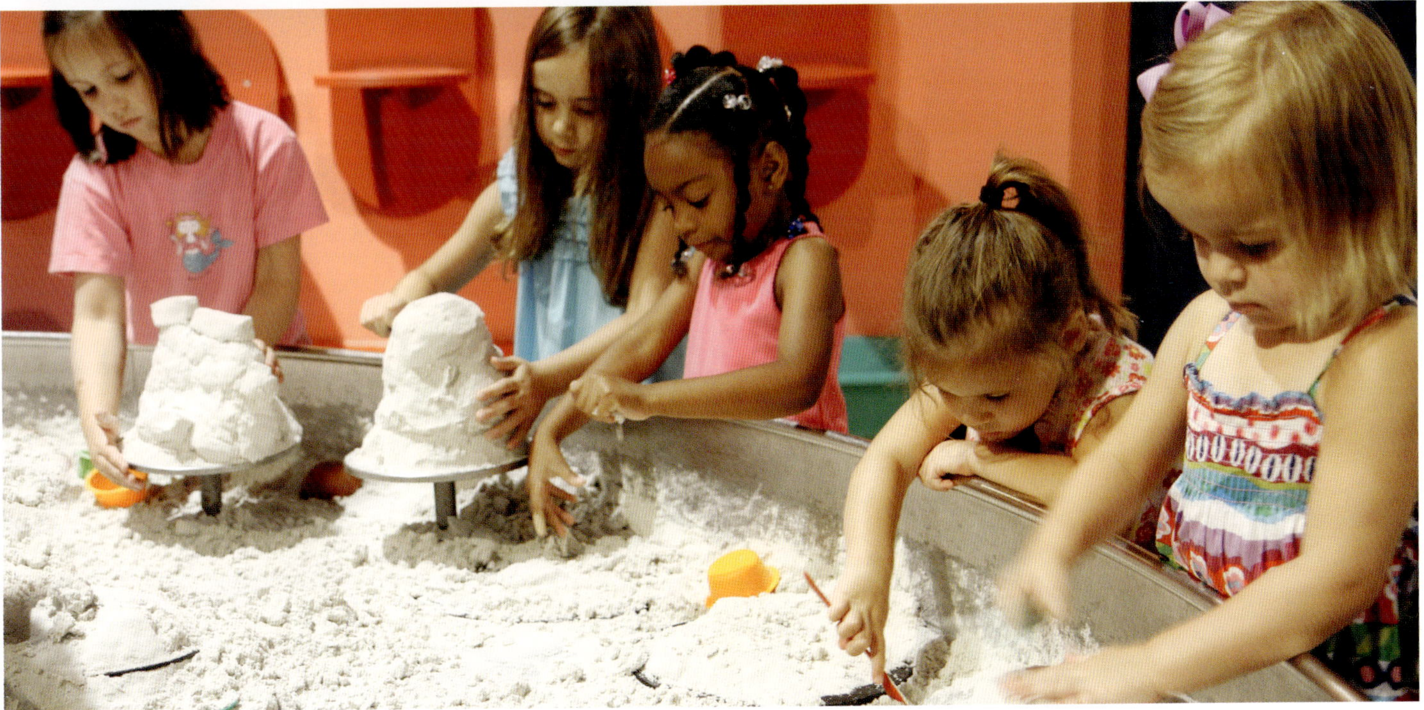

Interactive Play, Rotating Displays *(top)*

The Children's Museum of Atlanta has hosted over a million visitors since it opened in 2003. Besides interactive play, Imagine It! operates Museum Without Walls outreach programs, stages performances of the acting troupe *Imaginators*, has its own bio-friendly bus to bring children to the museum, and presents three new exhibits each year.

Paint and Sculpt, Imagine It!-Style *(bottom)*

Learn the power of play in the Morph Gallery, which presents an ever-changing lineup of programming – anything from a circus to fairytale land to a world of children's favorite television pals like Clifford The Big Red Dog. Even painting the walls is encouraged! Grab a smock and create a masterpiece or build a sand sculpture with secret-recipe sand.

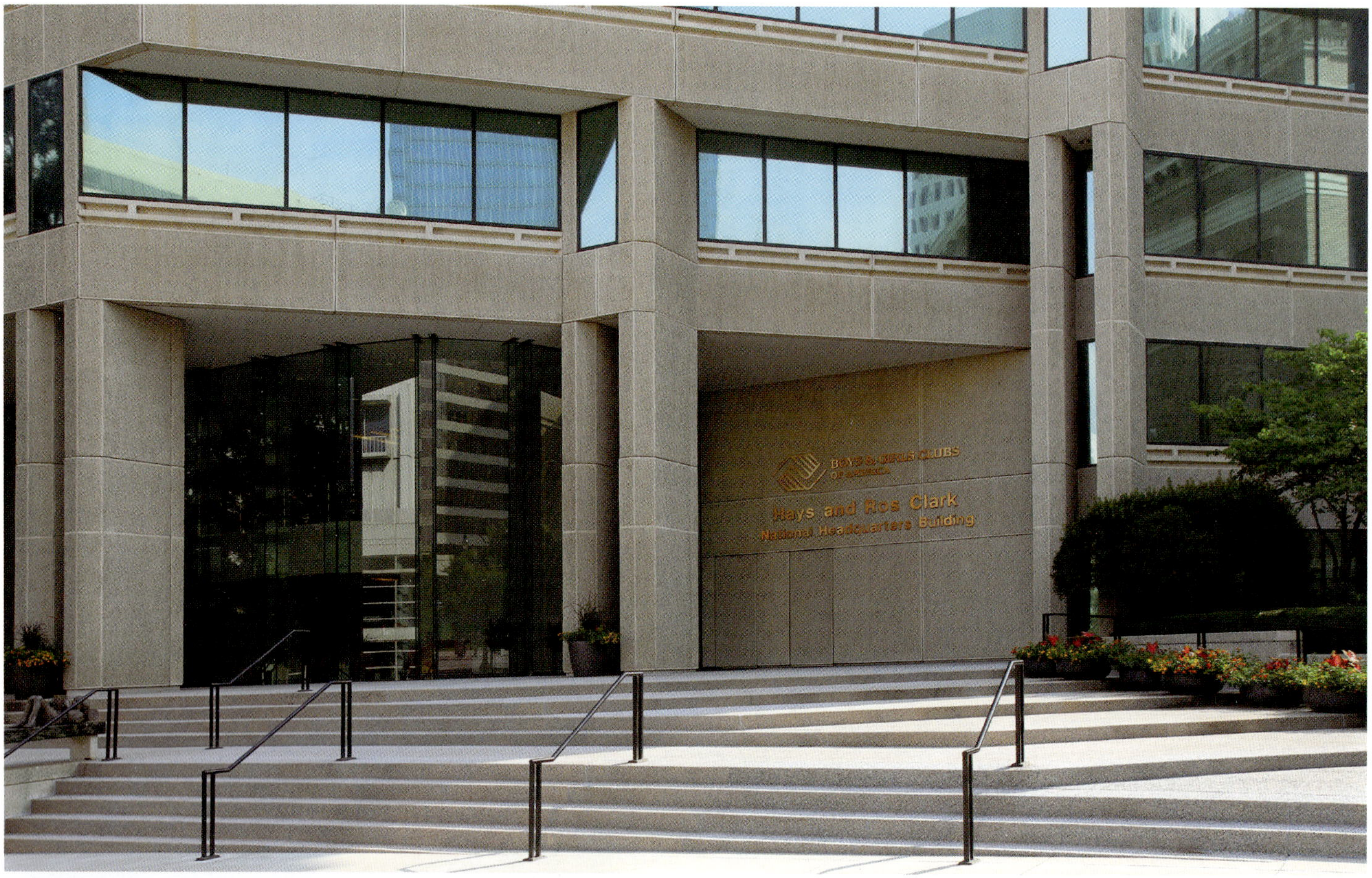

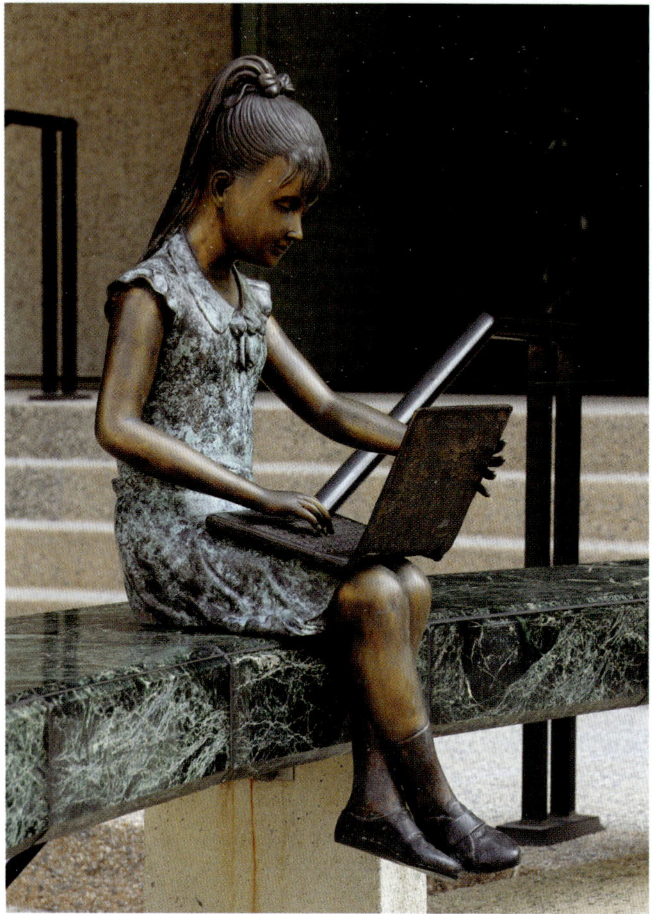

Boys and Girls Club *(above, left, and opposite)*

With a mission to empower Atlanta youth to become healthy, productive adults, the Boys and Girls Club of Metro Atlanta has provided a positive, enriching place to go, especially for disadvantaged children, since 1938. BGCMA operates 25 Clubs in 10 metro counties, plus Camp Kiwanis and Youth Art Connection, an art gallery and workspace in downtown Atlanta.

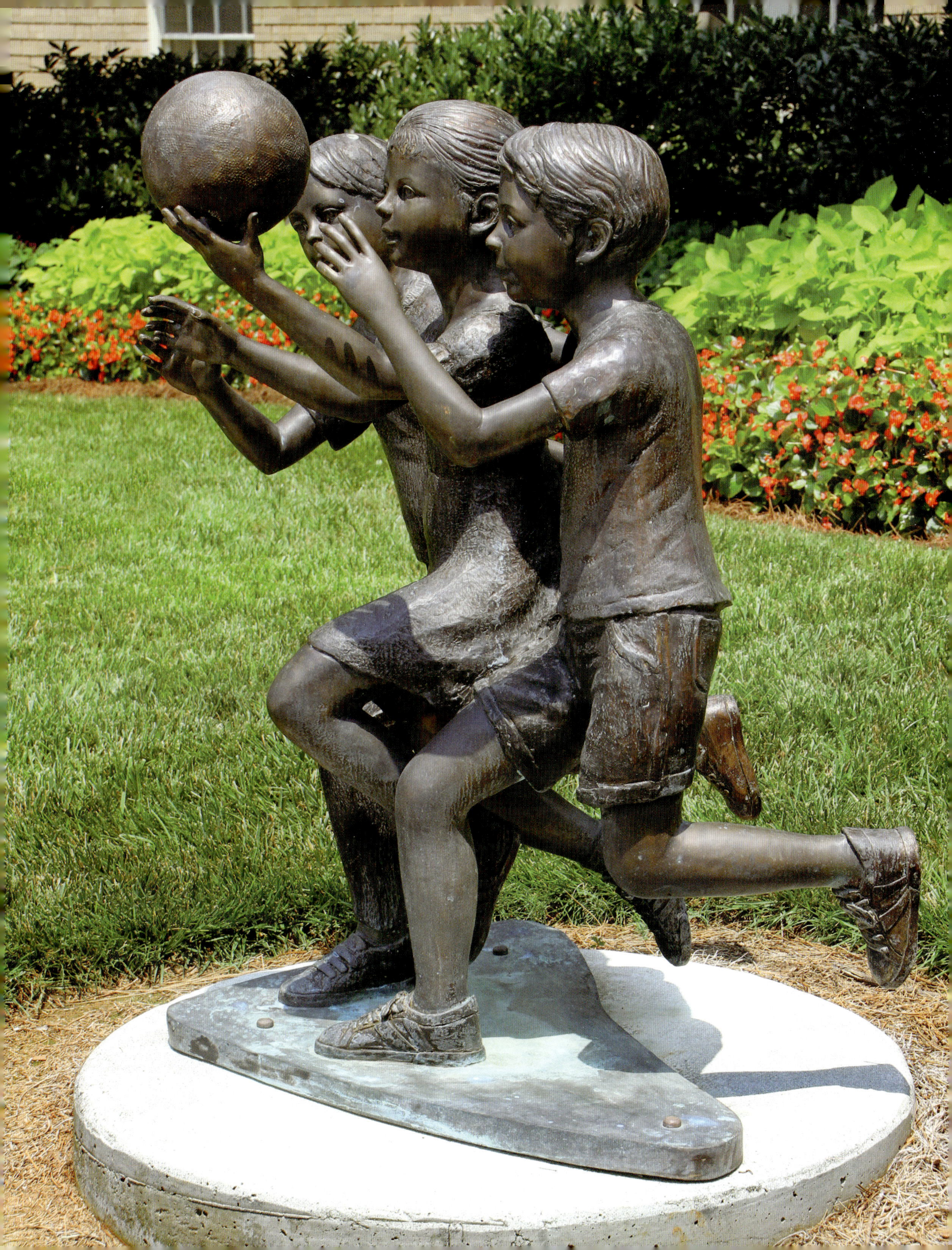

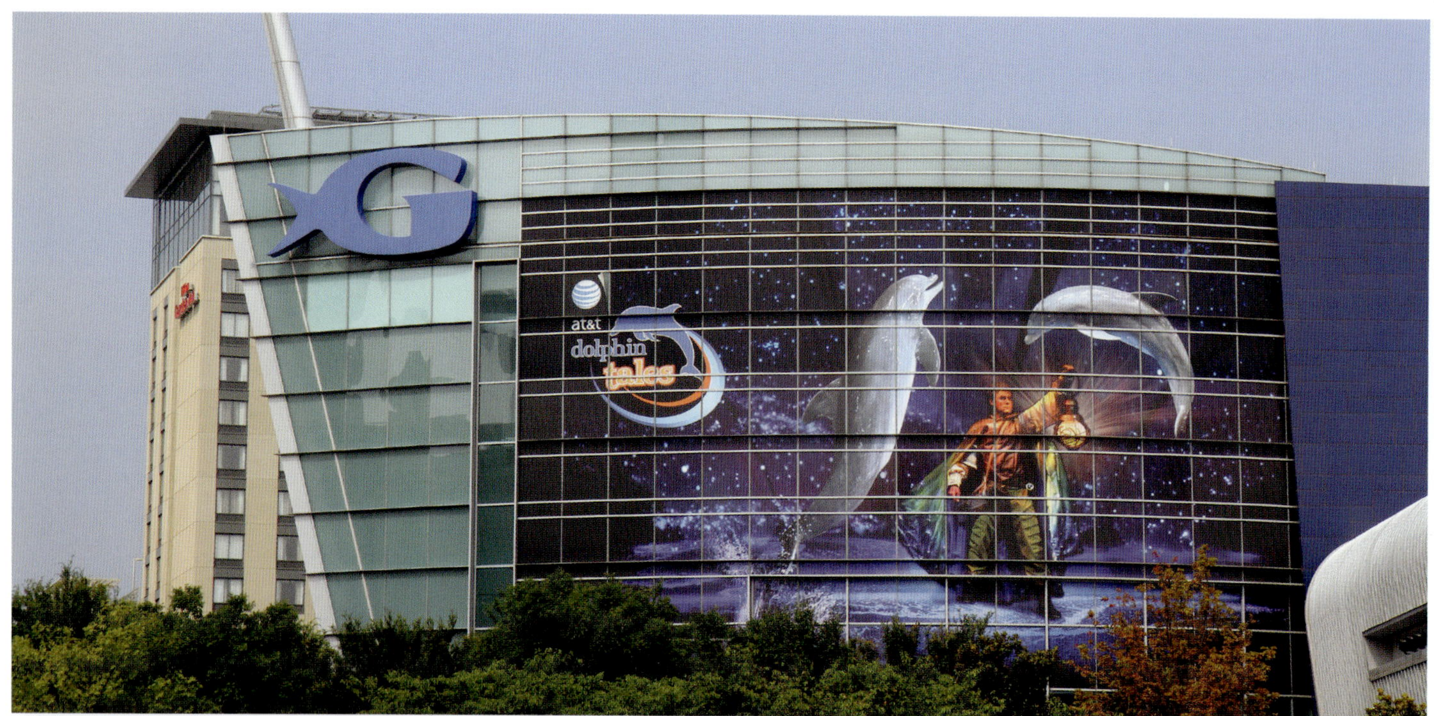

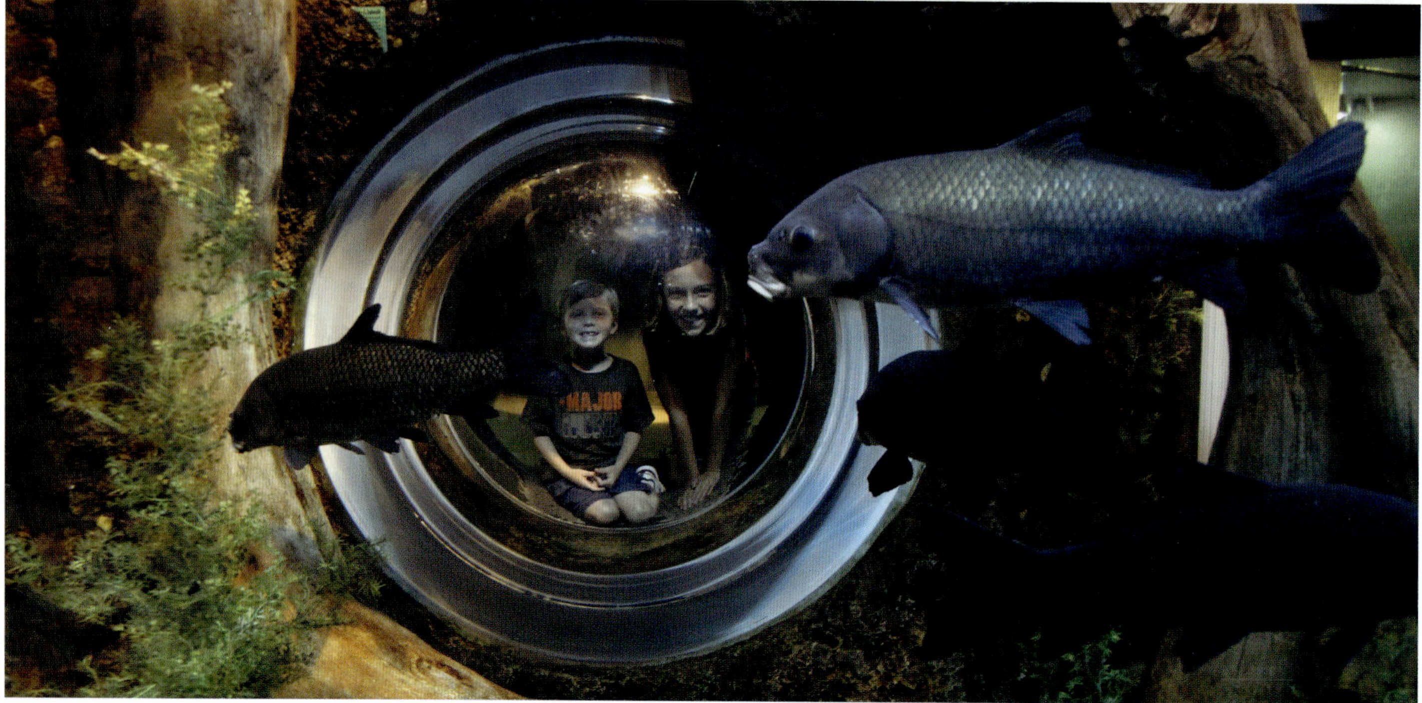

World's Largest Aquarium *(top)*

The world's largest aquarium – as certified by the Guinness Book of World Records by gallons of water (10 million), number of fish (thousands more than any other aquarium) and square footage (604,000) – is a multi-million-dollar gift to Atlanta and the people of Georgia from co-founder of The Home Depot, Bernie Marcus and his wife, Billi.

Georgia Aquarium *(bottom)*

Step inside the large blue metal and glass exterior of the aquarium – designed to evoke a ship on swelling ocean waves – and wander past "walls of fish" to six exhibit galleries, including the world's largest aquatic habitat, the new Dolphin Tales, and 4D Theater. Visitors from all 50 states, six continents, and 143 countries have come to explore.

Tropical Diver Gallery *(opposite)*

The Tropical Diver gallery showcases living art that is the beautiful Indo-Pacific tropical fish and temperate-water invertebrates. The 164,000-gallon reef habitat – 40 percent of which is live coral – is the largest in the United States and contains more than 90 species of fish. Here, jellyfish float in all their ruffled, tentacled, colorful glory.

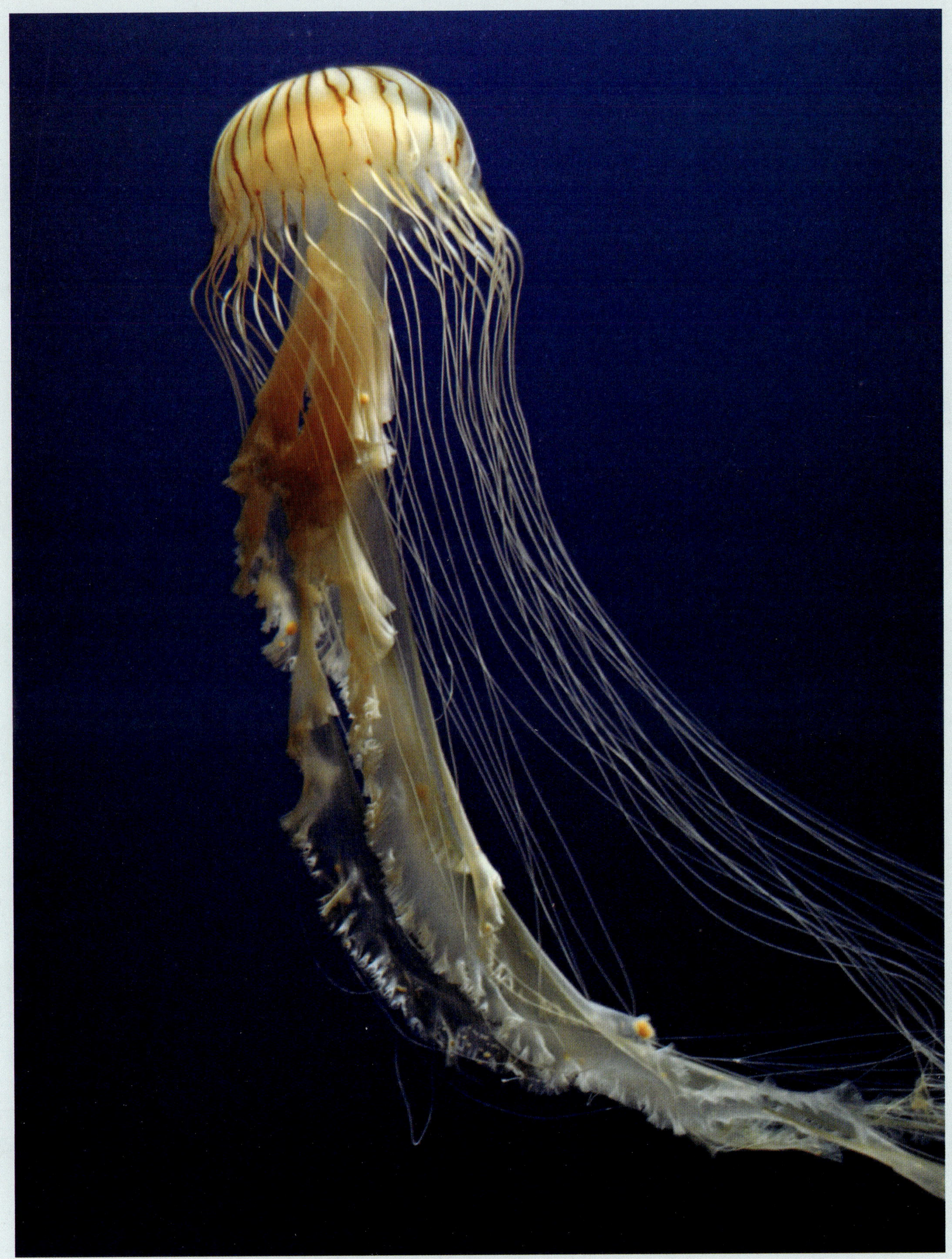

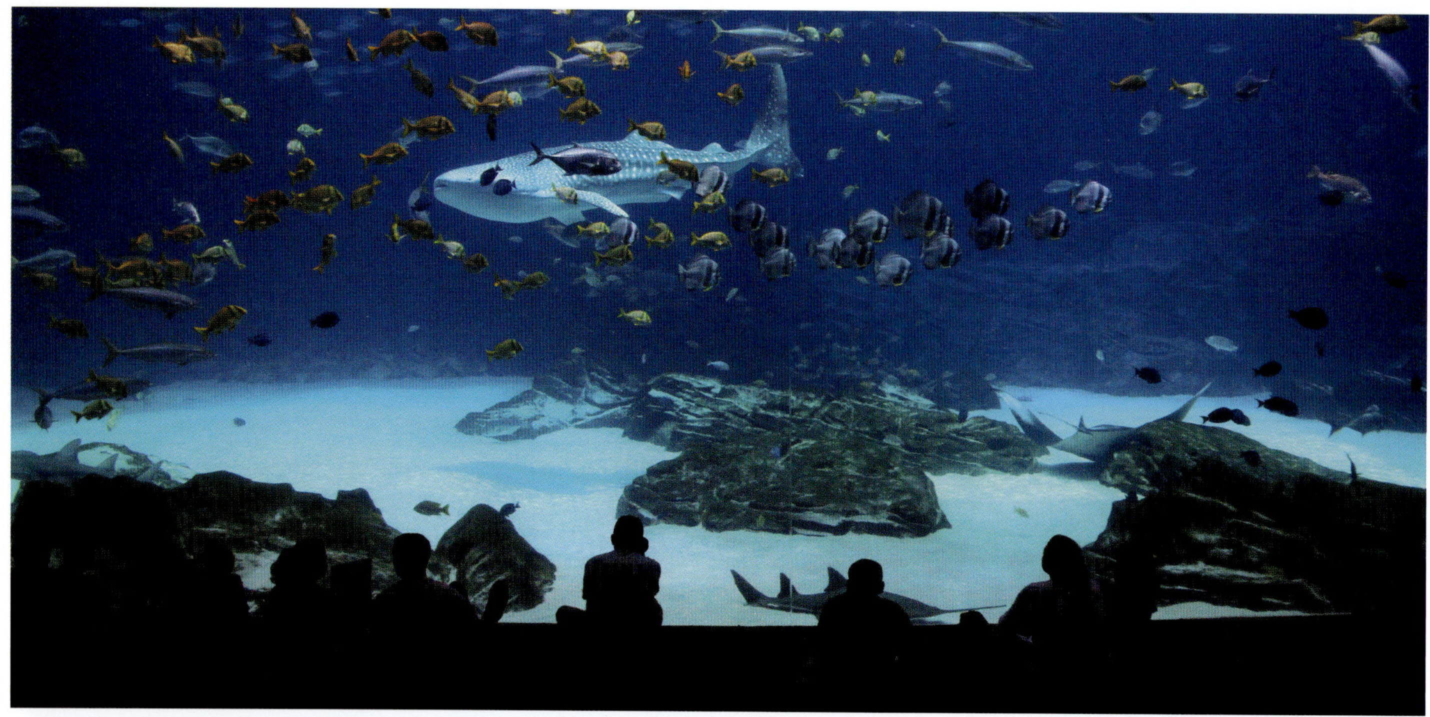

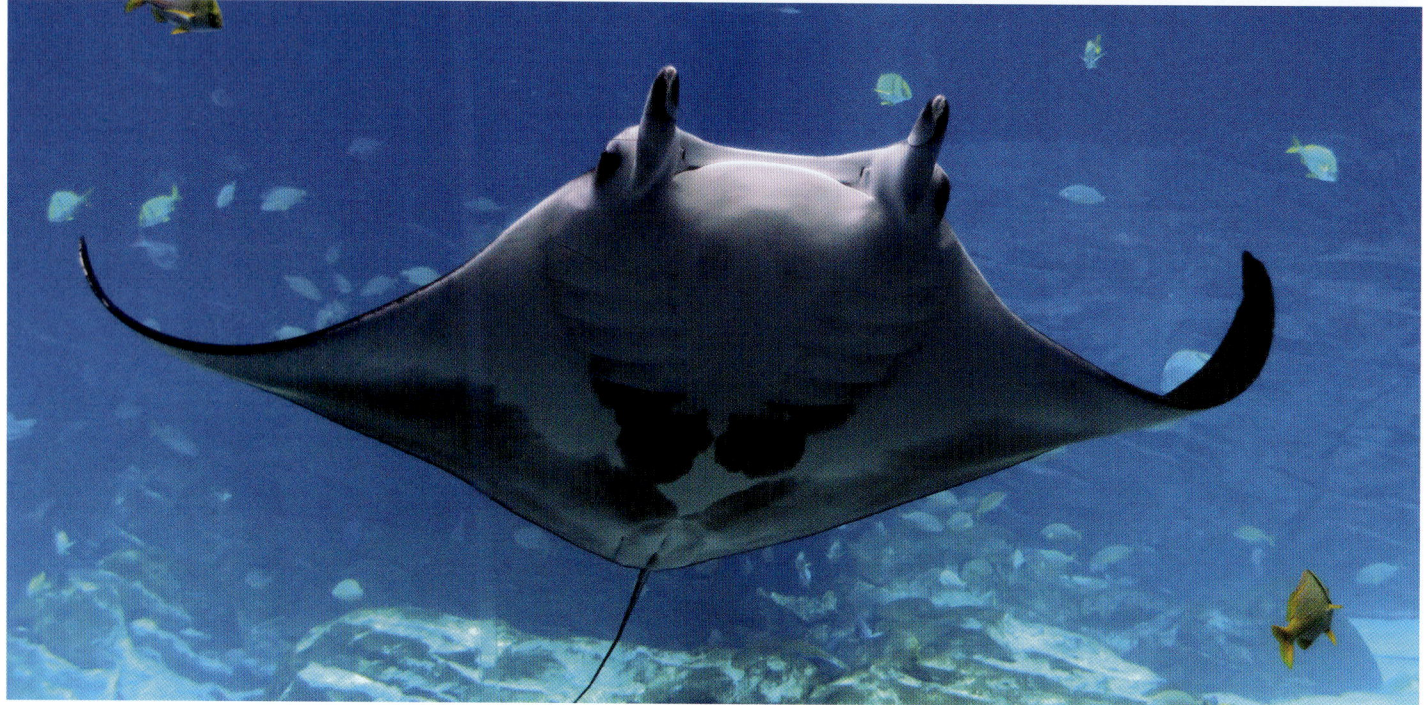

Sharks Play Here *(top)*

From the three-story atrium, guests are ushered into gift shops, the Café Aquaria, and six galleries, including Cold Water Quest, home to four beluga whales, four harbor seals, five Southern sea otters, and scads of penguins; freshwater River Scout with the only overhead river featured in an aquarium; and Georgia Explorer with its touch pools.

Ocean Voyager *(bottom)*

The world's largest aquatic habitat, the 6.3-million gallon Ocean Voyager, features species from the Atlantic, Pacific, and Indian Oceans. Meander through an acrylic tunnel and peer through the ginormous window to see sharks, including four mammoth whale sharks, and four manta rays – the first and only mantas in the United States.

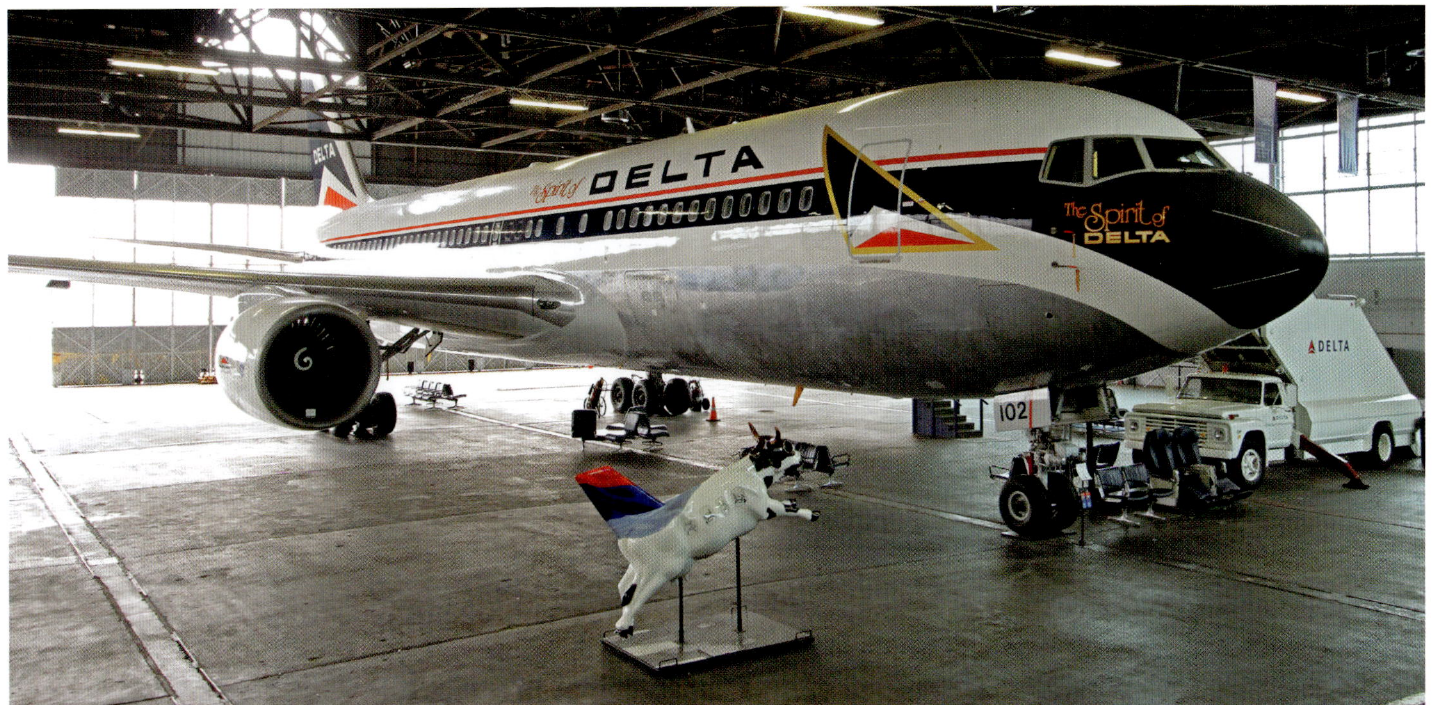

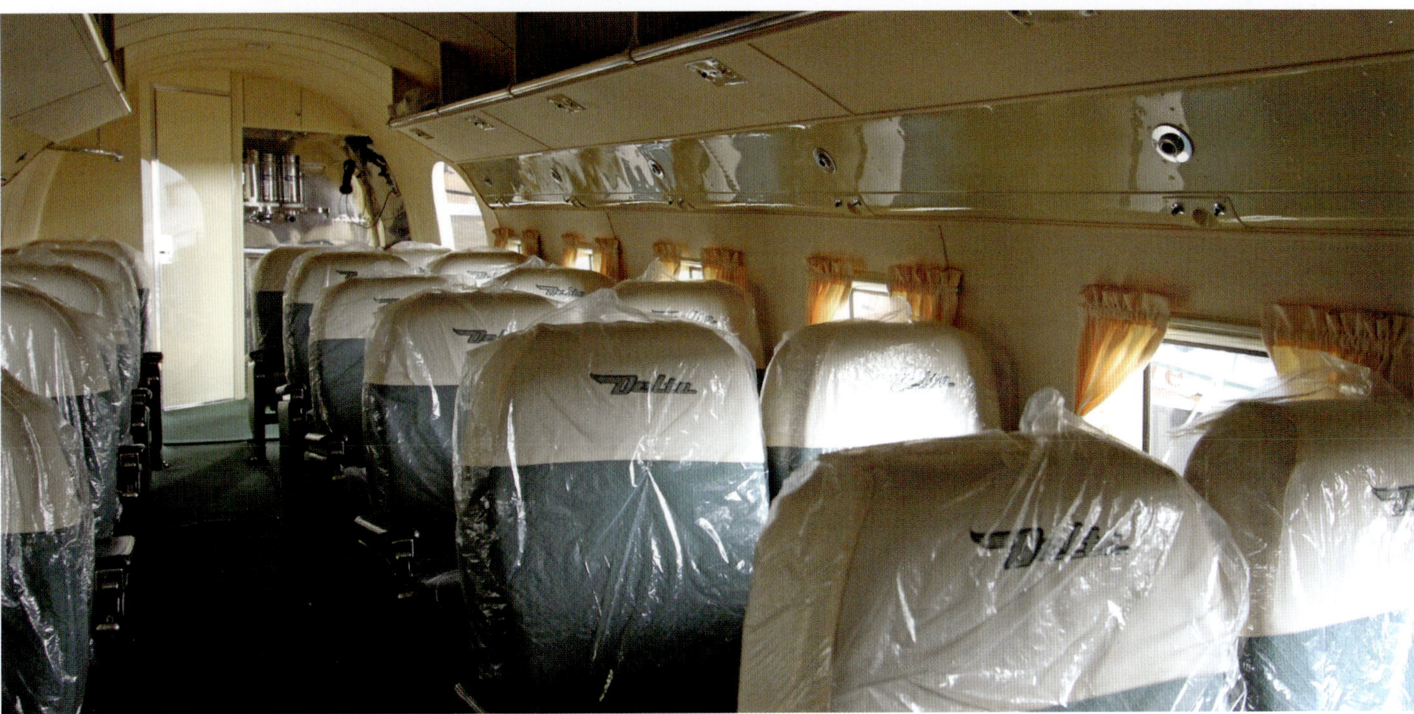

Delta Air Transport Heritage Museum *(top)*

Located in Atlanta's Delta World Headquarters, this award-winning museum is dedicated to collecting and preserving the history and heritage of Delta Air Lines and all the airlines that have merged with Delta, including the restored *Ship 41*, the first Douglas DC-3 to carry Delta passengers. It is open to the public by appointment.

Rare Delta Passenger DC-3 *(bottom)*

Walk back in time to see the *Spirit of Delta*, Delta's first 767. Also on exhibit are a 1931 Travel Air, symbolizing Delta's first passenger aircraft; a 1936 Stinson Reliant SE nicknamed the "Gull Wing"; and one of the world's largest airline uniform collections. Its archives maintains over 200,000 images and 1,000 films, plus an aviation reference library.

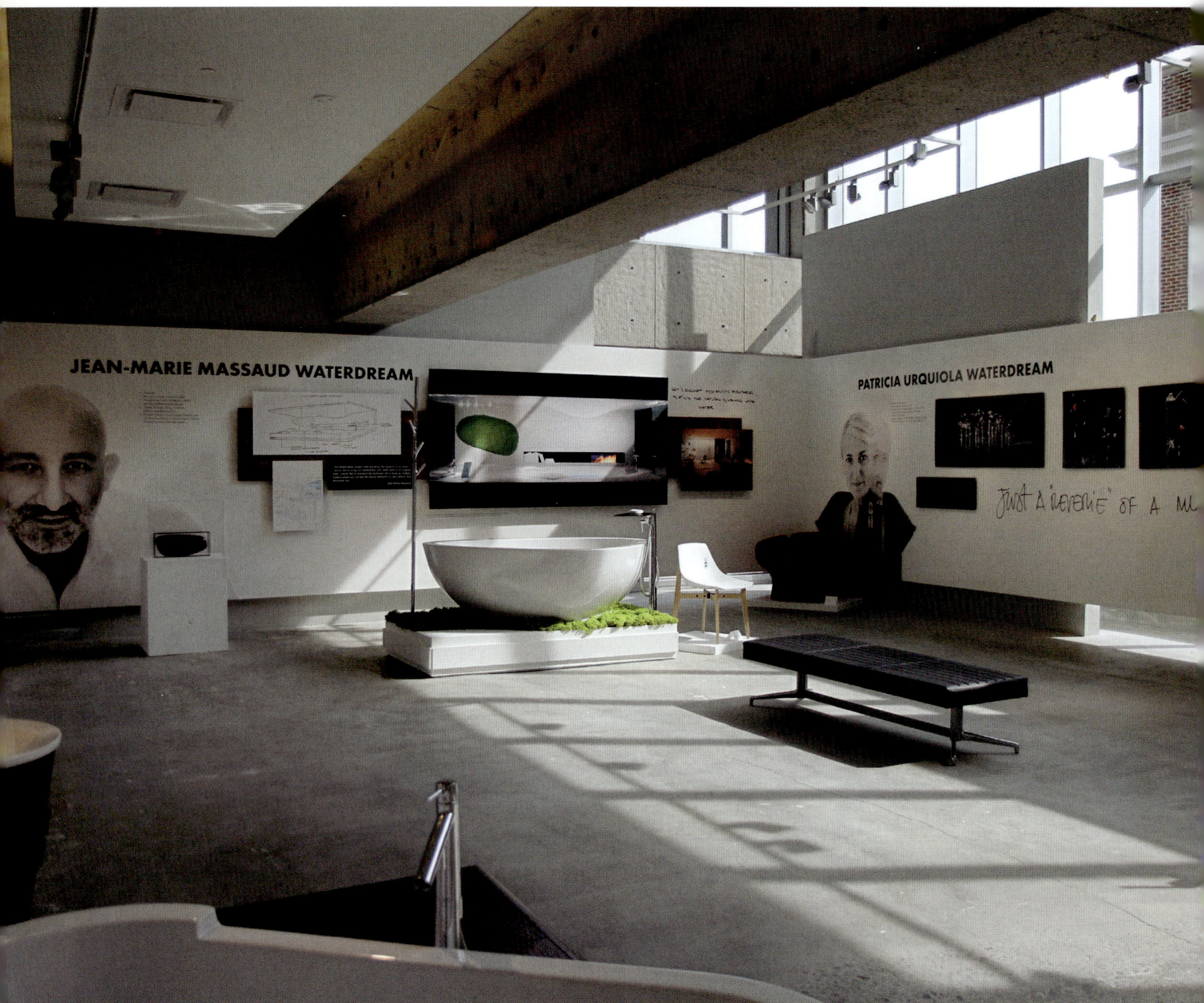

Curating Design

Located in the heart of the Midtown Arts Corridor and directly across the street from the High Museum of Art, the Museum of Design Atlanta (MODA), an affiliate of the Smithsonian Institution, is the Southeast's only museum dedicated solely to the design disciplines: architecture, fashion, furniture, graphic, jewelry, and media design.

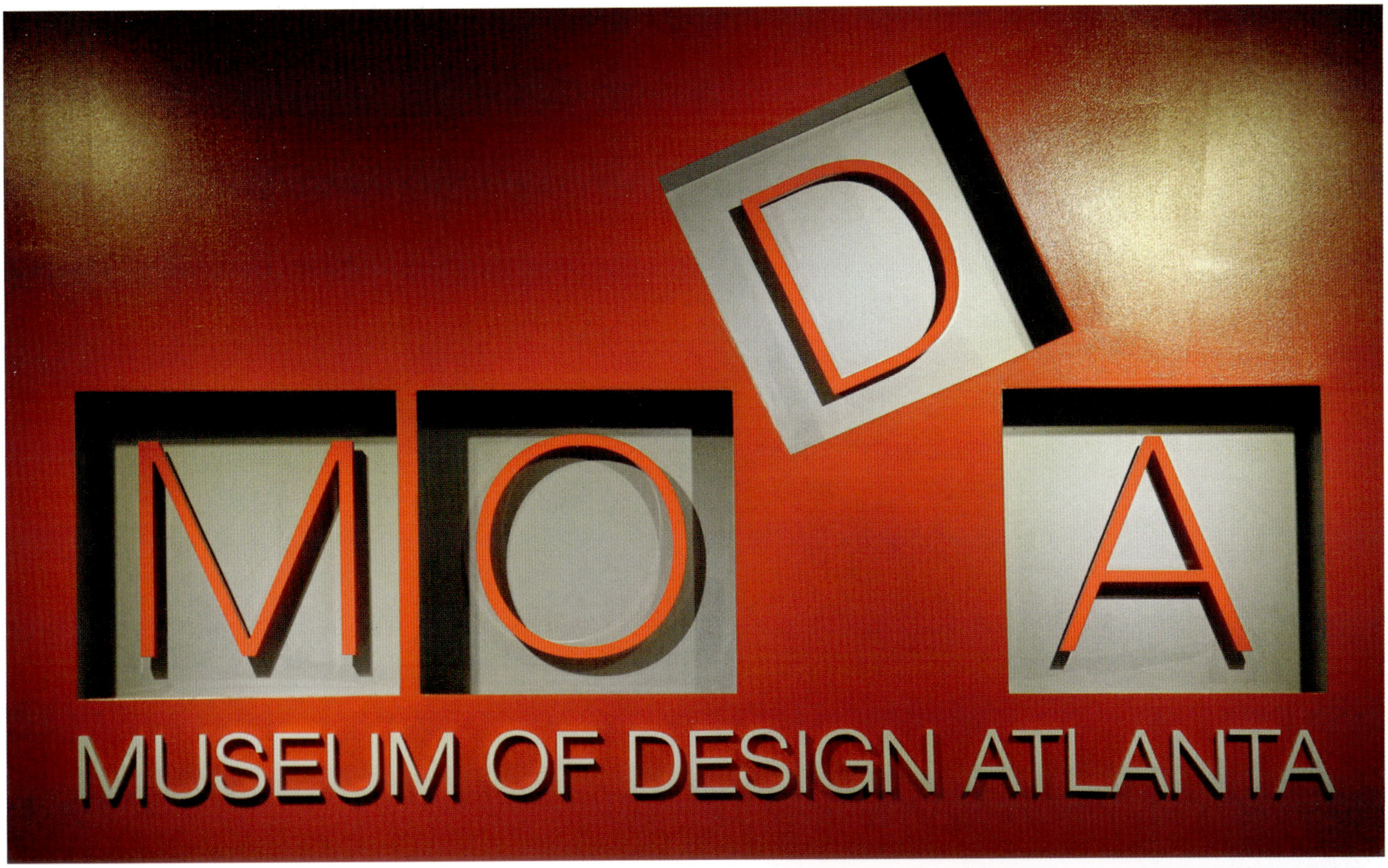

Museum of Design Atlanta *(above)*

Formed in 1989 by a group of art lovers who came together a few years earlier to form the Atlanta Committee for the Olympic Games, MODA expresses a design-centric mission. Its three galleries host rotating exhibits varying in length from four weeks to four months, allowing the museum to focus on as many aspects of design as possible.

The Alfie *(right)*

As a gathering place for all to exchange ideas, learn, and find inspiration, MODA's exhibits are constantly changing. Past exhibitions have included WaterDream: The Art of Bathroom Design, which was a journey through the evolution of bathroom design articulated through the works of some of the world's most famous architects and designers. This child's hand shower is the *Alfie* by Hansgrohe.

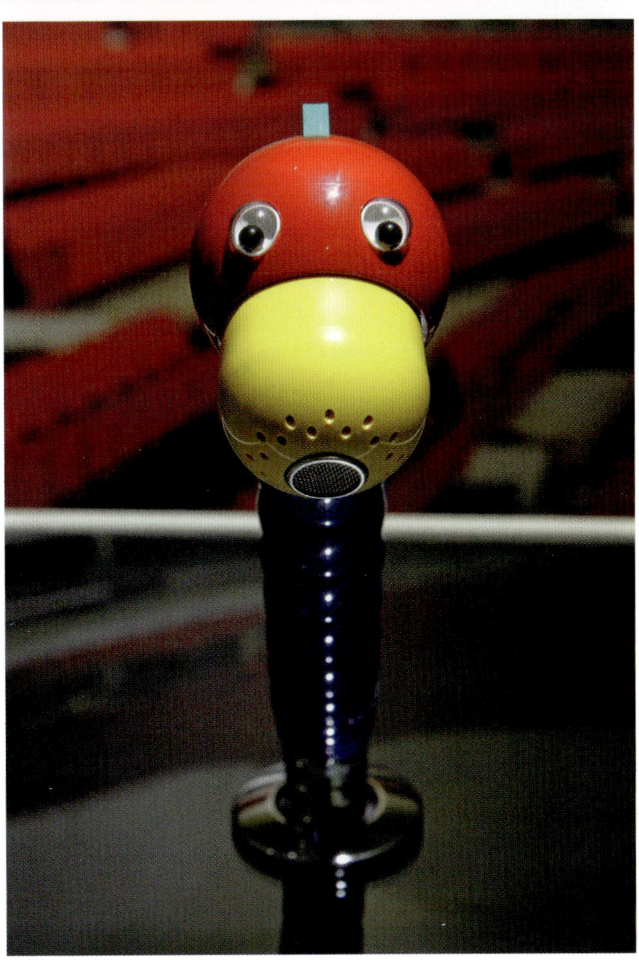

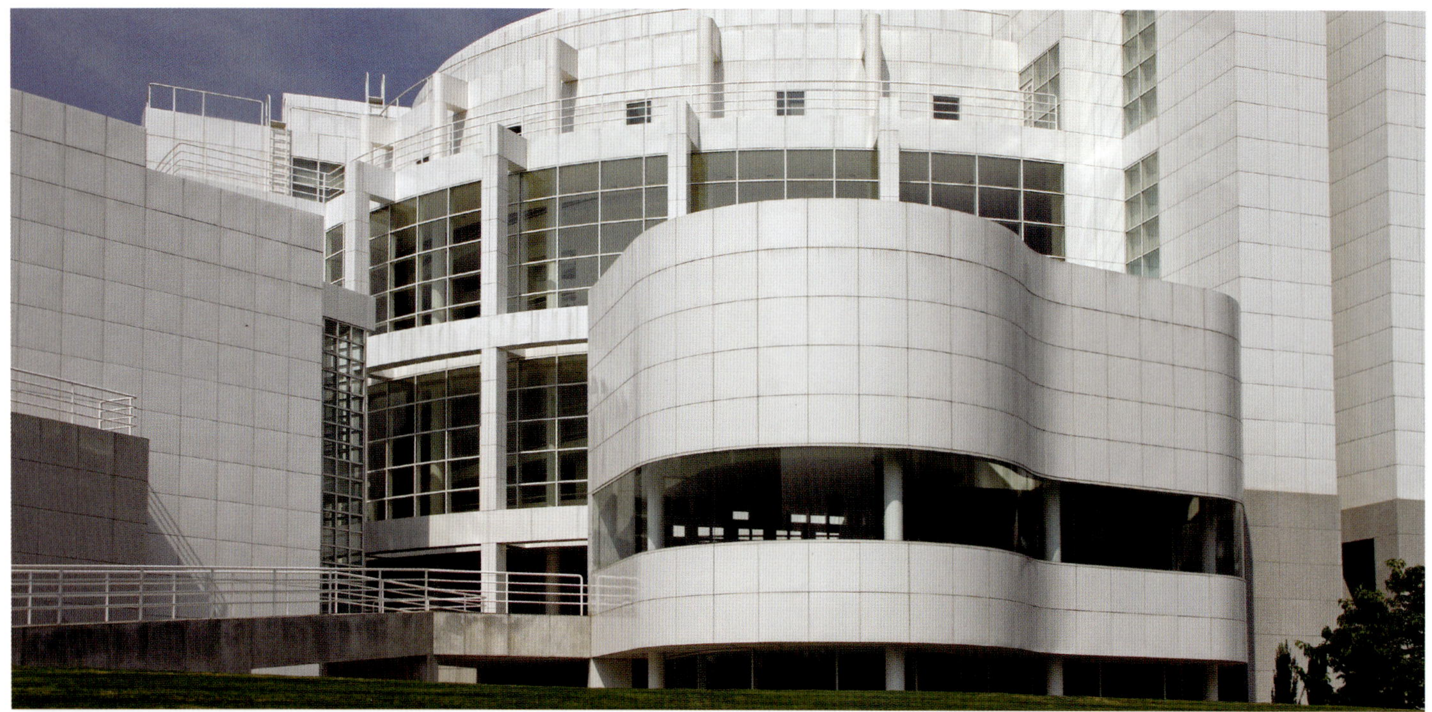

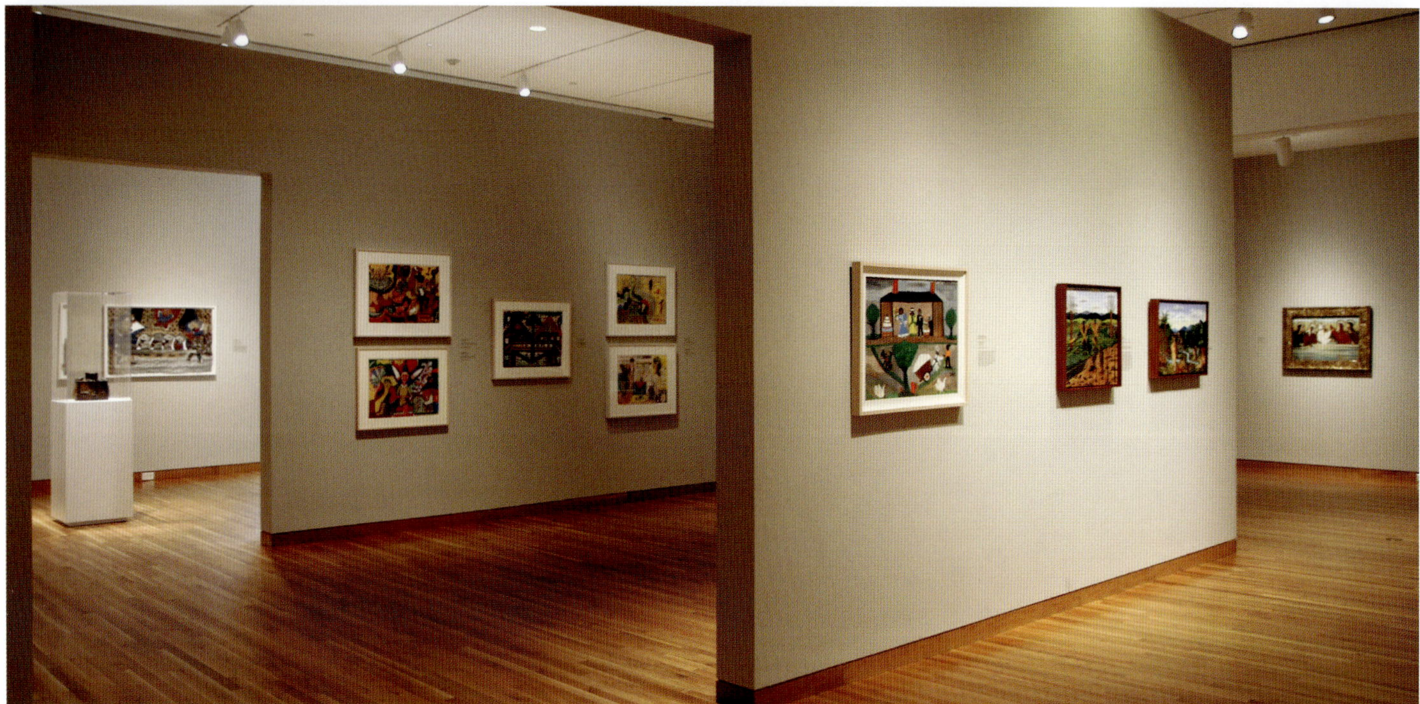

Village for the Arts *(top)*

A "village for the arts," the High Museum of Art is part of the Woodruff Arts Center, comprising the original 1983 Richard Meier-designed building and three additional buildings designed by Italian architect Renzo Piano. Connected by an outdoor piazza showcasing sculpture works, the High is one of the Southeast's premier art museums.

High Museum of Art *(bottom)*

With 312,000-square feet of exhibit space, the High Museum of Art has a staggering number of collection highlights: Italian works from the 14th through 18th centuries; an early 20th-century Ivory Coast "Elephant Mask"; nearly 100 years of decorative art masterpieces; American folk art; and American and European photography.

Renowned Collection *(opposite)*

More than 11,000 works of art fill the permanent collection of this Midtown landmark, including an extensive anthology of 19th- and 20th-century American art, significant European paintings, and decorative art; African-American art and photography; modern and contemporary art; and a premiere collection of American folk art.

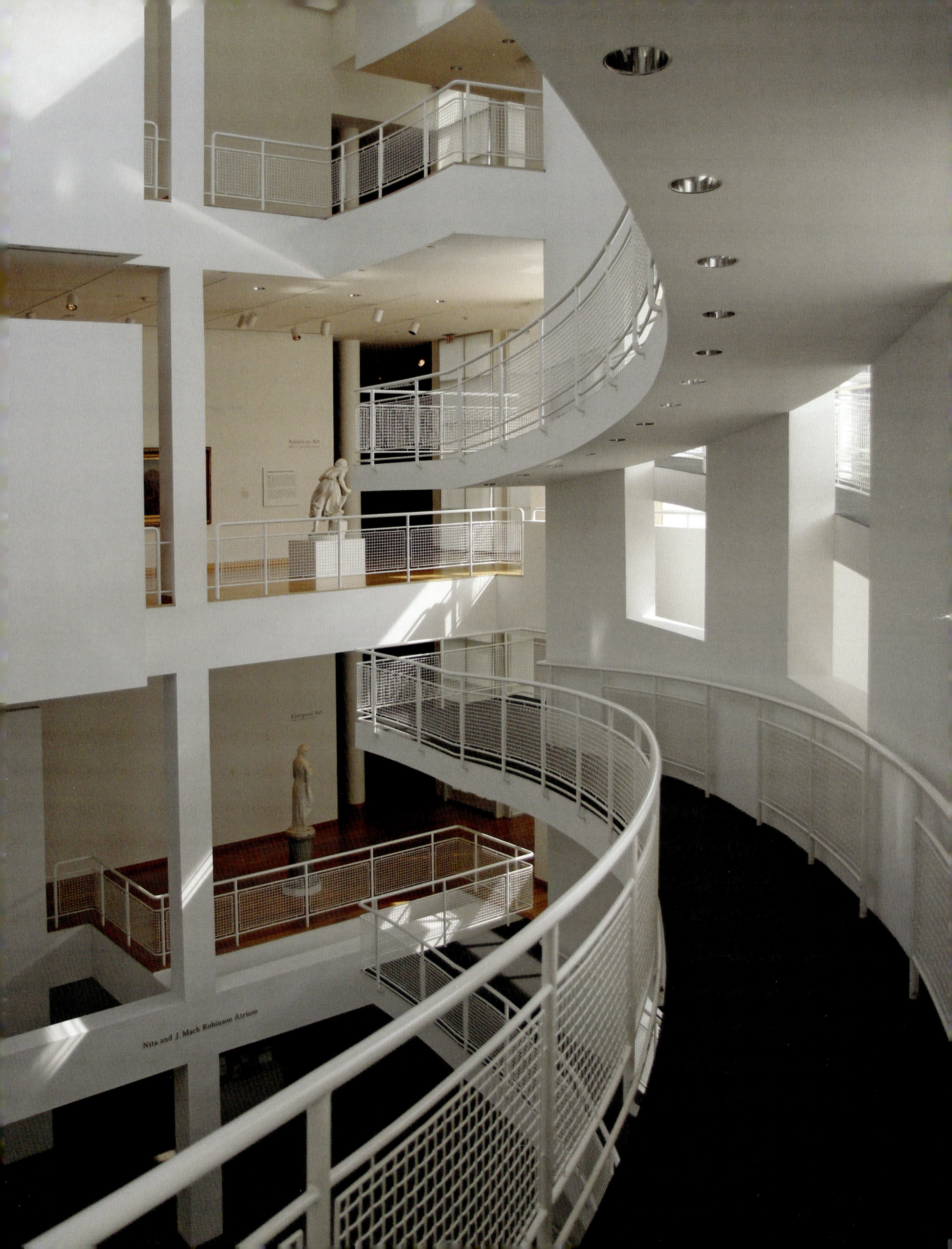
American Art
Nita and J. Mack Robinson Atrium

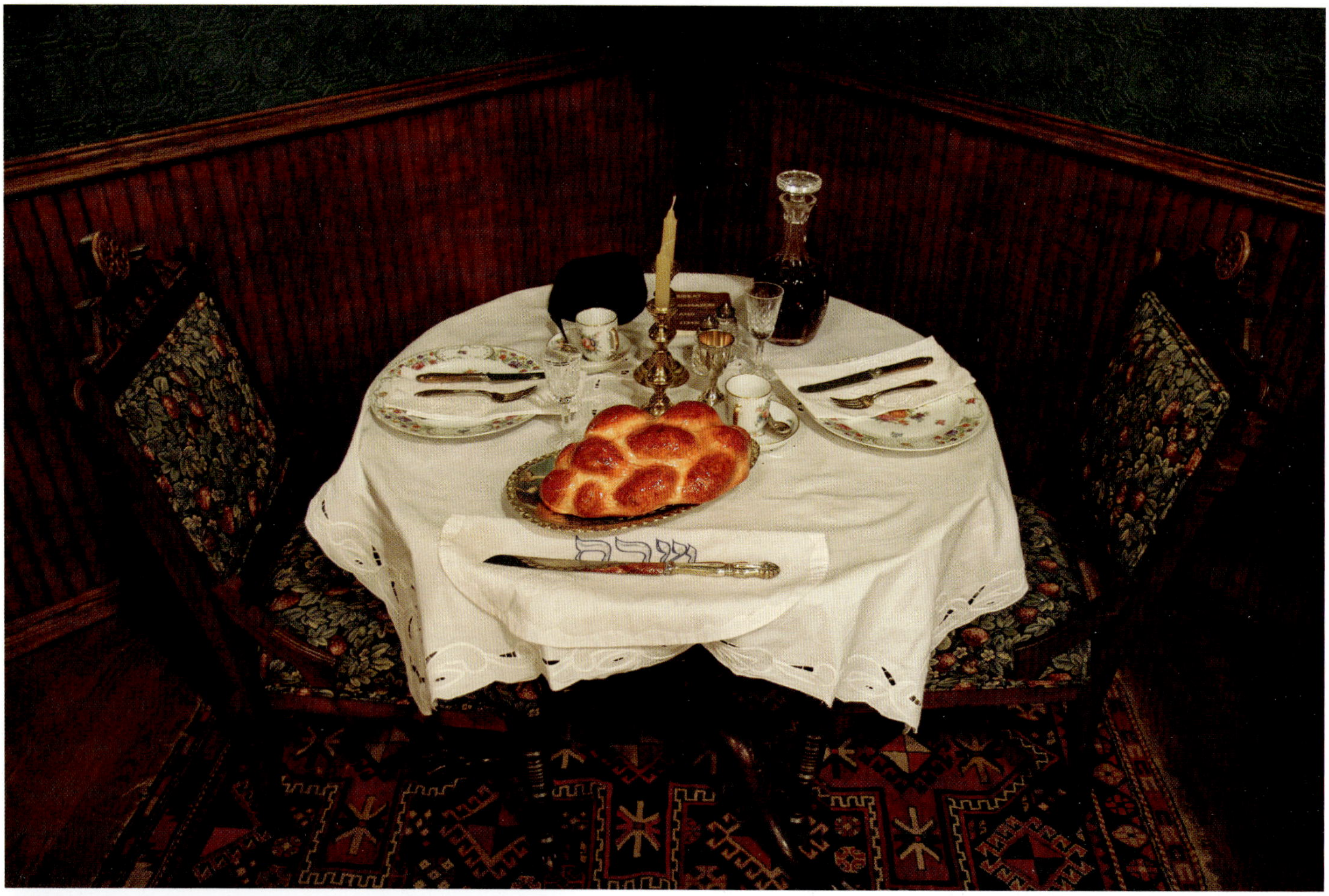

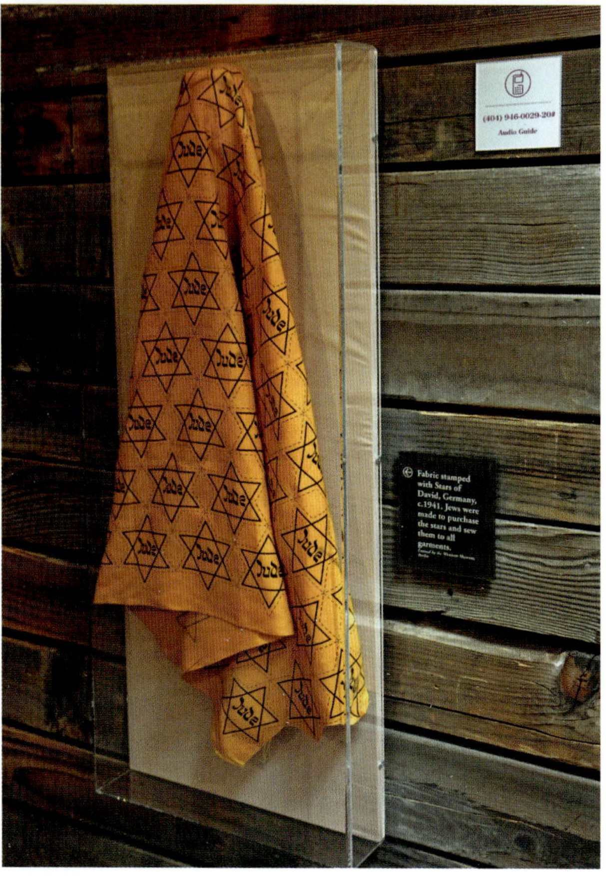

William Breman Jewish Heritage & Holocaust Museum *(above)*

A table set for the Sabbath resides at the William Breman Jewish Heritage & Holocaust Museum's exhibit, Creating Community: The Jews of Atlanta from 1845 to the Present, which depicts Jewish life in Georgia. Materials include diaries, documents, scrapbooks, photographs, audio and video recordings, oral histories, and an extensive newspaper collection that dates back to the 1850s.

Creating Community *(left)*

Through its public exhibitions and programs, The Breman explores the universal themes of respect for differences, responsible citizenship, human dignity, and community-building through the lens of the Jewish experience, providing visitors with a strong historical perspective, as well as a positive example of the strength of the human spirit and mankind's interdependence. It houses two permanent exhibitions.

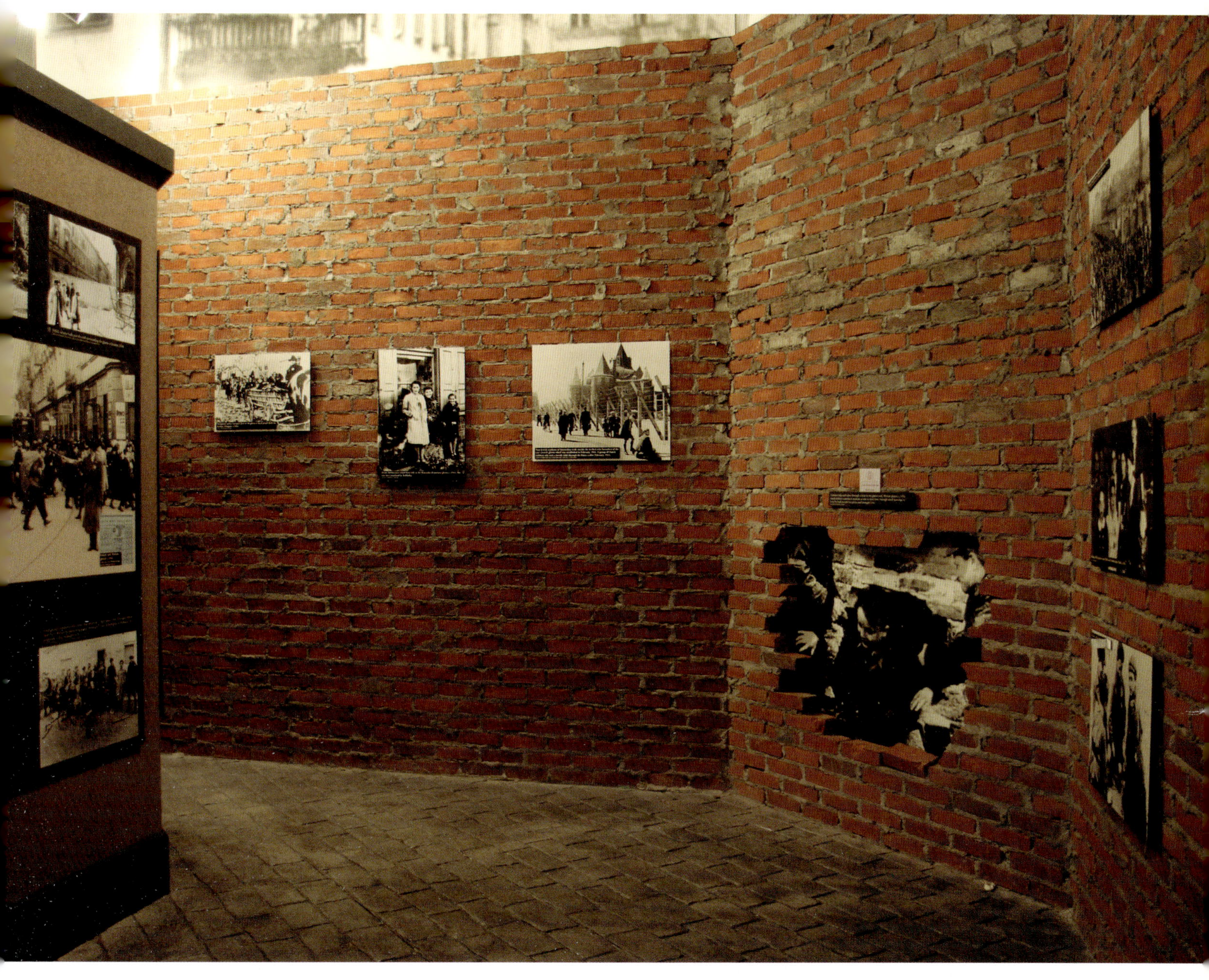

Holocaust Gallery

The exhibit, The Absence of Humanity: The Holocaust Years, 1933-1945, explores the historical context, events, and aftermath of the Holocaust through photographs, personal memorabilia, and videotaped interviews. Designed by Ben Hirsch, local architect and survivor, the gallery reflects the unfolding persecution of Jews in Europe.

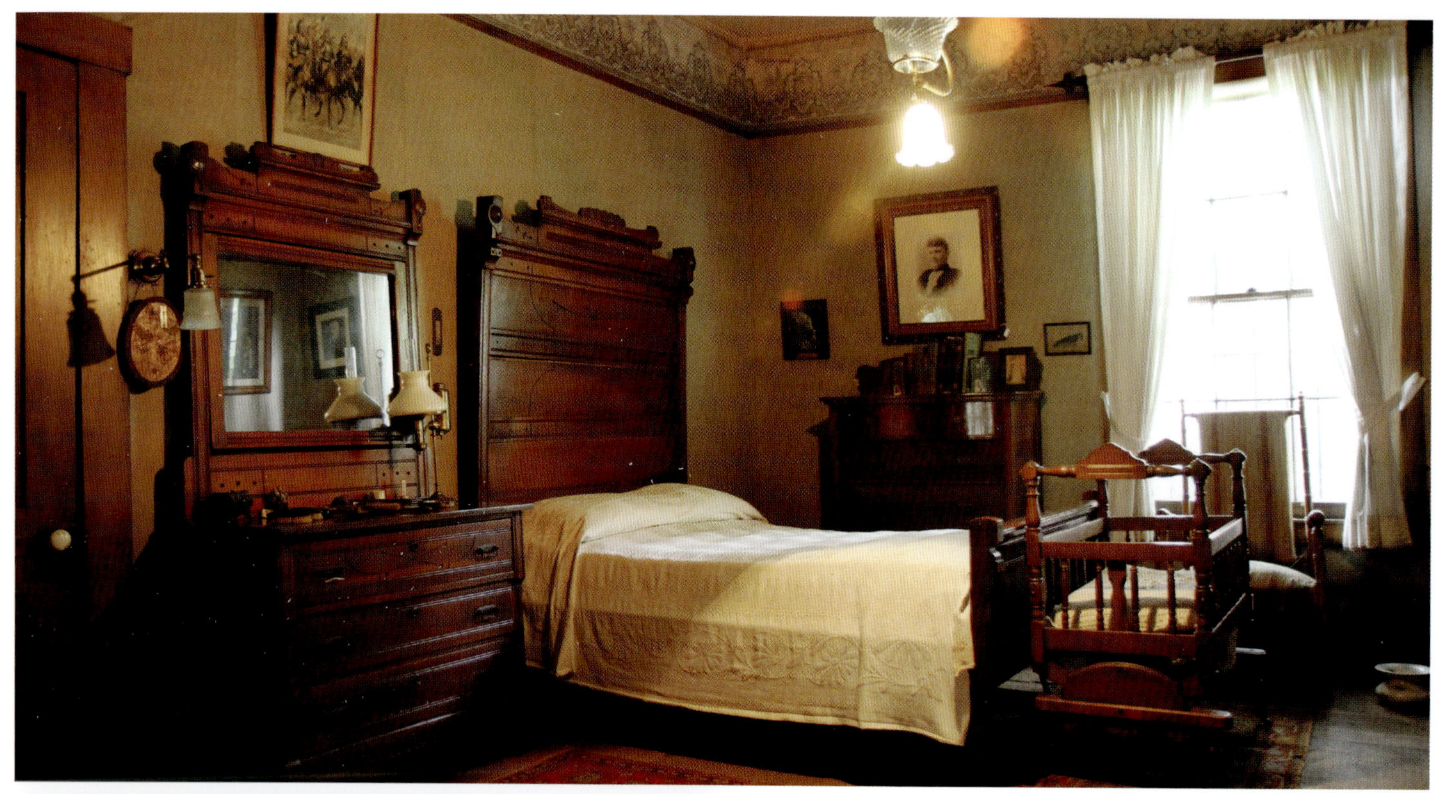

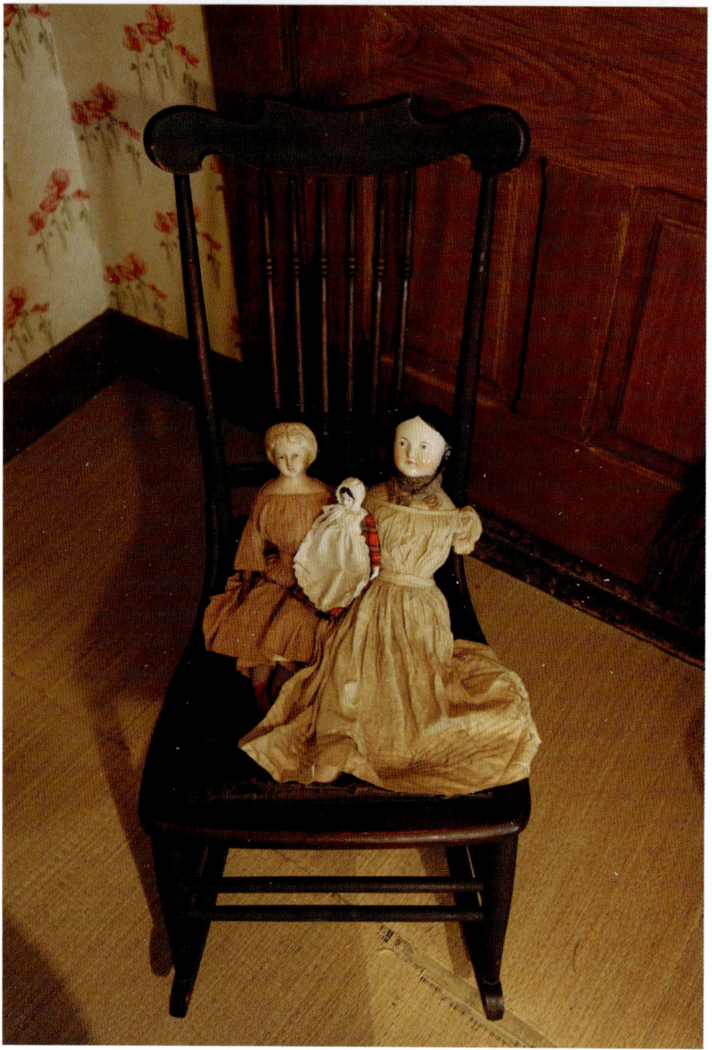

Wren's Nest *(above)*

Opened as a house museum in 1913, Wren's Nest shows off most of Joel Chandler Harris' family's original furniture and belongings. Following the famed author's death in 1908, Harris' wife, Esther LaRose, preserved his bedroom. It remains almost completely untouched to this day. In 1962, the National Park Service designated Wren's Nest a National Historic Landmark.

Brer Rabbit's Beginnings *(left)*

Wren's Nest is the historic home of Joel Chandler Harris, who lived here from 1881 until 1908. A journalist by trade, Harris was also a fiction writer, folklorist and children's author who penned the *Brer Rabbit* tales in the late 19th century. Wren's Nest preserves Harris' legacy, and the heritage of African-American folklore, through storytelling.

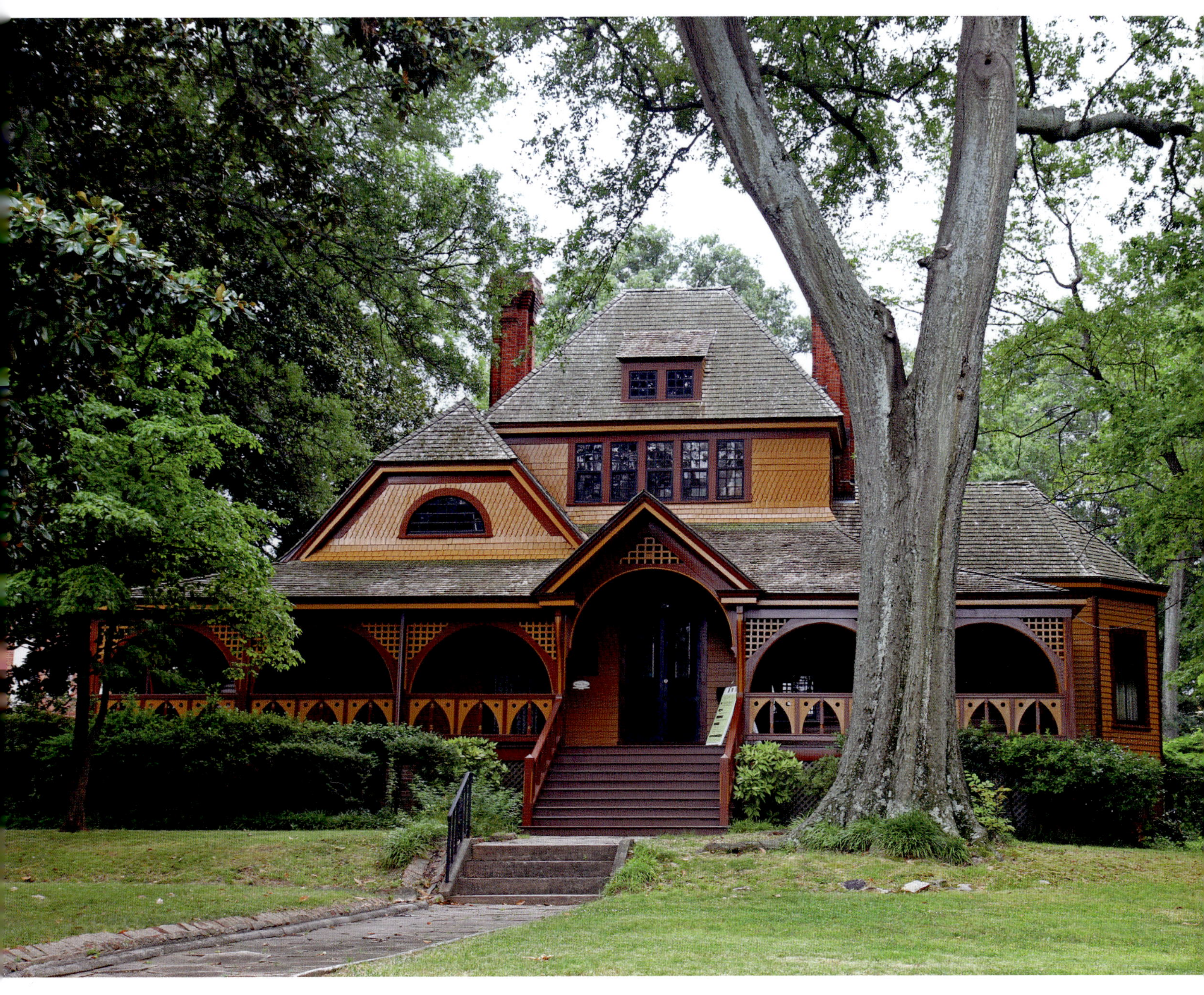

Victorian Home

One of just a handful of remaining Queen Anne Victorian homes in Atlanta, Wren's Nest presents a slice of life of upper middle class living around the turn of the 20th century. It took its moniker some 120 years ago after wrens built a nest in the home's mailbox – something they still do in the springtime.

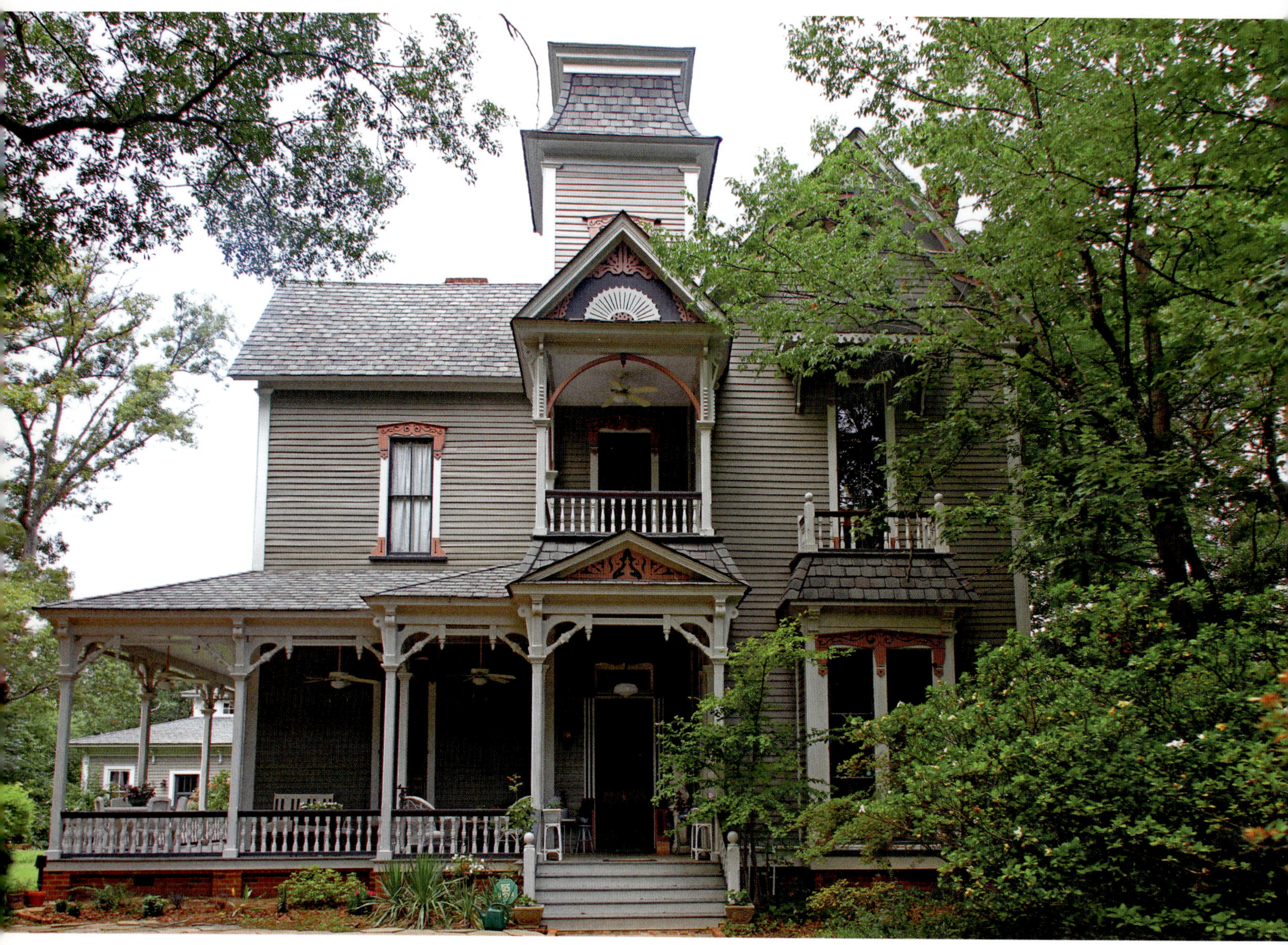

Smith-Benning House

The circa mid-1880s Smith-Benning House is located in one of Atlanta's first suburbs, Candler Park, which was founded originally as Edgewood in 1890. Recently restored, the home preserves the original Eastlake Victorian architecture including verandah and gable trim. Both house and neighborhood are on the National Register of Historic Places.

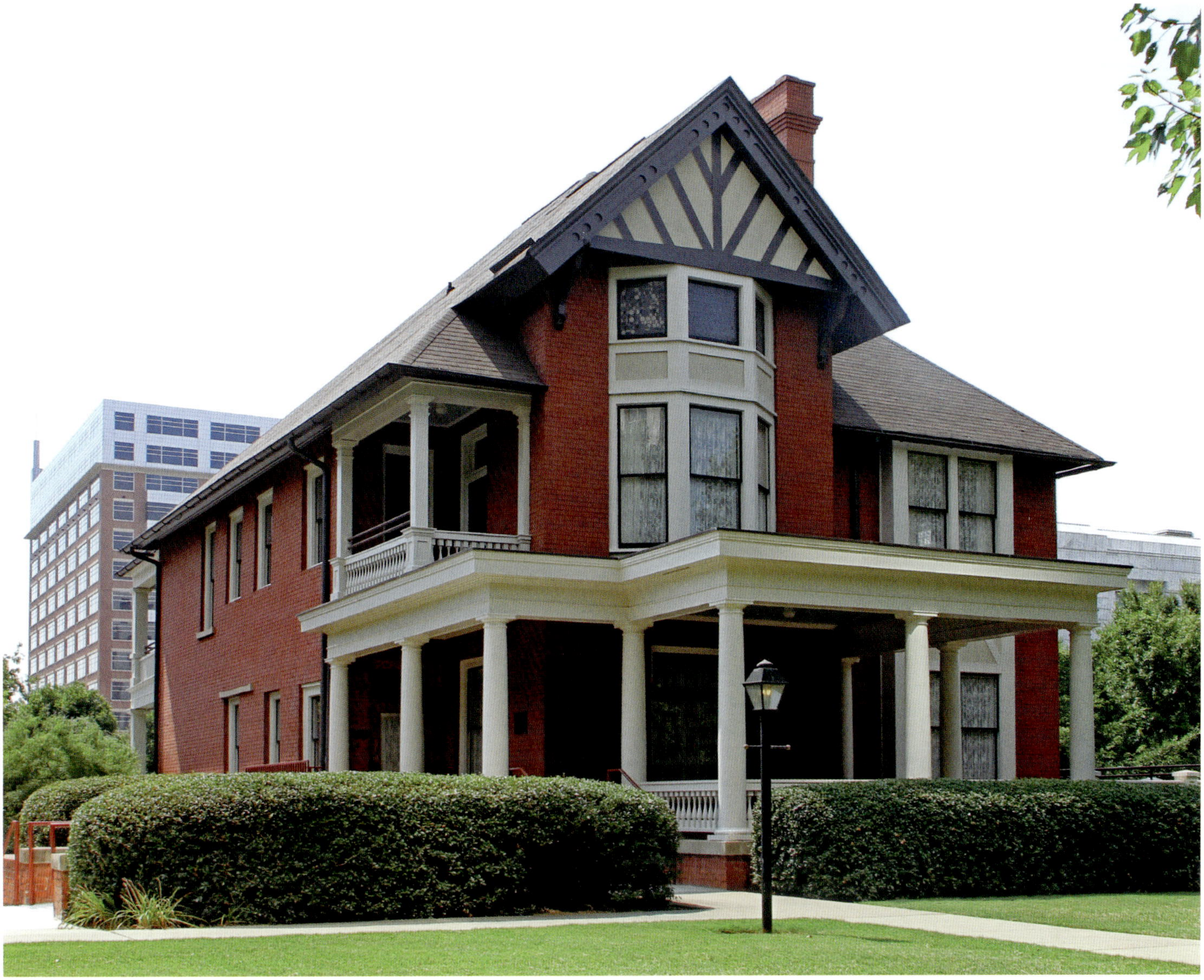

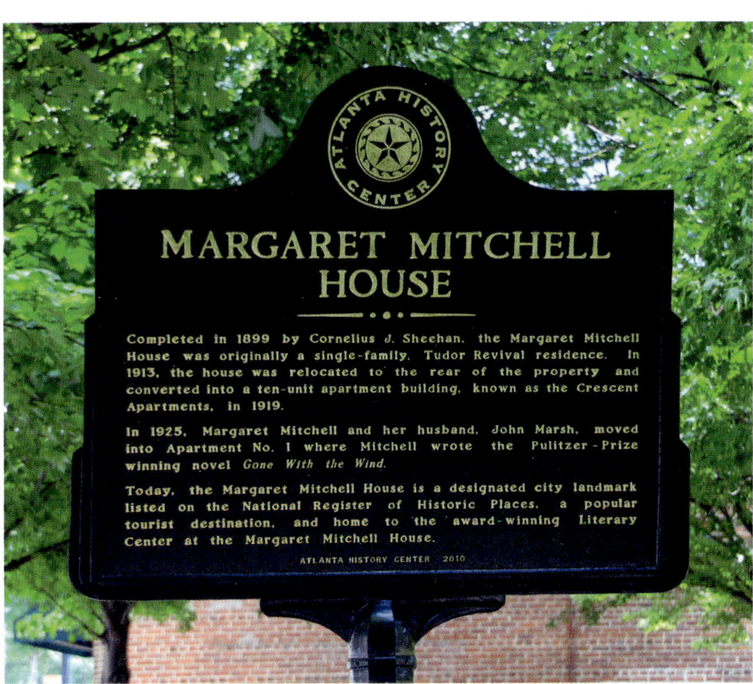

Margaret Mitchell House *(above and right)*

Take a guided tour of the Midtown apartment where Margaret Mitchell wrote her Pulitzer Prize-winning novel, *Gone with the Wind*, which was published in 1936. Operated by the Atlanta History Center, the three-story, Tudor Revival building, built in 1899, sits on two acres in Midtown. It is listed on the National Register of Historic Places.

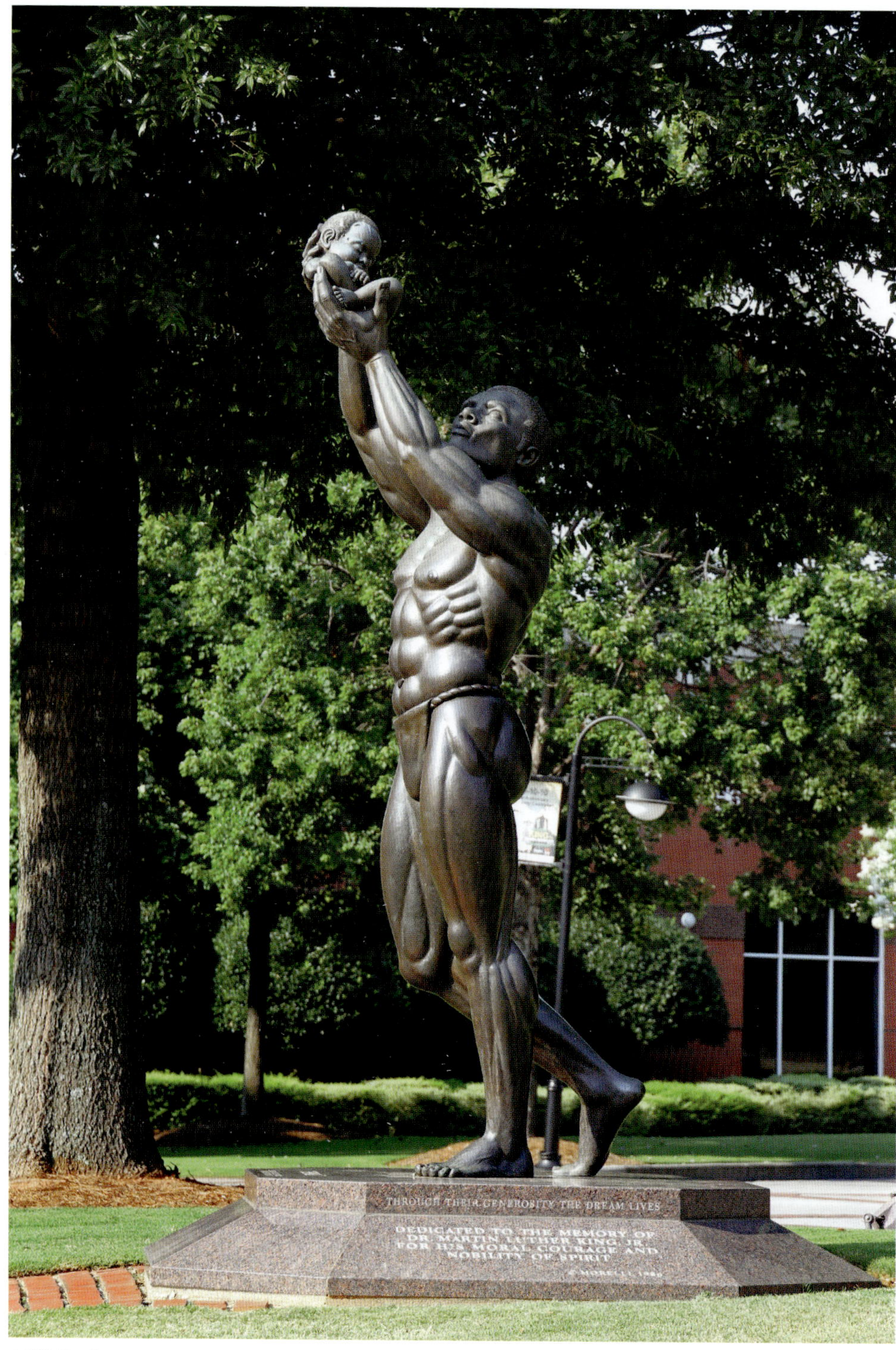

Behold Monument *(above)*

The bronze figure of a father raising his infant to heaven and looking toward Ebenezer Baptist Church stands majestically in Peace Plaza. Inspired by the ancient African ritual of lifting a newborn child to the heavens, *BEHOLD* embodies and commemorates the principles that guided the life and works of Dr. Martin Luther King, Jr.

National Historic Site *(opposite)*

The Martin Luther King, Jr. National Historic Site, established in 1980, encompasses several facilities operated in partnership with the National Park Service, Ebenezer Baptist Church, and The King Center. Peace Plaza, site of the inspirational "I Have a Dream" World Peace Rose Garden, is located between the Visitor Center and Auburn Avenue.

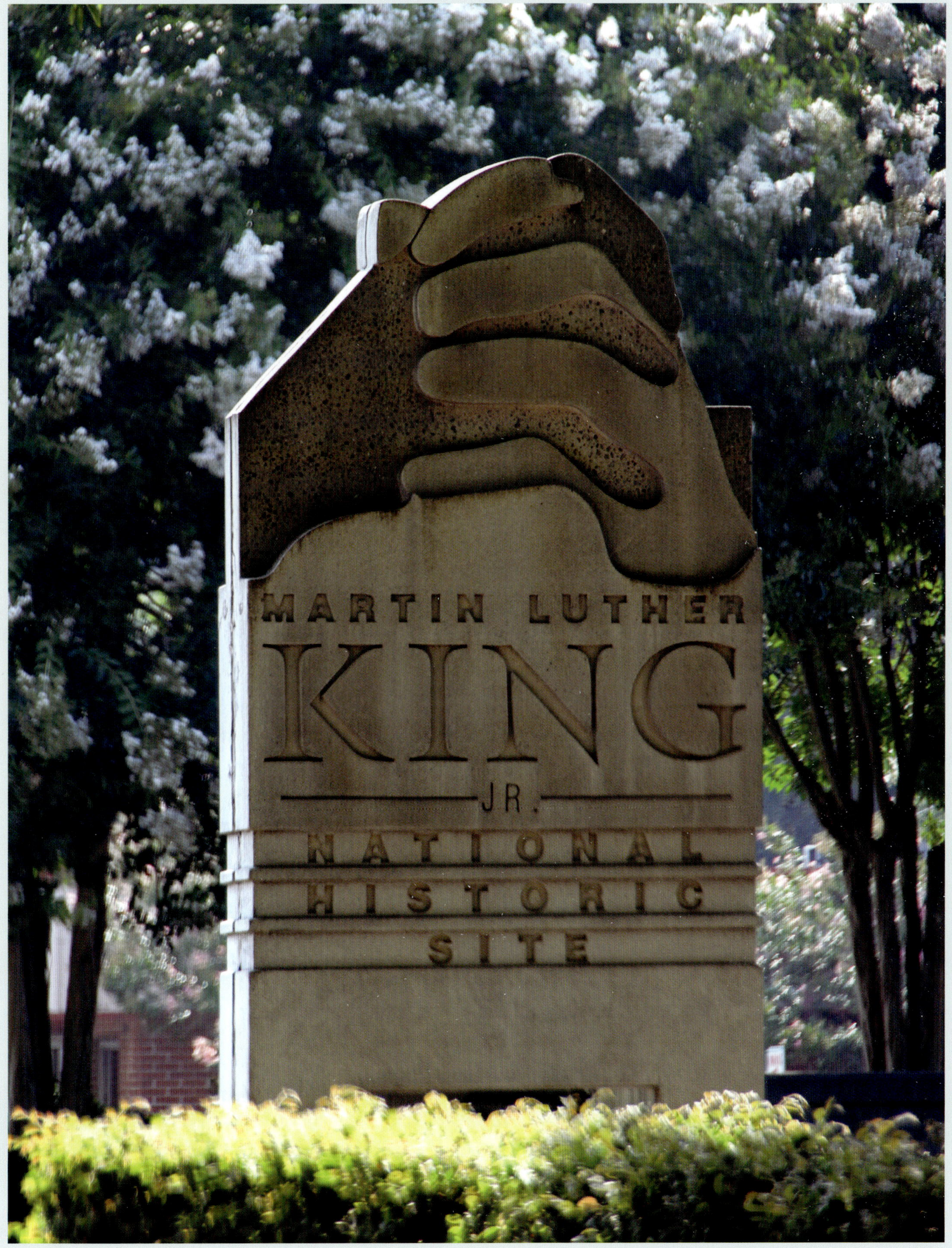
MARTIN LUTHER
KING
JR.
NATIONAL
HISTORIC
SITE

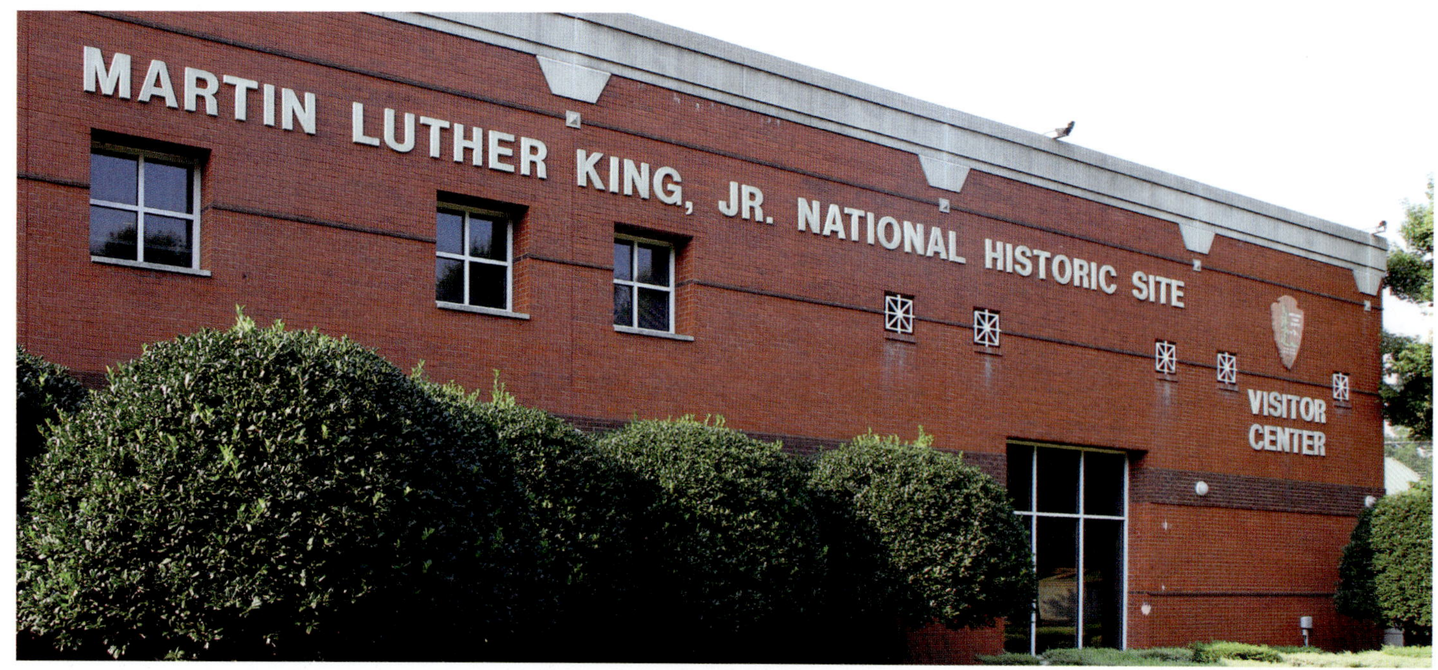

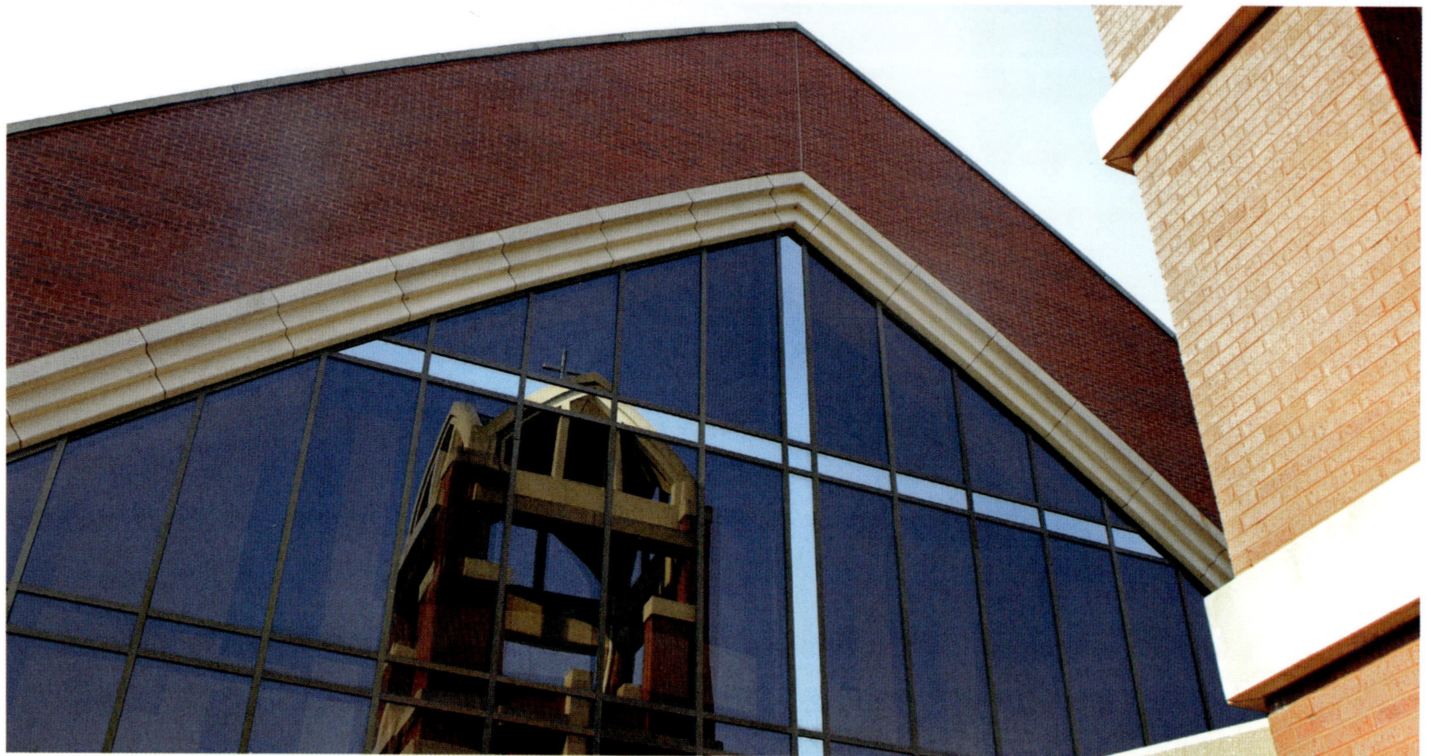

MLK Visitor Center *(top and bottom)*

Stop by the Visitor Center for a brief orientation to the site, watch ongoing videos, and tour the Children of Courage exhibit – geared to younger visitors – and the Courage to Lead exhibit, which follows the parallel paths of King and the Civil Rights Movement. The Freedom Road exhibit links the historic site to The Carter Center.

Martin Luther King Birthplace *(opposite)*

Dr. Martin Luther King, Jr. was born in an upstairs bedroom of this modest home at 501 Auburn Avenue in Atlanta. The Sweet Auburn neighborhood, also home to the Ebenezer Baptist Church, would play a significant role in King's life's work. Park ranger-conducted tours are filled on a first-come, first-served basis.

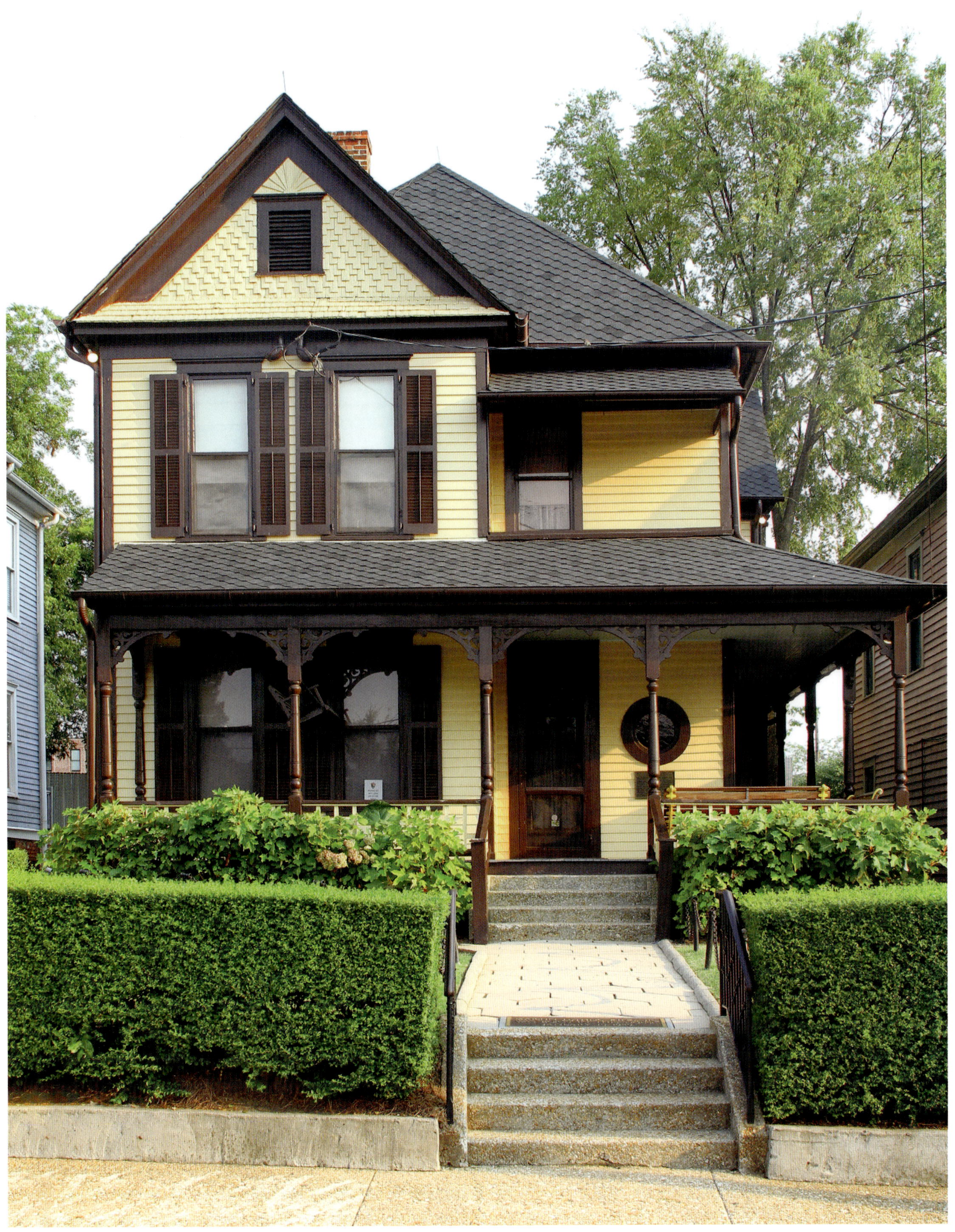

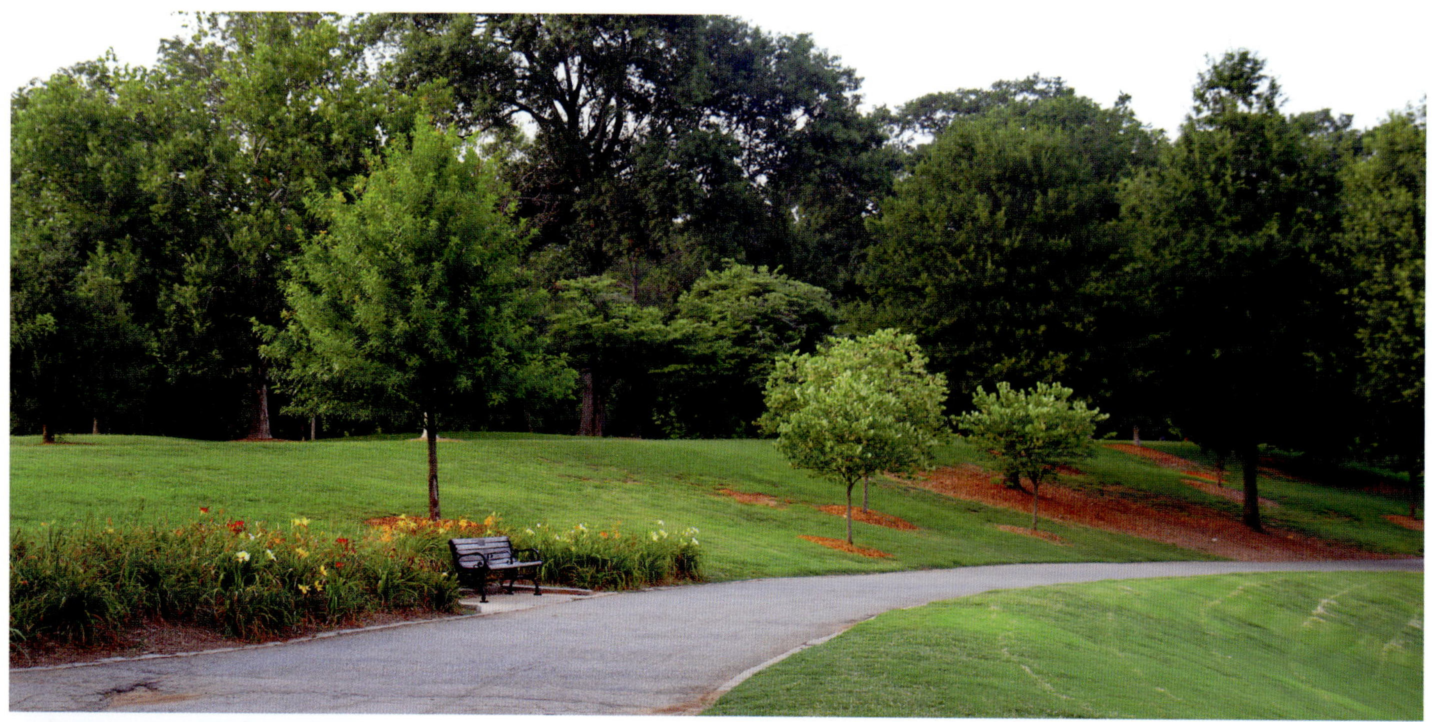

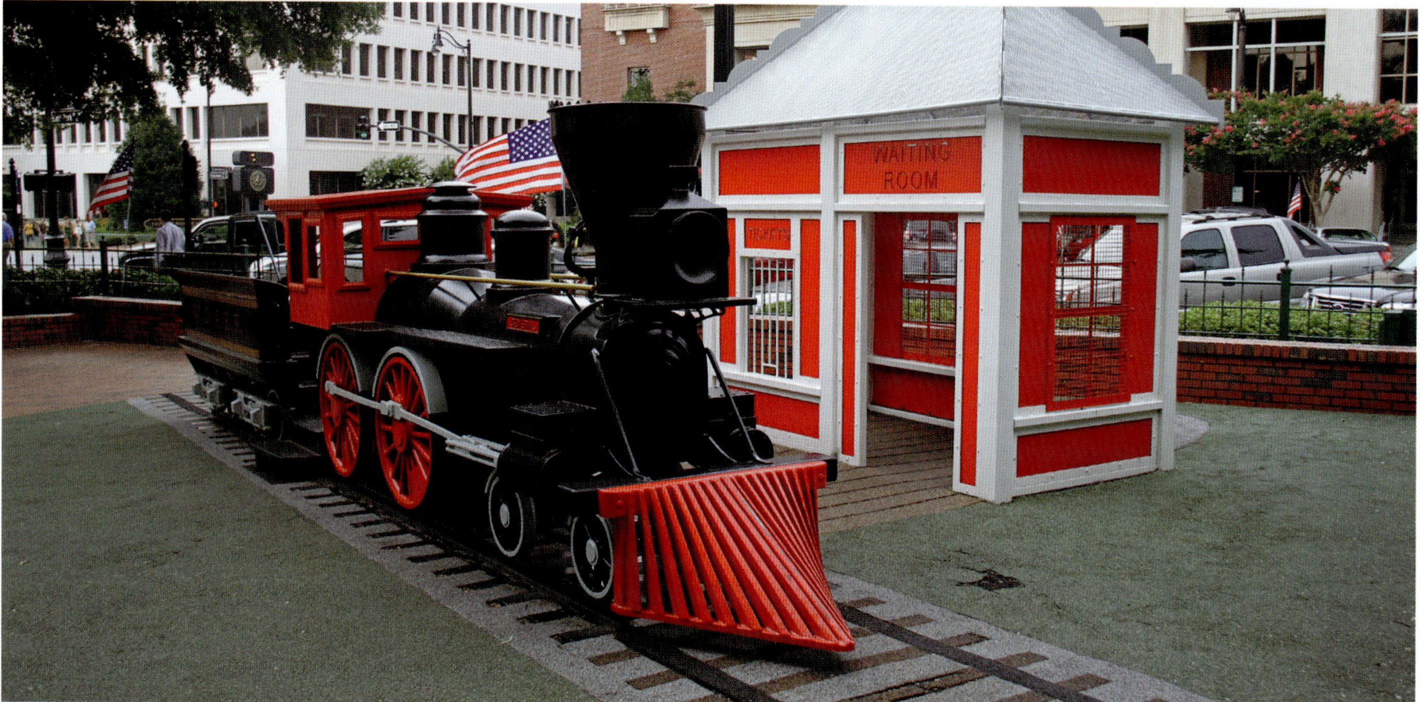

Piedmont Park *(top)*

Covering 211 acres of parkland in the heart of Atlanta, Piedmont Park is beloved for its meadows, woodlands, and wetlands. It also features sports fields, fishing, a dog park, and Aquatic Center with beach entry and lap lanes. Playgrounds include a playscape designed by renowned sculptor Isamu Noguchi. Park tours and bird walks are also offered.

The General *(bottom)*

An immaculate pocket park, Glover Park was a 19th-century bequest by Mayor John Glover, who stipulated the land must always remain a park. The park is famous for its fountain and its miniature replica of the famous locomotive, The General. The April 12, 1862 Great Locomotive Chase of the American Civil War started here.

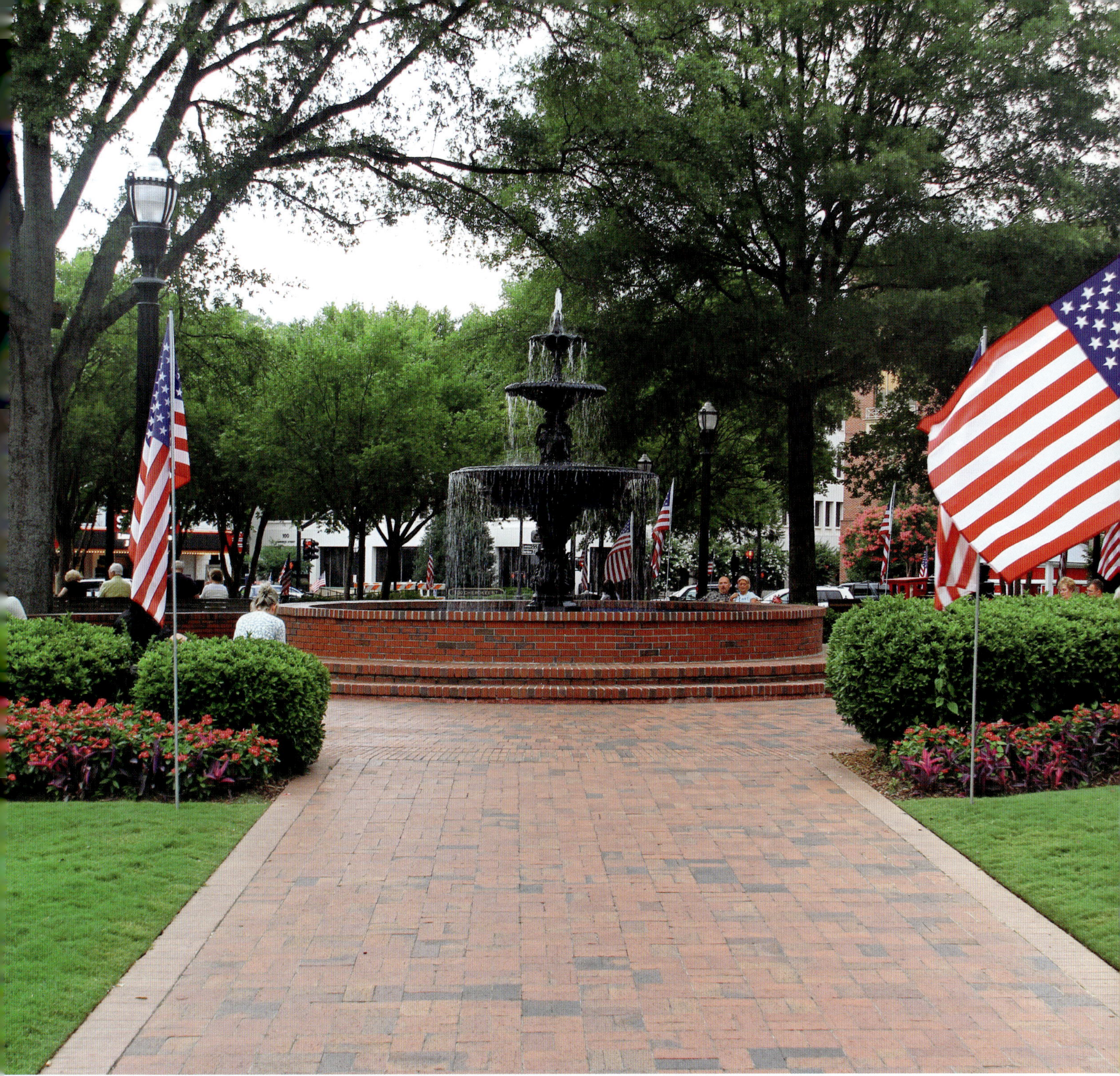

Glover Park at Marietta Square

Anchoring historic Marietta Square, victorianesque Glover Park is lined with shops, restaurants, and museums. With its magnificent multi-tiered fountain, statuary, and gazebo bandstand, it is the heart and soul of the community – abuzz with activity all year long with concerts, festivals, Broadway-style theatre, weddings, and more.

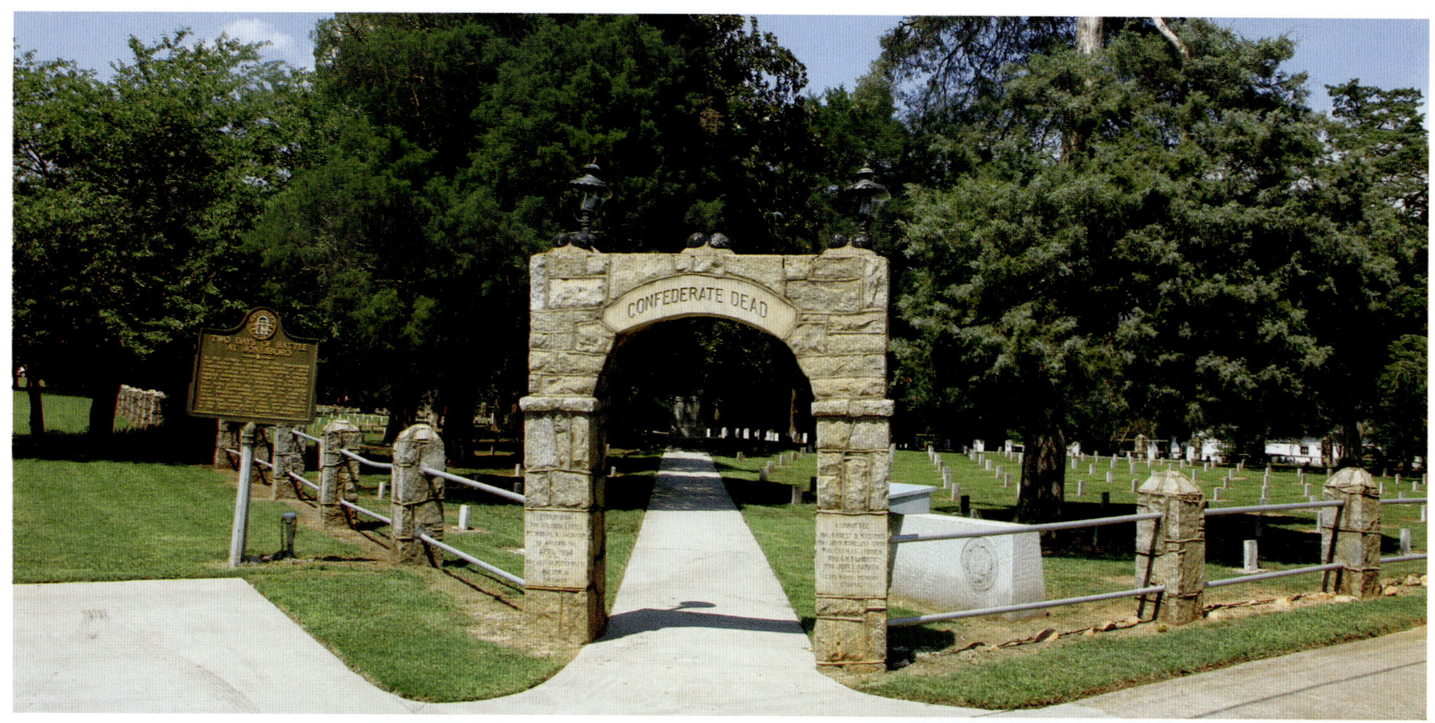

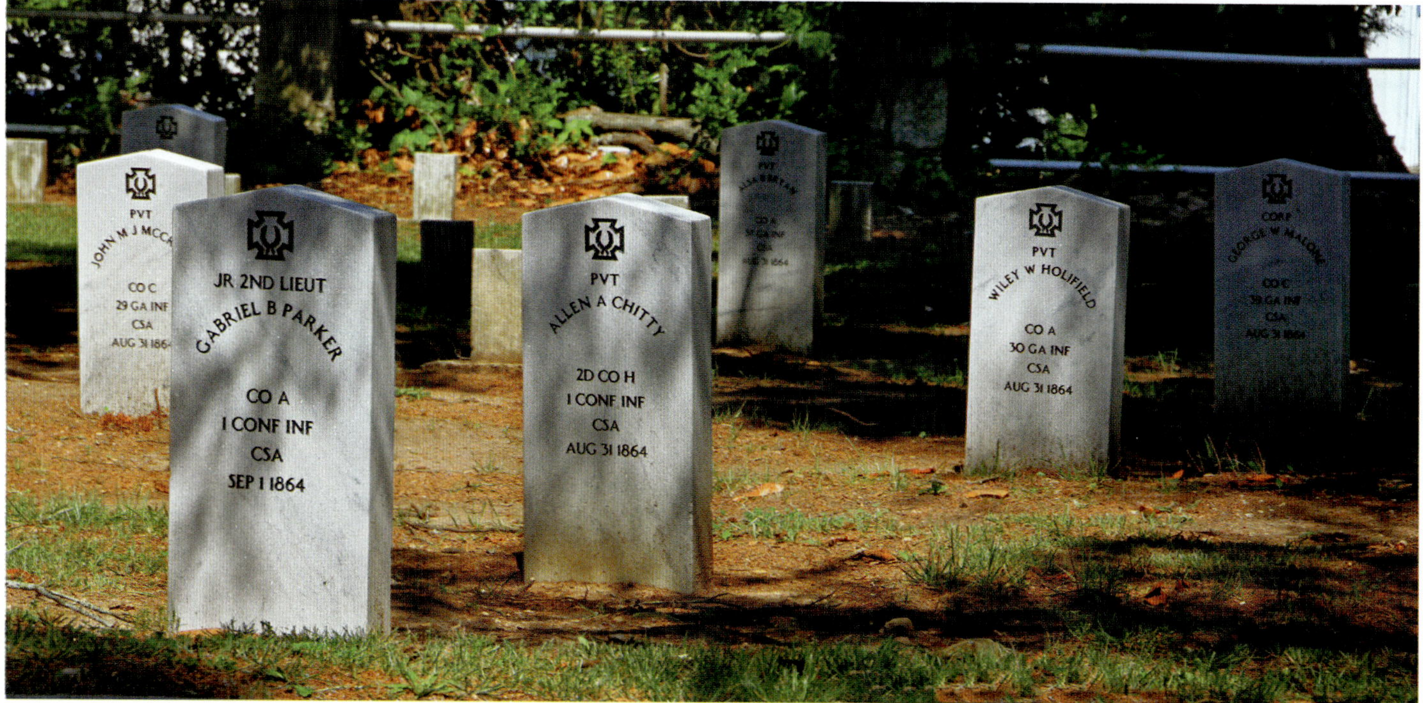

Unknown Confederates *(top and bottom)*

Dedicated by the Atlanta Ladies Memorial Association "To the Honored Memory of the Several Hundred Unknown Confederate Soldiers," Jonesboro's Patrick R. Cleburne Confederate Memorial Cemetery is the final resting place of nearly 1,000 soldiers whose unmarked headstones are laid out in the shape of the Confederate battle flag.

Marietta Confederate Cemetery

(opposite, top and bottom)

Established in 1863 on land donated by Mrs. Jane Porter Glover to bury 20 Confederate soldiers who died in a train wreck, this cemetery is the final resting place of some 3,000 soldiers. They represent every Confederate state, plus Kentucky, Maryland, and Missouri, including soldiers who fought nearby in the Battle of Kennesaw Mountain.

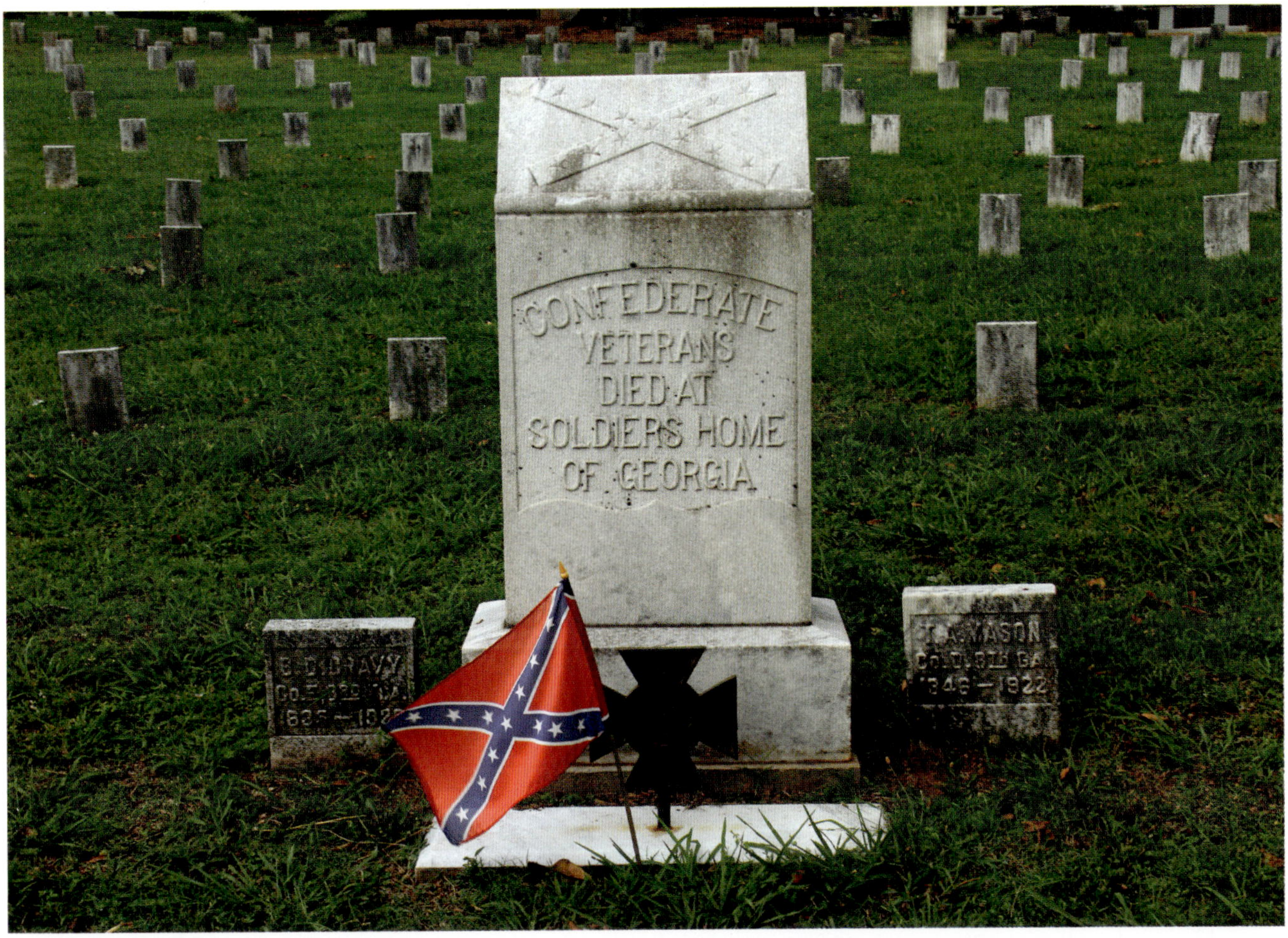

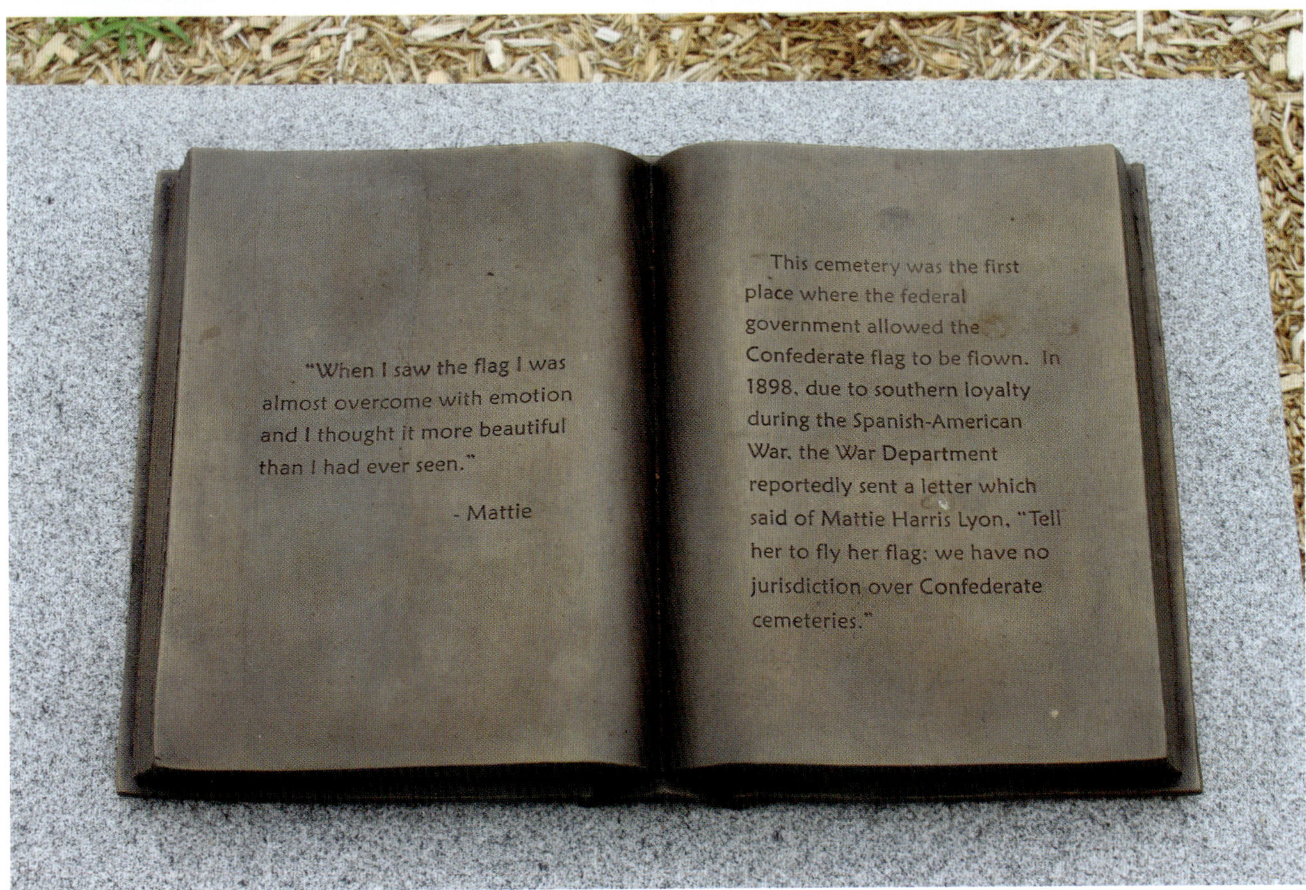
"When I saw the flag I was
almost overcome with emotion
and I thought it more beautiful
than I had ever seen."
- Mattie
This cemetery was the first
place where the federal
government allowed the
Confederate flag to be flown. In
1898, due to southern loyalty
during the Spanish-American
War, the War Department
reportedly sent a letter which
said of Mattie Harris Lyon, "Tell
her to fly her flag; we have no
jurisdiction over Confederate
cemeteries."

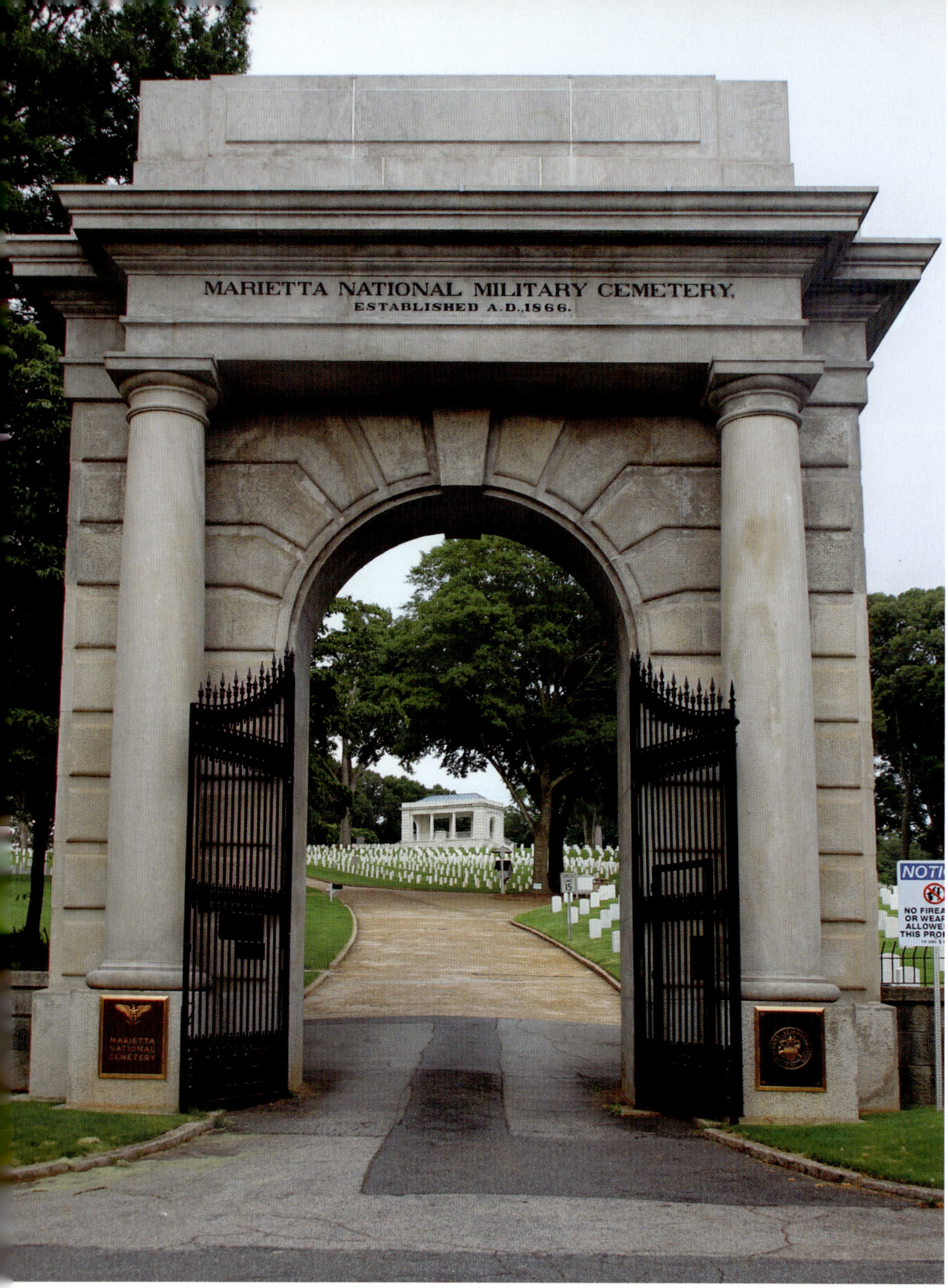

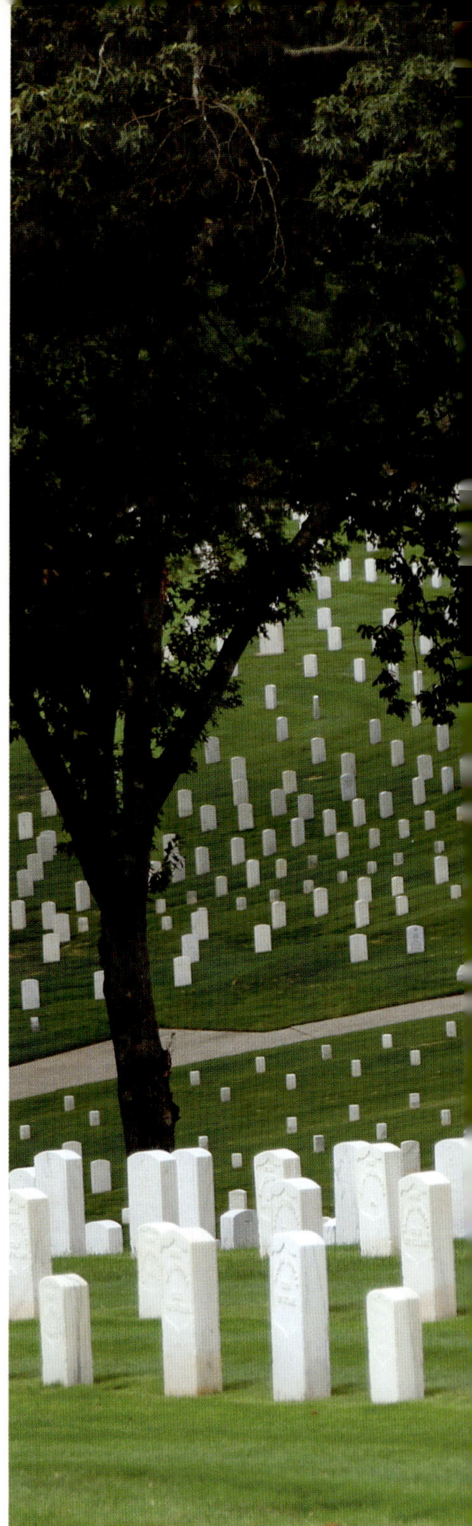

Monumental Masonry Archway

Built in 1883, this Roman-inspired masonry archway served as the formal entrance to the Marietta National Cemetery. Beyond the 35-foot-tall arch, trimmed with Doric columns and ornamental gate, is the final resting place of more than 10,000 Union soldiers. The cemetery was laid out by Union Army Chaplain Thomas Van Horne.

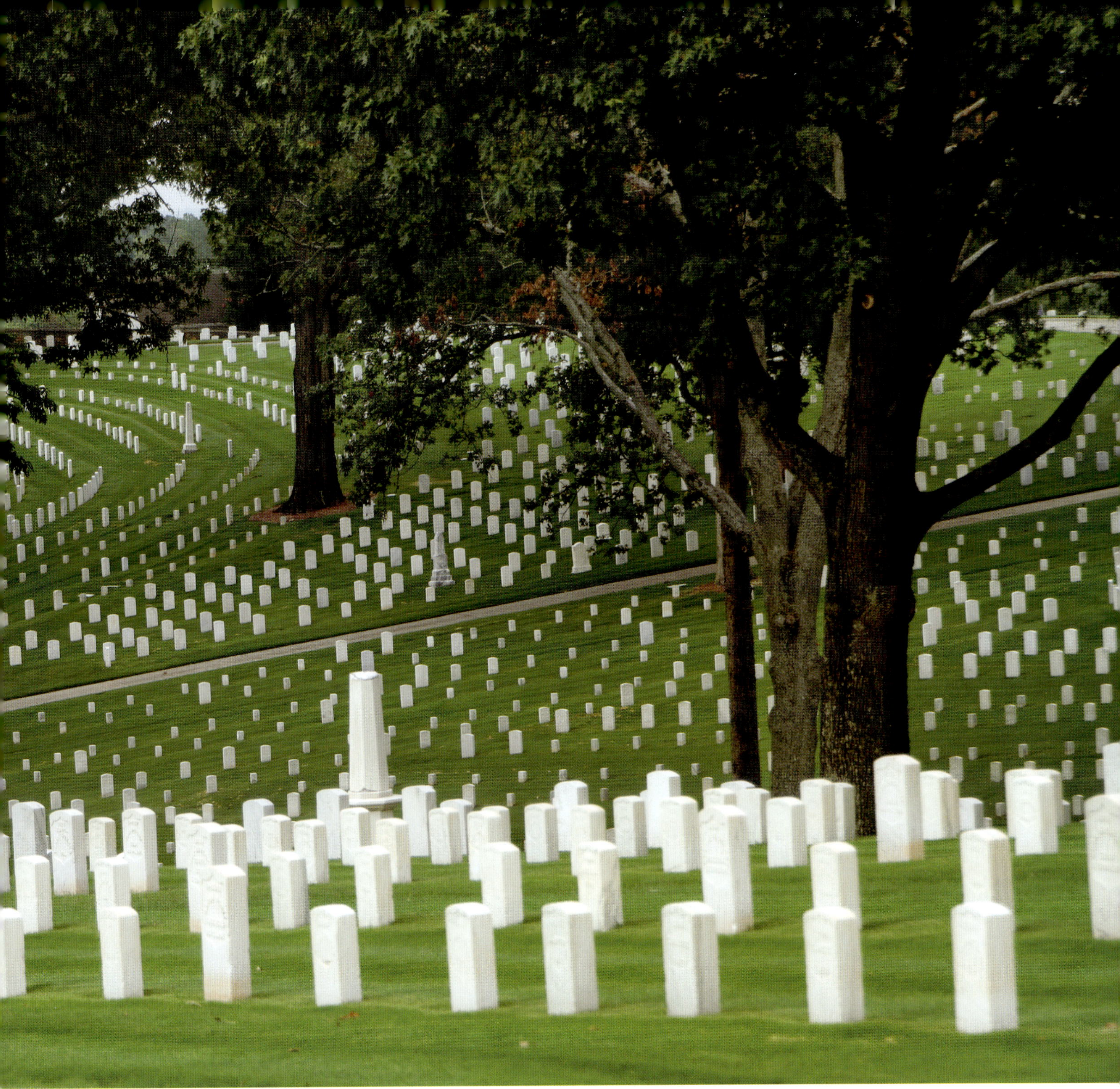

Marietta National Cemetery

Established as the Marietta and Atlanta National Cemetery in 1866 by General George Henry Thomas, a principal commander in the Western Theater, the Marietta National Cemetery is on the National Register of Historic Places. Notable monuments include a marble obelisk, erected in May of 1870 to honor the 20th Army Corps.

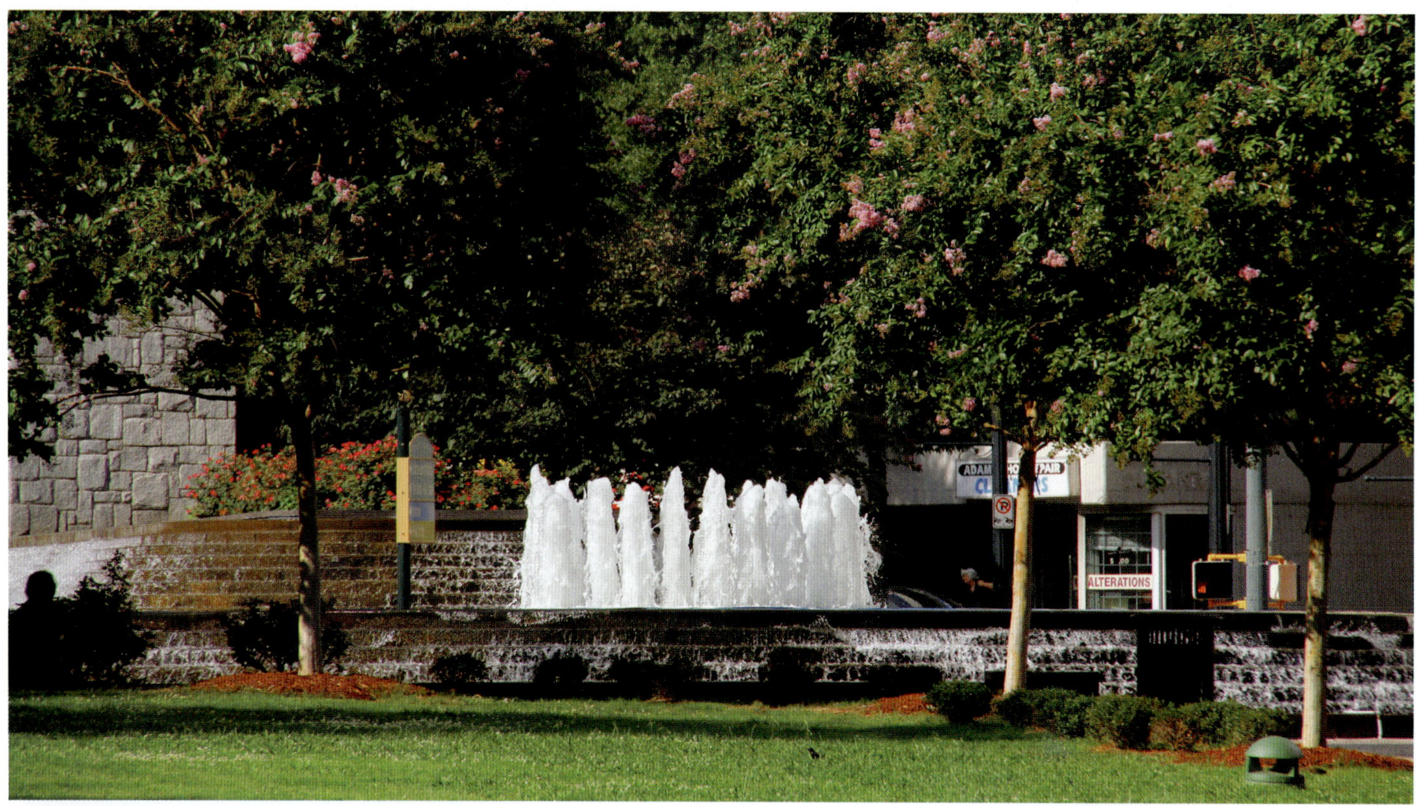

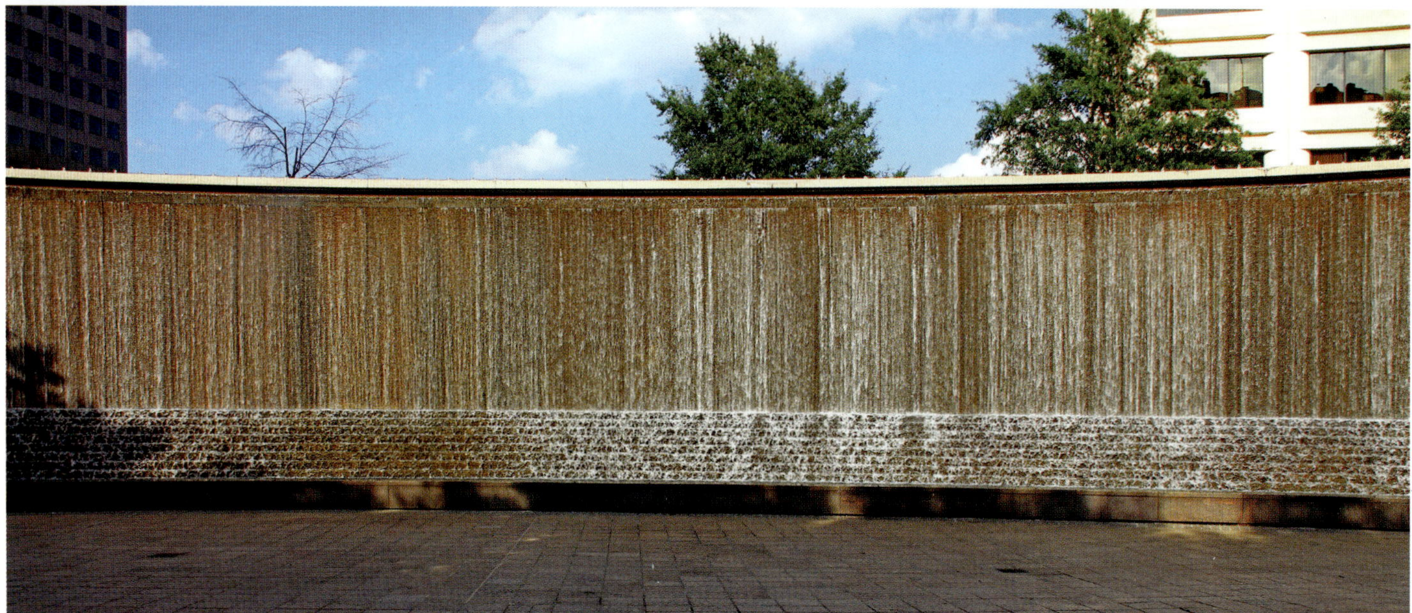

International Peace Fountain *(top)*

Commemorating Atlanta's key role in the Civil Rights movement, the *International Peace Fountain* at Woodruff Park, according to designer Nimrod Long III, symbolizes the "community relations between Atlantans of different cultures and Jimmy Carter's international peace efforts."

Waterwall *(bottom)*

Amidst the vibrant pedestrian spaces and urban energy of Woodruff Park, located at the intersection of Auburn Avenue and Peachtree Street, the *International Peace Fountain* features water cascading along a 180-foot-long curving wall and shooting 30 feet into the air from its geyser fountain. Like Atlanta, it is graceful and dynamic.

Woodruff Park *(opposite)*

This six-acre urban oasis, in the heart of Atlanta's financial, entertainment, and academic districts, boasts greenspace trimmed with florals and gardens of year-round color. Featured are a children's playground, exercise stations, monuments, Reading Room, chess court, outdoor movies and festivals, Speakers Corner, and food vendors.

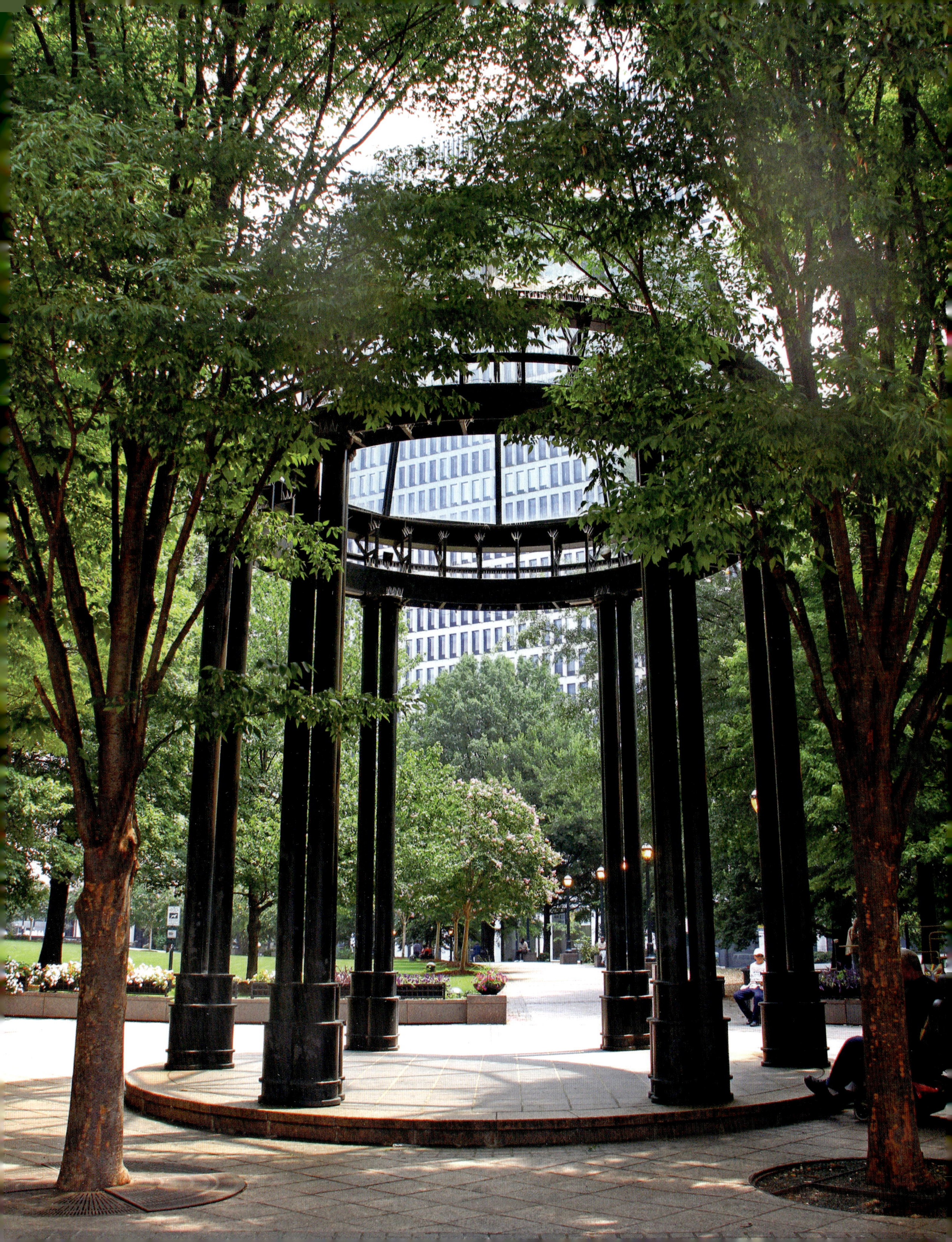

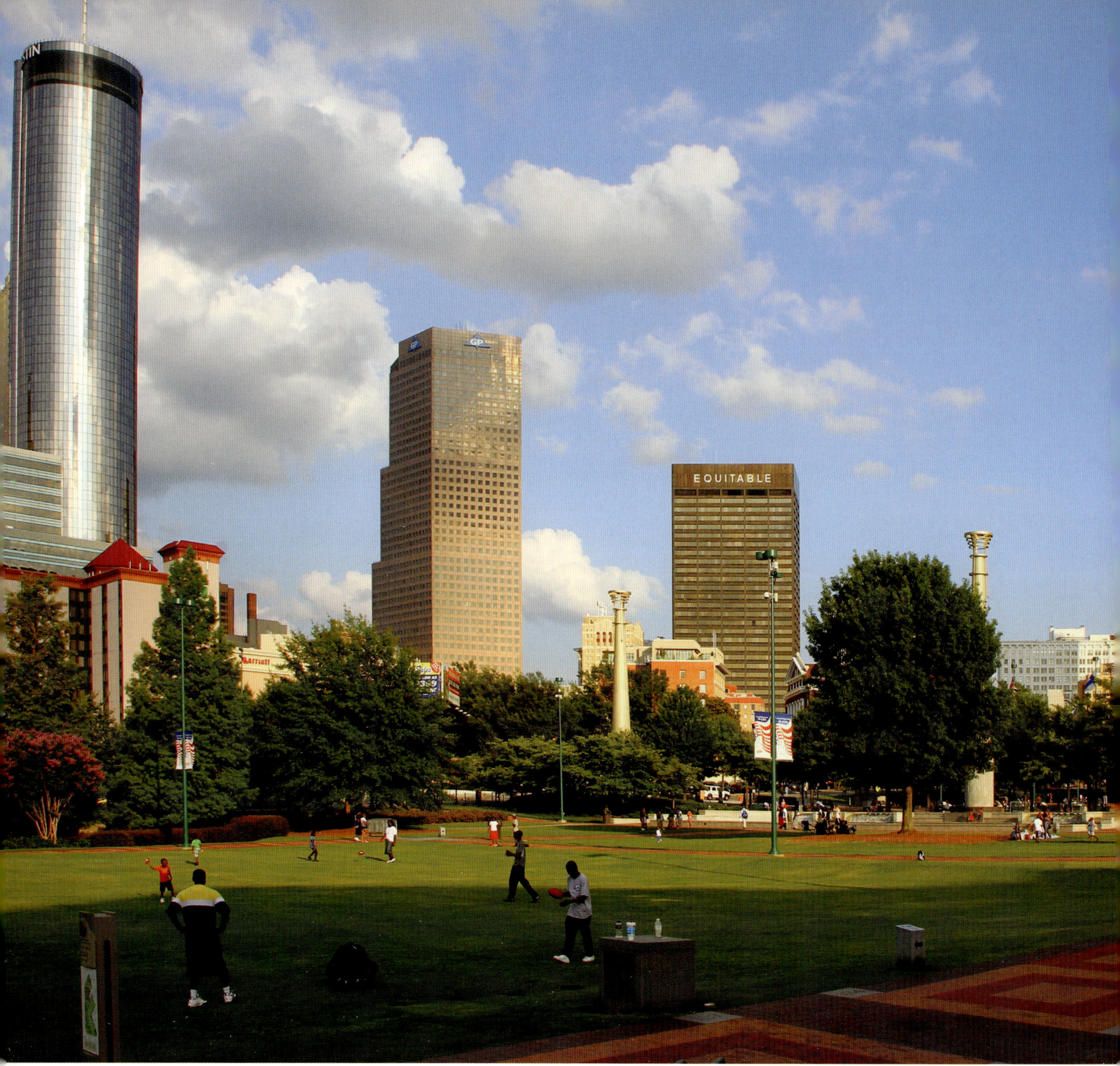

Centennial Olympic Park

Atlanta Committee for the Olympic Games CEO Billy Payne transformed this former multi-block eyesore into a vital 21-acre park. With enough grass to cover Turner Field three times, the park is landscaped with some 575 trees and 30,000 shrubs and includes granite from all five continents represented in the Games.

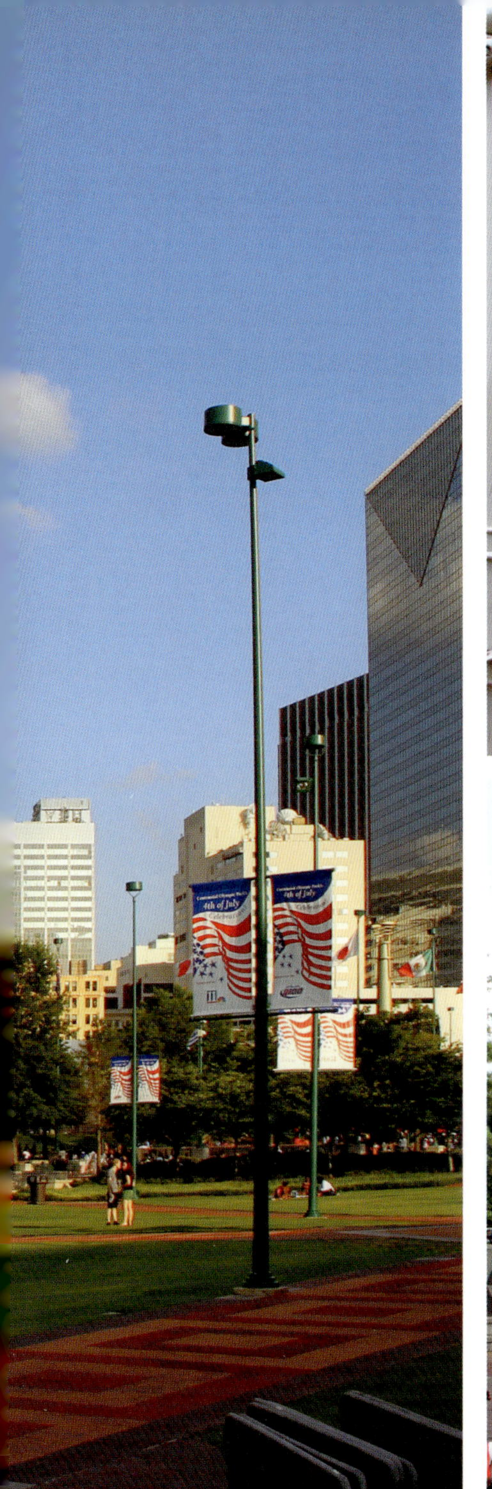

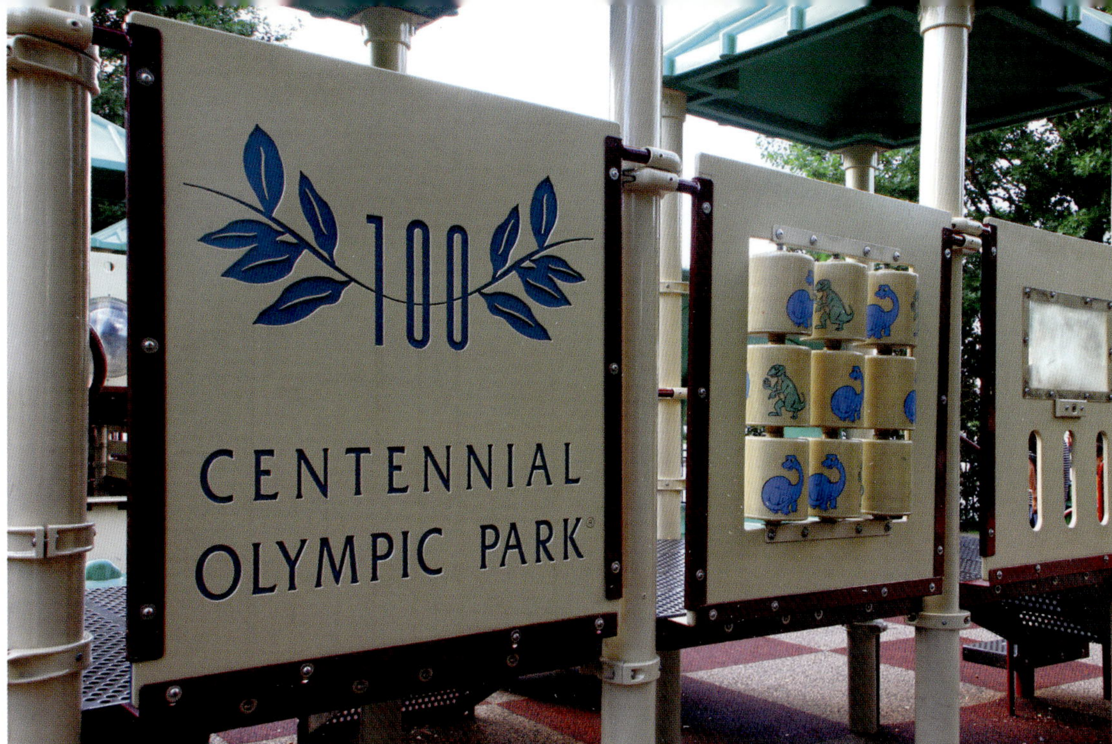

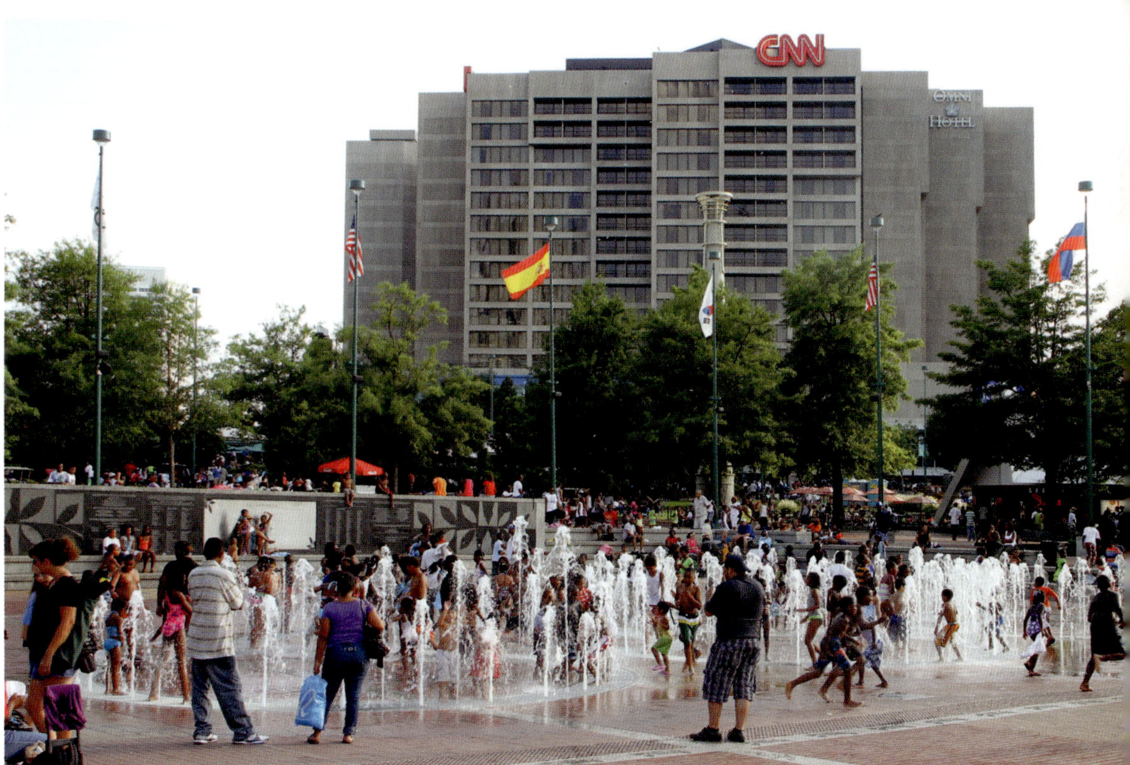

Olympic Legacy *(top)*

Created as the central gathering place for the 1996 Centennial Olympic Games, the park is located in the heart of downtown, within walking distance of some of the city's major attractions, including the Georgia Aquarium and CNN Center. The Park sponsors community-wide free events, including festivals and a Fourth of July Celebration.

Fountain of Rings *(bottom)*

Fountain of Rings is the centerpiece of the park and the world's largest interactive fountain. Utilizing the Olympic symbol of five interconnecting rings, it is one of the most recognized landmarks in Georgia. The *Fountain of Rings* show plays four times daily with 251 computer-controlled water jets, 410 fog jets, and sprays reaching 30 feet high.

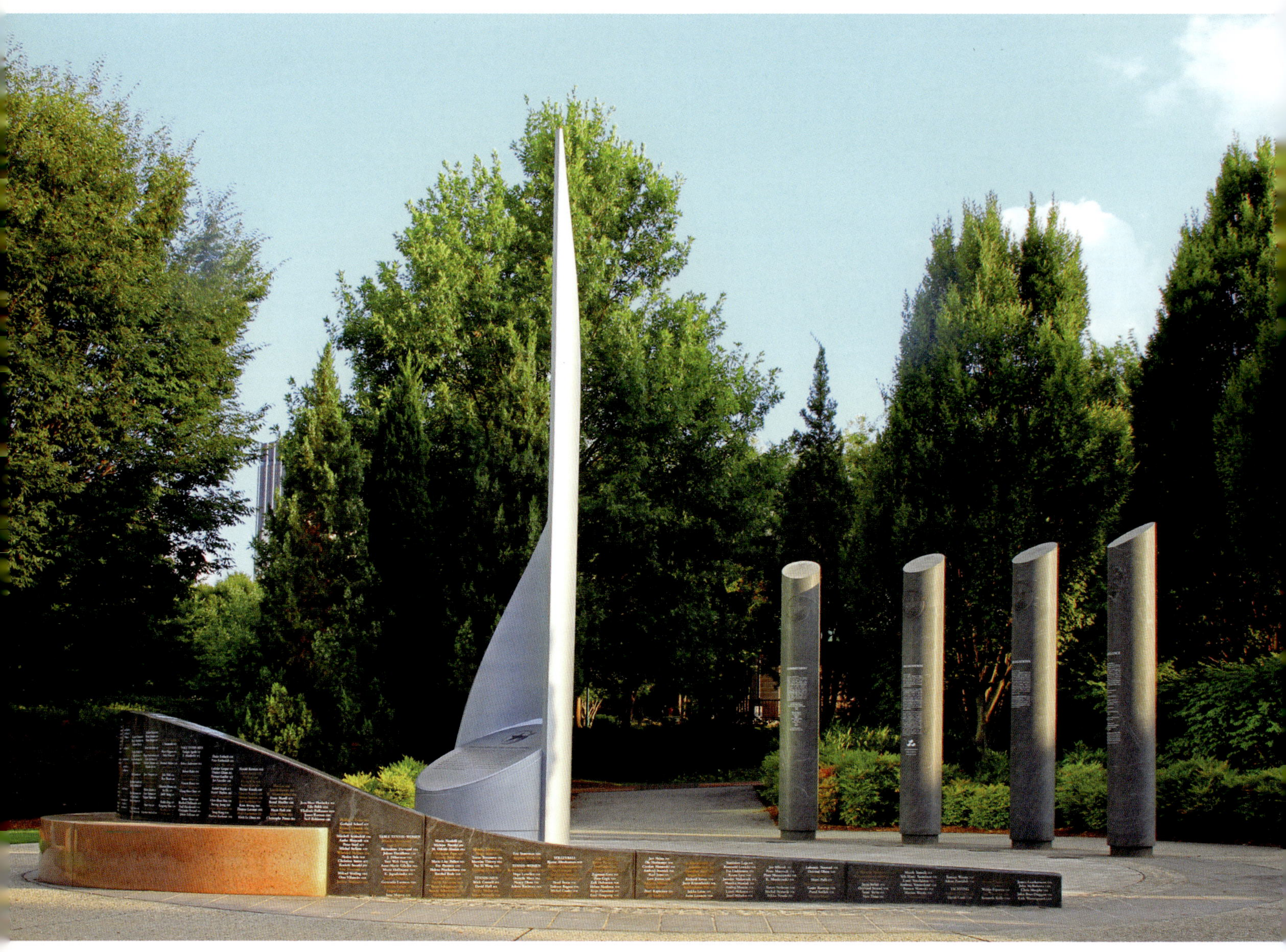

Paralympics Legacy

Paralympics Legacy honors the 1996 Paralympics Games, the Olympic-style events for disabled athletes that were first organized in Rome in 1960. In the 1996 Centennial Olympics, 3,310 athletes from 104 countries participated and set 268 world records. The names of these athletes are inscribed on the surrounding granite pillars.

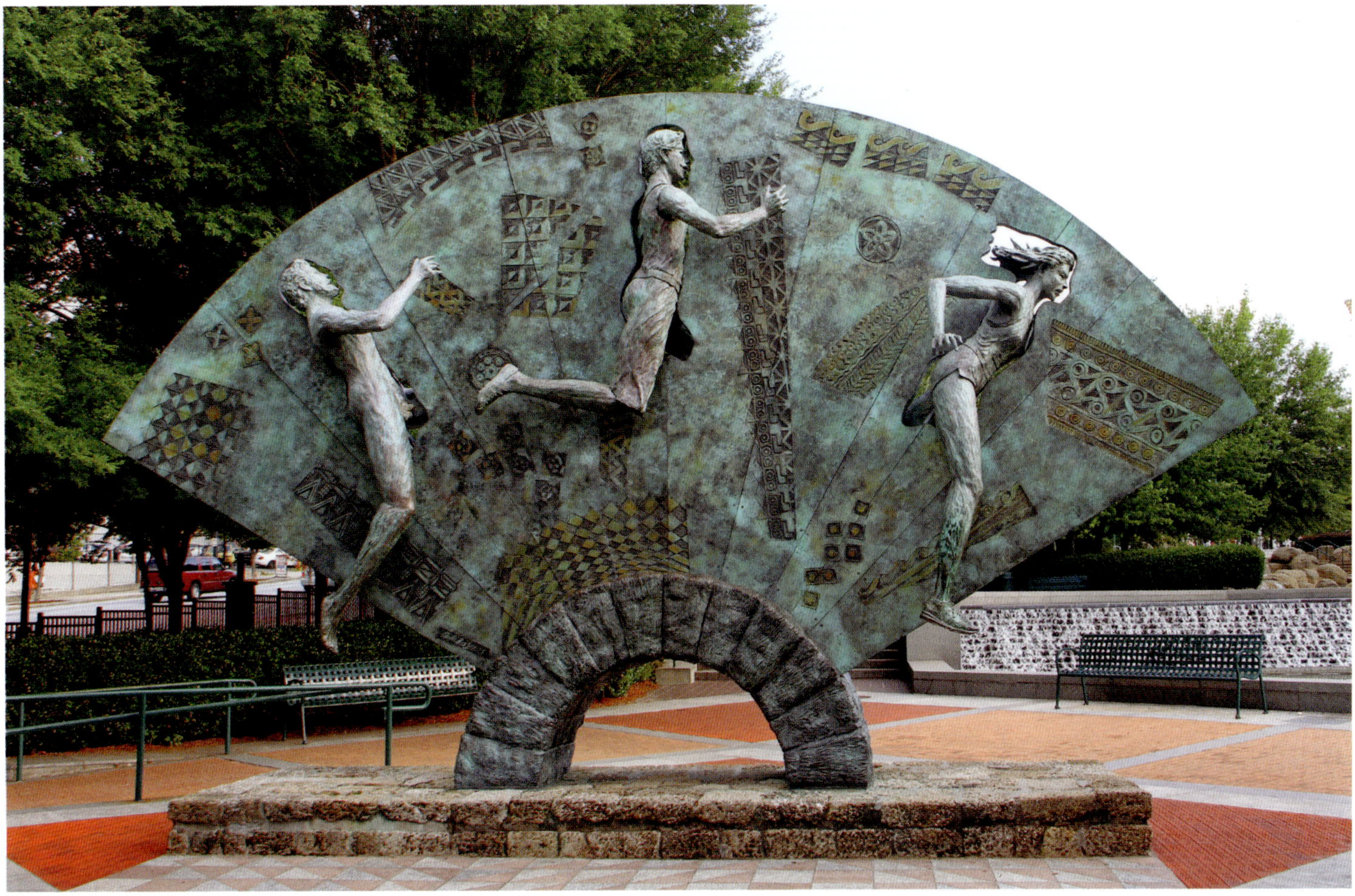

Quilt of Origins *(above)*

Presented by the Greek-American community in commemoration of the 100th anniversary of the Modern Olympic Games, *Quilt of Origins* depicts a nude male runner competing in the first Games in Olympia, Greece in 776 BC; a male runner competing in the first modern Games in Athens, Greece in 1896; and a female runner competing in the Centennial Games in Atlanta in 1996.

Gateway of Dreams *(right)*

This 15-foot sculpture was donated to the State of Georgia by the United States Pierre de Coubertin Committee. It depicts the founder of the modern Olympics, Baron Pierre de Coubertin of France, climbing the stairs to a gateway of ancient Greek columns. Seven doves descend the Olympic Rings to place a wreath of olive leaves on his crown.

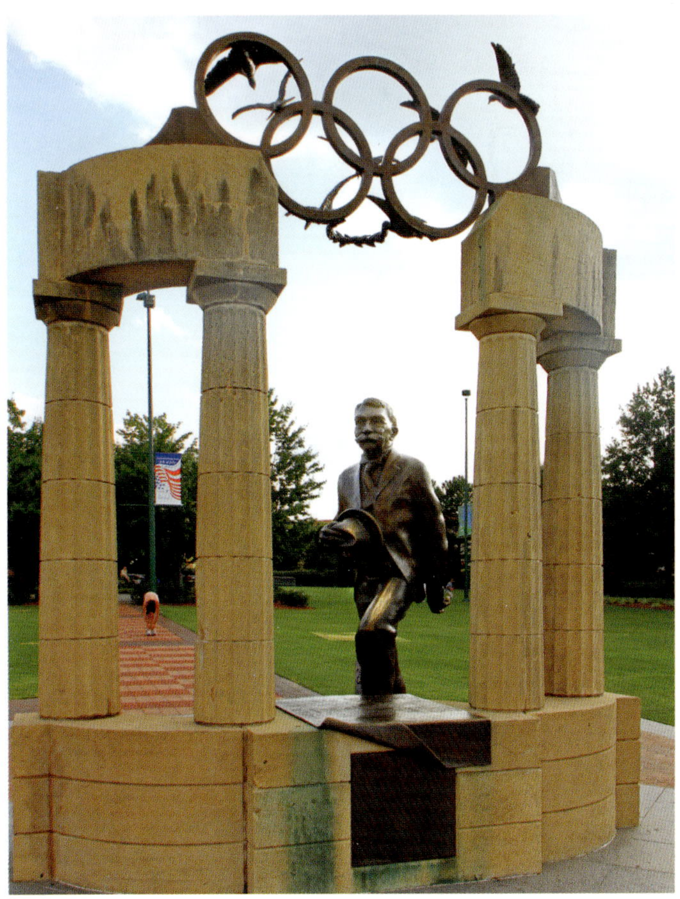

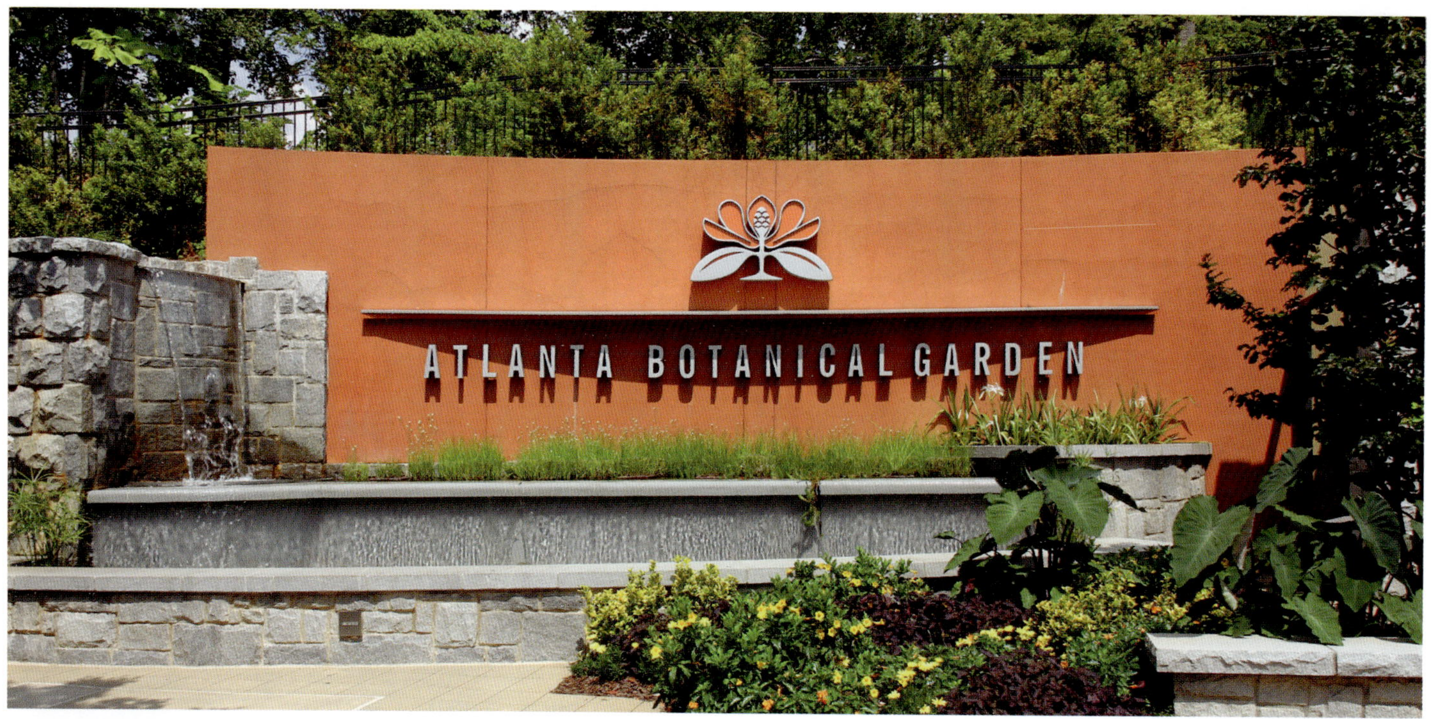

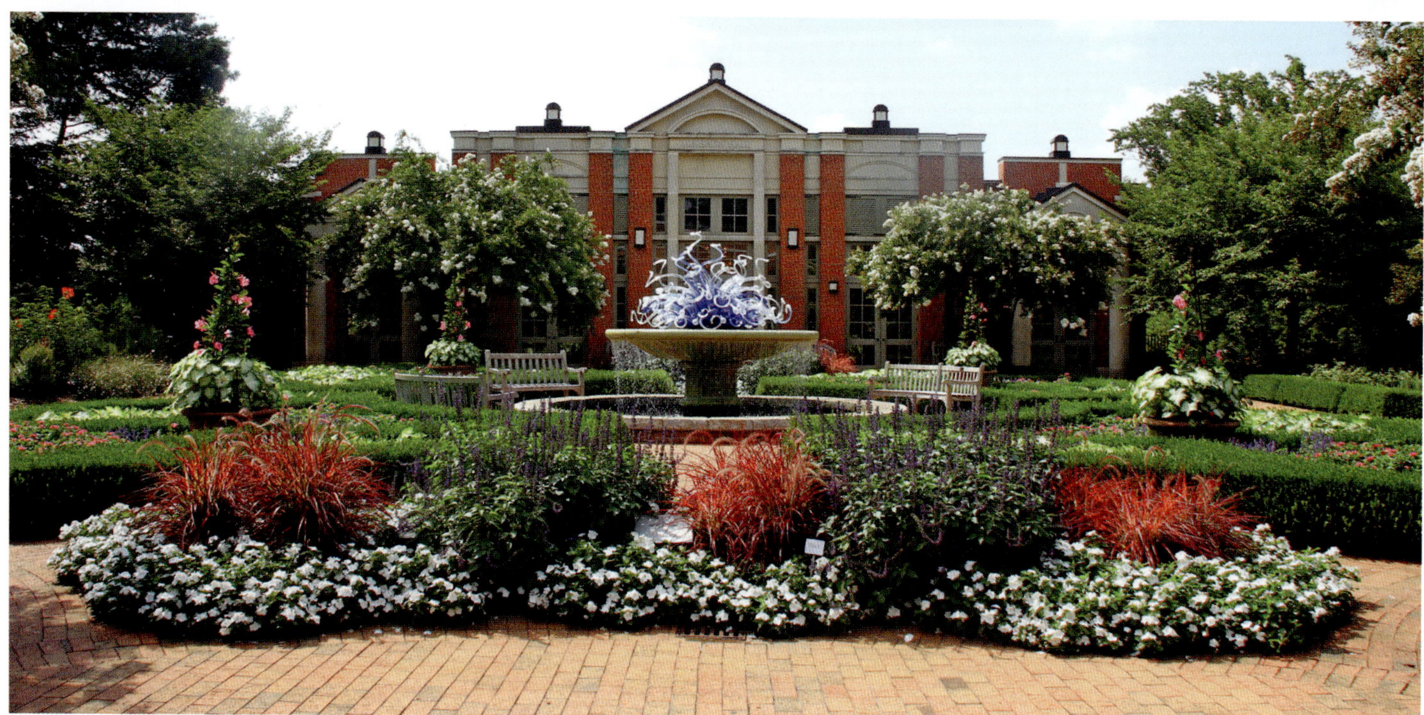

Atlanta Botanical Gardene *(top)*

The Atlanta Botanical Garden is an urban oasis in Midtown that includes 30 acres of outdoor gardens – roses, hydrangeas, dwarf and rare conifers, hardy palms, water plants, and winter-flowering plants – an award-winning Children's Garden, the serene Storza Woods with its unique Canopy Walk, and the Edible Garden and Outdoor Kitchen.

The Conservatory *(bottom)*

The Fuqua Conservatory is an organic biosphere housing tropical and desert plants. The Orchid Center has the leading collection of orchid species in the United States. Display areas include Tropical Rotunda, Desert House, and Orangerie. Permanent displays focus on plant diversity, ecological principles, conservation, and adaptation.

Trustees Garden *(opposite, top and bottom)*

The brick path beneath the gazebo leads into the secret Trustees Garden. Defined by four classical pavilions at its corners, this garden features formal dwarf boxwood edging to the flower beds. A balustrade wends up to the entrance, providing a breathtaking view over the Cascades Garden with its waterfalls and shady woodland garden.

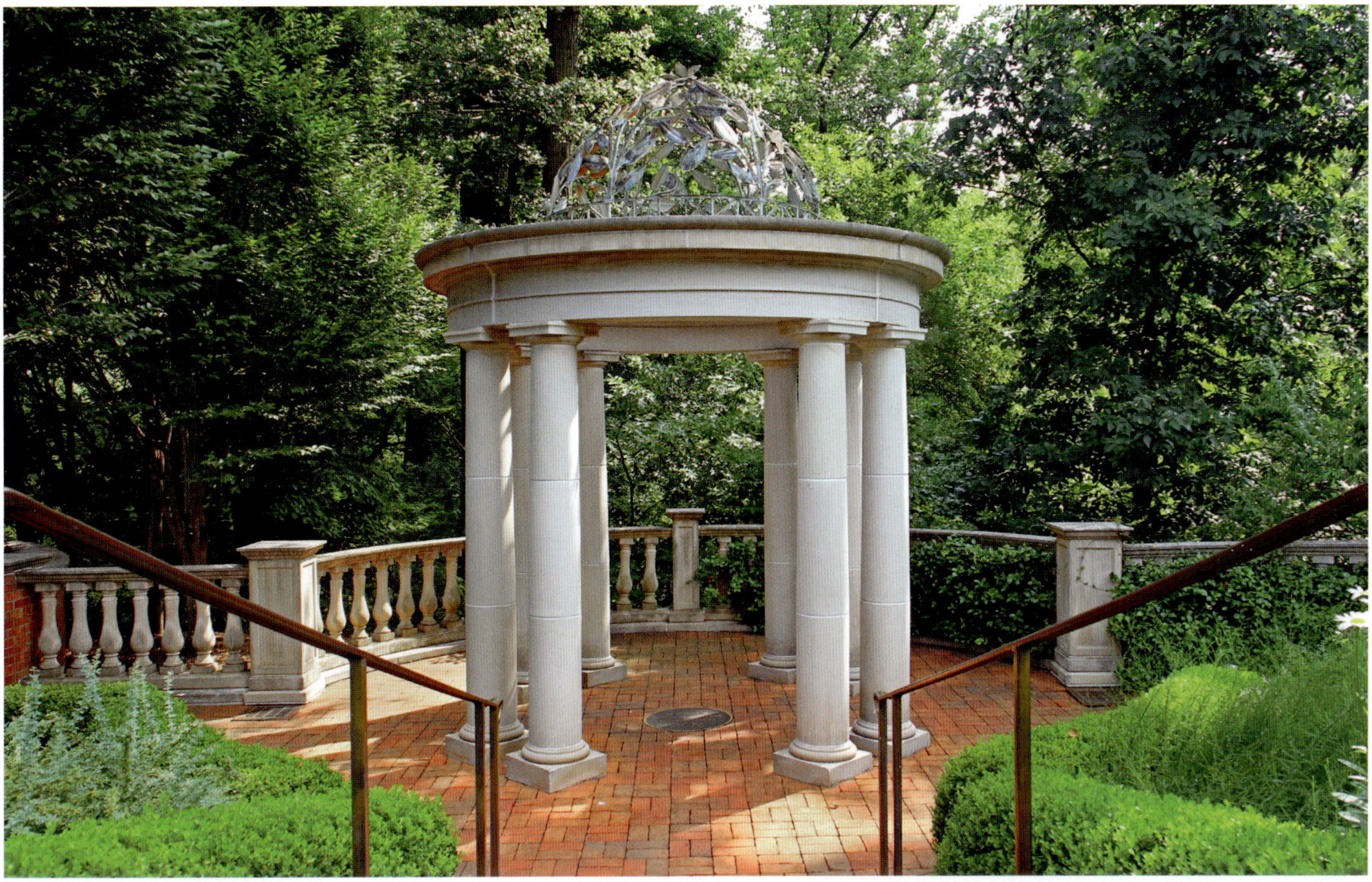

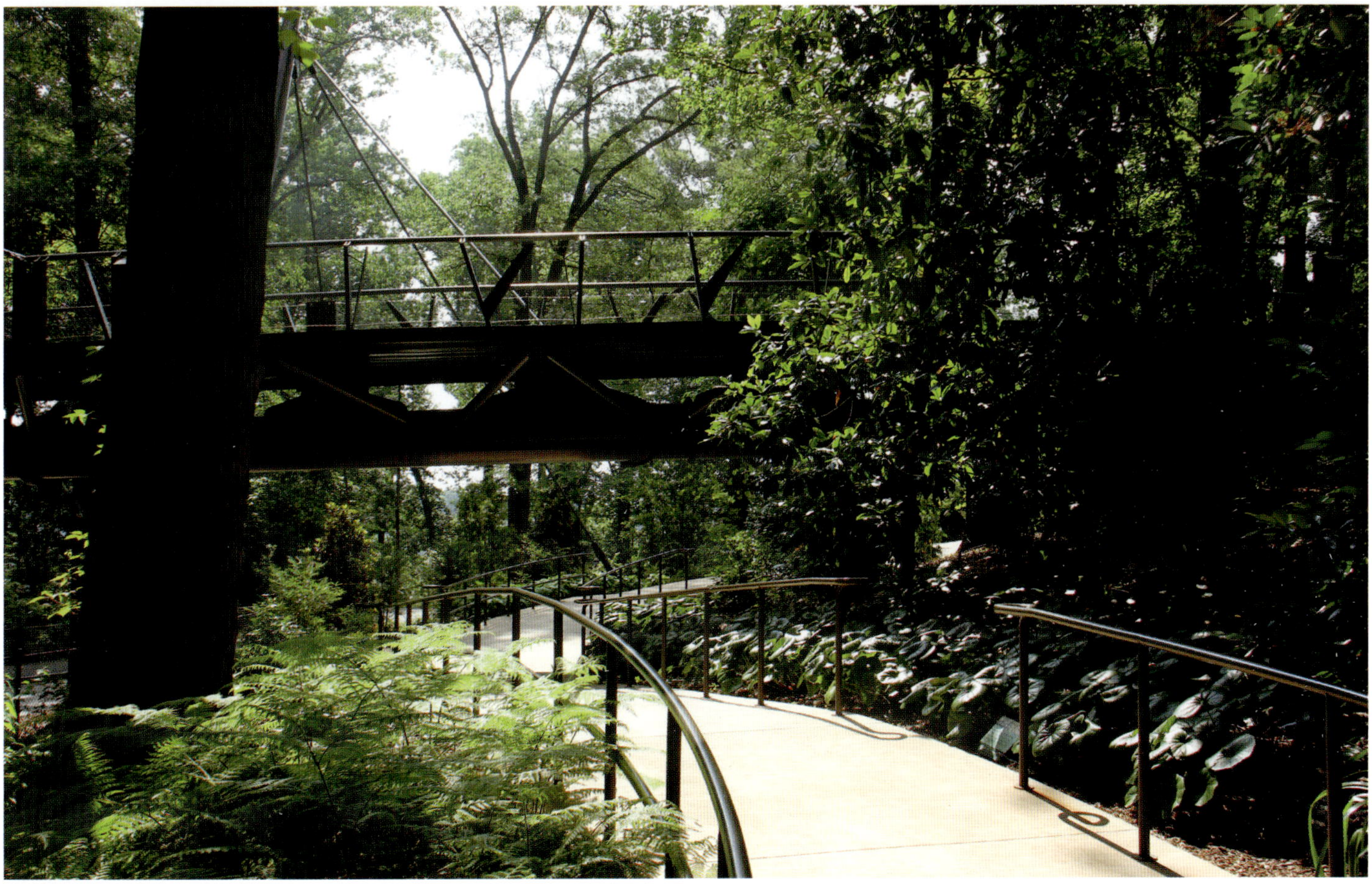

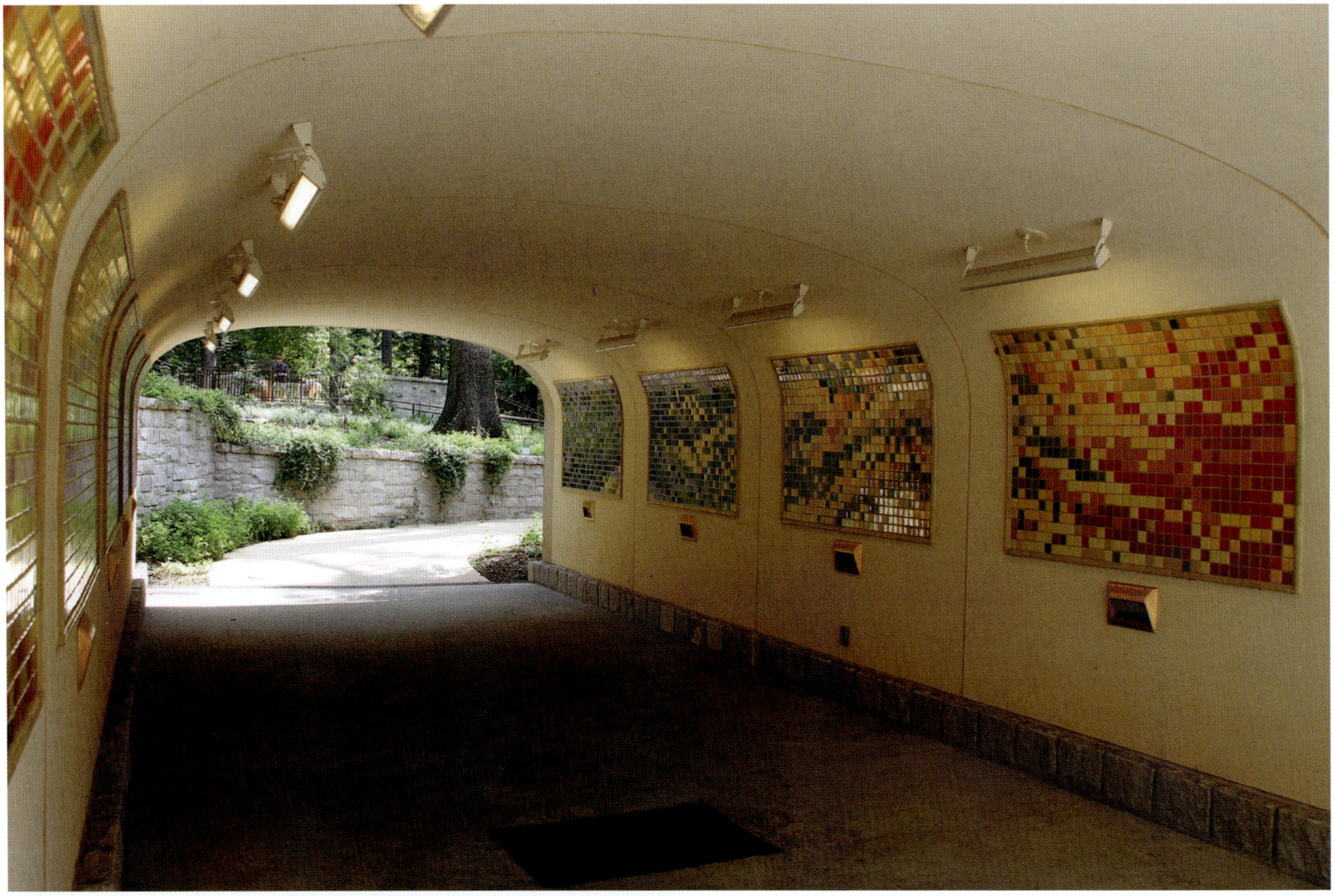

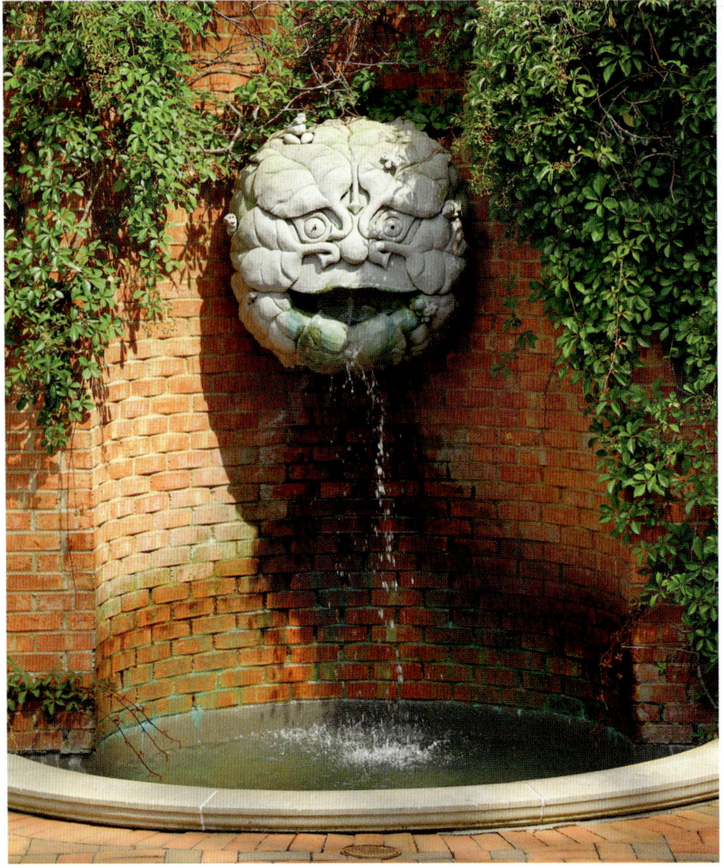

Garden Art *(above and left)*

Beyond each bend in the garden path or mosaic-filled tunnel there is something to see, from renowned plant collections and seasonally changing color to artwork in the Hardin Visitor Center and videos in the Garden Theatre. Throughout the year, the Atlanta Botanical Garden offers an array of activities and programs, including Cocktails in the Garden, Garden Chef Demos, Storybook Time, and the Wells Fargo Advisors Concerts in the Garden, as well as food festivals, lectures by noted environmental and horticultural experts, and classes ranging from watercolor painting to hands-on practical gardening workshops.

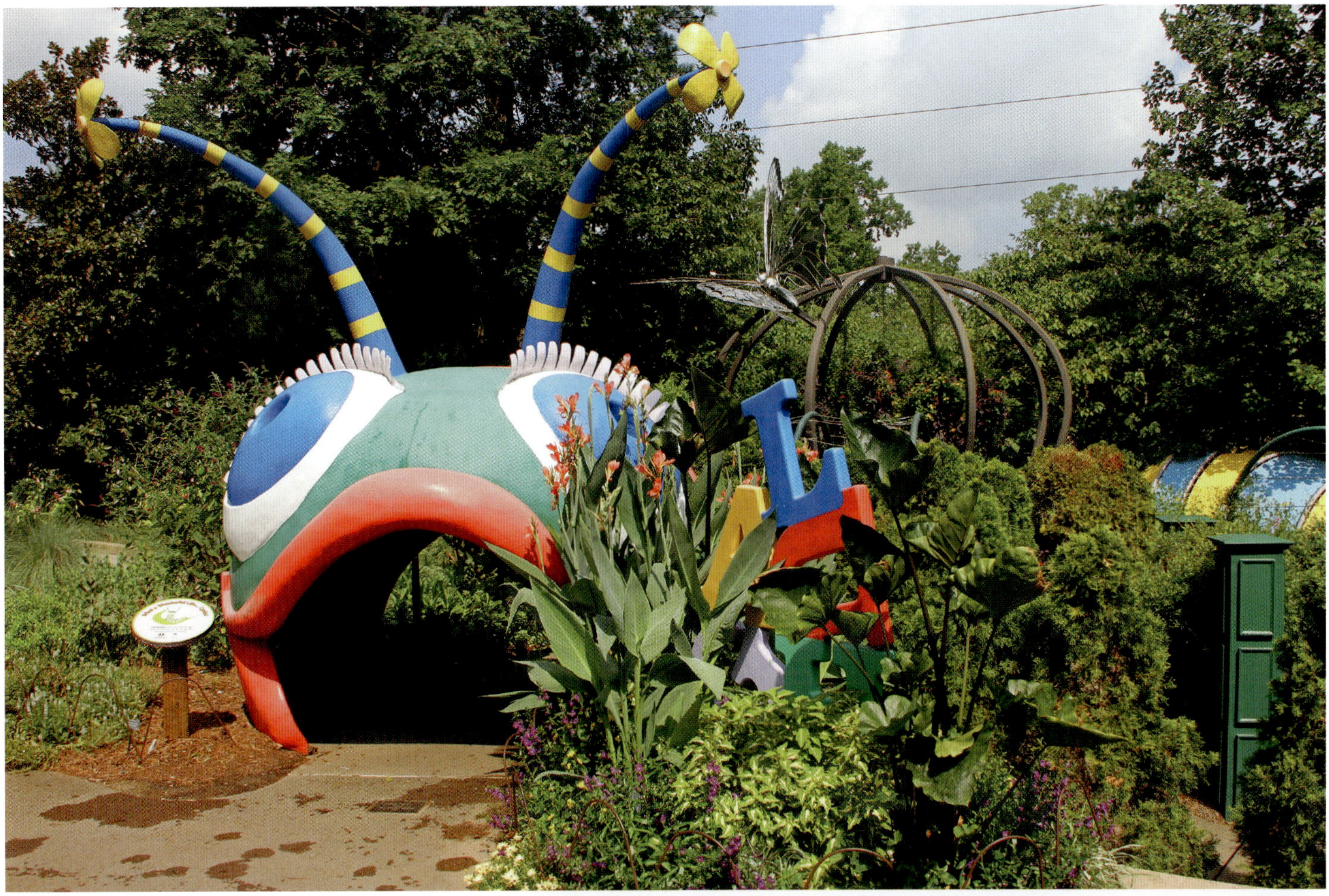

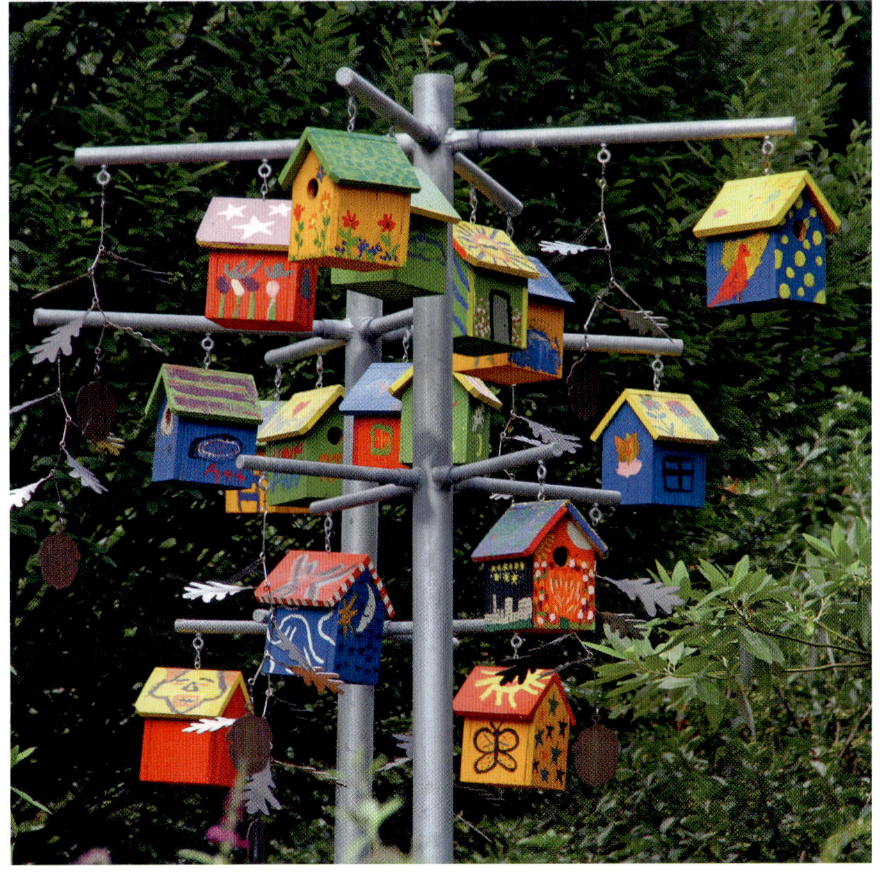

Children's Garden *(above)*

The Children's Garden combines plant education with interactive features such as slides, a green roof, and several water features to cool down junior botanists on warm days. Cross the Flower Bridge, which is planted with year-round color and fragrant herbs and overlooks the Cascades Garden, to reach the two-acre Children's Garden with its themed gardens.

Conservation at Atlanta Botanical Garden *(right)*

The Atlanta Botanical Garden is heavily involved in conservation programs in the areas of habitat restoration and rare species recovery, including working with 124 native plant species throughout the Coastal Plain and southern Appalachian Mountains. It has an active amphibian conservation program with live displays in the Fuqua Conservatory.

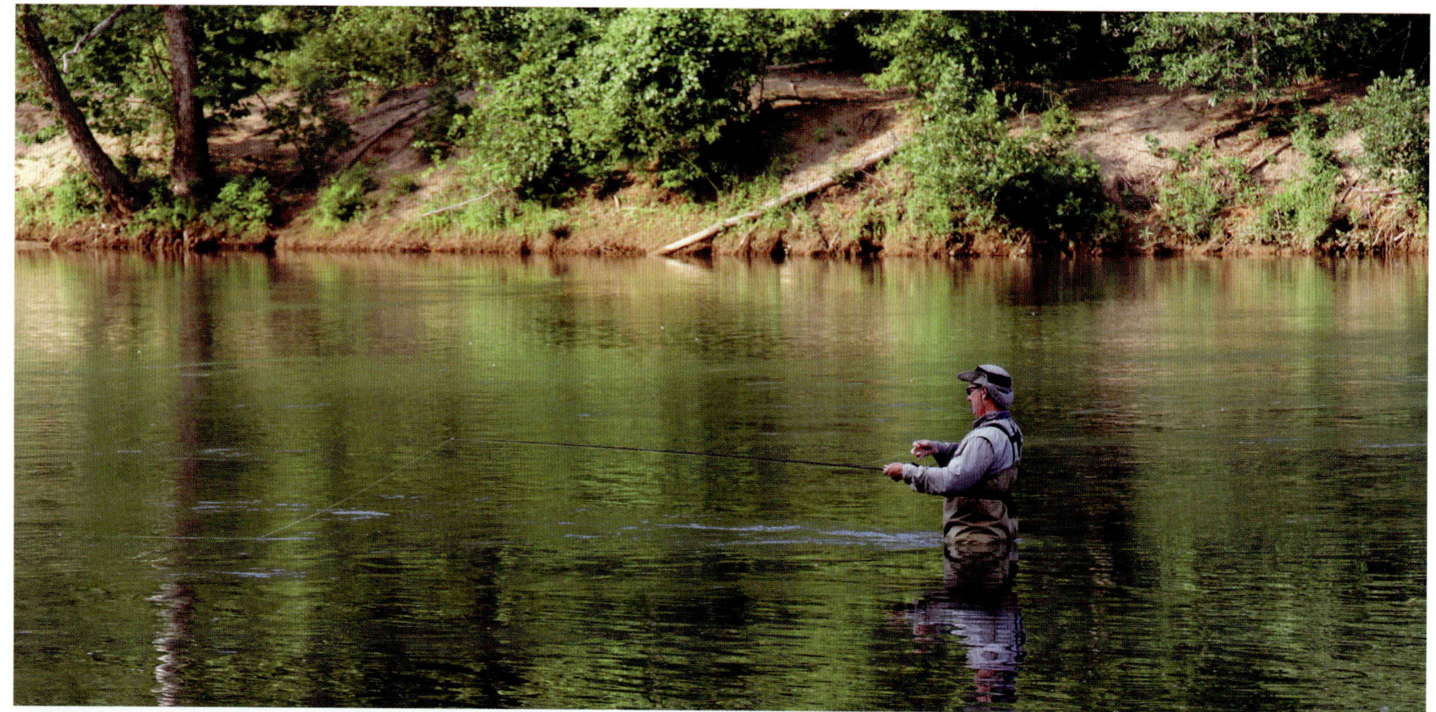

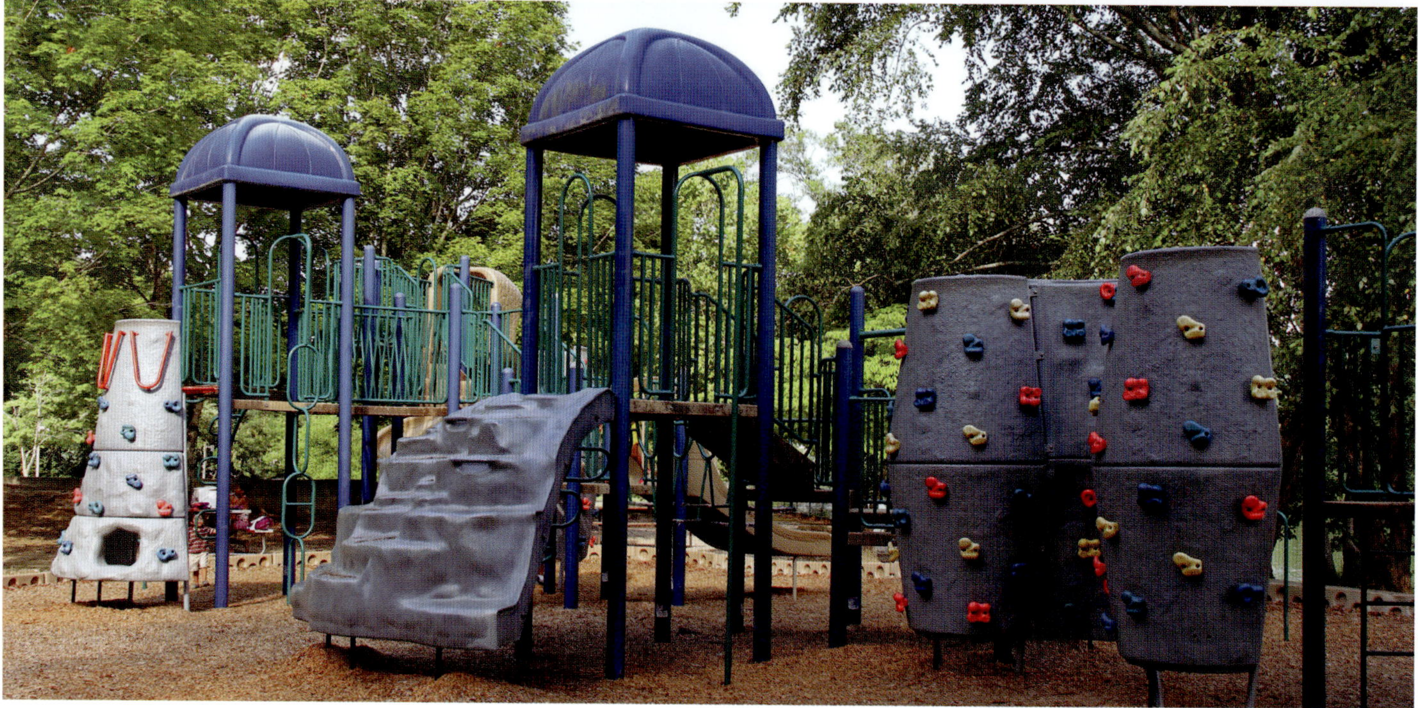

A Natural Paradise *(top)*

The Chattahoochee River National Recreation Area is a verdant world hidden away from Atlanta's northern suburbs by its lush foliage. Its rocky shoals, hidden ponds, miles of thickly forested trails, manmade waterfall, Civil War ruins, and 48 miles of the pristine Chattahoochee River lure fishermen, paddlers, boaters, and nature lovers.

A Place to Play *(bottom)*

Hike, fish, picnic, canoe, raft, splash. The Chattahoochee River stays a cool 50 degrees year-round, the perfect temperature for both water sports and wading. Playgrounds are shaded, colorful, and climbable and offer a respite from city life in a family-friendly pocket of nature.

Forty-Eight Miles of River *(opposite)*

Spend a few hours or all day at the Chattahoochee River National Recreation Area. The river offers myriad opportunities for lazily paddling a raft, canoe, or kayak to observe wildlife and wildflowers. Fish the river year-round for trout, bass, and catfish. Pack your camera and capture some of the most glorious scenery to be found in a city.

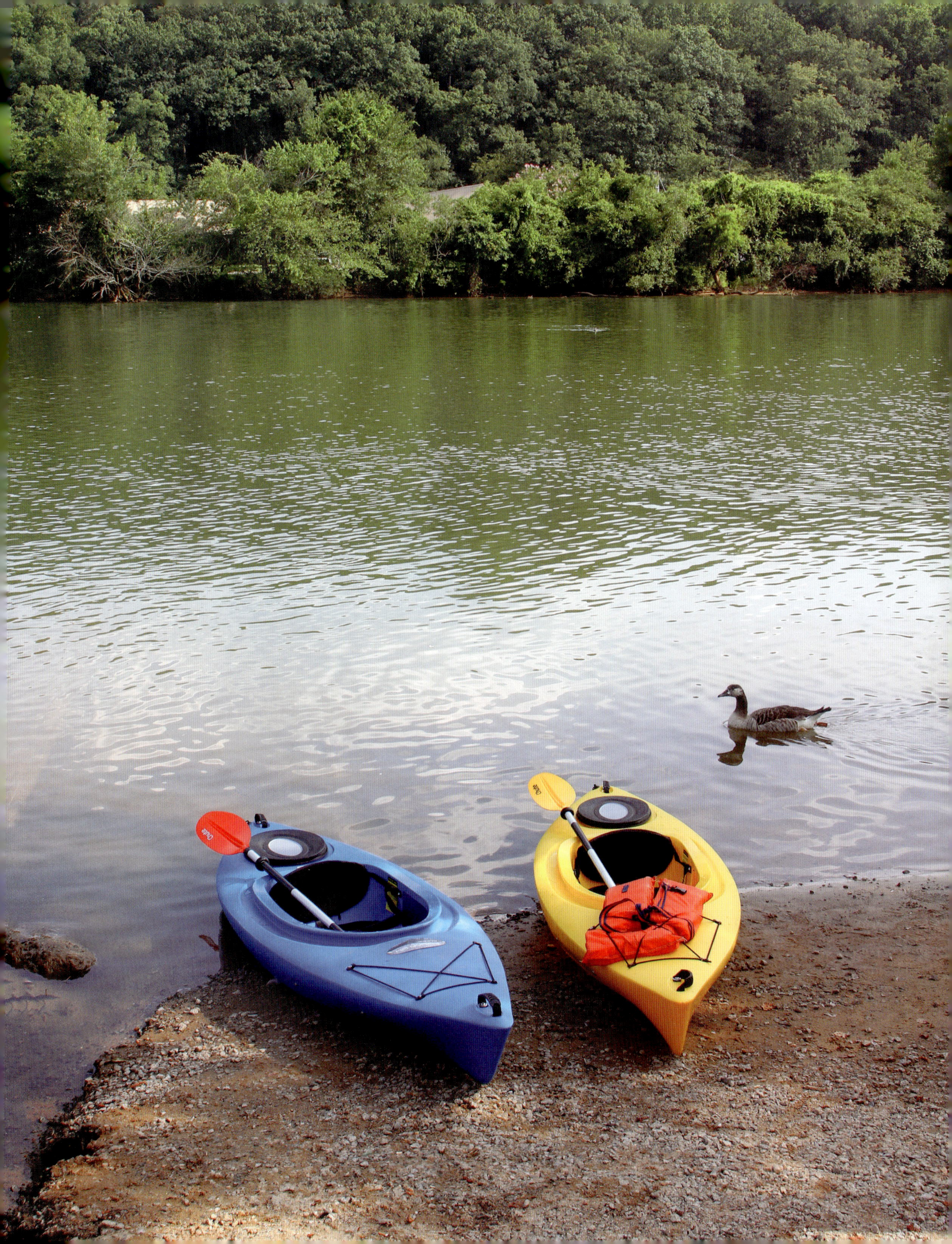

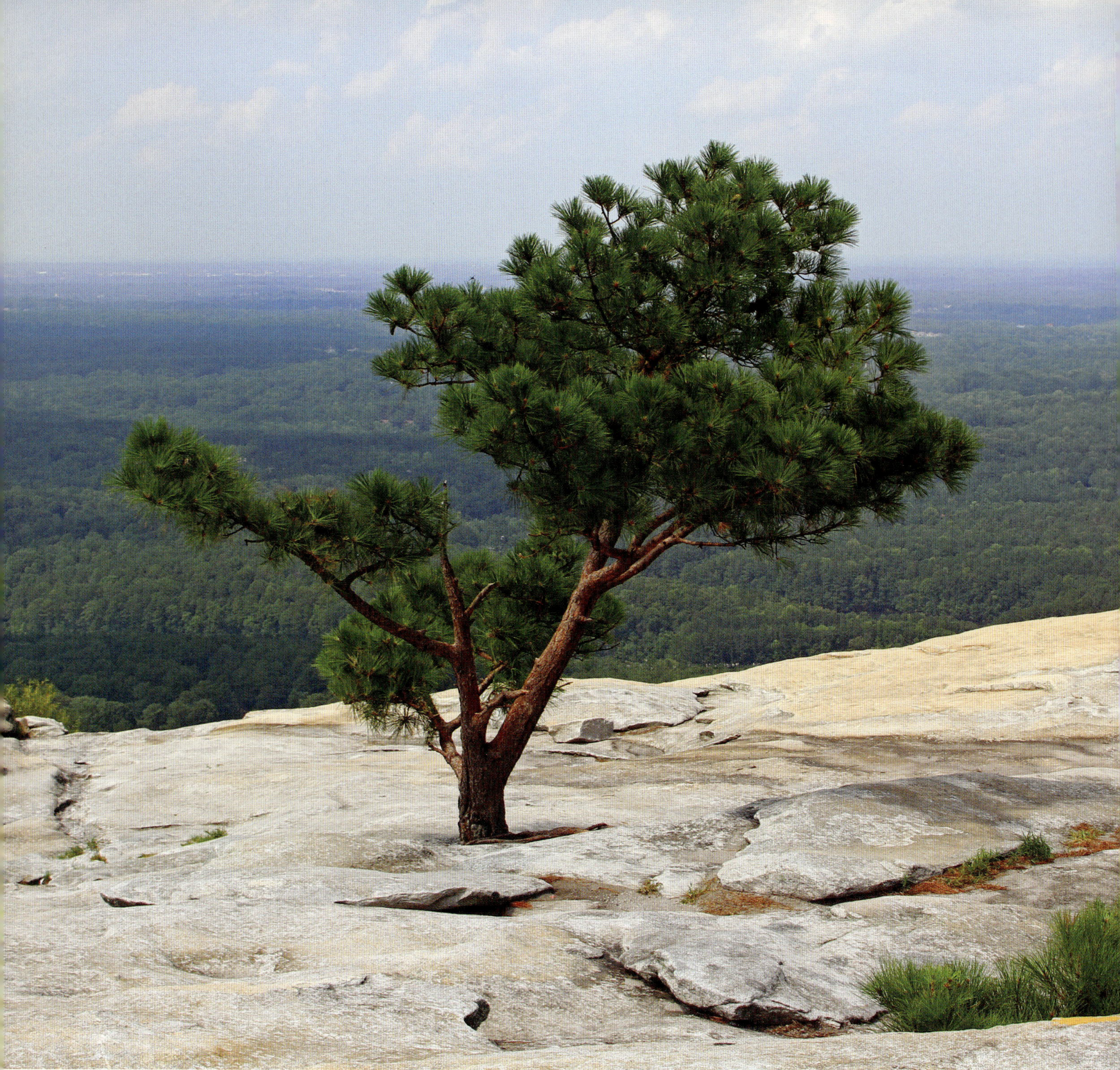

Stone Mountain Park

Visitors have been coming to this 825-foot-high mass of exposed granite since 1838 when the first tourist attraction – a 165-foot wooden tower that cost fifty cents to climb – was built atop the mountain. A 1.3-mile trek to the top affords sweeping vistas 60 miles beyond, including downtown Atlanta and the North Georgia mountains.

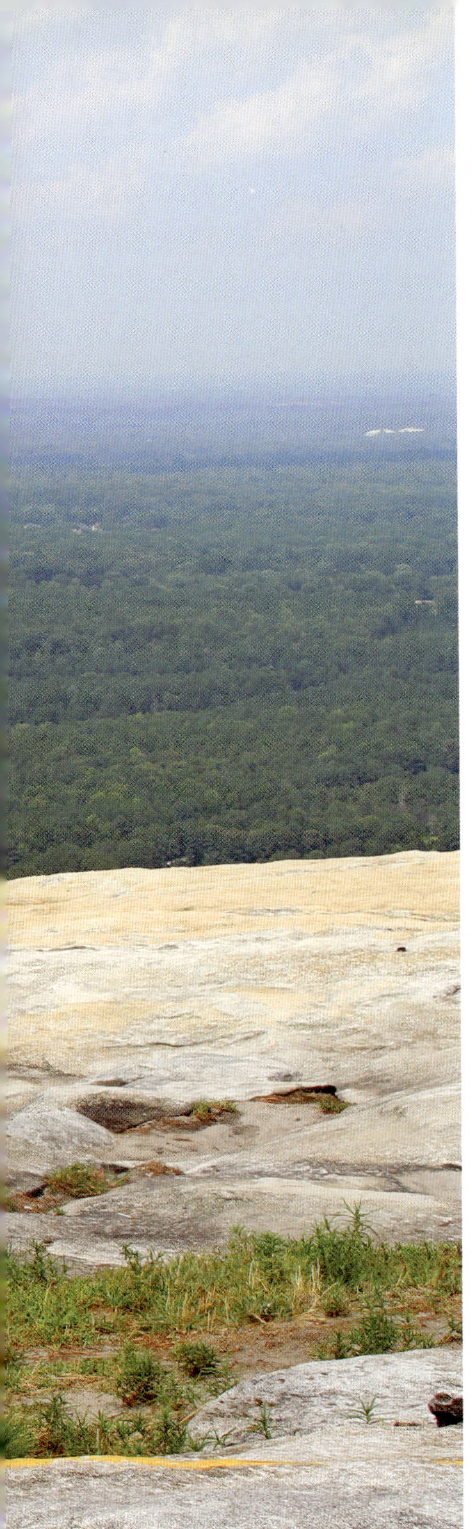

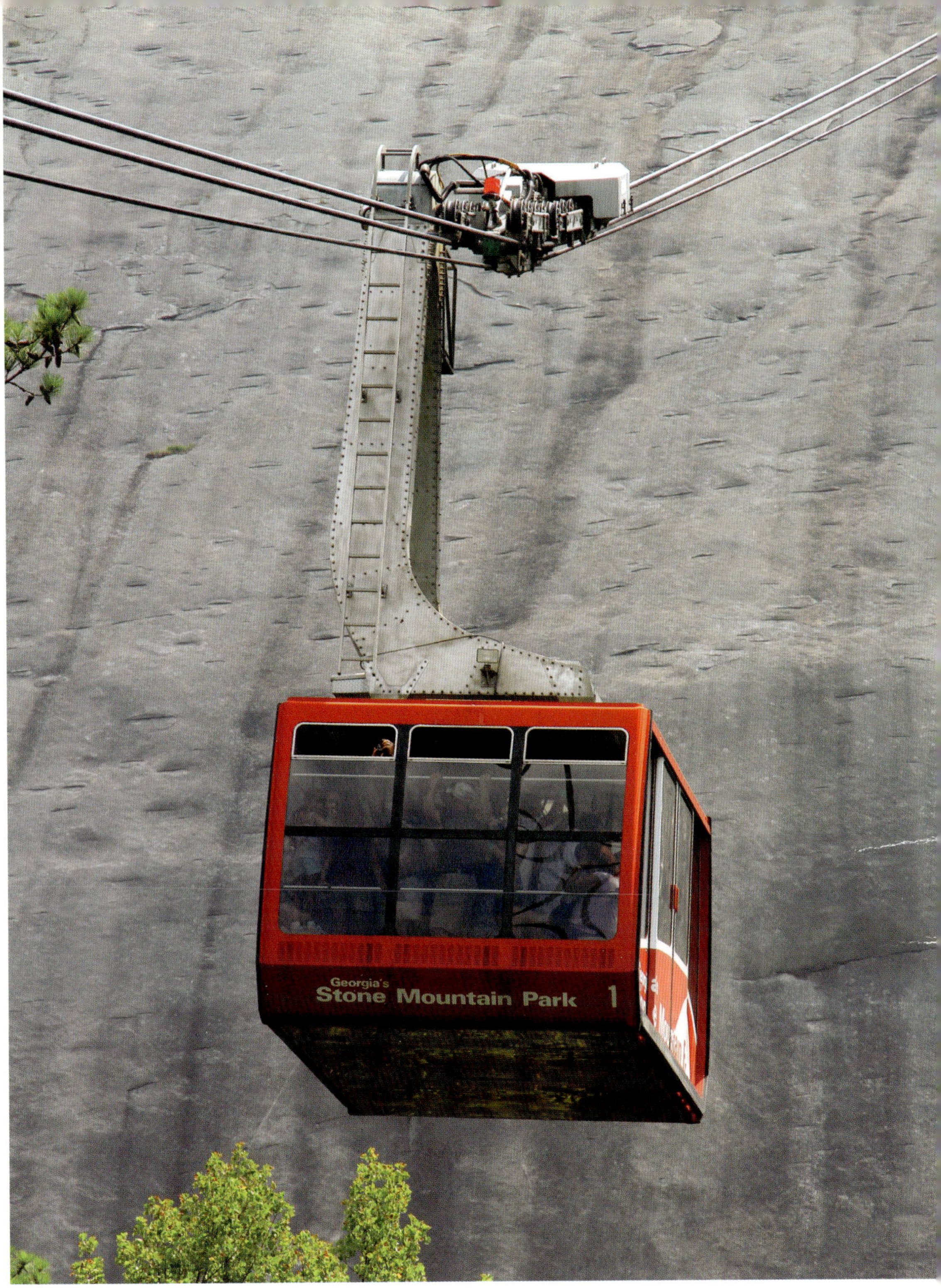

Skyride

The Summit Skyride at Discovering Stone Mountain Museum zips passengers to magnificent views of the world's largest relief sculpture, the *Confederate Memorial Carving*, featuring General Lee, Stonewall Jackson, and Jefferson Davis.

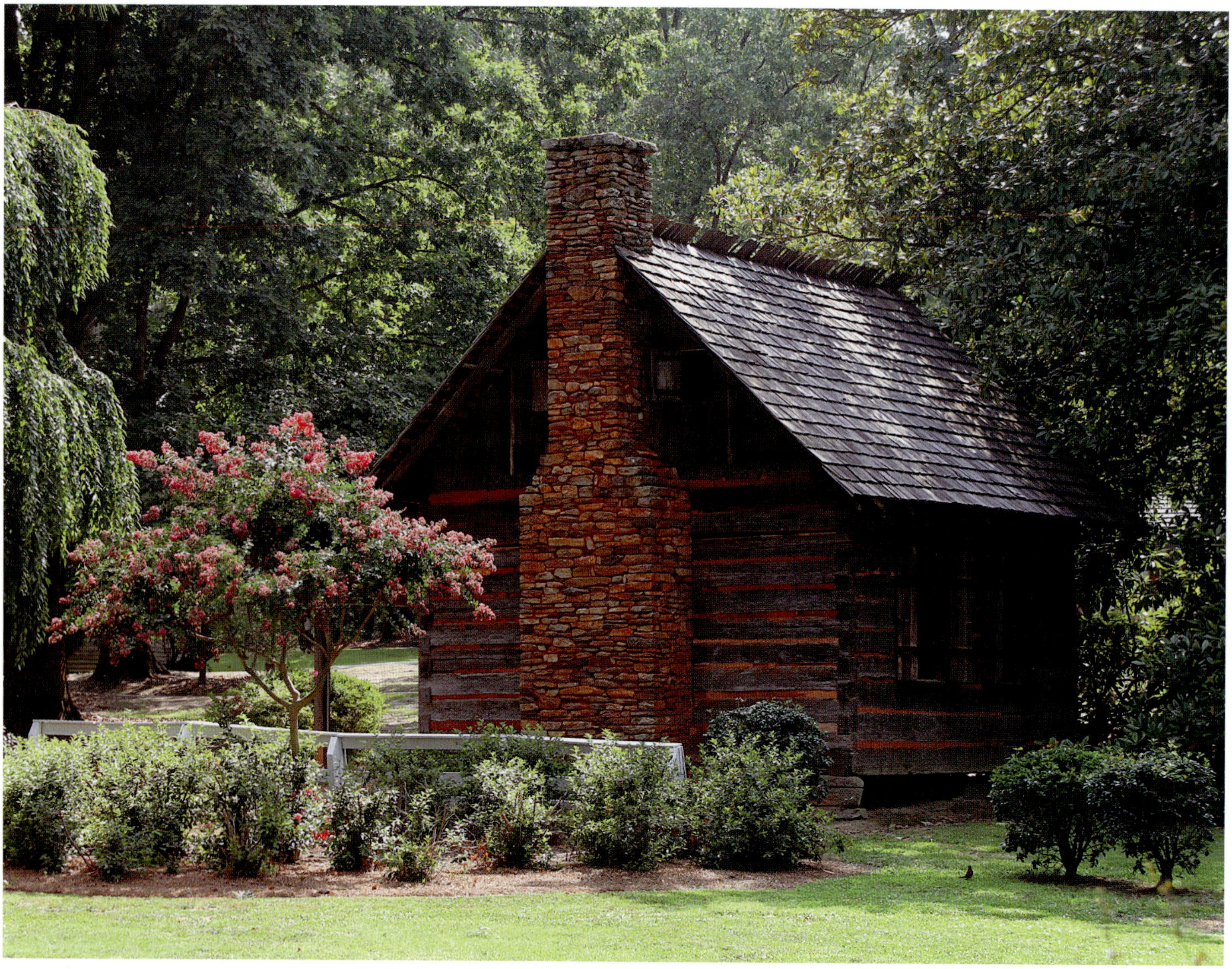

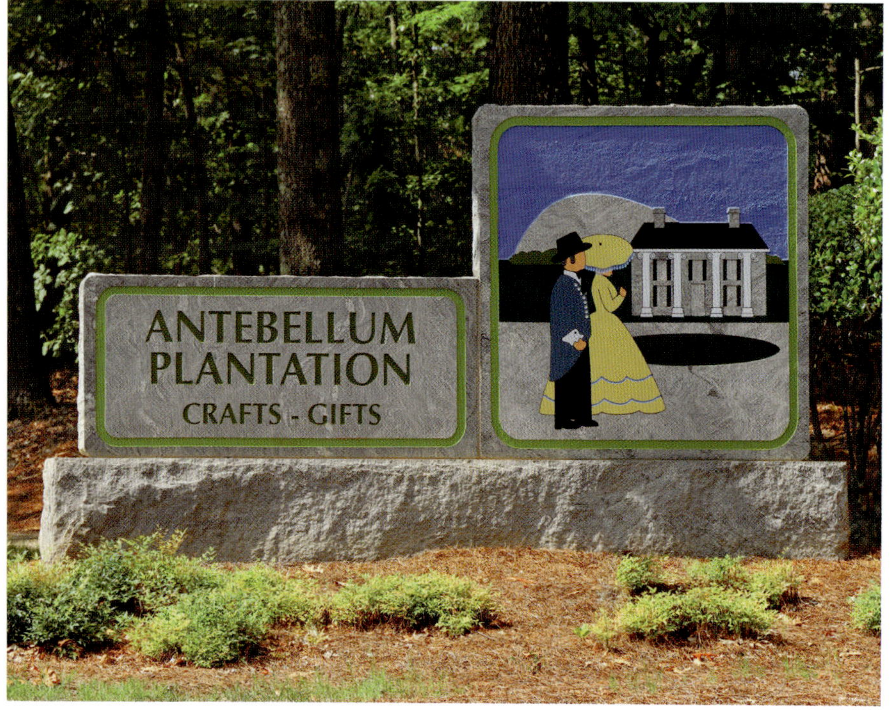

Antebellum Plantation *(above and left)*

Travel from Revolutionary America through the Reconstruction at the Antebellum Plantation and Farmyard at Stone Mountain Park. A collection of original buildings from Georgia was relocated here and restored with period furnishings. Take a self-guided tour of the buildings and garden and learn about the 18th- and 19th-century lifestyles of Georgia residents.

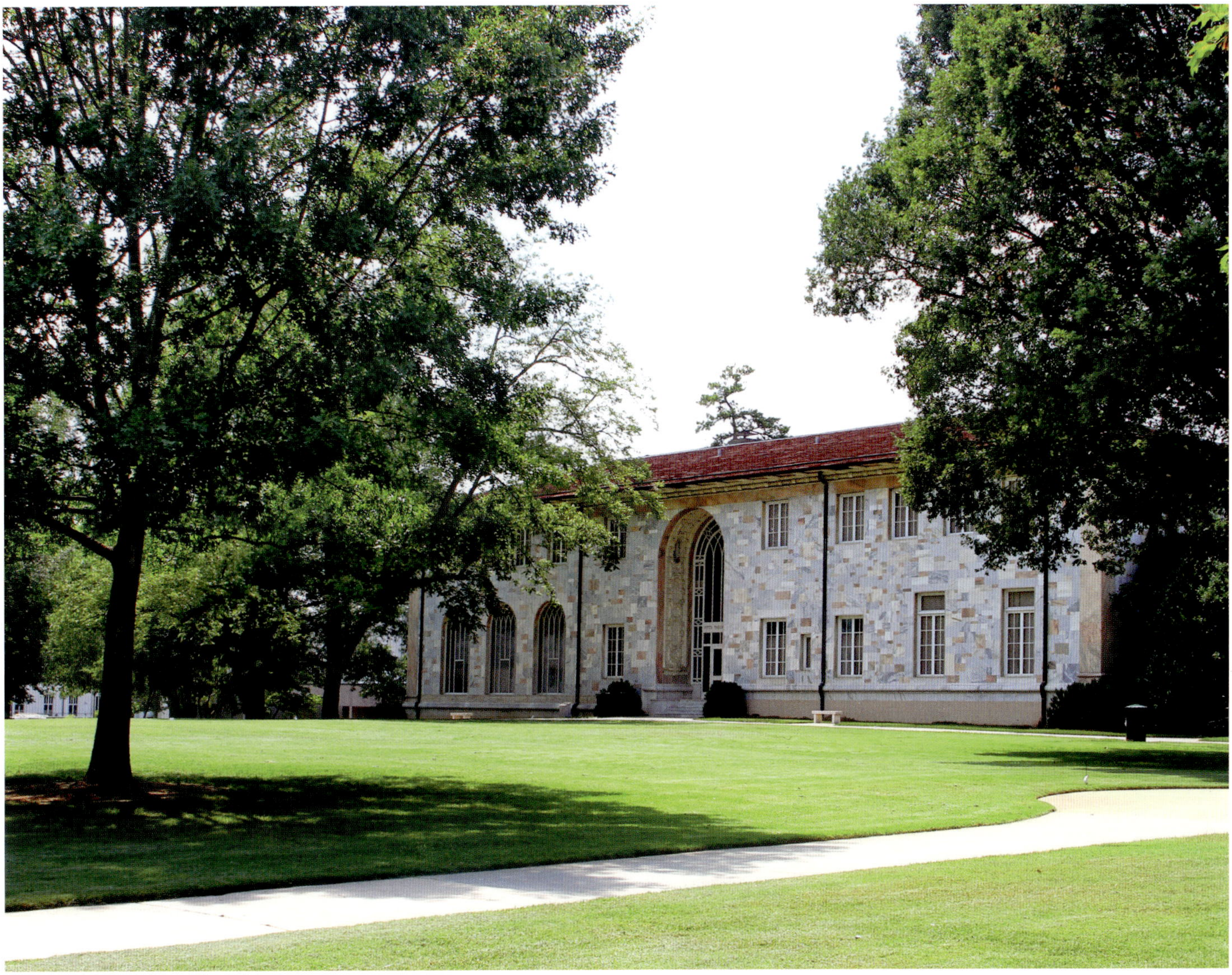

Emory University *(above and right)*

Established in 1836, Emory University, in Atlanta's historic Druid Hills suburb, ranks among the top national universities in *U.S. News & World Report's* "America's Best Colleges." Distinguished professors include former U.S. President Jimmy Carter and His Holiness the XIV Dalai Lama. Emory is recognized internationally for its superlative liberal arts college.

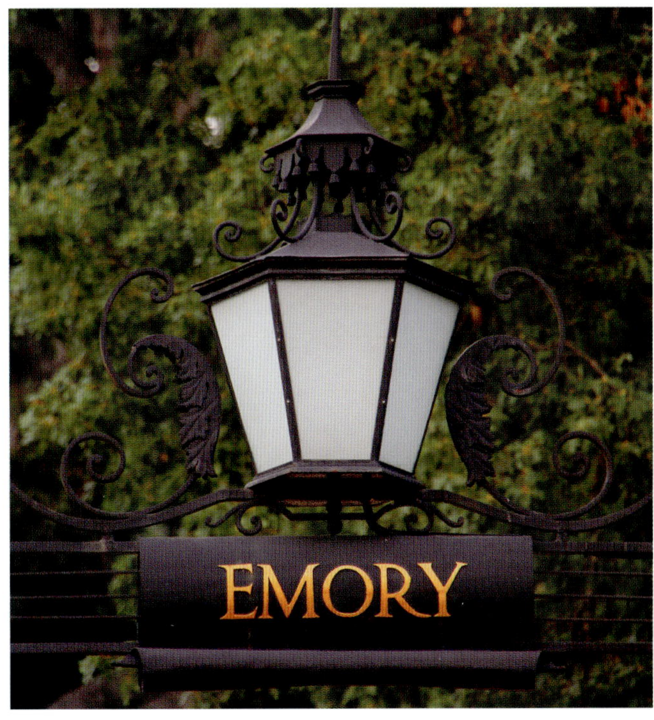

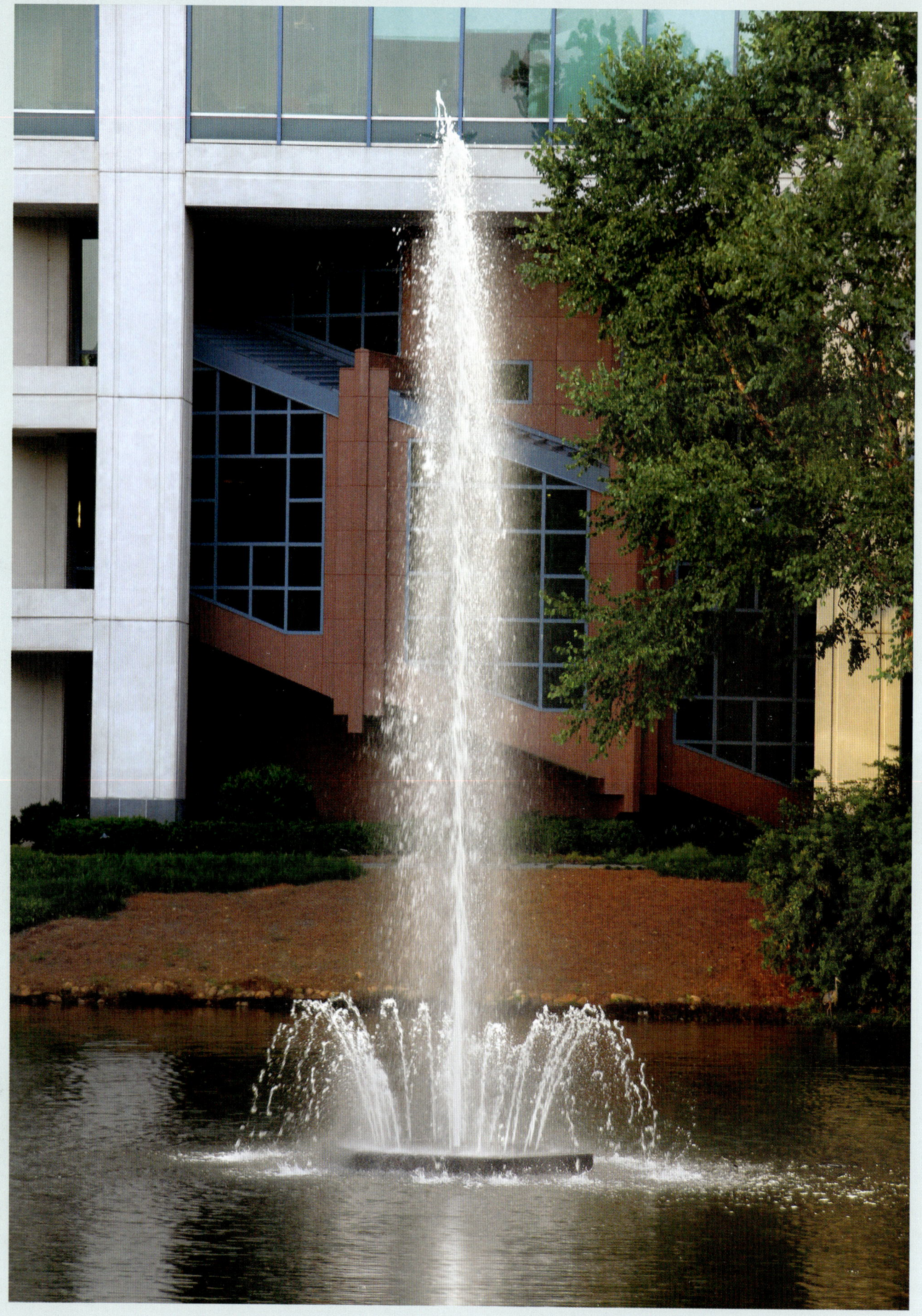

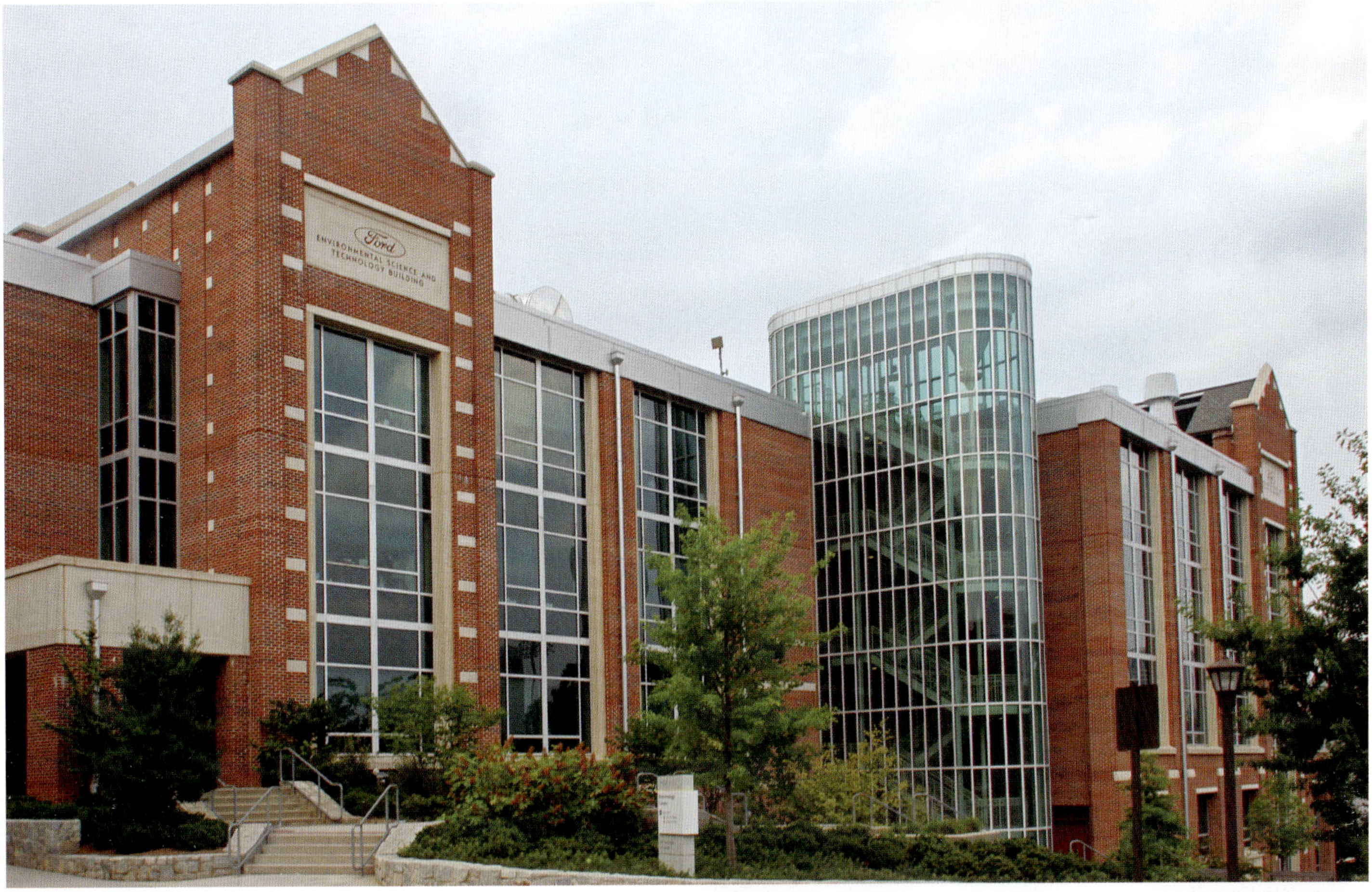

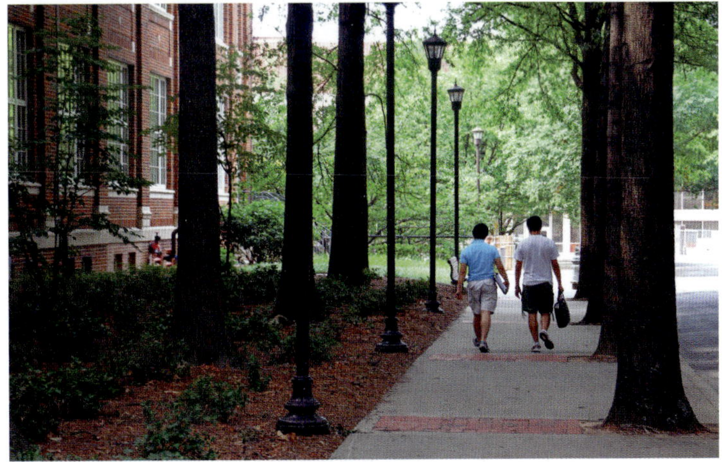

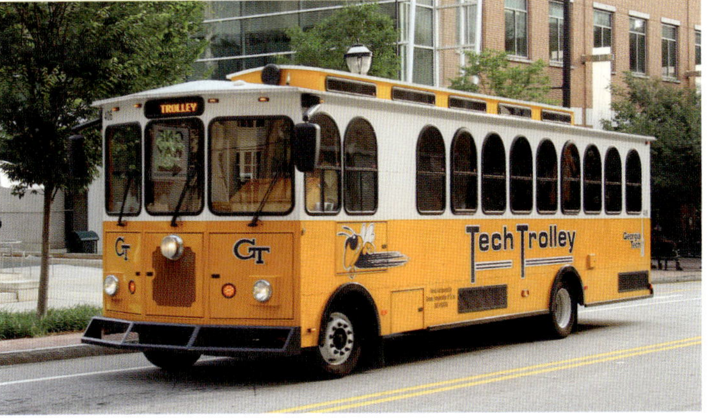

Georgia Institute of Technology *(above and right)*

Consistently ranked in *U.S. News & World Report's* top ten public universities in the United States, Georgia Tech is distinguished by its "commitment to improving the human condition through advanced science and technology" and nationally recognized, top-ranked programs. One of the top research universities in the country, its campus stretches over 400 acres in the heart of Atlanta.

Argosy University *(opposite)*

Learner-centered Argosy University, comprising five colleges within 19 campus locations across the U.S., including one in Atlanta, was formed in September 2001 by the merging of three separate academic institutions.

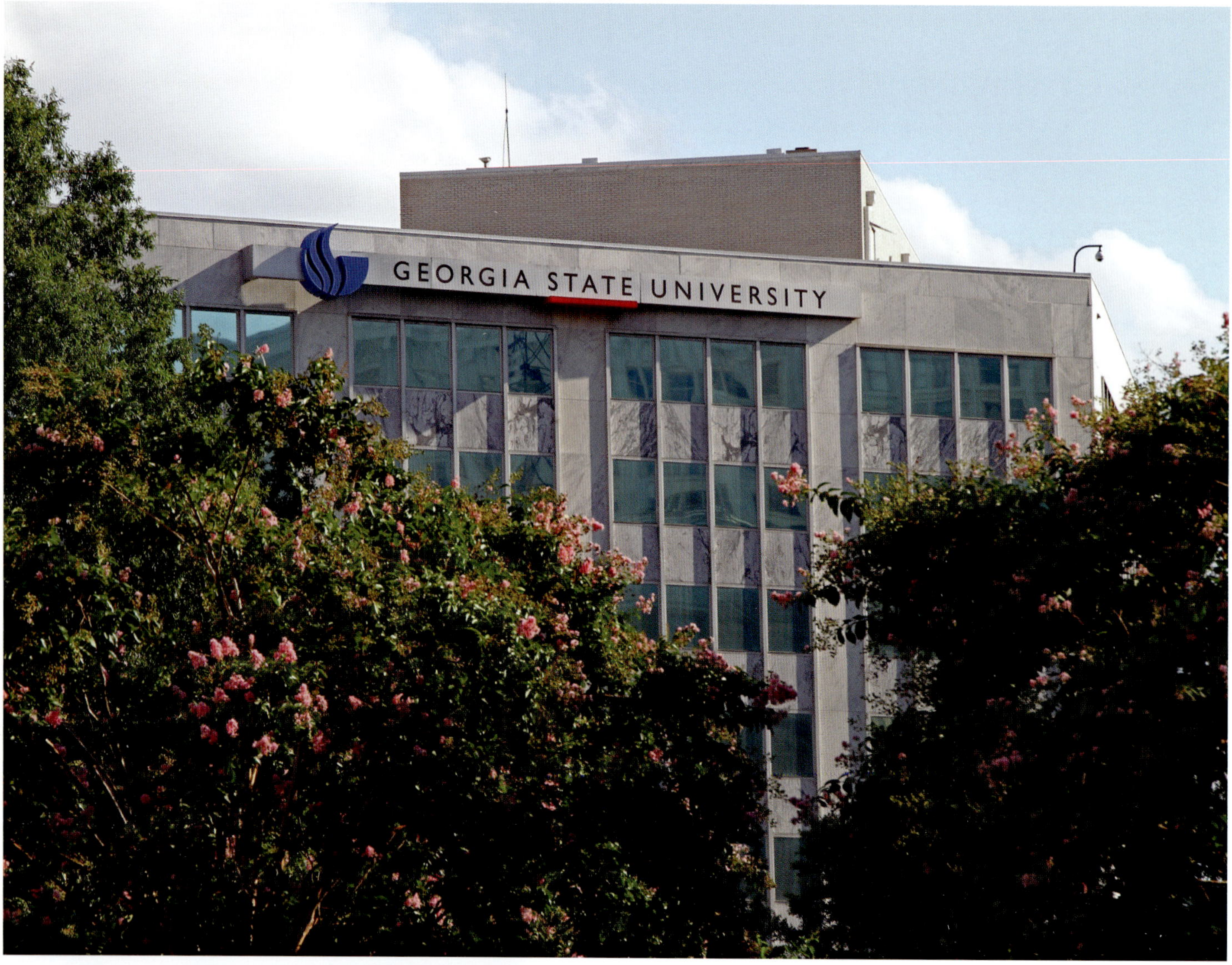

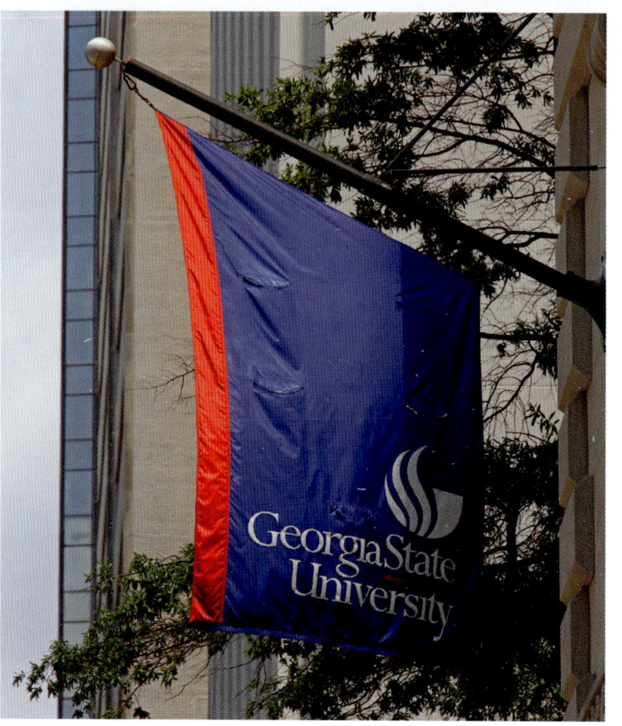

Georgia State University *(above and left)*

Founded in 1913, Georgia State University, the Southeast's leading urban research institution, is a top 100 public university for doctoral degrees awarded. It offers more than 250 degree programs with 100 fields of study through eight colleges.

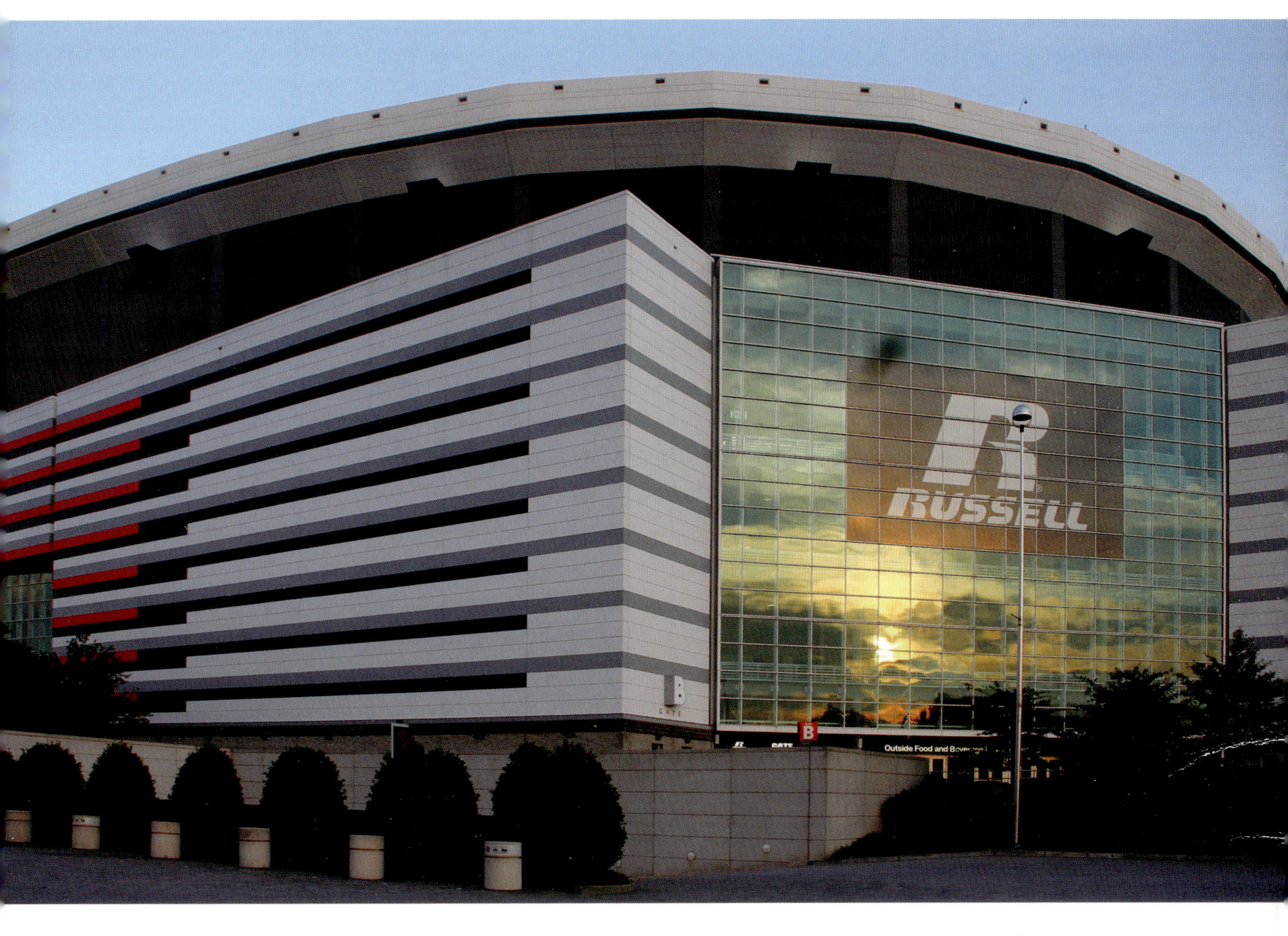

Georgia Dome

The largest cable-supported domed stadium, the Georgia Dome hosted events during the 1996 Olympic Games and is home to the Atlanta Falcons. Covering 8.9 acres and with a 290-foot-high roof composed of 130 Teflon-coated fiberglass panels, it has a seating capacity for 71,250 and over 660 television monitors scattered throughout.

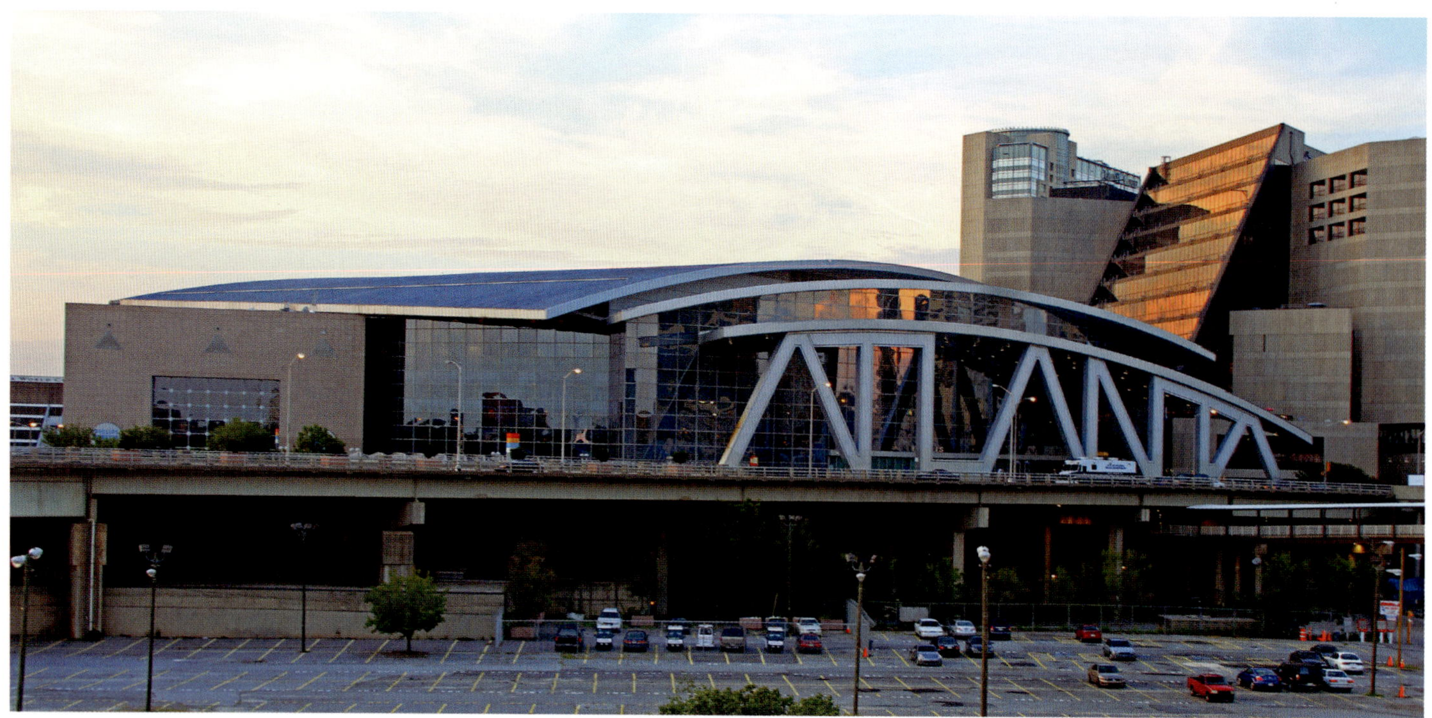

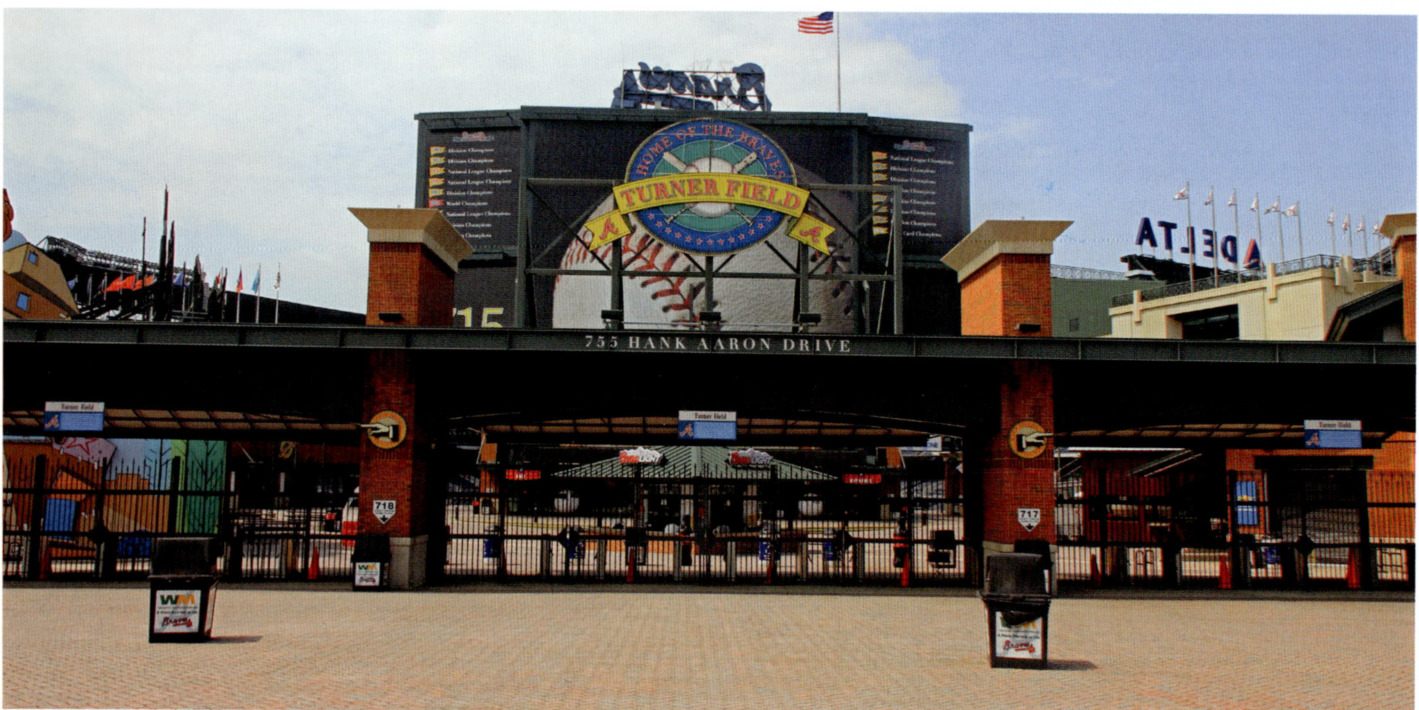

Phillips Arena *(top)*

Home of the Atlanta Hawks, part of the NBA's Southeast Division of the Eastern Conference, and the Atlanta Dream of the Women's National Basketball Association, the 18,371-seat Phillips Arena was built in 1999 to replace The Omni Coliseum. The arena also hosts a variety of events including musical concerts, comedians, and the circus.

Turner Field *(bottom)*

Originally constructed as Centennial Olympic Stadium, Turner Field – the "Home of the Braves" – combines the nostalgia of old-time baseball with a state-of-the-art park, unrivaled in its unique blend of high-tech prowess and entertainment. Guided tours include the Braves Museum & Hall of Fame, broadcast booth, clubhouse, and dugout.

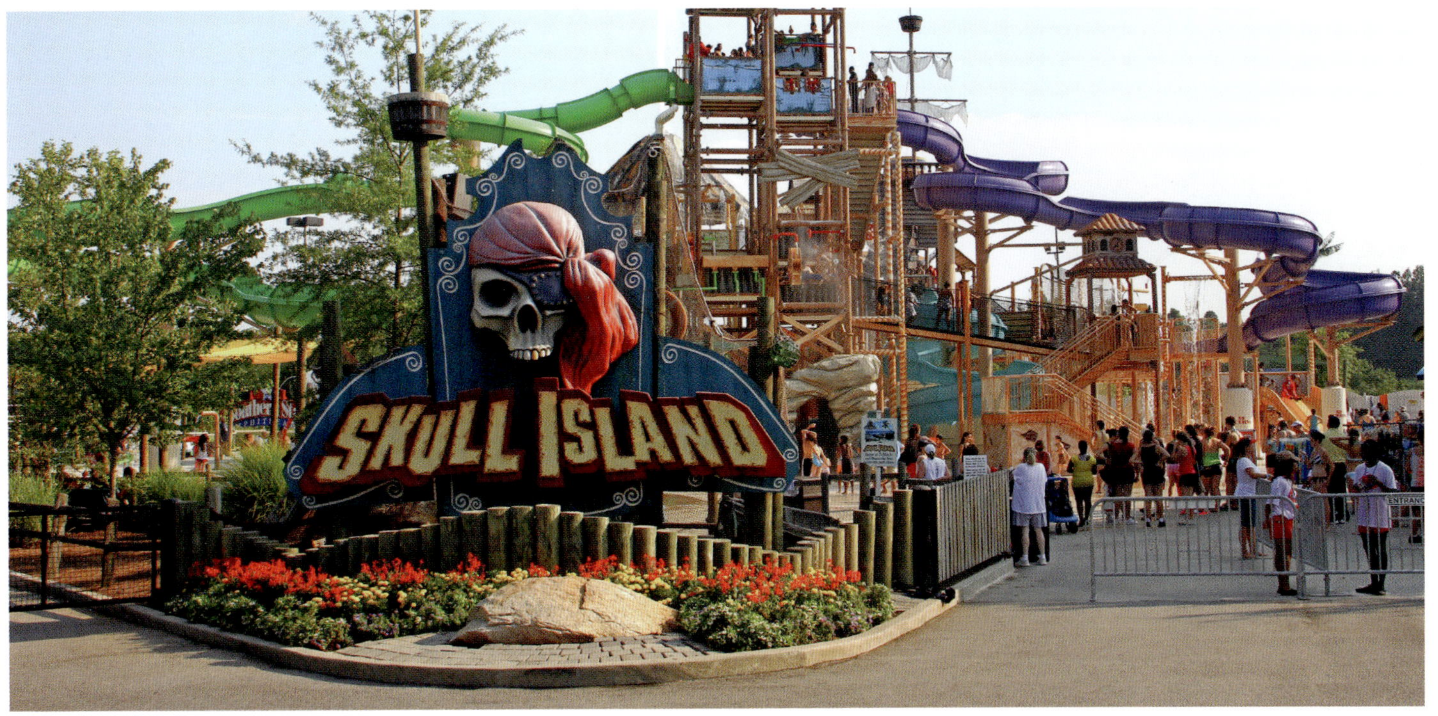

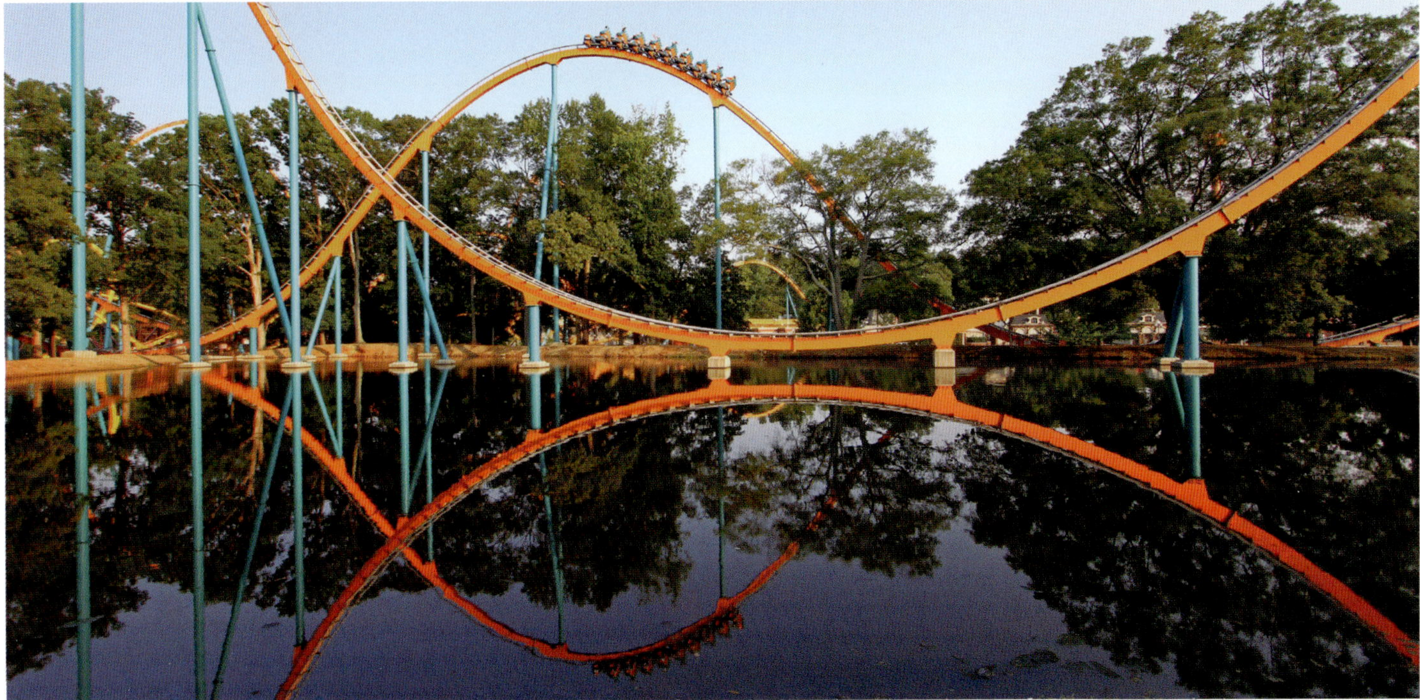

Skull Island *(top)*

Skull Island at Six Flags Over Georgia is a towering pirate-themed structure with hundreds of water elements guaranteed to soak all the mateys who enter these "high seas." A bathing suit and towel are a must!

Six Flags Over Georgia *(bottom)*

Take on Goliath, a giant steel coaster ranked one of the top in the world, or face your phobia on Acrophobia, the only stand-up tilting drop tower in the country. This 100-acre park has 35 rides – including 11 gut-wrenching coasters – three interactive children's areas, and the wild rafting adventure, Thunder River.

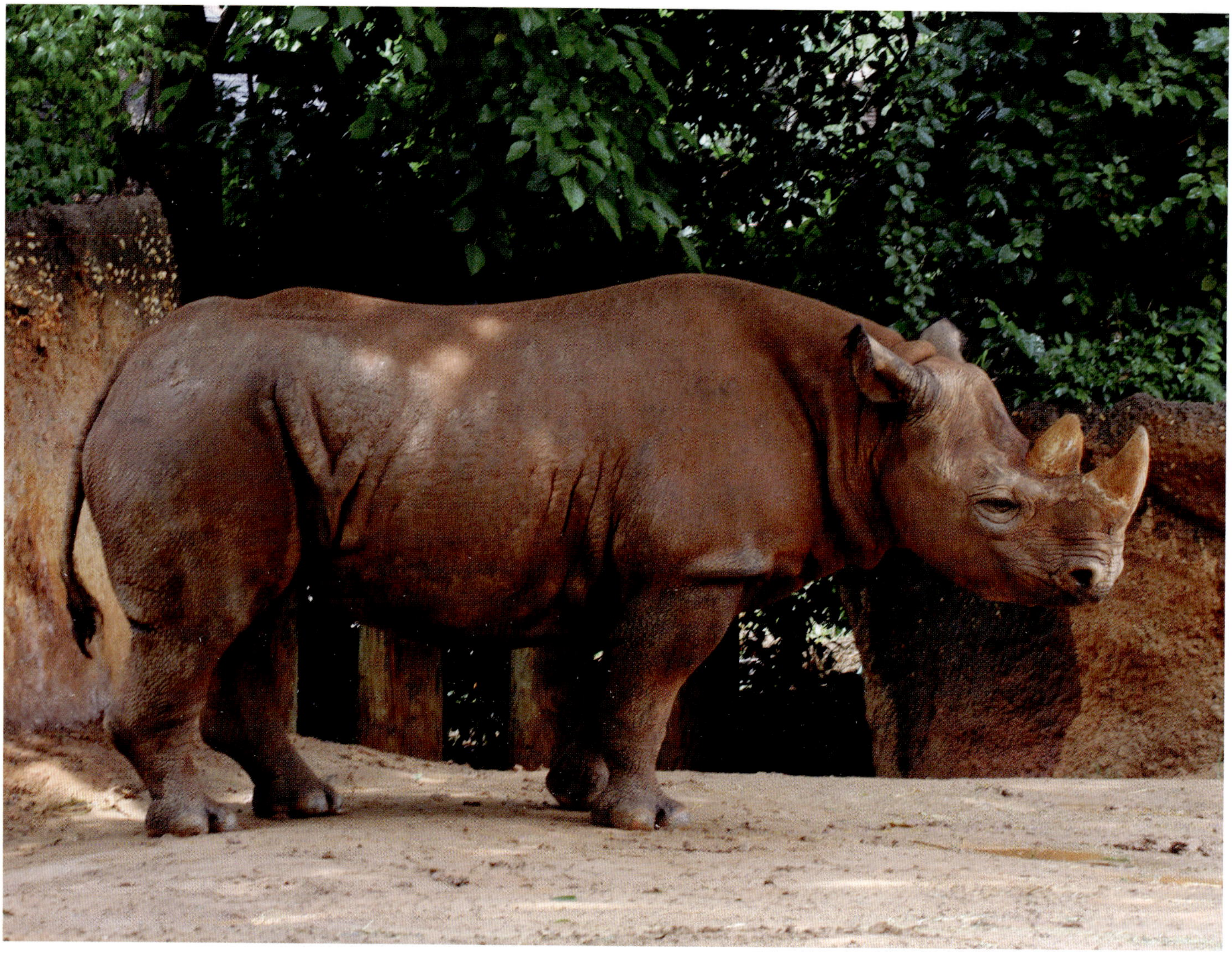

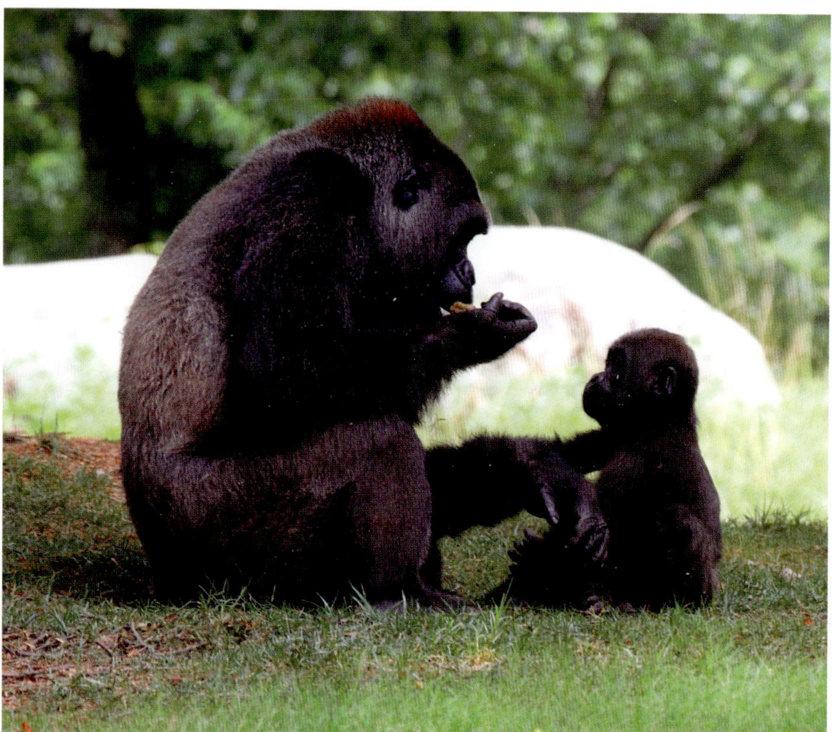

Zoo Atlanta *(above)*

When Atlanta's oldest cultural attraction was founded in 1889, it had a jaguar, hyena, black bear, raccoon, an elk, gazelle, Mexican hog, lionesses, pumas, camels, and snakes. Today, it maintains a collection of more than 1,000 animals, representing more than 200 species from around the world, including parakeets, bush dogs, Chilean flamingos, naked mole rats, and golden lion tamarins.

Leader in Naturalistic Habitats *(left)*

Spreading over 40 acres of lush landscapes and botanicals, the Zoo's naturalistic habitats include the African Rain Forest, home to the largest collection of gorillas in the country. Twenty-three gorillas, including a rare set of twins, live in the 1.5-acre series of verdant habitats. The Living Treehouse, an open-air aviary, is home to guenons, lemurs, and critically endangered drills.

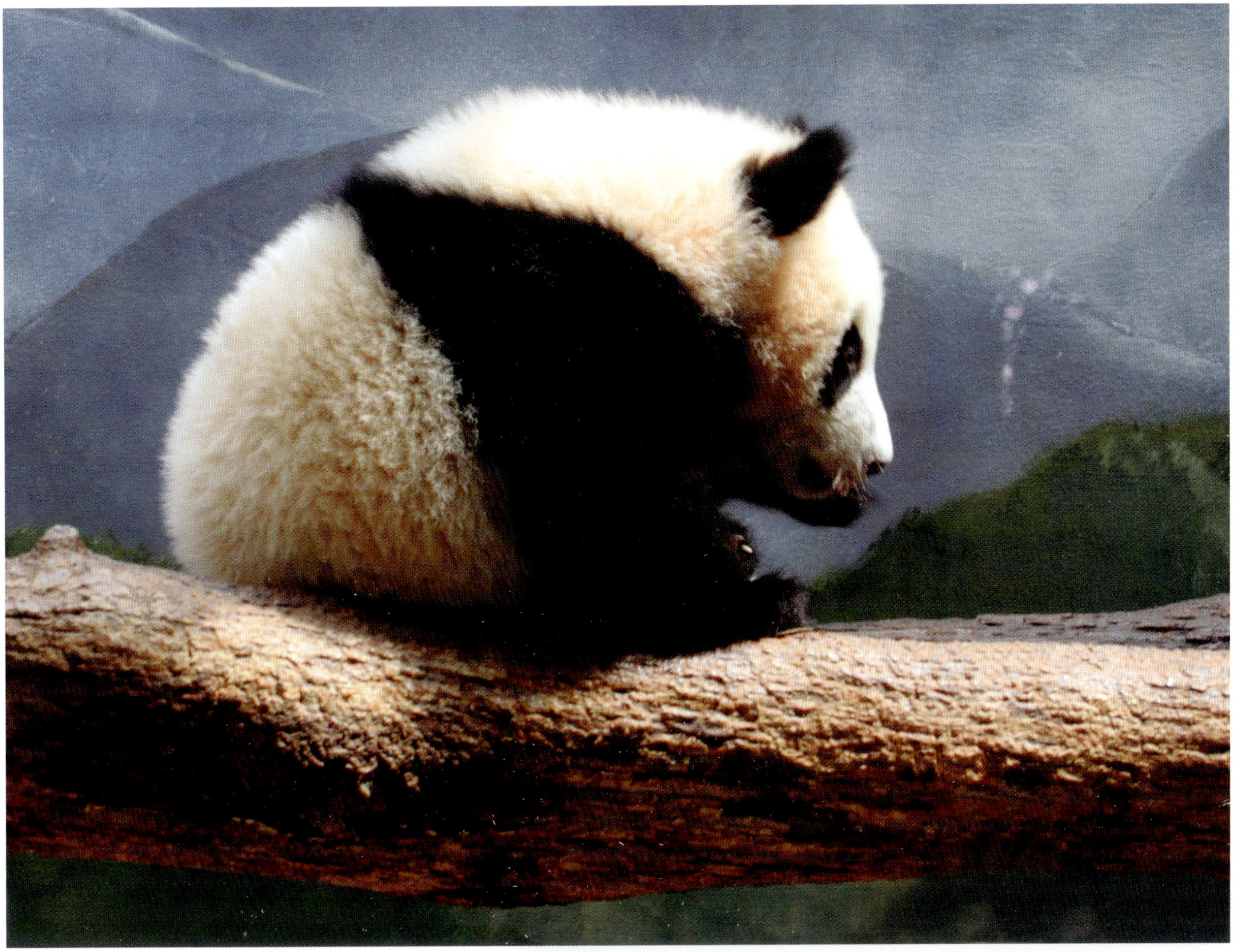

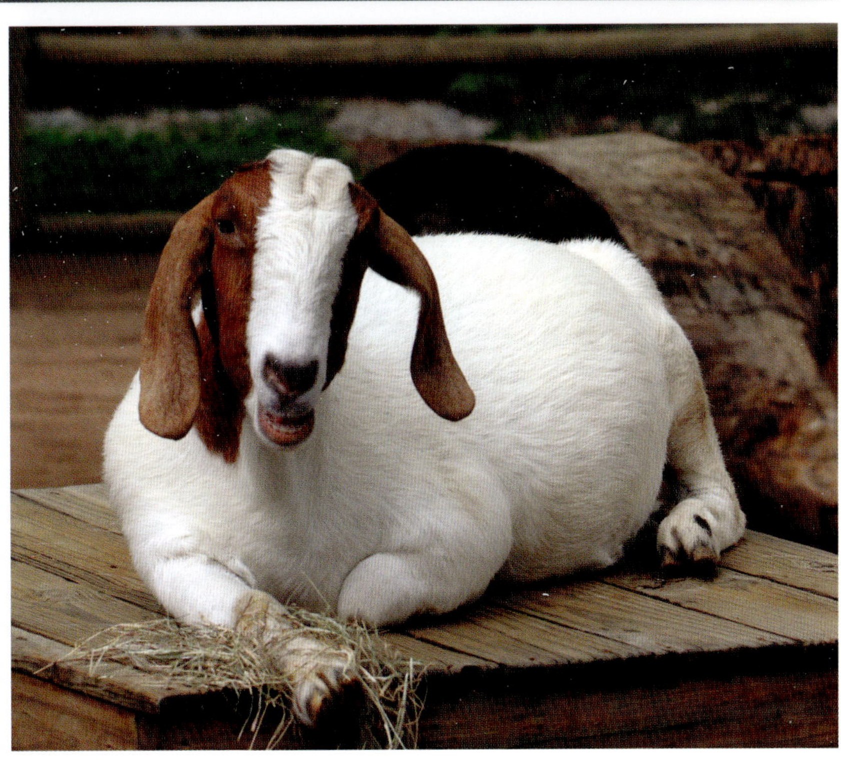

Giant Pandas *(above)*

Zoo Atlanta's Giant Panda Conservation Center has been researching giant pandas since 1997 and is one of four zoos in the country that houses giant pandas. In 1999, the zoo received a pair from Chengdu, China. Considered critically endangered, three cubs have since been born to the pair. Today, there are only about 1,600 giant pandas left in the world.

Beloved Family Destination *(right)*

One of the 10 oldest zoos in continuous operation in the U.S., Zoo Atlanta's Outback Station encourages children to pet their animals, including this sometimes rambunctious Boer goat.

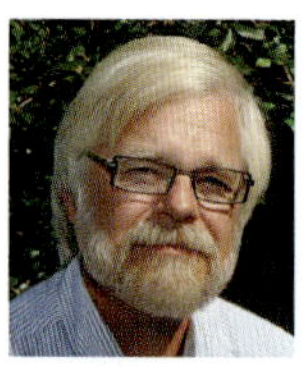

Photographer Paul Scharff has been captivated by light and nature his entire life. Over the years, his friends and family have learned to politely listen and nod as he repeatedly asks them to notice how the light is hitting this dirt road, that building, those waves, this flower, or that sand dune.

In addition, Paul has always looked at the world in a very non-traditional way, noting and zeroing in on a particular nuance or individual component of a much broader setting, or discerning an overarching design or geometric shape to an otherwise ordinary scene.

Paul's photography can be seen in a number of books from Twin Lights Publishers, including books on Cape Cod, Miami, Phoenix, and Philadelphia. Paul's work is also on display at several locations throughout the United States. Photographs from this book can be purchased as signed prints and note cards, and can be seen along with a wide range of photographs taken throughout North America and the Caribbean at www.PaulScharffPhotography.com.

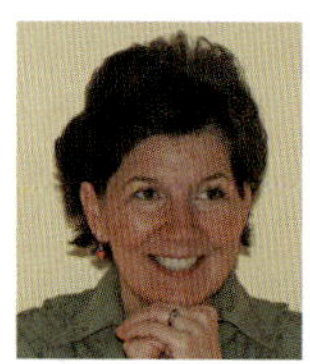

Kathryn Witt has explored Metro Atlanta on countless visits. It is a place she cherishes for its cultural arts and culinary diversity; historic, amble-worthy neighborhoods and charming town squares; optimistic nature and good Southern manners.

A prolific lifestyle and travel writer located in Kentucky, Kathryn has written a number of books, including the historical novel, *The Secret of the Belles*, which is based on Atlanta's 1939 three-day premiere for the movie, *Gone with the Wind*, and the Marietta Gone with the Wind Museum in Georgia. Atlanta and Marietta both play key settings in this book, one Cammie King Conlon ("Bonnie Blue Butler") called "a beautiful read."

Kathryn's other books include *Contemporary American Doll Artists and Their Dolls*, *Doll Directory*, and 26 children's books written for Malaysia's ESL program. She was a featured writer for the *Encyclopedia of Northern Kentucky* and has won numerous awards for her writing, including two Lily scholarships.

Visit www.KathyWitt.com to learn more about Kathy.